Encyclopædia Britannica, Inc.
Chicago · London · Paris · Rome · Seoul · Sydney · Tokyo

Medical&
Health
Annual
1999

1999 Medical and Health Annual

Editor
Ellen Bernstein

Senior Editor
Linda Tomchuck

Assistant Editor
Sherman Hollar

Editorial Assistants
Heather Blackmore, Julie Stevens

Creative Director, Art
Bob Ciano

Director, Art Production
Melvin Stagner

Systems/Technical
Michael Born, Jr., Bruce David Walters

Senior Picture Editor
John Judge

Picture Editors
Kathy Creech, Sylvia Ohlrich

Design Supervisor
John L. Draves

Designers
*Kathryn Syed, Jon Hensley,
Steven N. Kapusta*

Production
Ethan Persoff

Managing Artist
David Alexovich

Supervising Artists
Constance Sayas, Thomas Spanos

Artists
*James Alexander, Charles Goll, Paulina
Jiménez, Christine McCabe, Patrick
O'Neill Riley, Olga Sheynin*

Art Staff
*Michelle R. Burrell, Kimberly L.
Cleary, Karen M. Farmer, Carla M.
Whittington*

**Supervisor, Composition/
Page Makeup**
Danette Wetterer

Composition/Page Makeup Staff
*Griselda Cháidez, Carol A. Gaines,
Thomas J. Mulligan, Gwen E.
Rosenberg, Tammy Yu-chu Wang Tsou*

**Managing Director,
Art and Cartography**
Barbra A. Vogel

Supervisor, Cartography
John E. Nelson

Cartography Staff
*Amelia R. Gintautas, David A.R.
Herubin, Ashley Snyder*

Manager, Copy Department
Sylvia Wallace

Copy Supervisors
Lawrence Kowalski, Barbara Whitney

Copy Staff
*Locke Peterseim, Rebecca R. Rundall,
Lee A. Young*

Manager, Production Control
Mary C. Srodon

Production Control Staff
Marilyn L. Barton

Publishing Technology Group
*Oleg Barsukov, Steven Bosco, Troy
Broussard, Peter Davies, Ray
Goldberger, Vincent Star, Mary Voss*

Director, Information Management
Carmen-Maria Hetrea

Index Supervisor
Edward Paul Moragne

Index Staff
Noelle M. Borge, Catherine E. Keich

Librarian
Shantha Uddin

Assistant Librarian
Robert M. Lewis

Medical Advisers
Lois DeBakey, Ph.D.
Professor of Scientific Communication
Baylor College of Medicine
Houston, Texas

Bruce G. Gellin, M.D., M.P.H.
Staff Director, Vaccine Initiative
Infectious Diseases Society of America;
Adjunct Assistant Professor of Public
Health/Preventive Medicine
Vanderbilt University Medical Center
Nashville, Tennessee

Library of Congress Catalog Card
Number: 77-649875
International Standard Book Number:
0-85229-698-3
International Standard Serial Number:
0363-0366

Britannica Online may be accessed on
the Internet at <http://www.eb.com>.

Readers may notice that this volume is different from previous ones in the Britannica *Medical and Health Annual* series. It has a bold new design and might best be described as an anthology of "hot topics" in medicine and health. Over the years, the editors of the *Annual* have learned (from focus groups, reader feedback, reprint requests, reviews, etc.) that the articles readers appreciate most are comprehensive in their coverage and put the latest breakthroughs and developments in "proper perspective"—something the mass media rarely do. Because you (our readers) seem to want more-than-cursory coverage of the "real" world of medicine and health, we (the editors) have produced a volume composed entirely of "feature" articles—compelling in-depth reports that we hope consumers and health professionals alike will find "reader-friendly."

How did we decide what to cover in this all-feature volume? In a number of ways. As medical editors, we make it our business to keep as up to date in the field as is humanly possible. If I were to include anything close to a complete list of the lay and professional publications that we peruse on a regular basis—not to mention the ever-growing number of health and medicine sites we visit on the World Wide Web—I wouldn't have room to say anything else in this foreword!

Many of our past contributors—health professionals from all over the world—keep in close touch. Around the time we were planning this volume, Senior Editor Linda Tomchuck had a phone conversation with a health care law expert, who noted how often instances of malpractice and negligence in medicine are highlighted in the media, whereas the *honest* but inevitable mistakes that every doctor makes are rarely mentioned. That discussion led us to assign the thought-provoking article "Honest Errors in Medicine" (page 56).

We get occasional ideas from our colleagues at Encyclopædia Britannica. Last October, for instance, an editor in the geography and world data department passed along a news item from *Pacific Islands Monthly* about a very unusual study under way on the island of Nauru. (Nauruans have some of the highest rates of diabetes and obesity in the world.) We were intrigued—and had already commissioned a report on diabetes in the 21st century. The sidebar "No Man Is an Island" (page 187) looks at the fascinating research on Nauru, which could have important implications for people at risk for diabetes the world over.

This year the editors are indebted to the excellent counsel of two new medical advisers. Bruce Gellin, an infectious diseases expert, has been a frequent contributor to this publication. Lois DeBakey, a reader of the *Medical and Health Annual* since its inception (in 1976), has been called "the unchallenged champion of the proper use of medical English." (And, yes, she is related to the internationally acclaimed surgeon Michael E. DeBakey; he's her older brother.)

Michael DeBakey happens to be one of a select group of well-known individuals who contributed to this volume's pièce de résistance, "To Smoke or Not to Smoke: Celebrities Speak Out" (page 40). Some of the others who quite candidly reveal when and how they kicked the tobacco habit—or why they never took it up in the first place—are gourmet chef Julia Child, former surgeon general C. Everett Koop, political correspondent Cokie Roberts, star outfielder Ken Griffey, Jr., Indian yogi B.K.S. Iyengar, and British mystery writer P.D. James.

If you or someone you care about is still smoking, turn immediately to "Lighting Up for the Last Time" (page 26). There are lots of aids for quitters—from acupuncture to nicotine replacers to support groups to Zyban; author Tamar Nordenberg reviews them all.

In selecting topics for this volume, the editors took to heart a recent survey conducted by the International Food Information Council, which found foodborne disease to be the "number one" diet and nutrition topic covered by the mass media in 1997. The IFIC survey also found that the media often neglect "to provide the context necessary for consumers to make informed choices about their own food selections." *Our goal* in covering the subject ("It's Probably Something You Ate..."; page 240) was to provide that context—to give readers sound advice about reducing their personal risk of infection by foodborne pathogens.

If you are worried about pathogens that may be a threat to your health, don't miss the penetrating report on emerging infectious diseases, "Is There a Killer Flu in our Future?" (page 6), by Nobel Prize-winning scientist Joshua Lederberg.

Although it is not caused by a pathogen, an "emerging" malady that economist John Kenneth Galbraith writes about in "Contemplating Senior Citizenship" (page 294) is both prevalent and menacing. Find out if *you* might be suffering from the "Still Syndrome."

"If you've ever wondered what planet teenagers come from, you are not alone." This reassurance is offered by the internationally known psychologist Mihaly Csikszentmihalyi. "Teenage Turbulence" (page 104) is "must" reading for all parents of adolescents and other adults who are baffled by the behavior of today's teens.

I've run out of room and haven't mentioned so many of the other outstanding articles on the pages that follow—on leeches in medicine; road rage; the therapeutic effects of laughter; St. John's wort; state-of-the-art and alternative treatments for infertilty; attention deficit disorder; asthma; physician-activists; incontinence; and Lewis Carroll's migraine headaches.

—Ellen Bernstein

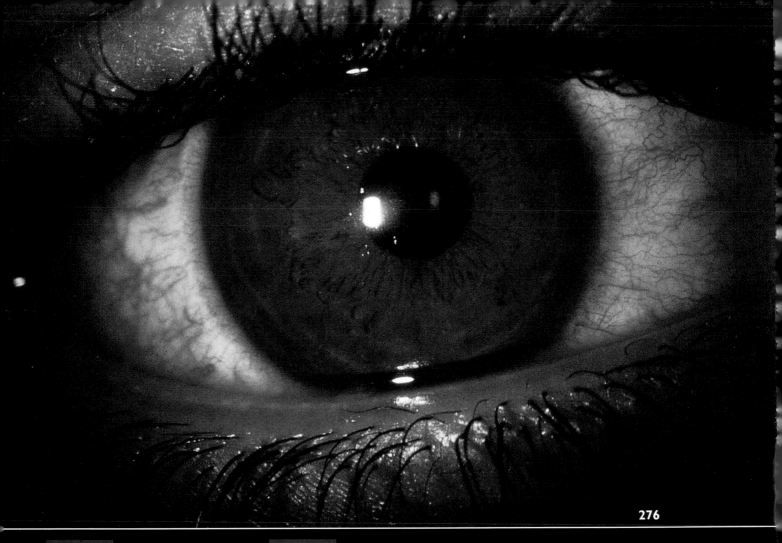

276

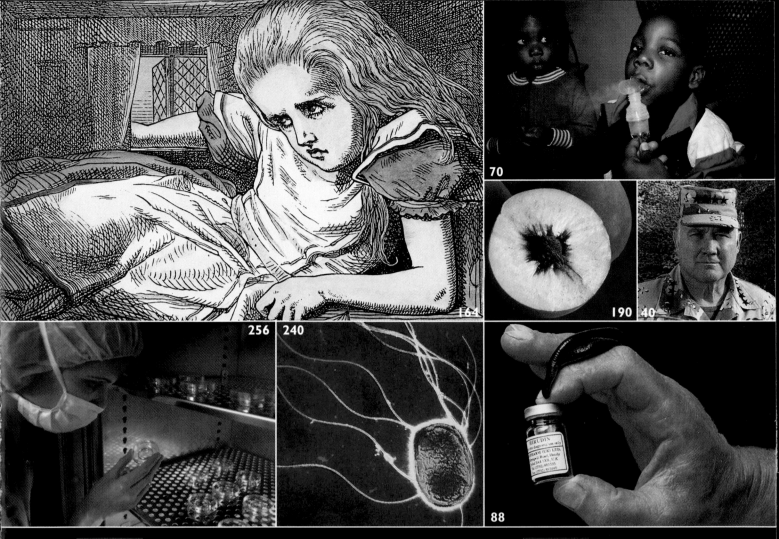

70

164

190 40

256 240

88

IS THERE A KILLER FLU IN OUR FUTURE?

BY JOSHUA LEDERBERG, PH.D.

PLAGUE: 1. an epidemic disease causing a high rate of mortality: PESTILENCE *2. a virulent contagious febrile disease that is caused by a bacterium of the genus* Yersinia *(Y. pestis).*

—*Merriam-Webster's Medical Desk Dictionary*

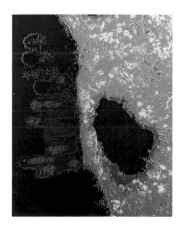

In May 1997 a three-year-old boy was admitted to a Hong Kong hospital with a high fever and serious illness. He died a few days later: a lamentable event, but not one so unusual as to make headlines. Three months later, when it was learned the child had been infected by a brand-new strain of influenza, one never before diagnosed in humans, there was community-wide panic. News of the new strain, called A(H5N1), reached the world in November and December, when nearly a score

7

Joshua Lederberg is Professor and President Emeritus and Sackler Foundation Scholar, the Rockefeller University, New York City. Lederberg received a Nobel Prize for Physiology or Medicine in 1958 and a National Medal of Science in 1989. He is a member of the National Academy of Sciences and the Royal Society, London, and has received 11 honorary degrees.

(Overleaf, left) Epidemiologist stands ready to confront the deadly Ebola virus; (right) false-color magnification of an influenza virus (red) infecting a cell. (Below) Allegorical representation of the Demon of the Plague, Germany, 1540.

(continued from page 7)
more new cases appeared, all in Hong Kong. With the late-fall cases came five more deaths—a situation grave enough to evoke visions of long-ago pestilences sweeping across huge sectors of the population.

PLAGUES AND PEOPLE

History, preceded by biblical and epic mythological accounts, attests to the fact that the human experience has been attended by devastating plagues. Plague, the exceedingly deadly human illness (second definition), struck Athens in 430 BCE, Constantinople in 542 CE, China and India in 1346, the entire European continent between 1347 and 1352 (when plague became known as the Black Death), and London in 1664. Each of these outbreaks achieved cataclysmic proportions, with anywhere from one-tenth to one-half of the people being afflicted. The defeat of the native peoples of the Western Hemisphere was a comparable event in that inadvertent infection of the population with measles and smallpox—"plagues" in their own right (first definition)—took a far greater toll than did the cavalry or the martial skills of the Conquistadores. In more recent times the misnamed "Spanish" influenza of 1918 exacted more than a half million American lives, and over 20 million worldwide.

Now, more than a century has elapsed since the foundations of scientific medicine were laid by Louis Pasteur in France and Robert Koch in Germany, culminating in the lifesaving vaccines and "wonder drugs" of the 1950s. Smallpox has now been eradicated from the face of the globe and polio nearly so. With antibiotics like penicillin and streptomycin, it appeared that most bacterial infections could be managed with a few pills. With that complacency, however, society, perhaps all too readily, let down its guard, and the major agenda of research and pharmaceutical development turned to other formidable challenges—chronic diseases like heart disease, cancer, and psychiatric disorders, which are not so easily attributed to external parasites or alien "bugs." (Even that judgment, it appears, may have to be revised, as medical scientists are increasingly finding infectious causes for afflictions of the human constitution; liver cancer has been linked to infectious hepatitis B, gastric ulcers [and perhaps stomach cancer] to helicobacteria, and, more controversially, heart disease to chlamydia infection and schizophrenia to "slow" neuroviruses.)

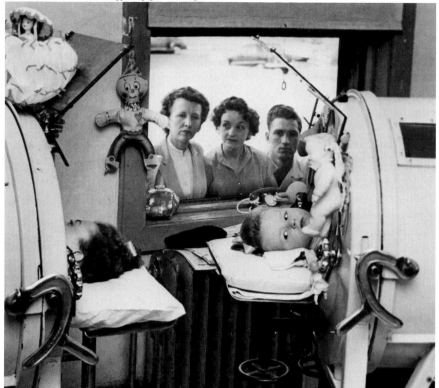

In 1952 polio epidemics reached their peak incidence in the United States. Here, anxious parents peer through an observation window at their quarantined daughters, both confined to iron lungs in the Memphis (Tennessee) Isolation Hospital.

RUDE AWAKENINGS

The complacency about infectious disease was brusquely shaken by the AIDS pandemic, starting in the early 1980s. Here was a brand-new disease unknown to medical science, for which, even now, neither a chemical cure nor a preventive vaccine is in sight. HIV/AIDS is still spreading—being on the rise especially in Africa and Asia—even as its acceleration in North America and Europe is being tempered by education and a class of highly effective, apparently life-prolonging drugs (though few medical scientists are optimistic that these agents will eventuate in long-term cures). A United Nations report released in June 1998 indicated that HIV/AIDS was hitting sub-Saharan Africa at levels even experts considered "shocking." Of the 30 million people infected with HIV worldwide 21 million were located in Africa alone.

Smallpox has now been eradicated from the face of the globe and polio nearly so.

Along with HIV/AIDS, the last 20 years have seen the emergence or reemergence of dozens of other infections, making headlines by the month: Ebola, Lassa fever, Lyme and Legionnaires' diseases, *Escherichia coli* O157:H7, hantavirus, cholera O139, cyclospora (in raspberries), cryptosporidium (in water supplies), and "mad cow" disease (in Great Britain). Equally alarming is the growing array of microbial infections for which long-used antibiotics are no longer effective. Many surgeons now fear that common postoperative wound infections will become untreatable, as in the preantibiotic era, and that many more patients will acquire "nosocomial" infections, those that are contracted in the hospital as a by-product of being treated in that environment.

None of these later outbreaks of illness has yet become a global scourge to match the 1918 flu or HIV/AIDS. At the very least, it is hoped that the headline makers have opened scientists' and society's eyes to the very real threat posed by emerging infectious diseases. Some key questions that presently demand answers are as follows: Which infections present the gravest risks to humanity? What biological and social factors account for the phenomenon of emergence? And, finally, what measures are needed for individual and collective security?

9

(Below) Mourners in Jerusalem observe World AIDS Day, Dec. 1, 1997. (Right) Red blood cell swollen with malarial parasites (*Plasmodium*); (opposite page) lungs infected by *Mycobacterium tuberculosis*. The causative organisms of both malaria and tuberculosis are growing increasingly drug-resistant on a global scale.

PREDICTING FUTURE ILLS

People's assumptions about what they can expect in the way of a healthy life have altered significantly over the 20th century. In the U.S. mortality rates from AIDS now appear to have peaked at about 17 deaths per 100,000 cases annually; this is just a bit less than the number that succumbed to syphilis each year between 1910 and 1940 or to diphtheria and typhoid fever between 1900 and 1920. The latter three diseases, in fact, are now rare in the industrialized world, thanks to the development and use of antibiotics and vaccines and the provision of sanitized water supplies. The death rate from the Spanish flu during its brief swath across the U.S. in 1918 was nearly 600 per 100,000. It came and went without any meaningful medical intervention; rather, the deadliest flu epidemic in history simply burned itself out when it could no longer find naive (*i.e.*, nonimmune) hosts—almost 99% of humans having been exposed and survived.

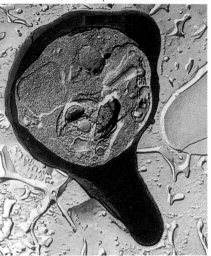

The world of microbes is enormously diverse and complex; new pathogens might arise from any of a thousand extant species. Furthermore, many pathogens have become quite "professional" in their activities—having evolved specific adaptations to life in the host, including means to circumvent the human immune system and, alarmingly, the drugs invented to defeat them. Their transmission from one victim to another is thereby ensured.

Knowing what they do about emergent diseases, experts predict that new infectious threats to human health are most likely to emerge as (1) further refinements of diseases already present in humans or (2) crossovers from animal diseases, known as zoonoses. (Rarely, as was the case with Legionnaires' disease, a bacterium whose normal habitat is in the soil manages to infect humans—its manifestation as a human disease being incidental to its life cycle.)

The most striking and well-documented examples of the first group are the drug-resistant variants of existing infections (among them, tuberculosis [TB], pneumonia, malaria, gonorrhea, and staph and strep infections). Plague, yellow fever, hantavirus, and very likely HIV are

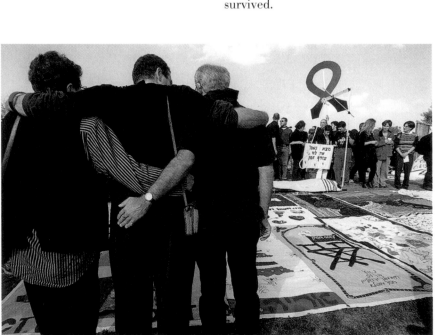

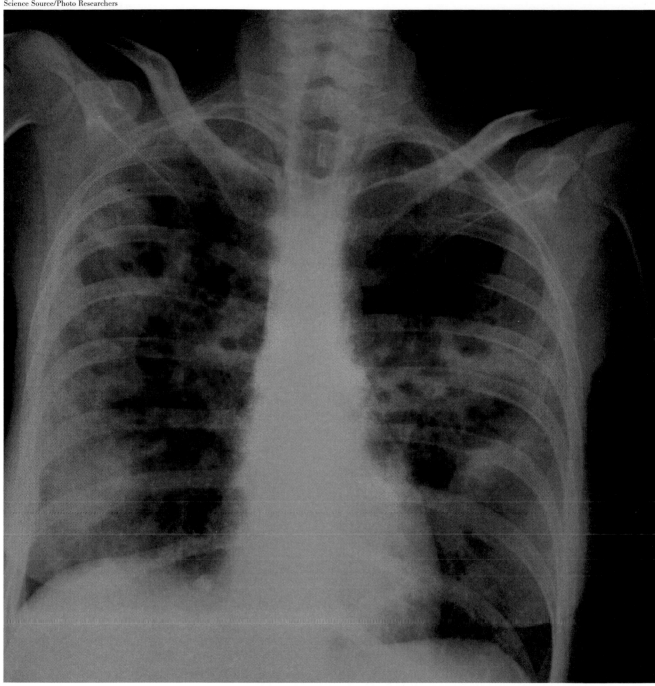

examples of the second group, the zoonoses. The catalog of existing diseases in this group is already a sizable one; in due course the reservoir of viruses infecting monkeys and rodents at the forest margin is likely to be exhausted. Nonetheless, new zoonoses may yet be discovered. The medical community must be especially cautious not to "ease the path" for the spread of these animal-based diseases—for example, by transplanting an animal organ that could be harboring a monkey virus into a human patient, particularly a recipient whose immune system is already compromised. If and when such experiments are done, as has been projected for treating AIDS, they should be governed by scrupu-lous monitoring of both the trans-plant tissue and the health of the human recipient, lest these new treatments become the seat of brand-new zoonoses. Medical scientists failed to predict AIDS; they must leave open the possibility of further infectious surprises.

Two infectious diseases that are prevalent and increasingly drug-

An Italian nun is buried in Kikwit, Zaire (now the Democratic Republic of the Congo), during a 1995 outbreak of the deadly Ebola virus. Ebola hemorrhagic fever struck the African continent again in 1996, taking lives in Gabon and South Africa.

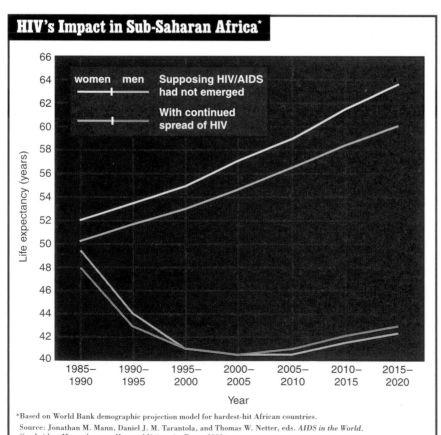

HIV's Impact in Sub-Saharan Africa*

women   men

Supposing HIV/AIDS had not emerged

With continued spread of HIV

Life expectancy (years)

*Based on World Bank demographic projection model for hardest-hit African countries.

Source: Jonathan M. Mann, Daniel J. M. Tarantola, and Thomas W. Netter, eds. *AIDS in the World.* Cambridge, Massachusetts: Harvard University Press, 1992.

resistant on a global scale, with grievous consequences, are malaria and TB. Thus far, preventive vaccines for both have had only limited success. The causative agents of these present-day scourges are a protozoan and a bacterium, respectively. In broad theoretical terms, it should not be difficult to devise new chemical treatments against them. Most "wonder drugs" directly reflect the level of research invested in their development. It is the industrialized countries of the world, by and large, that constitute the markets for these sophisticated new drugs, as they are the ones well able to pay for the technology required for developing them. Not surprisingly, the pharmaceutical industry has achieved many triumphs in responding to those markets. At the same time, though, it has largely ignored the many infectious diseases still prevalent in the less-developed countries (including

TB and malaria). Without marked increases in the funding for research on drugs and vaccines, a number of diseases, largely of the Third World, are sure to exact an ever-increasing toll on human life—and on the global economy. Furthermore, that disease burden will eventually cross the oceans in one form or another, as happened with HIV/AIDS.

Fortunately, the exciting science of "genomics" will enable scientists to overcome many of the technical challenges of responding to emerging infections. Researchers now have the tools to completely decode the genetic blueprints for each of a dozen—and, it is hoped, eventually hundreds—strains of pathogenic microbes. The gene studies already under way point to unique features of each pathogen that can be exploited in the search for chemical cures. It is

particularly exciting that scientists from Paris and Cambridge, England, announced in June 1998 that they had succeeded in decoding the complete DNA sequence for *Mycobacterium tuberculosis*, the microbe that kills more people annually than any other infectious agent in the world.

VIRUSES: FOES OF A DIFFERENT ORDER

Viruses are another matter. Rarely are there very effective chemicals against them. Put simply, viruses are autonomous genetic particles that reproduce in much the same manner as germs or genes, but they do so only within the cells they infect. They have evolved their own mechanisms for recognizing host cells, penetrating the cell membranes, and exploiting

Panic-stricken residents of Surat, India, cover their faces as they wait to receive prophylactic antibiotics during an outbreak of pneumonic plague that took the slum-ridden, rat-infested city of more than two million people by surprise in September 1994.

John Moore—AP/Wide World

(Below) Dr. R. Dourmashkin—Science Source/Photo Researchers; (opposite page) Scott Sady—AP/Wide World

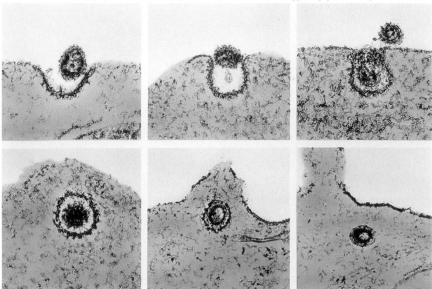

Series showing a flu virus at work. In the top three frames, the virus, which has a spiked outer coat, attaches to the host cell and then is enfolded by the cell's membrane. The lower three frames show the virus progressively penetrating and infecting the cell. Once inside the cell, the highly infectious agent will spread and invade mucous cells in the respiratory tract.

the cell's metabolism for their own benefit. They have also discovered specialized means of exiting the cell and then going on to infect new ones.

In order to do their damage within cells, viruses need strategies to penetrate the host organism in the first place and then escape it, surviving the intervening journey. There are numerous means by which viruses get from one host to another. They travel in body fluids (blood, mucus, semen). Other virus-carrying vehicles are contaminated needles, contaminated food or water, unwashed hands, and airborne droplets

There are numerous means by which viruses get from one host to another.

that get passed along when someone coughs or sneezes. Human skin usually provides an impermeable barrier to viruses; there are, however, certain viral diseases that are transmitted by biting insects, such as ticks, flies, and mosquitoes.

Within the human body, viruses face many hostile defenses in the form of a finely tuned immune system. The coughs and sneezes associated with respiratory viruses may well have evolved as a trait of the virus, enabling it to spread. Many of the other symptoms of viral infections are by-products of the host's natural chemical defenses— druglike substances (*e.g.*, cytokines) that are invoked in an effort to shed the invading virus. Some viruses have quite cleverly learned to manipulate those defensive reactions to their own benefit; the shedding of rotaviruses that cause severe diarrhea may facilitate the spread of infection to others at the same time it benefits the host by evacuating the offending virus particles.

The fact that viruses contain the same sort of genetic material (DNA or RNA) as is used in normal human cellular reproduction and physiology bedevils research scientists seeking therapies that are harmful to the virus but safe for the host. Furthermore, there is no firm evidence of how the scores of known viruses ultimately evolved, though it is safe to assume that they were rogue escapees from the normal cell, much as cancers are rogue cells that have shaken off the regulatory discipline of the integrated organism.

The difficulties inherent in attempting to thwart viruses are complicated by the acquired habit of many of these microbes to get inside the DNA of the host cell's chromosomes and for many generations simulate the normal genes therein.

Later (often years later), such viral pathogens may be remobilized as autonomous particles. The retroviruses, of which HIV is the most notorious example, are especially prone to playing this game. Many hundreds of such viruses are historically integrated into the normal human genome. There are odd examples of cancer or other diseases emerging from such remobilized viruses in animals (*e.g.*, Moloney murine leukemia). Their biological or pathological significance in the human—at least for now—remains quite mysterious. It can be said with some sureness, however, that the propensity for HIV to burrow into the chromosomes of some classes of white blood cells portends poorly for ever effecting a complete cure for AIDS.

All things considered, the likeliest viral candidate for the next great plague would be (1) a virus of high lethality that learns a new mode of spreading or (2) a virus that is highly communicable and then turns more vicious. A potential example of the first would be an HIV strain that mutates to a pneumonic form—*i.e.*, one that, like pneumonia, is capable of penetrating the lungs and is communicated via the respiratory route. Something akin to this did happen with a bacterial disease; the great plague of the 14th century began as "bubonic" plague—named for the "buboes," or huge skin pustules, that characterize it. But as the pandemic progressed, there were more and more cases of "pneumonic" plague spread directly from human to human, bypassing the fleas and rats that are the usual vectors and reservoirs, respectively, of *Y. pestis*.

Thus far, there is not a shred of evidence suggesting that HIV is pneumonically transmissible. But it should also be said that there has

been almost no direct research on the actual barriers to such transmission of the virus. If pneumonic transmission ever occurred, it would probably be in conjunction with other respiratory infections. Individuals whose lungs were already inflamed by another infection would probably be more vulnerable to the pneumonic intake of an HIV particle or, conversely, more likely to expirate such particles. It has already been well established that people with HIV are highly vulnerable to infection with pulmonary TB.

A child runs through stagnant water in a Haitian slum. Poverty, poor sanitation, political instability, crowded urban living, and microbial adaptation are among the many factors contributing to the emergence of pathogens that threaten global health.

A disease that might fall into a category between the first and the second is hepatitis A, which is very efficiently communicated and has already infected hundreds of millions of people. Hepatitis A, found in the excreta of infected individuals, is spread from person to person via the fecal-oral route—*i.e.*, by putting something in the mouth that has been contaminated by the stool of a person with the infection. Thus, it is especially prevalent in areas where

sanitation is poor and/or good personal hygiene is not observed. Hepatitis A can be lethal, but the severest manifestations occur infrequently, at least in its present-day form. Fortunately, highly refined versions of a hepatitis A vaccine produced by recombinant-DNA technology have been available for several years; thus, prophylactic immunization is ready to afford great relief at both an individual and a public health level. (*continued on page 19*)

DISCOVERING THE SECRETS OF THE DEADLIEST FLU EVER

BY M.J. FRIEDRICH

The influenza virus is a master of disguise, a shape-shifter that evades the body's immune system by transfiguring its protein facade. This transformation, which is brought about through frequent mutation of the genes that encode the virus's surface proteins (a process known as *genetic drift*), prevents previously infected individuals from developing resistance to future flu outbreaks; it also explains why new flu vaccines must be developed every year.

Every spring medical scientists from the World Health Organization in Geneva and the Centers for Disease Control and Prevention in Atlanta, Georgia, meet to forecast what strain of influenza virus pharmaceutical companies should use to prepare vaccines for the following fall-winter flu season. Their predictions are based on data collected from flu sufferers around the world. Though in the last several years this sophisticated system has produced very effective vaccines, infectious disease experts remain ever on the lookout for particularly virulent influenza strains that are known to emerge periodically. These unusually destructive variants often arise through the reassortment, or swapping, of genes that can occur between flu viruses of different species, such as humans, pigs, and birds. It is in pigs, which can be infected with both human flu viruses and avian (bird) viruses, as well as their own ("swine flu") viruses, that such gene reassortment, or *genetic shift*, most often occurs. When this happens, a new flu virus to which the human population is particularly susceptible can emerge.

Such an event occurred in 1918–19, when the most devastating influenza pandemic in history (also called the Spanish flu) killed about 675,000 Americans and between 20 million and 40 million people worldwide. The pandemic was notorious not only for its extremely high mortality rates but because most deaths occurred among persons between the ages of 15 and 34, an age group whose members normally recover from the illness. Because influenza viruses mutate so rapidly, the possibility of an-

This bit of lung tissue from a soldier who succumbed to the 1918 flu may reveal why that particular flu pandemic was so lethal.

other pandemic like that of 1918 is always present. If scientists today understood what made that particular virus so deadly, it might be possible for them to identify the most threatening strains as they emerge and, if they are clever or lucky, develop a vaccine rapidly enough to prevent such a deadly historical event from repeating itself.

Recently a number of investigators set out to discover just what genetic alteration transformed the influenza A virus into the lethal agent it was in 1918. But this has not been an easy task. Finding actual samples was the first hurdle to overcome. In 1995, to isolate the first genetic fragments of the 1918 virus, Jeffrey Taubenberger, the chief of molecular pathology at the Armed Forces Institute of Pathology, Washington, D.C., used a technique he had previously developed to extract viruses from decayed dolphin tissue. The viral fragments came from lung tissue of a 21-year-old flu victim, a soldier stationed at Camp Jackson, South Carolina. Taubenberger's initial analysis of the fragments, published in *Science* (March 21, 1997), indicated that the killer 1918 strain evolved from a classic swine flu virus, not an avian one, as some researchers thought.

Another scientific sleuth in search of the 1918 virus, retired Swedish pathologist Johan Hultin, contacted Taubenberger after reading his *Science* report. Hultin suggested that he might be able to help Taubenberger by coming up with more tissue samples containing the virus. Some 40 years earlier Hultin had attempted to recover the virus from the lungs of 1918 flu victims buried in the permafrost (permanent frozen ground) of the remote Alaskan tundra. Although that quest was unsuccessful, he was fairly confident that recent advances in molecular biology would improve his chances of securing actual viral samples from the lungs of frozen victims. He was right. In August 1997 he exhumed the bodies of four flu victims from a single grave site. One of the bodies—that of an obese Eskimo woman—was especially

(Below) Corbis/Bettmann; (opposite page) David Peterson

well preserved. Hultin sent the samples he recovered to Taubenberger, whose research team was indeed able to isolate the 1918 flu virus in the Eskimo woman's lung tissue. (Hultin is one member of an international team that is planning to exhume other 1918 flu victims' bodies—those of Norwegian miners buried in the permafrost of an island north of the Arctic Circle.)

Meanwhile, Taubenberger and his colleagues isolated still further fragments of the virus from tissue of another soldier who died in the 1918 epidemic—this one at Camp Upton, New York. With samples obtained from three geographically distinct regions, the researchers are hopeful that something unique in the virus's genes will finally reveal the secret of its lethality. Taubenberger acknowl-

Autumn 1918: New York City office clerks wear cloth masks on the job at the peak of the influenza pandemic that killed more than 20 million worldwide.

edges that his team's work is "just the beginning of the story." But he also thinks that following the genetic trail of the 1918 flu virus is vital. "Even if *we* don't understand it," he says, referring to the genetic basis of the virus's virulence, "in the future someone else will."

M.J. Friedrich *is an Associate Editor who specializes in science at Encyclopædia Britannica, Inc., Chicago.*

Photographs, Karen Kasmauski—Matrix

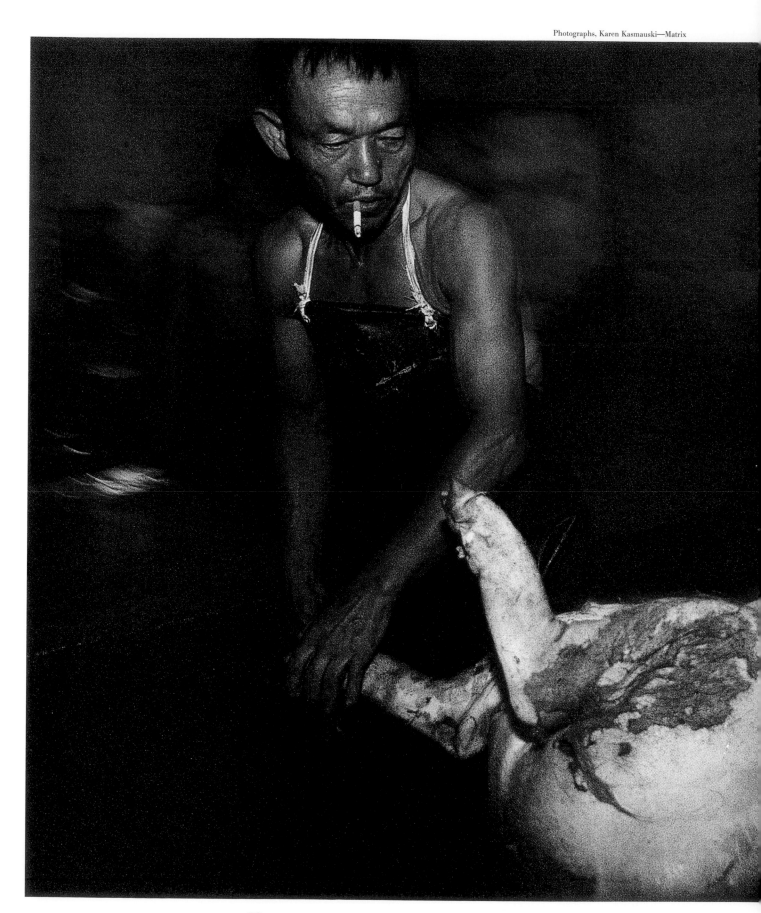

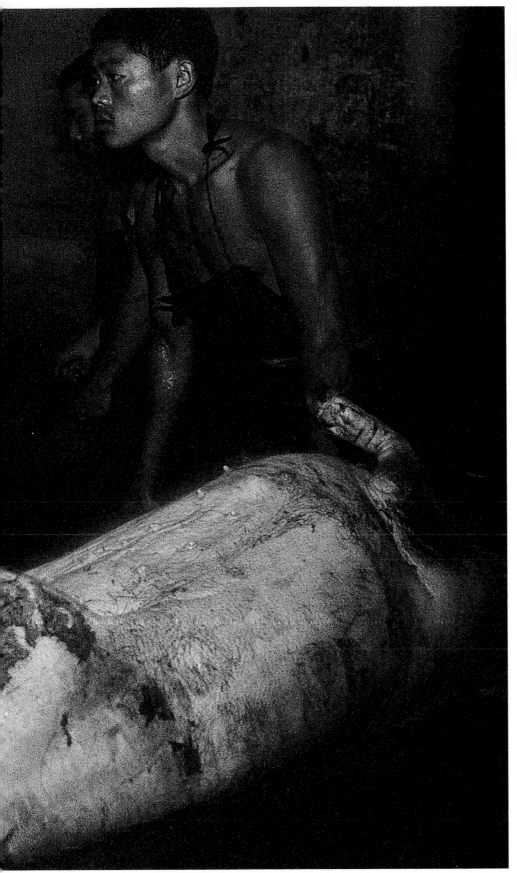

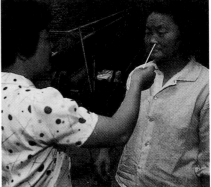

(*continued from page 15*)

FLU VIRUSES: CUNNING CONTENDERS

The exemplar of the second category of future viral threat—one that grows more vicious—is the influenza virus, which already afflicts a substantial percentage of the population every winter season. Because flu virus is subject to frequent mutational changes that alter its antigenic composition (the surface proteins that are capable of stimulating an immune reaction), each year calls for a fresh revision of the vaccines against it.

Influenza strains circulate through wild birds, including migratory ducks and geese; each year's hatch of these birds provides new nonimmune hosts. These influenza strains in birds (avian strains) are typically quite mild and have minimal disease

(Above) A swab from a Chinese farmer's nose and (left) specimens from slaughtered pigs will indicate which flu viruses are circulating—information that will help scientists concoct an appropriate vaccine for the next flu season. Swine are thought to be the "mixing vessel" for virulent new flu strains.

19

> # All the basic mechanisms are in place for the emergence of a [flu] strain as deadly as that of 1918.

impact; in fact, the bird flu may go unnoticed between episodes until it mutates to more devastating bird-killing varieties.

Swine appear to be the animals most readily accommodating to both bird and human strains of flu and therefore may be the reservoir, or mixing vessel, for recombined flu strains of high lethality. This has been the consensual model of what happened in the 1918 Spanish flu (which almost certainly got its start in the American Midwest, not Spain). South China is believed to be the ecologically favored site for the generation of new flu viruses in the contemporary world. It was there that the unusually virulent 1968 Hong Kong flu got its start. While the pandemic disease engendered by the '68 flu was hardly comparable to that caused by the 1918 strain, it was certainly not one to be sneezed at, as it killed some 46,000 people. Today influenza specialists are almost unanimous in their conviction that all the basic mechanisms are in place for the emergence of a strain as deadly as that of 1918. If anything, today's

patterns of global air traffic—over a million passengers daily board an aircraft bound for an international destination—would ensure a much more rapid spread of disease than has ever occurred before.

It might seem like the world is better prepared to cope with a major flu pandemic today than it was early in the century. Pneumonia, for example, a common complication of the flu, presumably would be managed more successfully in today's hospitals than it was in 1918, and the wide assortment of antibiotics now available would make the treatment of secondary bacterial infections possible. Unfortunately, however, drug resistance is spreading rapidly among many respiratory bacteria; already pneumonia secondary to influenza accounts for tens of thousands of deaths annually. In the course of a major pandemic, hospital facilities worldwide would be so overwhelmed by caseloads that it would be nearly impossible to provide the ideal level of supportive care for influenza's unlucky victims.

HONG KONG ALERT

Against this historical backdrop, the sudden appearance in Hong Kong of a new type of influenza in humans in May 1997 was a source of considerable consternation for infectious disease experts. Because similar flu strains were known to be circulating in birds, authorities quickly turned a watchful eye on the situation. The 17 new human cases of H5N1 that occurred in November and December triggered a global alert, at which time infectious disease experts from the U.S. Centers for Disease Control and Prevention (CDC) laboratories in Atlanta, Georgia, were enlisted to carry out extensive epidemiological studies. Those efforts pointed to

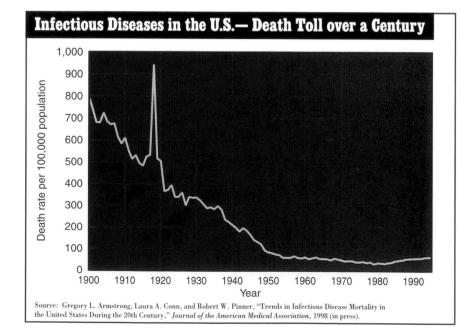

Infectious Diseases in the U.S.— Death Toll over a Century

Death rate per 100,000 population (y-axis: 0 to 1,000) vs. Year (x-axis: 1900 to 1990).

Source: Gregory L. Armstrong, Laura A. Conn, and Robert W. Pinner, "Trends in Infectious Disease Mortality in the United States During the 20th Century," *Journal of the American Medical Association*, 1998 (in press).

Emerging and Reemerging Infectious Diseases, 1996-98

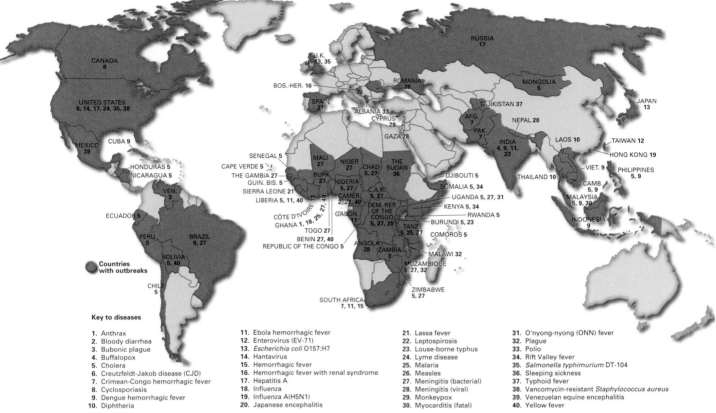

Countries with outbreaks

Key to diseases

1. Anthrax
2. Bloody diarrhea
3. Bubonic plague
4. Buffalopox
5. Cholera
6. Creutzfeldt-Jakob disease (CJD)
7. Crimean-Congo hemorrhagic fever
8. Cyclosporiasis
9. Dengue hemorrhagic fever
10. Diphtheria

11. Ebola hemorrhagic fever
12. Enterovirus (EV-71)
13. *Escherichia coli* O157:H7
14. Hantavirus
15. Hemorrhagic fever
16. Hemorrhagic fever with renal syndrome
17. Hepatitis A
18. Influenza
19. Influenza A(H5N1)
20. Japanese encephalitis

21. Lassa fever
22. Leptospirosis
23. Louse-borne typhus
24. Lyme disease
25. Malaria
26. Measles
27. Meningitis (bacterial)
28. Meningitis (viral)
29. Monkeypox
30. Myocarditis (fatal)

31. O'nyong-nyong (ONN) fever
32. Plague
33. Polio
34. Rift Valley fever
35. *Salmonella typhimurium* DT-104
36. Sleeping sickness
37. Typhoid fever
38. Vancomycin-resistant *Staphylococcus aureus*
39. Venezuelan equine encephalitis
40. Yellow fever

©1998, Encyclopædia Britannica, Inc.

direct human contact with infected chickens as the main, if not the only, source of contagion. There was no clear evidence of person-to-person spread, and the number of new H5N1 cases did not escalate.

At the end of December, the Hong Kong authorities decided to sacrifice the entire flock of chickens, as well as a number of quail, pigeons, ducks, and geese (an estimated 1.5 million birds), in the affected territory as a precaution against further cases. They were especially intent on wiping out the bird flu epidemic *before* the arrival of the annual winter flu season. Had the two flus been present simultaneously, the mixing of strains would have been a distinct possibility—and with it generation of still more deadly strains. As of

midsummer 1998, there had been no new H5N1 cases in humans. Although six deaths out of a total of 18 cases speaks of a highly lethal variant of the flu, the H5N1 strain is not one that is readily transmitted. That is indeed fortunate because hundreds of thousands of travelers have transited Hong Kong, flying everywhere around the globe.

The latest word from the CDC is that the Hong Kong birds were experiencing not one but two similar lethal flu viruses, which would have significantly complicated the task of preparing an appropriate vaccine. Public health officials cannot just turn their backs on the situation, as the biological cauldron churning out new viral strains continues to simmer. For the last several years, representatives of government agencies, medical centers, and the vaccine industry have been conferring to generate a better-founded plan for dealing with future flu epidemics. The evolving "influenza pandemic preparedness plan" for the U.S. is focused on six major areas: (1) improvements in ongoing virological and disease-based surveillance systems; (2) vaccination of high-priority target groups (*e.g.*, the elderly, immunologically compro-

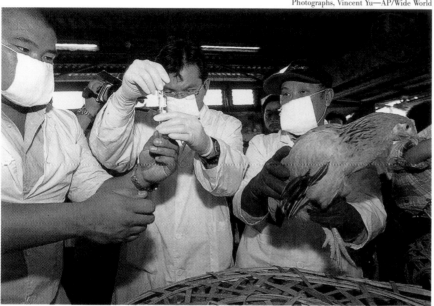

Dec. 17, 1997: veterinary officers take samples of chicken feces at a Hong Kong poultry market after two humans died from a flu virus previously known to infect only birds. (Opposite page) Considering the vast numbers of international travelers who pass through Hong Kong every day, it is indeed fortunate that there were so few human cases of "bird flu."

mised individuals such as cancer and HIV/AIDS patients, hospital workers), and, given sufficient vaccine supplies, the entire U.S. population; (3) establishment of indemnification programs for vaccine manufacturers and health care providers that would provide "no-fault" protection to all sides in the event of mishaps following vaccination (provided federal standards are met); (4) research to improve detection of new microbial variants and to increase the availability of vaccines and antiviral agents; (5) development of integrated, multicomponent communication systems for rapid dissemination and exchange of emerging

infectious disease information; and (6) emergency preparedness plans to provide for adequate medical care and maintenance of essential community services during a severe epidemic.

Such planning is indispensable if today's global village is to have any chance of coping with future pandemics. It has to be said that existing flu vaccines are only barely satisfactory, and current methods for their production are hampered by logistic issues like the amount of time it can take to verify the existence of new flu types and the ongoing need for the crash production of vaccines. Further, because vaccines are made by growing influenza virus in fertile hens' eggs from acceptable breeds, there must be ample quantities of such eggs available when they are needed, and the viral strain in question must be able to grow in the eggs. The H5N1 flu virus was so lethal to birds that it killed inoculated eggs intended for the making of vaccines before they could deliver a sufficient yield of virus. Great efforts are now under way to overcome these obstacles.

The situation is hardly better for the chemotherapeutic treatment of the flu. The antiviral drugs amantadine and rimantadine can be used to mitigate flu symptoms, but the potential for mass prophylaxis (prevention) with either of these virtually identical agents is, unfortunately, limited by their toxicity. Furthermore, widespread use of rimantadine or amantadine would almost certainly ensure the development of viral resistance.

Investment in research on influenza has long been insufficient, owing in part to the misperception that flu is just a bad cold. Only now is research in this area beginning to receive the attention it deserves. Real flu in humans is too often under-estimated. In epidemic seasons it can account for 10% of overall mortality, the majority of deaths being in people already debilitated by other disease. In the U.S. alone it is responsible for some 20,000–40,000 deaths each flu season.

All present indications are that humanity experienced a "close call" in Hong Kong in 1997. The global community is indebted to the local and international health authorities for the professional and responsible way in which they handled a truly alarming situation. This author, for one, hopes that the six fatal encounters in Hong Kong with a strain of flu entirely new to humans served as an exhortation that will be heeded to universal benefit during the present "breathing spell."

FOR FURTHER INFORMATION

Books

Collier, Richard. *The Plague of the Spanish Lady: The Influenza Pandemic of 1918–1919.* London: Allison and Busby, 1996.

Crosby, Alfred W. *America's Forgotten Pandemic: The Influenza of 1918.* Cambridge: Cambridge University Press, 1989.

Ewald, Paul M., and Ewald, Paul W. *Evolution of Infectious Disease.* Oxford: Oxford University Press, 1994.

Garrett, Laurie. *The Coming Plague.* New York: Farrar, Straus and Giroux, 1994.

Henig, Robin Marantz. *A Dancing Matrix: How Science Confronts Emerging Viruses.* New York: Vintage Books, 1994.

Kilbourne, Edwin D. *Influenza.* New York: Plenum Medical Book Co., 1987.

Lederberg, Joshua; Shope, Robert E.; and Oaks, Stanley C., Jr., eds. *Emerging Infections: Microbial Threats to Health in the United States.* Washington, D.C.: National Academy Press, 1992.

McNeill, William H. *Plagues and Peoples.* New York: Anchor Press/ Doubleday, 1976.

Wills, Christopher. *Yellow Fever, Black Goddess: The Coevolution of People and Plagues.* Reading, Massachusetts: Addison-Wesley Publishing Co., 1996.

Web site

OUTBREAK
http://www.outbreak.org

MENINGITIS IN MOSCOW, EBOLA IN GABON: REPORTING OUTBREAKS ON THE INTERNET

BY JOHN P. ("JACK") WOODALL, PH.D.

Ebola, hantaviruses, toxic *Escherichia coli*, flesh-eating bacteria, chicken flu. The world needs to know about outbreaks of these and other potentially virulent "emerging diseases" as soon as they appear anywhere on the globe. Public health workers need to take steps to prevent epidemics from spreading, and the public needs to know how to protect itself.

Imagine more than 10,000 computers with an equal number of users—scientists, health officials, journalists, laypeople—in 150 countries across the globe, keeping watch for disease outbreaks round the clock. That is precisely what the world's first—and so far only—global emerging disease reporting network can do. Moreover, it can get the word out even before official reports appear.

Rapid response, vital connections

The network's name is ProMED-mail. Established as a nonprofit project of the Federation of American Scientists in 1994, it receives reports by E-mail from subscribers; these reports are analyzed by disease experts ("moderators") and sent back out over the Internet via satellite, radio, and telephone. All of the ProMED-mail messages are archived and searchable.

- When a British travel medicine outfit wanted confirmation of a meningitis outbreak in Moscow, its query was posted on the Internet by ProMED-mail. First came an official denial, closely followed by confirmation of the epidemic from the Moscow Laboratory for Meningococcal Infection and Bacterial Meningitis.
- When Ebola broke out in Gabon in October 1996, ProMED-mail posted the news as soon as it was released by the World Health Organization's (WHO's) Regional Office for Africa, four days before it was disseminated on WHO's own outbreak-reporting system.
- After a tourist visiting the Amazon died of yellow fever, ProMED mail alerted travelers of the need for vaccination and sparked the vaccination of the at-risk resident population of the Brazilian city of Manaus.
- In June 1996 an epidemiologist in Los Angeles wanted to confirm a story he had heard concerning an outbreak of *E. coli* O157:H7 in Japan. Within four days the doctor in charge of the Hiroshima (Japan) Quarantine Station began to post a day-by-day account of the spread of what became a major epidemic.
- When it received reports from both sides of the Atlantic of similar illnesses caused by a rare type of *Salmonella*, ProMED-mail linked the unusual outbreaks. In so

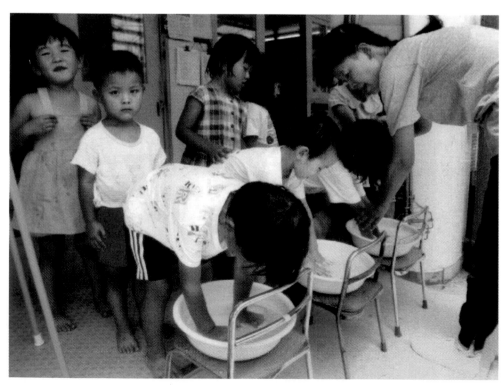

Following a major food poisoning outbreak, Japanese schoolchildren take special precautions before eating.

doing, the network demonstrated what would be a critical capability in the event of the use of biological weapons by terrorists.

• When the worst epidemic ever recorded of the rat-transmitted viral illness Lassa fever struck war-torn Sierra Leone in 1997, the only drug known to be effective against it (ribavirin) was found to be in critically low supply. This led ProMED-mail moderator and viral disease expert Charles H. Calisher to post this notice: "Here we have a drug we know is effective against numerous viruses that cause life-threatening illnesses and, disgracefully, it is neither licensed nor readily and cheaply available in the U.S., which has international responsibilities as well as the responsibilities for maintaining the good health of laboratory and field workers who study these viruses. As Hawkeye Pierce [of *M*A*S*H* fame] might have said, 'Who's in charge here?'" Thanks to the lively Internet discussion that ensued, the U.S. Navy was warned of the peril in a timely fashion. And enough ribavirin was secured to protect a fleet evacuating expatriates from Sierra Leone following a violent coup d'état.

In May 1997 foreigners are evacuated from Sierra Leone, at a time when the country was experiencing a major outbreak of Lassa fever.

Emerging diseases soap opera?

Although some have questioned the value of ProMED-mail's "unofficial" reports, and at least one subscriber has described ProMED-mail as "much more entertaining than anything Hollywood could come up with...a Peyton Place of microbes," many others are quick to point out the "incredible educational value" of the postings. To learn more about or subscribe to ProMED-mail, go to these Web sites:

• http://www.healthnet.org/programs/promed.html
• http://www.fas.org/promed

*ProMED-mail Director **Jack Woodall** is Director of the Nucleus for Investigating Emerging Infectious Diseases, Institute of Biomedical Sciences, Federal University of Rio de Janeiro, and Director, Arbovirus Laboratory, New York State Department of Health, Albany.*

LIGHTING UP FOR THE LAST TIME

BY TAMAR NORDENBERG

Now that I'm gone, I tell you, "Don't smoke. Whatever you do, just don't smoke." If I could take back that smoking, I wouldn't be talking about any cancer. I'm convinced of that.

—Actor Yul Brynner in a TV commercial aired after his death from lung cancer in 1985

Suppose that two jumbo jets crashed every day without a single survivor. That's the number of Americans killed by cigarettes—1,000 plus each day—more than the combined casualties from car accidents, AIDS, fires, alcohol, and murders. Smokers not only suffer disproportionately from lung and other cancers, heart disease, stroke, bronchitis, emphysema, and other illnesses that compromise the quality of their lives, they die an average of seven years earlier than nonsmokers.

27 *Tamar Nordenberg is a freelance writer living in Bethesda, Maryland.*

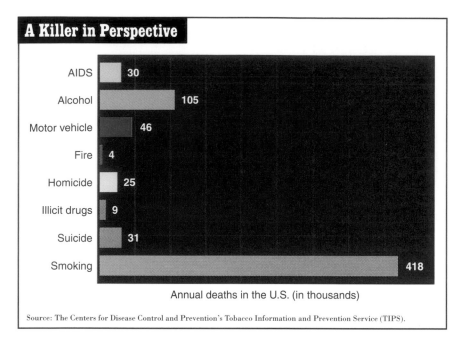

A Killer in Perspective

	Annual deaths in the U.S. (in thousands)
AIDS	30
Alcohol	105
Motor vehicle	46
Fire	4
Homicide	25
Illicit drugs	9
Suicide	31
Smoking	418

Annual deaths in the U.S. (in thousands)

Source: The Centers for Disease Control and Prevention's Tobacco Information and Prevention Service (TIPS).

Nowadays, those who still smoke have few places *but* the street to light up.

Paul S. Howell——Gamma/Liaison

True, not every smoker dies young. "There are survivors of almost everything. Even the bubonic plague killed 'only' one out of three people," says addictions specialist Michael Smith, director of the Substance Abuse Division at Lincoln Medical and Mental Health Center, Bronx, New York. "Most people will know someone who smoked and lived a long time, but you don't know if you're the one who will be immune to smoking's negative effects until you're 52 and somebody finds a 'thing' on your lung." Unlike the victims of bubonic plague or passengers on a doomed jet, however, smokers have the opportunity to shape their own fate. According to the Centers for Disease Control and Prevention, 70% of smokers want to kick their killer habit.

A BURNING DESIRE

Eugene Sapiro, a 32-year-old restaurant owner from Gaithersburg, Maryland, first tried to give up cigarettes after having smoked heavily for more than 10 years. "I reached a point where I couldn't think about any-

thing but my next cigarette," he says, "and I couldn't get my work done because I was always outside smoking. I didn't want to depend on cigarettes any more than I would want to be dependent on drugs or alcohol." But like alcohol and other drugs, cigarettes can command a powerful physical and mental hold that can be tough to overcome. "I had become a slave to the habit," Sapiro says. "I was so addicted that I continued to smoke up to two or three packs a day even after it stopped being enjoyable." Challenging as it is to quit, Sapiro and millions of others have done it, usually after several tries. U.S. government statistics suggest that for every one of the country's current 47 million smokers, there is an ex-smoker who has conquered the addiction.

Like many smokers, Jacquelyn Rogers knew that cigarettes could cause lung cancer and other deadly diseases but continued to smoke anyway. After 22 years of heavy smoking, she finally triumphed over her habit and then founded Smok-Enders to teach others to do the same. Focusing on smoking's dire health consequences, Rogers contends, is counterproductive; it only enhances the smoker's anxiety. "The motivation must come from a feeling that you want to quit rather than you ought to or you must or the doctor told you to." Smoking-cessation expert Douglas Jorenby, a psychologist at the Center for Tobacco Research and Intervention at the University of Wisconsin, agrees. People may decide to quit on the basis of the health consequences, he says, but "it's not the health scares, by and large, that will pull people through. It's feeling that they're better off not smoking, for reasons that vary from person to person."

In addition to the long-term health benefits, there are many other personal rewards to be gained from quitting.

- Nonsmokers feel healthier, perform better in sports, and have greater endurance for most physical activities. While smoking, people often experience shortness of breath and aggravation of asthma.
- People who quit don't need to feel guilty about exposing their spouses, children, and others to smoke. Secondhand, or passive, smoke, also known as environmental tobacco smoke (ETS), has been linked to over 3,800 cases of lung cancer in nonsmokers each year in

Conor Caffrey—Photo Researchers

There are countless reasons for parents of young children *not* to smoke. Their youngsters' respiratory health is one of them.

(Clockwise from top center) Davies & Starr—Tony Stone Images; Brian Yarvin—Photo Researchers; Jean-Marc Bouju—AP/Wide World; Patricia Agre—Photo Researchers; Rafael Macia—Photo Researchers

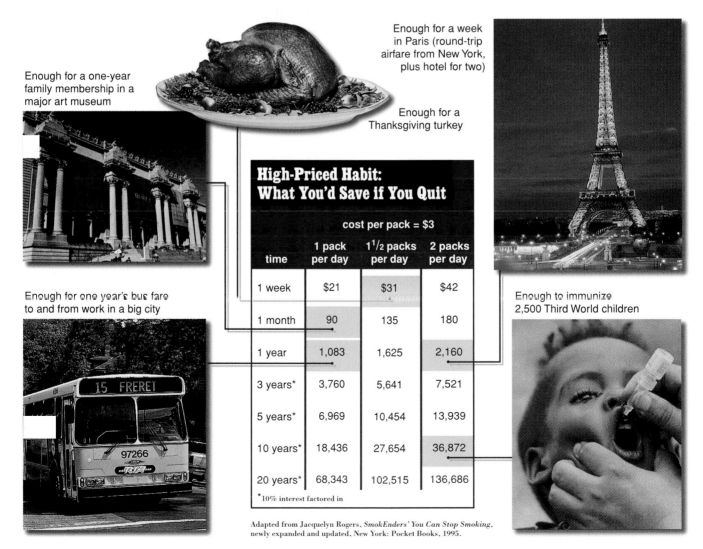

Enough for a one-year family membership in a major art museum

Enough for a week in Paris (round-trip airfare from New York, plus hotel for two)

Enough for a Thanksgiving turkey

Enough for one year's bus fare to and from work in a big city

Enough to immunize 2,500 Third World children

High-Priced Habit: What You'd Save if You Quit

cost per pack = $3

time	1 pack per day	1½ packs per day	2 packs per day
1 week	$21	$31	$42
1 month	90	135	180
1 year	1,083	1,625	2,160
3 years*	3,760	5,641	7,521
5 years*	6,969	10,454	13,939
10 years*	18,436	27,654	36,872
20 years*	68,343	102,515	136,686

*10% interest factored in

Adapted from Jacquelyn Rogers, *SmokEnders' You Can Stop Smoking*, newly expanded and updated, New York: Pocket Books, 1995.

the United States alone, as well as to a doubled risk of heart attack in nonsmoking women. Children exposed to ETS are more likely than those who grow up in smoke-free households to have respiratory ailments—asthma, pneumonia, bronchitis, and tonsillitis.

- Nonsmokers have healthier babies. Studies show that babies born to women who smoke are more likely to be premature or underweight and to have decreased lung function; they are also three times more likely to die from sudden infant death syndrome than other babies.
- Parents who give up their unhealthy habit set a good example for their kids. Children of smokers are more likely to become smokers themselves.
- Quitters save money. SmokEnders founder Rogers has calculated the dollars and cents that can be saved by giving up smoking (*see* table on previous page). She determined, for example, that if a parent quits smoking when a child is born and saves all the money that would have been spent on cigarettes, 18 years later he or she will have enough to pay for that child's college education.

There are, of course, other important benefits of quitting; these include improved senses of taste and smell, fresher breath, a better-smelling home and automobile, enhanced self-esteem, and, perhaps most important, freedom from a powerful addiction.

> # Nicotine...may be as addictive as heroin or cocaine.

NICOTINE'S HOLD

A robust resolve makes it possible—but by no means easy—to give up smoking. One reason quitting can be so tough is that the nicotine in cigarettes is an addictive drug. Nicotine, in fact, may be as addictive as heroin or cocaine. Rogers knows addicts who have managed to quit those substances but couldn't quit smoking. For genetic or other reasons, nicotine is less addictive for some people than it is for others. "Everyone has an Uncle Charlie who was driving down the road and threw his cigarettes out the window and never looked back," says Richard Hurt, director of the Nicotine Dependence Center at the Mayo Clinic in Rochester, Minnesota. There are various ways of predicting how difficult it is likely to be for an individual smoker to give up cigarettes. A convenient test that rates smokers' physical dependence on nicotine, developed and refined by Swedish researcher Karl-Olov Fagerström, appears on page 36 (*see* Sidebar: "How Hooked Are You?").

As a rule, people experience some uncomfortable withdrawal effects when their bodies begin to get less nicotine. These symptoms, which can include anxiety, irritability, frustration, anger, difficulty concentrating, and a craving for tobacco, tend to be worst during the first few days but can last a month or more. With a medical aid that helps combat these pangs, however, almost all smokers can raise their odds of quitting successfully. Such help, experts point out, is available in numerous forms. Whereas 15% of smokers are successful at quitting cold turkey, studies show that the chance of success almost doubles with the help of a nicotine-replacement product—patch, gum, nasal spray, or inhaler.

THE HIT WITHOUT THE HAZARDS

The nicotine replacers deliver nicotine into the body in small, steady doses. Because they do not deliver the nicotine into the lungs like cigarettes, they do not produce the addictive "buzz" that smokers experience. Also, they don't contain the tar, carbon monoxide, and other toxic ingredients that are largely responsible for smoking's health hazards. Each of the four types of nicotine replacers can help fight cravings, and each has pluses and minuses. Personal preference is usually the best determinant of which one to use. For those who want something that is easy to use, a patch a day may be the best choice. Others may want a fast-acting drug in their system when they feel a craving coming on; for them the gum, nasal spray, or inhaler may be better.

Patch.
- Availability: Over the counter.
- Use: A new patch is applied to a

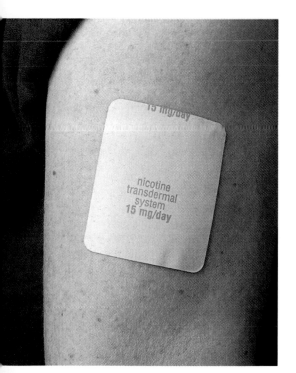

different area of dry, clean, non-hairy skin each day and left on for the amount of time recommended by the manufacturer (16 or 24 hours, depending on the brand).
- Possible side effects: Mild itching, burning, or tingling at the site of the patch. People with skin problems, including certain allergies, should consider a different form of nicotine replacement.

Gum.
- Availability: Over the counter.
- Use: The gum is "chewed and parked"—*i.e.*, chewed until it tastes peppery, then placed between the cheek and gums for about 30 minutes to allow the nicotine to be absorbed through the mouth's mucous membrane. "It won't be effective," cautions Jorenby, "if you just chomp away like it's a piece of Juicy Fruit." The U.S. government's guideline on smoking cessation, issued in 1996 by the Agency for Health Care Policy and Research (AHCPR), recommends a fixed schedule (one piece of nicotine gum every one to two hours over a period of one to three months).
- Possible side effects: Mouth soreness, hiccups, and jaw ache. People who have had extensive dental work, wear dentures, or suffer from temporomandibular joint pain should try a different nicotine replacer.

Nasal spray.
- Availability: By prescription only.
- Use: The nicotine is inhaled into the nose from a pump bottle and absorbed through the nasal lining.
- Possible side effects: Very com-

"Nicotine replacers" are just that: they give smokers a decent "hit" of the substance they crave but spare them the lung-clogging tar, carbon monoxide, and other toxic ingredients in cigarettes. (Clockwise from bottom left) Nicotine patch, gum, and nasal spray.

(Top) SmithKline Beecham

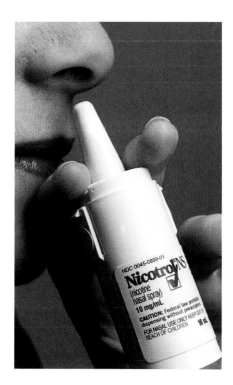

31

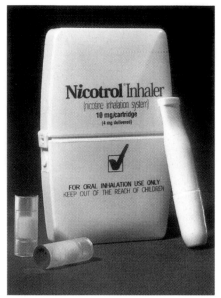

The newest smoking-cessation aids on the market: (above) a nicotine-inhalation system that can be used up to 16 times a day for three months and (below) Zyban, an antidepressant drug that may alleviate withdrawal symptoms. Both products require a doctor's prescription.

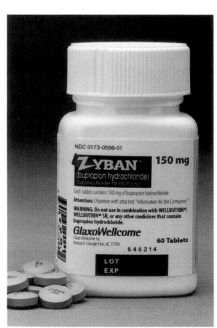

monly, nasal and sinus irritation. The spray is not recommended for those with nasal or sinus conditions, allergies, or asthma.

Inhaler.

- Availability: By prescription only.
- Use: A nicotine-inhalation system was approved by the Food and Drug Administration (FDA) in May 1997. An aerosolized form of nicotine is sucked in through the plastic mouthpiece of a handheld device. The nicotine never reaches the lungs of the user; rather, it is absorbed through the mucous membranes of the mouth and throat. Although some have likened the inhaler to a fat plastic cigarette, it is not known whether the similarity of the hand-to-mouth ritual provides any psychological advantage over the other modes of nicotine replacement.
- Possible side effects: Cough or throat irritation. Those with asthma or other bronchial ailments should use the inhaler cautiously.

People trying any nicotine replacement for the first time should consult a physician if they have a medical problem such as heart disease or high blood pressure; are taking any other medications, especially drugs for asthma or depression; or are pregnant or breast-feeding. It's possible to get an overdose of nicotine. Therefore, when using any of the nicotine replacers, people should not smoke, chew tobacco, or use snuff or other nicotine-containing products. Signs of overdose include headaches, dizziness, weakness, fainting, upset stomach, vomiting, diarrhea, or mental confusion. Finally, nicotine-replacement products, including those that have been used and thrown away, should be kept out of the reach of children and pets; ingesting even a small amount of nicotine can make them seriously ill.

PROMISING NEW MEDICATION

The newest nonnicotine antismoking option on the market is the prescription drug bupropion hydrochloride (Zyban). The drug, which had been previously approved by the FDA as an antidepressant (under the brand name Wellbutrin), seems to reduce withdrawal symptoms and the urge to smoke by affecting the neurotransmitters dopamine and norepinephrine (brain chemicals that transmit signals between nerve cells and are thought to be linked to nicotine addiction). In the largest study to date, published in *The New England Journal of Medicine* (Oct. 23, 1997), 615 men and women who had tried and failed to quit previously were given either 100, 150, or 300 milligrams per day of a sustained-release preparation of bupropion or a placebo. After seven weeks, smoking-cessation rates were 19% for the placebo group and 28.8%, 38.6%, and 44.2%, respectively, for the groups taking the ascending dosages of the drug. After one year, however, quit rates among all four groups had declined substantially. Hurt, who was the lead author of the study, describes the results as "good" but adds, "There is not going to be a magic bullet for this very difficult addiction."

An earlier trial had found that subjects who simultaneously took bupropion and used a nicotine patch for 10 weeks had higher success rates than those who took a placebo or used a patch alone. In studies of Zyban, which involved nondepressed people, most subjects reported no noticeable mood changes while using the drug. Insomnia and dry mouth were the most common side effects. Tremor and skin rash were occasionally reported. The usual dosage recommended by the manufacturer, Glaxo Wellcome, is 150 milligrams once a day for three days, then twice a day for 7 to 12 weeks, with or without concurrent treatment with a nicotine-replacement product. Zyban is not recommended for women who are pregnant or breast-feeding.

NOT BY DRUGS ALONE

Drugs alone cannot "cure" a smoker, experts point out, because the smoking addiction involves a psychological component on top of the nicotine dependence. Certain daily cues can trigger a smoker's desire for a cigarette. Jesse Nichols, who is struggling to give up his 40-year pack-a-day habit, reports that he "can go the whole workday without thinking about a cigarette, but on the way home the cravings begin." Cigarettes have become so much a part of his leisure-time activities that he can't imagine an evening social engagement or a Saturday-afternoon golf game without them. "It would be like a club was missing from my bag," he says.

To get through the most trying times, Jorenby recommends a two-part strategy. First, think about when the urge for a cigarette is greatest. Is it first thing in the morning? in the car? after a meal? with a cup of coffee? Second, have a distraction ready for each of those vulnerable times. It could be deep breathing, getting up and leaving a stressful situation, drinking a glass of water, sucking on a mint, or taking a brisk walk. Jorenby's promise: "The craving will come, but in a few minutes the urge will pass."

Beyond this mental preparation, some form of emotional support is also critical. The support can come from a structured stop-smoking pro-

Ted Soqui—Sygma

gram or a pep talk from a doctor, nurse, dentist, pharmacist, psychologist, or other health professional. Counseling needn't be time-consuming or expensive. The more support one gets, the better, but studies show that even very brief counseling—as little as three minutes total—can make a difference. Despite the fact that brief physician counseling has been shown to increase quit rates, a recent study published in the *Journal of the American Medical Association* (Feb. 25, 1998) found that American physicians as a group fell far short of meeting national health objectives when it came to identifying smokers among their patients and advising them to quit.

"Hang in there. This is a good thing you're doing for yourself."

An encouraging word from a family member or friend, perhaps someone who has successfully quit, can help prevent relapse, too. Smokers may want to ask for the

The public health community is waging an all-out war on smoking. Many public service advertisements, like the one on the city bus above, tell consumers the grim truth about a categorically harmful habit.

understanding of those around them, including co-workers. "It's about getting feedback from other people when you're feeling run-down," Jorenby says. "Everyone needs someone to say, 'Hang in there. This is a good thing you're doing for yourself.'"

BEYOND THE CONVENTIONAL

Some smokers have found hypnosis and/or acupuncture helpful in quitting cigarettes. Among health professionals there are advocates of these techniques and others who remain skeptical about their usefulness.

Forty-year-old Ann Marks never managed to abstain from smoking for more than three days, despite several tries. Cold turkey didn't work for the 32-year smoker, and neither did weaning or using the nicotine patch or gum. When her father died from lung cancer, Marks became motivated as she had never been before. She did not want to die the way he did, uncomfortable and unable to breathe or talk during his last days. Less than a year after her father's death, on what would have been his 76th birthday, Marks underwent hypnosis by her psychology professor, Edward Frischholz, at the University of Illinois at Chicago. Marks can now report, "I know I've quit for good. I have cravings, but I'm not a smoker anymore. The hypnosis helped me focus on my reasons for quitting."

Frischholz, who is editor of the *American Journal of Clinical Hypnosis*, has had notable success with the thousands of smokers he has hypnotized. In his single-session treatments, he helps people focus on the urge to "protect and respect" their bodies rather than on the urge to smoke. Other hypnotherapists get their clients to imagine themselves in the future as healthy nonsmokers or suggest that they focus on the noxious taste of cigarettes.

To determine the "hypnotizability" of each potential candidate, Frischholz administers a five-minute test. The more hypnotizable a person is, he says, the more likely the treatment is to work. He estimates that one in four people can benefit from his type of therapy, which makes its effectiveness comparable to that of other smoking-cessation therapies. Frischholz recommends that people contact the American Society of Clinical Hypnosis to find a certified hypnotherapist who treats cigarette addicts. (*See* "For Further Information," page 39.)

Many experts, including the authors of the AHCPR guideline,

A patient trying to give up smoking undergoes acupuncture therapy. Although *solid scientific* evidence that this traditional Eastern form of medicine helps curb addictions is lacking, there are many former nicotine addicts who swear by it.

Blair Seitz—Photo Researchers

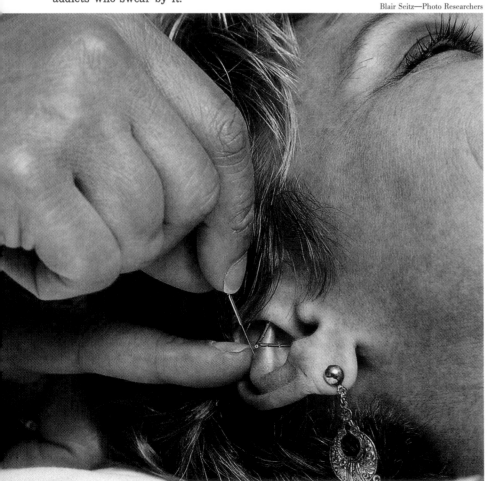

Precisely placed acupuncture needles help the body help itself.

contend that there is no proof that hypnosis is effective for smoking cessation. Hurt notes that he has had patients who "have gone to hypnotists and have quit smoking, and that's great. But there just isn't enough scientific evidence that it works."

Many doctors are equally skeptical about the use of the ancient Chinese medical technique acupuncture for the treatment of cigarette addiction. Proponents, however, report that the method has been shown to reduce nicotine cravings. Although it is not clear exactly how acupuncture works, it is said to promote homeostasis, the balanced functioning of the whole person. Addiction specialist Smith, whose Bronx substance-abuse program treats thousands of addicts a year, regularly uses acupuncture as "a nonverbal, nonthreatening first step in treatment," no matter what the addictive substance is. Precisely placed acupuncture needles help the body help itself, Smith says.

One approach to smoking cessation uses "press" needles that are usually inserted into the "lung point" on both ears. The lung point (said to be associated with pain, excess sweating, and various respiratory symptoms) is one of five main ear points used in acupuncture. The needles, which stay in place for a week or two at a time, are gently manipulated by the patient several times a day. Treatment continues for one to two months. Smith has seen dramatic results among the few hundred smokers he has treated. He says acupuncture gives most heavy smokers "a free ride to a very low amount of smoking." The confidence gained in curtailing excessive smoking may then help the person continue on to total abstinence. But acupuncture will help only those who are committed to quitting, Smith emphasizes. Also, he points out, the method appears to be far more effective for those with a serious habit than for "light smokers."

STUMBLING BLOCKS

Many things are known to undermine a quitter's resolve, such as being around smokers, being under stress, and drinking alcohol. Quitting pangs can be minimized by avoiding these temptations as much as possible and removing cigarettes, ashtrays, and other such reminders from one's home, car, and office.

Another common stumbling block for would-be quitters, especially women, is the fear of gaining weight. Although the extra 5 or 10 pounds that most people put on when they quit is not enough to present a health (*continued on page 37*)

Waistline Realities

Smoking status	Men		Women	
	Percentage who are overweight	Average weight gain in last 10 years (pounds)	Percentage who are overweight	Average weight gain in last 10 years (pounds)
Never smoked	37	0.7	42	1.7
Quit 10 or more years earlier	40	1.1	35	2.2
Quit within last 10 years	47	2.4	42	3.8
Current smokers	28	0.8	33	1.3
Other tobacco users	41	0.2	52	1.8

Source: K.M. Flegal, R.P. Troiano, E.R. Pamuk, R.J. Kuczmarski, and S.M. Campbell, "The Influence of Smoking Cessation on the Prevalence of Overweight in the United States," *The New England Journal of Medicine* (Nov. 2, 1995), pp. 1165–70.

HOW HOOKED ARE YOU?

The Fagerström Test for Nicotine Dependence was developed for research purposes. The scoring range is 0–10 points with [0] indicative of minimum dependence and [10] of maximum dependence. This adapted version of the test is used with permission of Karl-Olov Fagerström.

1. How soon after you wake up do you smoke your first cigarette?

Within 5 minutes. [3]
Within 6–30 minutes. [2]
Within 31–60 minutes. [1]
After 60 minutes. [0]

2. Do you find it difficult to refrain from smoking in public places where it is expressly forbidden?

Yes. [1]
No. [0]

3. Which cigarette would you hate most to give up?

The first one in the morning. [1]
Any others. [0]

4. How many cigarettes per day do you smoke?

10 or fewer. [0]
11–20. [1]
21–30. [2]
31 or more. [3]

5. Do you smoke more frequently during the first hours after waking than during the rest of the day?

Yes. [1]
No. [0]

6. Do you smoke if you are so ill that you are in bed most of the day?

Yes. [1]
No. [0]

(*continued from page 35*)
risk, it can be a major deterrent to trying to quit or a reason for relapse. It is common for weight-conscious people to resort to a cigarette because it provides a quick fix of appetite-suppressing, metabolism-speeding nicotine. Studies show that women who quit tend to gain slightly more than their male counterparts and that African-Americans, people under 55, and heavy smokers are at somewhat greater risk than others for excessive weight gain.

Several years ago a Canadian study found that weight gain associated with smoking cessation was temporary. Subjects who had stayed off smoking (usually for about two years) gradually shed the five or six pounds they had gained initially. For weight control, experts recommend adopting a healthy lifestyle that includes moderate exercise and a diet rich in fruits, vegetables, whole grains, and other low-fat foods. More than other forms of nicotine replacement, nicotine gum seems to stave off weight gain while it is used.

More often than not, successful quitters tackle one problem at a time: they give up cigarettes first; then, once they are secure in their "nonsmoker" status, they cope with the extra pounds. How long does it take to gain that security? It may come in three to six months; it may take years. Even after abstaining through the most precarious period, however, people shouldn't kid themselves that they can be "occasional" smokers. Nicotine's addictiveness makes that virtually impossible. "Not even a single puff after the quit date," the government's guideline on smoking cessation advises. Finally, smokers should know that cigars, smokeless tobacco, and low-tar, low-nicotine cigarettes are not safe alternatives. They too can be addic-

tive and cause cancer, heart disease, and a number of other serious health problems.

JUST DO IT!

What's the best time to quit? "Pick a date, and go for it," Hurt says. Come what may, try to maintain your focus on the short- and long-term rewards of being a nonsmoker. The American

---

What's the best time to quit? "Pick a date and go for it."

Cancer Society points out that blood pressure drops to a normal level within 20 minutes of the last cigarette. In the first one to nine months, the ex-smoker will cough less, be less likely to experience shortness of breath, and feel less tired than previously. In the long run,

On Dec. 30, 1997, two nights before a strict new law banning smoking in all California drinking establishments would take effect, these San Francisco nightclub-goers indulge in a last *legal* cigar.

Eric Risberg—AP/Wide World

Penny Tweedie—Tony Stone Images

Every day in the U.S., some 3,000 young people join the ranks of regular smokers. About one-third of them will die prematurely as a result of their tobacco use.

although quitting may not completely reverse smoking's ill effects on the heart, lungs, and blood vessels, it can dramatically lessen the chances of developing life-threatening cardio-pulmonary disease.

It takes most people several tries to quit for good, so would-be quitters shouldn't get discouraged after a single failure. With each try, chances of succeeding improve. Specialists suggest that those who are trying again after a few failures think about the things that helped in the past and the things that got in the way. If one type of nicotine replacement didn't work, it's worth trying another. Similarly, if one program was not helpful, another might be. The AHCPR guideline suggests that the most effective smoking-cessation programs are those that focus on behavior modification and involve at least four to seven sessions.

What ultimately enabled Sapiro to accomplish what two years of sampling different medical approaches couldn't? In his words, "powerful motivation." After trying the patch, gum, hypnosis, and acupuncture without lasting success, he was determined to quit "for good." He resolved that he didn't "want anybody or anything running my life but me." Finally, in August 1997, he knew he would never light up again.

FOR FURTHER INFORMATION

Books

Allison, Patricia, and Yost, Jack. *Hooked, but Not Helpless: Kicking Nicotine Addiction.* Portland, Oregon: BridgeCity Books, 1996.

Brigham, Janet. *Dying to Quit: Why We Smoke and How We Stop.* Washington, D.C.: National Academy Press, 1998.

Rogers, Jacquelyn. SmokEnders' *You Can Stop Smoking,* newly expanded and updated. New York: Pocket Books, 1995.

Stevic-Rust, Lori, and Maximin, Anita. *The Stop Smoking Workbook.* Oakland, California: New Harbinger Publications, 1996.

Who's Lighting Up?[1]

	Men (%)	Women (%)	Total (%)
Race/ethnicity			
White	27.1	24.1	25.6
Black	28.8	23.5	25.8
Hispanic	21.7	14.9	18.3
American Indian/ Alaskan Native	37.3	35.4	36.2
Asian/Pacific Islander	29.4	4.3	16.6
Years of education[2]			
≤8	28.4	17.8	22.6
9–11	41.9	33.7	37.5
12	33.7	26.2	29.5
13–15	25.0	22.5	23.6
≥16	14.3	13.7	14.0
Age group			
18–24	27.8	21.8	24.8
25–44	30.5	26.8	28.6
45–64	27.1	24.0	25.5
≥65	14.3	11.5	13.0
Poverty status			
At or above	25.9	21.8	23.8
Below	36.9	29.3	32.5
Unknown	26.9	21.0	23.5
Total	**27.0**	**22.6**	**24.7**

[1] Latest available data on smokers in the United States (from the National Health Interview Survey, 1995).
[2] Persons aged ≥25 years.
Source: *Morbidity and Mortality Weekly Report,* vol. 46, no. 51 (Dec. 26, 1997).

Whelan, Elizabeth M., ed. *Cigarettes: What the Warning Label Doesn't Tell You: The First Comprehensive Guide to the Health Consequences of Smoking.* Amherst, New York: Prometheus Books, 1997.

Organizations

The Agency for Health Care Policy and Research (AHCPR) offers the pamphlet *You Can Quit Smoking*, a consumer version of the *Clinical Practice Guideline on Smoking Cessation* for doctors; a Smoking Cessation Consumer Tools Kit; and other materials in both print and electronic forms.
AHCPR Publications Clearinghouse
PO Box 8547

Silver Spring MD 20907-8547
800-358-9295
InstantFAX (24 hours a day) 301-594-2800, push 1, then press start button for instructions and a list of publications
Web site: http://www.ahcpr.gov/
American Cancer Society
1599 Clifton Rd NE
Atlanta GA 30329-4250
800-ACS-2345 (800-227-2345)
Web site: http://www.cancer.org/
American Lung Association
1740 Broadway
New York NY 10019-4374
800-LUNG-USA (800-586-4872)
Web site: http://www.lungusa.org/
American Heart Association
7272 Greenville Ave
Dallas TX 75231-4596

800-AHA-USA1 (800-242-8721)
Web site: http://www.amhrt.org/
Office of Smoking and Health
Centers for Disease Control and Prevention
1600 Clifton Rd NE
Atlanta GA 30333
800-CDC-1311 (800-232-1311)
Web site: http://www.cdc.gov/tobacco/
American Society of Clinical Hypnosis (ASCH)
Suite 291
2200 East Devon Ave
Des Plaines IL 60018-4534
(Prospective clients can obtain the names of clinical hypnotherapists in their area by sending a request, along with a self-addressed stamped envelope, to ASCH.)

TO SMOKE OR NOT TO SMOKE: CELEBRITIES SPEAK OUT

Actress and comedienne
Carole Lombard, 1937.

Who, these days, *doesn't* know that smoking is harmful to health—one's own health *and* that of others? The foregoing article took a close look at the many benefits of giving up cigarettes—among them, fresher breath and freedom from a powerful addiction. It also evaluated smoking-cessation methods, from acupuncture to support groups to Zyban. Surveys indicate that 70% of current smokers want to quit, but swearing off cigarettes is easier said than done.

Knowing that there is no one-size-fits-all way to kick the habit and that the public—especially young people—is easily swayed by the words and actions of "celebrities," the editors of this volume asked a variety of prominent individuals about their own experiences with tobacco.

The responses to our admittedly unscientific survey run the gamut from "I never touched a cigarette" to "I'd rather die than quit." At the same time, the stories of many of those we contacted were alike in several ways, which suggests some common factors that inform a person's decisions to smoke—or not.

Jane Brody, *New York Times* health writer.

Antismoking activist Stanton Glanz.

Respondents were asked:

↩ What prompted you to start smoking? How old were you?

↩ If you've never smoked, how did you manage to avoid it? What factors enabled you to resist peer pressure and the other influences that typically persuade young people to adopt the habit?

↩ Did you consider smoking an extremely pleasurable activity?

↩ What finally prompted you to quit?

↩ Did you try and fail a number of times, or were you able to quit on the first try?

↩ Did you do it on your own or with help? Did you join a program? Use a nicotine substitute or medication?

↩ Was weight gain a problem?

↩ Was abstaining at certain times of the day—or during certain activities—more difficult than at others?

↩ As a smoker, did you underestimate the degree to which you were addicted?

↩ Now that you are a nonsmoker, how tolerant are you of those who still smoke?

The 24 responses that follow have been edited slightly.

SMOKE? NEVER!

Jane E. Brody, whose background is in medicine and biology, is a nationally known health columnist for the *New York Times*. She is the author of nine books, among them *Jane Brody's Nutrition Book* (1981) and her latest, *Jane Brody's Allergy Fighter* (1997). Brody also writes regularly for magazines and lectures frequently on health and nutrition.

I never smoked. If you never start, you never have to quit!

Topping almost any list of antismoking activists is the name of **Stanton A. Glanz**, Ph.D. Trained as a cardio-vascular physiologist and presently holding the position of senior fellow for cardiovascular research at the University of California, San Francisco, he has conducted research on many public health issues, including the dangers of exposure to "secondhand" smoke. Glanz gained public prominence in 1994 when thousands of pages of a major tobacco company's internal research and analysis documents mysteriously appeared on his desk. He posted the documents on the Internet and subsequently published them as a book, *The Cigarette Papers* (1996). Glanz led the efforts that resulted, briefly, in a total ban on smoking in bars in California. He continues to spearhead the campaign for antismoking legislation.

Smoking never appealed to me. I knew I was a nerd in junior high and high school. Even Marlboro couldn't cure that.

Mike Moore has been attorney general of the state of Mississippi since 1988. He first received national attention in 1994 when he filed suit against 13 tobacco companies, making Mississippi the first state to insist that cigarette manufacturers bear the health care costs of smoking. He is the recipient of numerous special awards for his efforts to improve public health and hold the tobacco industry accountable for tobacco-related illnesses. In December 1997 the *National Law Journal* named Attorney General Moore Lawyer of the Year for his achievements in tobacco litigation on behalf of the states. *People* magazine named him one of the 25 Most Intriguing People of the Year in 1997.

I never smoked a cigarette, probably because both my parents smoked and I hated the smell. Smoke has always bothered me, made my eyes red, etc. My hope is that we will be able to persuade young people never to start....If we do that, we will save millions of lives.

According to the *Guinness Book of World Records*, **Ann Landers** is the most widely syndicated columnist in the world; her column appears in over 1,200 newspapers and has an estimated readership of 90 million. She began writing her column in 1955. A 1978 World Almanac Poll showed Landers to be the "most influential woman in the United States." The American Medical Association presented her its Citation for Distinguished Service. In 1985 Landers was the first journalist to receive the Albert Lasker Public Service Award, in recognition of her efforts to pressure Congress to approve millions of dollars for cancer research and her referral of her readers to a wide variety of heath care agencies. She is the recipient of 32 honorary degrees and the author of six books, the most recent of which is *Wake Up and Smell the Coffee* (1996). In private life she is Mrs. Eppie Lederer and lives in Chicago.

Mississippi Attorney General Mike Moore enlists schoolchildren in his crusade against tobacco.

I have never smoked. When I was 15 years old, I made up my mind that I would never smoke or drink alcohol. I am pleased to say I have abstained from both, and that decision has served me well. I am not very tolerant of those who smoke. On several occasions I have asked someone to please "put that thing

Advice columnist Ann Landers: intolerant when "some clod decides to light up."

Lifelong nonsmokers:
(below) nonagenarian sur-
geon Michael DeBakey and
(bottom) senator and song-
writer Orrin Hatch.

*out" when I am in a car and some
clod decides to light up. I feel that no
one has the right to make my eyes
water and my clothes smell. So far
as I know, I've never lost any friends
because of my outspokenness. Sad to
say, however, I have lost some
friends to lung cancer.*

Fourth-term Republican senator from
Utah **Orrin Hatch** is one of the most
visible men on Capitol Hill. Not only
has he held a host of influential committee assignments, including the
chairmanship of the Senate Judiciary
Committee and membership on the
Finance and Foreign Relations committees, but he is often embroiled in
one or another high-profile legislative
battle. His name is indelibly linked
with the campaign for a balanced budget amendment to the U.S. Constitution, and he has earned a reputation as
champion of the American small busi-
nessman. He has also promoted legislation on public health, diet, and drug-
control issues, notably the Child Care
and Development Block Grant, which
he cosponsored with Democratic Sen.
Edward M. Kennedy of Massachusetts.
Hatch is a lifelong member of the
Church of Jesus Christ of Latter-day
Saints. In his spare time he plays piano
and composes songs.

*It was faith, religion, and a deter-
mination not to use anything to de-
tract from physical strength that
allowed me to resist the peer pressure and other influences to smoke.*

Michael E. DeBakey, M.D., is an
internationally recognized surgeon,
teacher, and innovator who is currently chancellor emeritus and distinguished service professor of surgery at
Baylor College of Medicine and director of the DeBakey Heart Center,
Houston, Texas. A pioneer in lifesaving surgery, in 1964 DeBakey was the
first to perform a successful coronary
artery bypass operation. For half a century he has served as adviser to almost
every U.S. president and to many
heads of state throughout the world. In
his role as international medical
statesman, he was chief consultant to
Renat S. Akchurin, who performed
coronary bypass surgery on Russian
Pres. Boris N. Yeltsin in the fall of
1996. DeBakey is the coauthor of several books aimed at lay audiences, including, most recently, *The New Living
Heart Diet* (1996).

*Since I have never smoked, I have
not had the problem of quitting. Early in my life, my parents instilled in
me the value of self-discipline and of
independent thinking, which helped
me resist peer pressure and the im-
portunings of the cigarette ads.*

*It is always easier to avoid any
adverse habit-forming activity than
to stop once the habit is established.
This is why it is important for young
people to resist superficially appealing or popular activities that have
subsequent deleterious effects on
their health and well-being.*

ONCE (OR TWICE) WAS ENOUGH!

Jimmy Carter served as the 39th president of the United States (1977–81). In 1982 he established the Carter Center in Atlanta, Georgia, a nongovernmental, nonprofit organization that promotes peace and human rights; resolves conflicts; fosters democracy and development; and fights hunger, poverty, and disease throughout the world. He is the author or coauthor of numerous books, including *Living Faith* (1996), *Always a Reckoning: And Other Poems* (1994), and the children's book *Talking Peace: A Vision for the Next Generation* (1995).

Thanks to my father, I have never been a smoker. He was my hero—strong, fair, hardworking, fun-loving, and a good athlete. When I was a child, I followed him everywhere he would let me go.

During World War I the government gave out free cigarettes to soldiers, and like a lot of other young men, my Daddy started smoking. He smoked two or more packs of cigarettes every day from then on. He tried on many occasions to quit but was never successful. In those days he had no way of knowing that cigarettes would ultimately cause his early death from cancer, but he resented the grip of a habit he could not break. When I was 12 years old, he asked me not to smoke until I was 21. I agreed.

On my 21st birthday I bought a pack of cigarettes and lit one up. My reaction was the same as that of most young people—I hated it. I gave the package away and never touched them again. Most people who first try cigarettes in their 20s or later don't get hooked. Peer pressure and other factors are not as strong when you're older, so it is imperative that we keep cigarettes out of the hands of our young people.

Christiane Northrup, M.D., is a pioneer in the field of women's health. A graduate of Dartmouth Medical School and a board-certified obstetrician-gynecologist with nearly 20 years of clinical and medical teaching experience, she was a cofounder in 1986 of Women to Women, an innovative health care center for women in Yarmouth, Maine, where she maintained a clinical practice for over 12 years. She is past president of the American Holistic Medical Association and current clinical assistant professor of obstetrics and gynecology at the University of Vermont College of Medicine. Through her highly successful monthly newsletter, *Health Wisdom for Women,* Northrup has created a network that provides ongoing and integrated support, education, and health-assessment services for women. Northrup is

One puff was enough for both former president Jimmy Carter (right) and women's health advocate Christiane Northrup (below).

(Below) Lee Crum—Outline; (bottom) Jon Randolph

45

the author of the best-selling book *Women's Bodies, Women's Wisdom* (1994; revised and updated edition, 1998).

When I was 12, my parents sat all five of us children down and said, "Today we're going to smoke so you'll know about it." Dad lit up a Salem and then passed it around. I got a bloody nose and found the whole thing disgusting. My parents immunized us well when it came to peer pressure by pointing out what it was. I have never felt pressured to smoke or drink.

The world's foremost advocate of Hatha yoga, **B.K.S. Iyengar** has dedicated his life to the study of this ancient art, philosophy, science, and therapy. He began teaching in 1936 and over the years developed the school of yoga that bears his name. He heads the Shrimati Ramamani Iyengar Memorial Yoga Institute in Pune, India; through Iyengar institutes all over the world, he continues to inspire and educate several million students. His classic *Light on Yoga* (1966) has become the bible for Hatha yoga practitioners the world over. As his student the violinist Yehudi Menuhin wrote in the introduction: "[Yoga] is a technique ideally suited to prevent physical and mental illness and to protect the body generally.... This book will serve to spread the basic art and will ensure that it is practiced at the highest level." Iyengar has modified many of the basic yoga postures for the benefit of people with physical impairments and is recognized by medical professionals around the world for his expertise in treating complex medical problems. In December 1998 he celebrates his 80th birthday.

When I was 10 years old, my contemporaries were already smoking and drinking. My association with them caused me to succumb to temptation. One day they coerced me into taking a puff from a cigarette. I was a physically weak child and immediately began to cough, which strained my chest and caused unbearable pain. This negative experience put an end to my smoking.

My friends continued to indulge in addictive habits. I practiced yoga, remaining friendly but aloof. I was able to observe the effect their behavior had on their moods and their lives and the effect my practice had on mine. I learned a great deal. Yoga transformed my life, and I became a teacher. Hundreds of students who have studied with me and emulated my lifestyle and eating habits have been relieved of addictions to cigarettes, drugs, and alcohol. Yoga transformed their lives as well as mine.

Nature has provided us with air to breathe that is loaded with energy and oxygen. Healthy lungs are able to transport these nutrients into the blood, which improves the quality of one's life. Those who learn to breathe slowly and deeply, imitating the style of smoking a cigarette, experience pleasurable sensations in the nerves, improvement of the mood, and a sense of exhilaration. None of those are realized by breathing in the tainted toxic alkaloid nicotine provided by tobacco smoke.

Yogi B.K.S. Iyengar with his youngest grandson, Sharan Kumar, in Pune, India.

(Below) Homer Sykes—Network/Matrix;
(bottom) Paul Warner—AP/Wide World

Home-run slugger **Ken Griffey, Jr.,** outfielder for the American League West Seattle Mariners since 1987, was born into a baseball-playing family; his father is hitting coach for the Cincinnati Reds and a former outfielder with four major league teams, and his brother Craig was an outfielder in the Mariners' minor league organization. Griffey shares the major league record for the most consecutive games with one or more home runs. Twice he has hit three home runs in one game, and he boasts a career tally of nine grand-slam homers in major league games. Early in the 1998 season, he was among three players in pursuit of Roger Maris's all-time record of 61 home runs in a season. He was the top vote getter (for the sixth time and by a large margin) in the balloting for the American League in the All-Star Game played on July 7, 1998.

I tried smoking a cigarette once and will never do it again. My head didn't feel right afterward, and I don't like that feeling of being out of total control.

Best-selling British novelist **P.D. James** was engaged in public service for 30 years, first as an administrator in the National Health Service and then in the Home Office, from which she retired in 1979. She has written 14 crime novels, 10 of them featuring the poet-detective Commander Adam Dalgliesh. The latest, *A Certain Justice*, was published in October 1997. All the Dalgliesh novels have been dramatized for television. James was a governor of the BBC from 1988 to 1993. She is a fellow of the Royal Society of Literature and the Royal Society of Arts. She has served on numerous public and private literary advisory panels and committees. In 1987 she was chairman of the Booker Prize panel of judges, and she is currently president of the Society of Authors.

She was honored with the title O.B.E. (Officer of the Order of the British Empire) in 1983 and since 1991 has been Baroness James of Holland Park.

I lit a cigarette at the age of 16, didn't like it, and have never lit another. I have never had peer pressure. I am not tolerant of those who still smoke in restaurants.

Henry J. Heimlich, M.D., Sc.D., president of the Heimlich Institute, Cincinnati, Ohio, is best known as the developer of the Heimlich maneuver, a technique for saving the lives of choking victims by dislodging foreign objects from the windpipe. The maneuver also resuscitates drowning victims by expelling water from the lungs and helps some asthma sufferers. Heimlich is the inventor of the Heimlich Chest Drain Valve, the Heimlich Micro-Trach (for rehabilitat-

P.D. James (above) thinks it's a crime to smoke in restaurants. Ken Griffey, Jr. (below), would rather hit home runs than smoke.

47

Chest surgeon Henry Heimlich knows a tar-damaged lung when he sees one.

One herb alternative medicine advocate Andrew Weil never prescribes is tobacco.

ing emphysema patients), and the Heimlich Esophagus Replacement Operation. He is currently researching cures for cancer and AIDS and serving as head of A Caring World, a campaign that relies on TV, computers, and economic interdependence for promoting universal peace and health. The term *Heimlich maneuver* appears in most standard dictionaries, and its developer is credited with having saved more lives than anyone else in the world.

When I was in the sixth grade, a couple of friends and I sneaked into the fields once or twice to a secluded spot to smoke cigarettes. The taste, the smell, the coughing were supposed to make us feel brave and grown up. It was horrible. I remember a local grocer looking sternly at us and saying, "Are you sure these are for your parents?" To lie and say "yes" was the worst feeling.

On these occasions I cashed in two milk bottles for five cents each to buy the cigarettes. One day, walking nervously to the store, I hit the two milk bottles together a couple of times, and suddenly one broke. To a 10-year-old in the Depression, the loss of five cents earmarked for carrying out an illicit act was more than my

conscience could bear. I never smoked again.

When I became a chest surgeon exposed to patients with cancer of the lung or emphysema who gasped for every breath on the road to death, I was compelled to stop that murder.

When I married Jane, my wife of 47 years, she smoked one or two cigarettes at social functions, which we attended every few weeks. I told her it was a foolish thing to do, and she said, "Oh, it's only occasionally." One day I said to her, "You know, when you smoke even occasionally you have tobacco breath, and it's unpleasant for me to kiss you." That was the last cigarette she put in her mouth, and our kisses are still sweet.

THE LURE OF A CIGAR —OR A PIPE

The full beard, bald pate, and amiable countenance of **Andrew Weil,** M.D., are familiar to health-conscious people in the U.S. and many other countries. His picture graces the covers of his best-selling books—*Spontaneous Healing* (1995) and, most recently, *Eight Weeks to Optimum Health* (1997). He also makes frequent TV appearances, runs the popular World Wide Web site "Ask Dr. Weil," and edits a monthly newsletter, *Self Healing.* He is a Harvard-trained physician who became an early proponent of alternative medicine and approaches that integrate traditional methods of healing, preventive medicine, and both Eastern and Western medical practices. Weil teaches at the University of Arizona and founded the Program in Integrative Medicine at the University of Arizona Health Sciences Center in Tucson.

I always disliked smoking, and attempts to smoke cigarettes always made me sick. I briefly flirted with cigars in college but got sick from them too. I'm not very tolerant of smokers in my presence, but I have great compassion for tobacco addicts, most of whom had no idea of the magnitude of risk of addiction when they began to use this substance.

C. Everett Koop, M.D., was surgeon in chief of the Children's Hospital of Philadelphia for 33 years, serving in that capacity until 1981, when he was appointed U.S. surgeon general by Pres. Ronald Reagan. He served in that post until 1989. He is remembered as one of the most forthright and independent individuals ever to have held the office, campaigning tirelessly against smoking and raising public consciousness about AIDS. Koop continues to educate the public about health issues through his frequent speaking engagements, books and articles, and appearances on TV and radio. In 1992 he established the C. Everett Koop Institute at Dartmouth College with the mission of reshaping medical education and improving U.S. health care delivery. In 1995 he was awarded the Presidential Medal of Freedom.

I never smoked cigarettes. Avoidance of smoking when I was a youngster was cultural, not based upon health knowledge. More members of my extended family did not smoke than did smoke. Cigarettes were routinely referred to as "coffin nails." Although my father was a heavy smoker until I went to college, it was the expectation of my parents that I would never smoke.

When I was in the middle years of my surgical life, I smoked a pipe for a while—for perhaps eight years. Looking back on it, I see that it was all theater. I loved the smell of other people's pipes and the aroma of the tobacco, but it was never that satis-

fying when I did it myself. I quit smoking a pipe because I was getting too many holes in my suits.

I stopped the day I wanted to and without any help; I was never addicted. Smoking is a very strange habit when you come to think of it. I don't think it's truly pleasurable outside the terrible problem of addiction to nicotine.

I'm tolerant of kids who are seduced into smoking by a number of factors. I can't understand why the 15% or so of smokers who start after the age of 18 do so. They know exactly what they are getting into; they understand addiction and mistakenly think that unlike others, they can quit.

A pathologist by training, **George D. Lundberg,** M.D., has worked in the areas of tropical medicine and forensic medicine. His major professional interests are toxicology, the public health consequences of violence, communication, physician behavior, strategic management, and health system reform. Since 1982 Lundberg has been on the staff of the American Medical Association, where he is edi-

Former surgeon general C. Everett Koop never tires of telling kids about the dangers of smoking.

49

Medical editor George Lundberg knows a thing or two about smoking and health.

Best actress Susan Sarandon was not a convincing on-screen smoker.

tor in chief of scientific information and multimedia with responsibility for the AMA's 39 medical journals and is the editor of the *Journal of the American Medical Association*. He holds academic positions at Harvard Medical School and Northwestern Medical School.

I tried to learn to smoke under intense peer pressure while in the U.S. Army. I never learned how to inhale—I would cough and sputter, and my eyes would water, so I never started cigarettes. I did later try a pipe—it seemed sexy and intellectual. But it tasted awful and smelled bad close up and was dirty and so much trouble. So I quit before getting really started.

I believe that addicts of all types (including tobacco/nicotine) should be treated with compassion. Smokers should be allowed to use tobacco in private, in the presence of consenting adults only.

QUITTING WAS EASY

Susan Sarandon is one of today's most intelligent and versatile actors, having built a singular reputation for portraying strong, independent women on the screen. She won the 1995 Academy Award for best actress and was named the Screen Actor's Guild best female actor of 1995 for her performance in *Dead Man Walking*. Her prior work earned her four best actress Academy Award nominations. Her most recent films are *Twilight*, in which she stars opposite Paul Newman and Gene Hackman, and *Stepmom*, costarring Julia Roberts and Ed Harris. On Broadway, Sarandon appeared in *An Evening with Richard Nixon* and was critically lauded for her performances off-Broadway in *A Coupla White Chicks Sitting Around Talking* and *Extremities*. A strong supporter of many social causes, Sarandon is an ac-

tive campaigner for people with AIDS and an advocate for women's rights.

It took me a long time to be able to smoke because I wasn't very good at it, but I persisted because the man I was with at the time was a smoker. I was in my mid-20s. On the set of The Front Page, the director, Billy Wilder, told me not to bother smoking because I was so bad at it. I finally quit because of pregnancy.

Readers depend on **Marian Burros's** two weekly columns for the *New York Times*, "Eating Well" and "Plain and Simple," for inspiring recipes and thoughtful appraisals of whatever nutrition issues are making news. She is the author of numerous cookbooks and books about food, the latest of which is *The New Elegant but Easy Cookbook* (1998).

I started smoking when I was 13 like every other stupid little child. Then it was time to give it up, and I gave it up and never missed it. I nev-

New York Times food writer Marian Burros has no taste for cigarettes.

er had any withdrawal symptoms. No problem. Then I went through a period in my life where I seemed to be under some kind of pressure, so I went back to cigarettes for about two weeks. I was never addicted. I mostly got dizzy when I smoked too much.

Julia Child would probably be the first chef most people would think of if asked to name a television cooking-show host. Child is the author of 10 cookbooks, beginning with *Mastering the Art of French Cooking* (1961), which she wrote with her colleagues at L'École des Trois Gourmandes, the Paris cooking school she ran in the 1950s with Simone Beck and Louisette Bertholle. This two-volume classic precipitated a revolution in American cuisine, which Child furthered in her popular PBS television program "The French Chef." She has starred in other television series as well, including the acclaimed "Master Chef" series, in which she serves as host to 26 of the top chefs in the United States, and "Baking with Julia," in which she trades licks with a similar number of top-flight pastry chefs and bread bakers. Her most recent book is *Baking with Julia* (1996), based on that TV series.

Everyone smoked in the 1930s, and I couldn't wait to start, but I had promised my father not to smoke until I was 21. At age 21 and one second, I started smoking, and I was a heavy smoker for 30 years.

My husband had given up smoking, and I knew I should too. Finally one day, leaving him off at the dentist, I took out a cigarette, and the first big puff made me dizzy. I threw my cigarettes out of the car, came home, and threw all of the rest of the cigarettes away. That was it! I quit entirely on my own, but I was motivated by knowing the dangers, and

my voice was getting hoarse. That is not good for anyone who speaks publicly and is on television.

Edward Koren has long been associated with *The New Yorker* magazine, for which he has drawn more than 850 cartoons as well as many covers. He has also contributed to many other publications, including the *New York Times*, *Newsweek*, *Time*, *GQ*, *Esquire*, *Sports Illustrated*, *Vogue*, *Fortune*, *Vanity Fair*, *The Nation*, and the *Boston Globe*. He has illustrated many books, written and illustrated a book for children, and published six collections of cartoons. Koren's latest book is *The Hard Work of Simple Living: A Somewhat Blank Book for the Sustainable Hedonist* (1998). A New York City native, Koren trained at the Pratt Institute and taught at Brown University, both in Providence, R.I., for many years. He lives in Vermont, where he is a captain of the Brookfield Volunteer Fire Department.

What prompted me to start was the widespread acceptance of smoking. The fact that it was never ques-

Julia Child, who probably knows more tantalizing ways to cook a turkey than any other chef alive, quit smoking "cold turkey."

51

Cartoonist, illustrator, author, volunteer fireman, and ex-smoker Edward Koren.

tioned, from either a social or a health standpoint, made smoking an inevitable aspect of adulthood! I started in college at 18. I never felt smoking to be unpleasant or difficult. I don't remember ever feeling any exaltation from smoking—just the addict's relief.

I never thought I was very seriously addicted. I rarely smoked a whole pack in one day, and I often smoked much less. I finally quit, quite easily and entirely on my own, at age 36 (27 years ago) when I started to run seriously. Running seemed to replace the need for cigarettes, which had become an impediment to my newfound athleticism. Indeed, I felt that my lungs were claiming independence. I was never drawn back to start again. The cleansing I felt, coupled with an increasing ability to run faster and longer, made smoking unattractive.

I think substituting aerobic intensity prevented my gaining weight, and if I did crave a cigarette substitute in food, I suspect I burned the excess off as fuel.

I'm terribly intolerant of those who continue to smoke. I simply don't understand how, with all the information that has become available about its dangers (and its harmful effects on nonsmokers), any thinking person can continue to smoke. I feel assaulted by smokers and their by-products and offended by the sight of someone with a cigarette.

AFTER DINNER: THE HARDEST TIME TO REFRAIN

Many would say that **H. Norman Schwarzkopf** is the quintessential "military hero." Schwarzkopf attended military academies as a boy and graduated from the U.S. Military Academy at West Point in 1956. He served two tours as an officer in Vietnam, rose quickly in rank, and distinguished himself as deputy commander of the 1983 invasion of Grenada. Schwarzkopf served as de facto commander of the U.S. forces in the Persian Gulf War in 1990–91. Intelligent, decisive, cou-

Retired general and former three-pack-a-dayer Norman Schwarzkopf.

Dennis Brack—Black Star

Anne Hall

rageous, affable, and possessing a sense of humor atypical of a military man, he attained celebrity in his frequent television and other media interviews during Operation Desert Storm, the liberation of Kuwait from Iraqi occupation. Upon his return to the U.S., "Stormin' Norman" led military victory parades of a kind not seen since the end of World War II. Schwarzkopf published his autobiography, *It Doesn't Take a Hero*, in 1993. Now retired from the military and a survivor of prostate cancer, he is an advocate for cancer patients.

I started smoking as a result of peer pressure. In those days smoking was an "adult" thing to do, and since so many of my friends smoked, I felt I had to smoke also. I never enjoyed it. The first several times I tried it, I got ill, and I particularly did not enjoy the taste.

Eventually I realized I was smoking too much (three packs a day) and was killing myself. I actually quit smoking several times. Each time I did it cold turkey and was able to stay away for a couple of years. Then, for some reason, I started smoking one or two cigarettes again and soon found myself back up to smoking three packs a day.

I quit on my own, without any nicotine substitute. Weight gain was a small problem but not a major consideration. The most difficult time of the day for abstaining was in the evening after a big meal, particularly if it was a social setting. A good cigar always went very well with cognac.

I never felt that I was addicted, even though I was a chain smoker. I felt it was a nervous habit more than an addiction. I am not very tolerant now of smokers. I do not want people around me who smoke, because I am concerned about secondhand smoke health hazards. I do, how-ever, sympathize with them, since I used to smoke.

Marcia Angell, M.D., is executive editor of *The New England Journal of Medicine* and lecturer in the department of social medicine at Harvard Medical School. Angell is a member of the Institute of Medicine and serves on the advisory boards of several leading medical institutions and foundations. She writes frequently for the *Journal* and other publications on a wide range of topics and is particularly interested in health policy, the ethics of biomedical research, the use of medical evidence in courts of law, and care at the end of life. She is the author of *Science on Trial: The Clash of Medical Evidence and the Law in the Breast Implant Case* (1996).

I started smoking because I liked the smell. I was 16.

I quit because I had recurrent bronchitis, and I knew cigarettes were harmful in general. I quit twice. The first time was when I was 23, just before entering medical school. I resumed smoking while studying for exams and during my internship but stopped again when I became pregnant during my residency. Altogether I smoked about two packs a day for roughly nine years. I stopped cold turkey both times—no program, no nicotine substitute, no medication. I gained about 10 pounds the first time.

The second time, I'm sure it contributed to my weight gain during pregnancy. I knew it would be hard to quit. (I prefer not to use the ambiguous term "addicted.") I found I had to avoid all activities that were emotionally intense, including good conversation. I also could not drink alcohol or coffee, both of which I associated with cigarettes. I put myself on automatic for three weeks and ate a lot of celery.

Physician and medical editor Marcia Angell substituted celery for cigarettes.

53

All smiles: Cokie Roberts, coanchor, special correspondent, political analyst, and author (above); and Secretary of Health and Human Services Donna Shalala (below right), who often dons the hat of antismoking campaigner.

I am very tolerant of those who still smoke. I understand them. Still, I know it is possible to quit and that it is worth the difficulty.

Cokie Roberts is coanchor of the ABC News program "This Week" and a special correspondent for ABC News covering politics, Congress, and public policy; she often serves as substitute anchor on "Nightline." Roberts is also a news analyst for National Public Radio. She previously was a panelist on "This Week with David Brinkley." Roberts has won numerous honors for her journalism, including the Edward R. Murrow Award, the Everett McKinley Dirksen Award for coverage of Congress, 12 honorary degrees, a Distinguished Alumnae Achievement Award from Wellesley College, and an Emmy for her contribution to the ABC News Special "Who Is Ross Perot?" She is the author of the best-selling *We Are Our Mothers' Daughters* (1998).

I started smoking because it was "in," "cool," etc. I was probably 15 or 16. Smoking was more an exciting and sinful activity than pleasurable.

I quit on my first real try and on my own—I was 20 by the way—so

it's been many, many years. I quit because I had asthma and my boyfriend hated smoking. I wasn't really addicted. Abstaining from a cigarette with after-dinner coffee was the hardest. I did gain a few pounds.

Intellectually, I'm tolerant of smokers and intolerant of antismokers; practically, I stay away from the smell because I'm allergic to it.

ADMIT TO BEING ADDICTED

Prior to being named U.S. secretary of health and human services in 1993 by Pres. Bill Clinton, **Donna E. Shalala** served as chancellor of the University of Wisconsin for six years. For more than a decade, she was a member of the board of the Children's Defense Fund, and she became its chairperson in 1992, the same year that *Business Week* magazine named her one of the top five managers in U.S. higher education.

When I started smoking, I was 19 and editor of the student newspaper

at college. All journalists seemed to be smoking then.

I made some halfhearted attempts to quit over the years. Then I woke up one morning with an awful taste and couldn't stop coughing. "That's it," I said, and I called the American Cancer Society. I joined a group program. It was cold turkey. I am an addict.

I feel sorry for smokers but understand the addiction and the difficulty of quitting.

QUIT? NEVER!

Humorist **David Sedaris**—who has been known to describe his occupation as "typist"—is a playwright, fiction and nonfiction writer, regular commentator on National Public Radio, and contributor to *The New Yorker*. He is the author of three collections of essays, short stories, and personal reminiscences, *Barrel Fever* (1994), *Naked* (1997), and *Holidays on Ice* (1997). Sedaris and his sister Amy have written three plays, *Stitches, One Woman Shoe*, and *The Little Freida Mysteries*. Sedaris was described in the *Washington Post Book World* as "wickedly funny…one of America's most prickly, and most delicious, young comic talents."

I've been smoking for 21 years and have no intention of quitting. I started at the age of 20. A friend and I were traveling through Canada, and I took up smoking cigarettes because I didn't know where to find any pot. I consider smoking to be an extremely pleasurable activity. The first cigarette of the day is the best, but there's still a lot to be said of the 17th and 35th.

I have never tried to quit and arrange my life so that I'll never find myself searching for good-sized butts at the bottom of the trash can. Someone gave me a nicotine patch, and I

Humorist David Sedaris thinks he'll be more at home in France, "a smoker's paradise."

wore it over my eye, pirate style, hoping to get a few laughs. The only time I've abstained was during jury duty. After six hours without a cigarette, I would have sent my own father to the electric chair.

I understand that I am addicted. The word doesn't bother me in the least. I still smoke and am intolerant of those who have quit. We need to build an army of smokers, well trained in hand-to-hand combat. Smoking is the only sport in which quitting is an acceptable goal.

Nothing irritates me more than the recent nonsmoking legislation enacted by cowards and [expletive deleted] They continue to tax cigarettes but would never think of placing a 50-cent-per-gallon tax on gasoline. It enrages me, and as a result, I'm moving to France in August 1998. France is a smoker's paradise. Cigarettes cost more, but still you can enjoy them on planes, on trains, and in restaurants. I like going to France and watching the health-conscious American tourists wave their arms in protest. Nothing is funnier than listening to an American beg the bus driver to put out his cigarette.

HONEST ERRORS IN MEDICINE

BY ABIGAIL ZUGER, M.D.

The incident took place in March of my internship year, an important detail only because it means I had been working 100-hour weeks for most of the previous nine months and had reached a zenith of fatigue. The patient was José, a whale of a man who had been rushed by ambulance to the emergency room spouting blood from veins that had suddenly ruptured in his throat. When José was up and walking around, as I was eventually to see for myself, he was a big, likable drunk with a beer belly and a rotten liver. But José horizontal

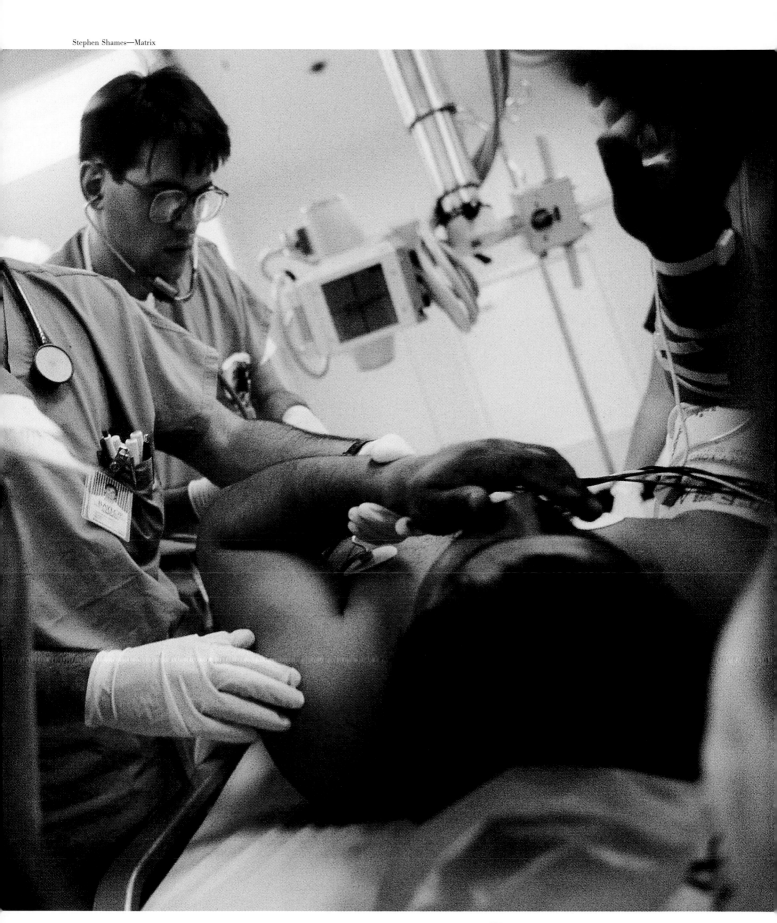

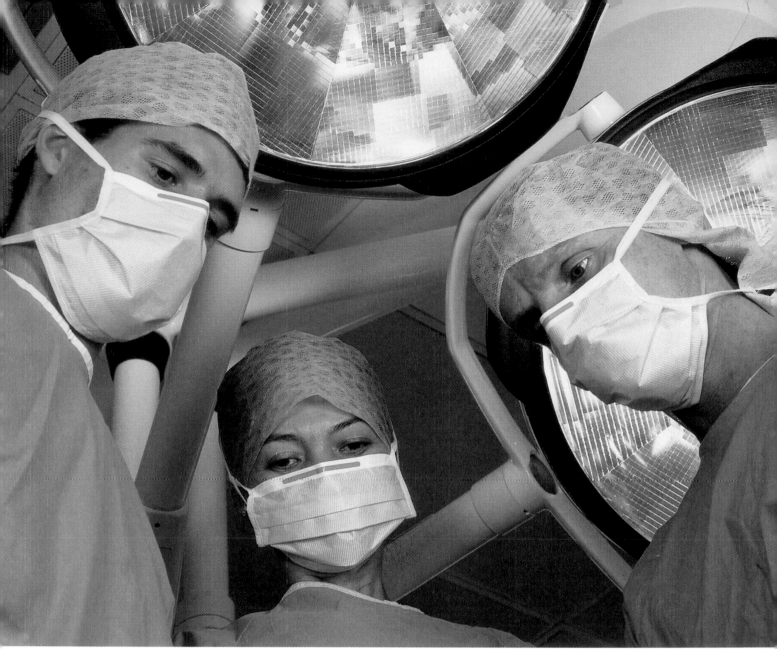

Despite the godlike qualities patients often endow them with, doctors too make mistakes—sometimes with disastrous consequences.

Simon Fraser—Science Source/Photo Researchers

Abigail Zuger is *Associate Clinical Professor of Medicine at the Albert Einstein College of Medicine, New York City. A widely published freelance writer and regular contributor to the* New York Times, *she is also the author of* Strong Shadows: Scenes from an Inner City AIDS Clinic *(1995).*

(continued from page 56)
on a stretcher, blood gushing from his mouth, fat arms flailing, was a living, bellowing nightmare. The more blood he lost, the lower his blood pressure dropped and the more disoriented and violent he became, spattering the exam cubicle and everyone in it with blood. Two burly male nurses could barely hold him down. Every minute he headed deeper into shock. He was far too strong and too agitated for the first step in his treatment—the insertion into one arm of an intravenous line through which fluids could be administered and lost blood replaced.

Fortunately, with nearly a year's experience, I knew well what to do next. If José's arms couldn't be successfully immobilized, I would have to start a line in his neck or his chest. I sponged an iodine solution onto his bare chest. He roared and struggled even harder, straining free of the nurses' grip. "Better numb him up a little," one of them suggested, panting. I headed over to the cart stocked with emergency medications and grabbed a blue-and-green-striped bottle of lidocaine, a local anesthetic.

Back at José's bedside I drew some of the lidocaine into a syringe, poked

58

the needle into the skin beneath his collarbone, squirted in a generous dose, waited a few seconds for the numbness to take effect, and then jabbed a big intravenous catheter into the middle of the area. José's bellowing escalated, but I was too preoccupied with finding the vein and setting up the intravenous fluids to pay much attention. Then Eric, one of José's nurses, picked up the lidocaine bottle I had tossed on the stretcher, looked at it incredulously, looked at me, then stared at the bottle again. It was when Eric raced off to telephone my supervisor and the local poison control center (in that order) that I realized something had gone seriously amiss.

It turned out that in my haste I had picked the wrong blue-and-green-striped bottle from the jumbled emergency cart. Instead of lidocaine, I had squirted a hefty dose of the drug atropine into José's chest. The atropine bottle was smaller than the lidocaine bottle, and of course the tiny type on the label read "Atropine Sulfate" rather than "Lidocaine 2%," but otherwise their design was identical: bright blue and green stripes on a white background. Lidocaine would have left José's chest numb for an hour or so and then worn off. Atropine might speed his heartbeat and make him disoriented and violent for hours. It was unquestionably not the drug that José needed at that particular moment.

A SIMPLE MISTAKE

The next hour has mercifully blurred in my memory. Eric came back to the bedside to give me a piece of his mind. My boss, his boss, and a handful of hospital lawyers and administrators showed up at the scene. I was presented with a hefty stack of forms to fill out and sign.

José got a quart of fluid and a pint of blood through his intravenous line and stopped shouting. His heartbeat sped up for about 20 minutes but then slowed down again. There were no signs that the atropine was affecting his brain. Instead, he actually became coherent and began to thank everyone for saving his life. The bosses, lawyers, and administrators slowly drifted away. By the time I had signed the last incident report, my hand had stopped shaking.

It had been a mistake, no more and no less—a mistake made possi-

> # Mistakes like this happen every day, every hour, at every hospital in the country.

ble by a good half-dozen separate factors, ranging from my haste, inexperience, and fatigue to the larger issues of the drug vials' ill-conceived labeling and the chronic understaffing of the emergency ward, where no one had the time to straighten out the chaotic medication cart. Mistakes like this happen every day, every hour, at every hospital in the country. There is no doctor in the world who hasn't made similar ones—and who doesn't spend the occasional sleepless predawn hour reviewing them all. The fact that José and I ultimately could smile and reminisce about this incident years after it occurred means that I am able to think and write about it with some equanimity, but it doesn't

change the event itself. It was an accident that should not have happened.

THE MYTH OF INFALLIBILITY

Mistakes are part of every field of human endeavor. Every day, cashiers hand shoppers the wrong change, diners ordering the baked potato get the french fries instead, and cars roll off the assembly line with misaligned windshield wipers. It is likely that somewhere in this book at least one typographical error has eluded zealous editors and proofreaders. But medical mistakes are different somehow. Partly, their potential life-or-death consequences distinguish them from other, less-momentous errors. Then, too, although we know intellectually that doctors are only human, it is one of those truths that even the wisest person just doesn't want to believe. When we or our loved ones are sick, we need to believe irrational things—that a desperately ill person will beat unbeatable odds, that a medicine known to be only moderately effective will have miraculous results, that doctors will function with smooth infallibility. We know it isn't possible, but we want so badly for it to be possible that each departure from our expectations stuns and wounds us.

Until very recently the medical profession itself colluded in the illusion that doctors were somehow better than the average mortal. In 1912 the American Medical Association (AMA) specified the doctor's qualifications as follows: he (the vast majority of physicians were, of course, male) was to be "an upright man," "pure in character," "modest," "sober," "patient," "prompt," and "pious." Members of the profession "deficient either in moral character

In the 19th century the family physician (above) epitomized the sober, upright member of society. Following the precepts set forth in Thomas Percival's seminal treatise (right), the medical profession saw to it that members' mistakes were shrouded in secrecy.

or education" should be exposed by their peers "before the proper medical or legal tribunals." By implication, practitioners with the requisite education and moral character were unlikely to disgrace the profession with errors.

When errors actually happened, time-honored principles saw to it that they were kept quiet. They were reviewed in closed rooms by tight-lipped committees composed solely of other medical professionals. In his treatise *Medical Ethics* (1803), the document from which all modern codes of medical ethics stem, the English physician Thomas Percival specified that the honor of the profession depended on the secrecy he diplomatically referred to as "esprit de corps." About disagreements within the profession, Percival wrote that they should be mediated "by a sufficient number of physicians or of surgeons, according to the nature of the dispute." They should not be communicated to the public, "as they may be personally injurious to the individuals concerned, and can hardly fail to hurt the general credit of the faculty."

DOCTORS IN THE CONFESSIONAL

It is only in the past few decades that the doors of those closed rooms have begun to open, exposing the proceedings to the scrutiny of the world at large. Some of the most widely publicized medical mistakes have been those aired in courts of law. Others surfaced when social scientists began to study the practice of medicine. In *Forgive and Remember: Managing Medical Failure* (1979), a classic of medical sociology, Charles Bosk, then at the University of Pennsylvania, devoted an entire book to an analysis of how surgeons at one

U.S. teaching hospital in the 1970s handled the errors in judgment and technique committed by students and professors alike. He found that the doctors actually maintained not one but two "conspiracies of silence"—first, carefully keeping their errors out of the public eye, and then, shielding them from open analysis even within the hospital, where professors often assumed responsibility for the mistakes of their trainees and thereby reinforced the prohibition against open discussion. "There must be public forums for discussing problems and allocating blame," Bosk concluded. "The patient deserves the protection of not only the individual's but also the collectivity's conscience." He called for the medical profession to "raise its conscience about its public responsibilities," and he suggested that the profession should "build stronger accounting mechanisms into everyday practice."

More recently, doctors themselves have come forth to discuss their own errors in confessions that would have been inconceivable a generation ago. In 1984 when David Hilfiker, then a general practitioner in Minnesota, wrote an essay in *The New England Journal of Medicine* describing a nightmarish mistake he had made in a patient's care, an outpouring of letters from other doctors ensued. Hilfiker had been misled into a tragic error of judgment by a series of false-negative pregnancy tests in a woman who had missed several menstrual periods. On the basis of the test results, he assumed his patient was not pregnant. He performed a standard procedure called dilation and curettage, in which the contents of the womb are removed, and in the process terminated a viable and much-wanted pregnancy.

Hilfiker's frank discussion of the circumstances of the error—and his

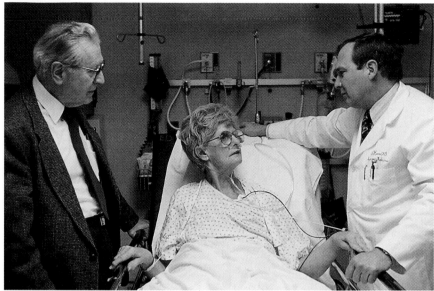

Sarah Leen—Matrix

Whereas doctors once made medical decisions unilaterally, today's patients—and their families—demand to be involved.

feelings about it—elicited praise from some readers and censure from others. Some letters hailed his candor and called for physicians to forgive themselves. "Making a bad mistake must not be equated with being a bad doctor," wrote one

---

Doctors... maintained not one but two "conspiracies of silence."

Connecticut practitioner. Other letters from doctors deeply uncomfortable with this kind of soul baring in an eminent academic journal condemned Hilfiker's piece as "neurotic" and accused him of "obvious obstetric blunders."

Despite its critics and detractors, the essay was one of the first signs that the closed world of medical errors was finally beginning to open. "If the medical profession has no

room for doctors' mistakes, then neither does society," Hilfiker wrote. He went on:

At some point we must all bring medical mistakes out of the closet. This will be difficult as long as both the profession and society continue to project their desires for perfection onto the doctor. Physicians need permission to admit errors.... The practice of medicine is difficult enough without having to bear the yoke of perfection.

DISCLOSURE: THE "RIGHT THING"?

The spirit of openness Hilfiker advocated has not yet materialized, but many voices have joined his in calling for it. Some are those of doctors, seeking, like Hilfiker, to break free from the "yoke of perfection." Increasingly, though,

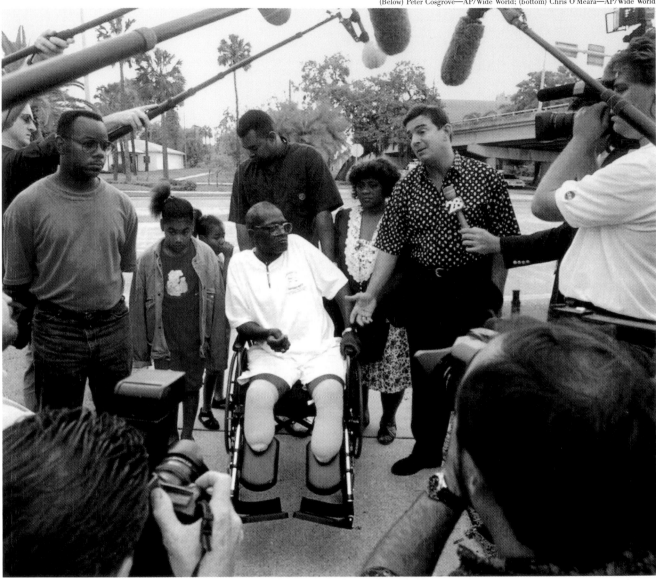

Willie King (above) was the victim of a highly publicized Florida malpractice case. King was confined to a wheelchair in 1995 after a doctor amputated his healthy foot; the diseased extremity was removed later. (Right) The accused physician in the case faces the state medical board.

support for full disclosure comes from outside the profession. In this last decade of the 20th century, no aspect of medical ethics remains under the sole proprietorship of doctors. Patients now demand to be involved in decision making and want to be provided with all the information they need to make reasonable, considered choices about their care. Medical administrators and insurers have become acutely aware that medical ethics is more than a mere abstraction; the resolution of ethical dilemmas sometimes comes with a sizable price tag.

Medical errors are now everyone's business. ...They feature prominently on the nightly news.

(Below) Karl Deblaker—AP/Wide World; (bottom) Lisa Quinones—Black Star

Medical errors can range from the confusion of one drug name for another to the mixing-up of patients' records. Some mistakes can be easily remedied; others are lethal.

And so, along with such previously jealously guarded issues as whether to provide life-prolonging care to a patient who is clearly near death and when to forgo resuscitation, medical errors are now everyone's business and everyone's problem. They feature prominently on the nightly news: a Florida surgeon amputates the wrong leg, a woman in New York has the wrong side of her skull opened in an operation to remove a tumor, and a Boston woman dies after receiving a massive overdose of a cancer chemotherapy drug.

For years the AMA successfully lobbied against the publication of the federal government's National Practitioner Data Bank, a list of physicians who have paid malpractice claims or had their licenses revoked. Although hospitals and managed-care organizations have traditionally had access to this information, patients—and potential patients—have not. In 1998, however, the list was made public by the Public Citizen's Health Research Group, a consumer-protection organization. Articles in academic journals now urge doctors who make a mistake to tell the patient the truth about the incident. Not only is it "the right thing to do," according to Albert Wu and colleagues at the Johns Hopkins School of Public Health, Baltimore, Maryland (*Journal of General Internal Medicine*, December 1997), but it will strengthen the patient's faith in the doctor's integrity, inspire goodwill, and lessen the chances of a lawsuit.

A SUBTLE SPECTRUM

Many health care professionals disagree. Medical errors are complex entities, they say, and full disclosure of the profession's failures without full understanding of the circumstances behind them will benefit no

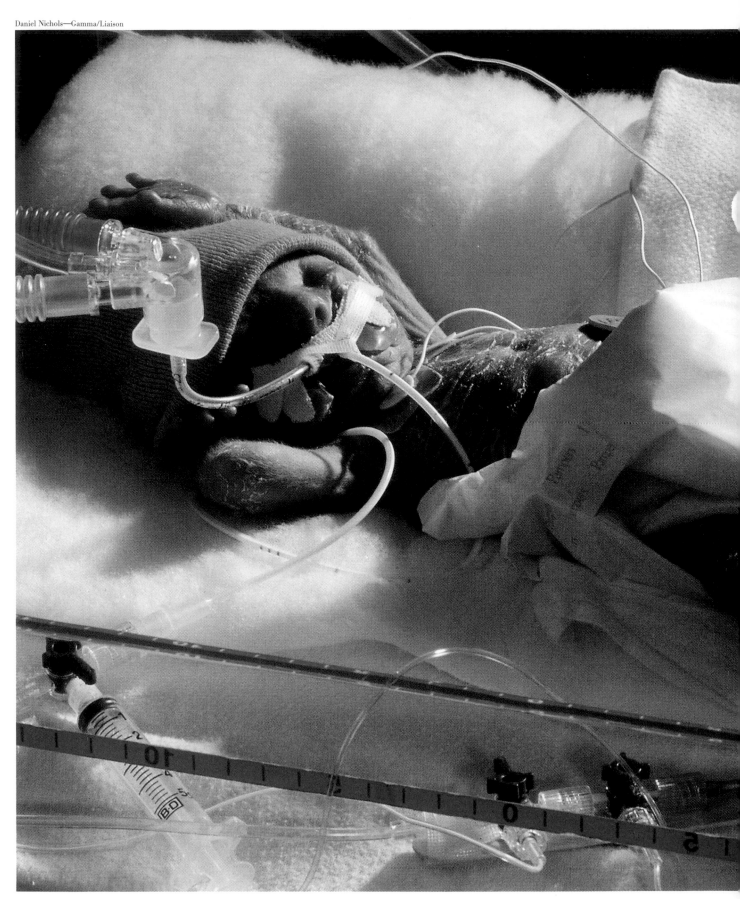

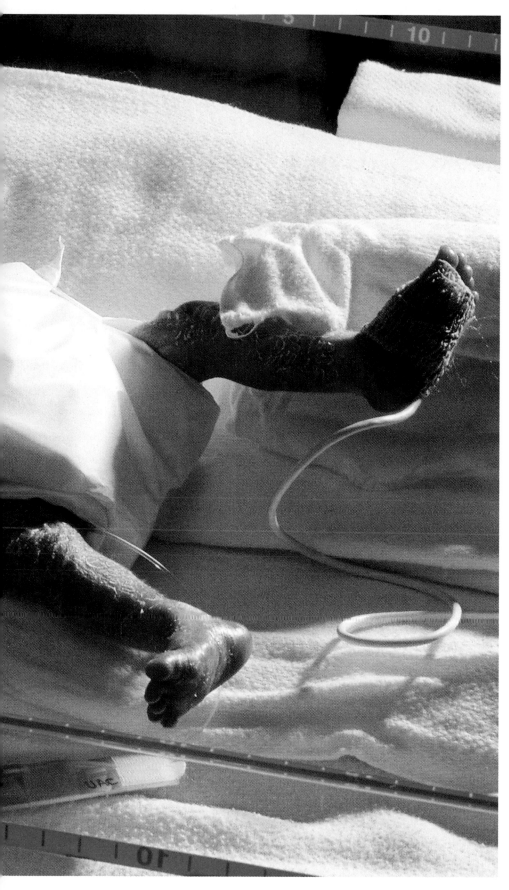

When the doctor caring for the baby calculates the dose of the heart drug digoxin suitable for the baby's weight, he forgets to "carry the zero." ...The infant receives 10 times the correct dose of the drug and dies.

Who knows how many medical errors are the consequence of fatigue due to overwork? In New York state, where one tragic patient death was blamed on a young doctor's exhaustion and inexperience, laws were subsequently passed limiting the work hours of medical residents.

one. As Hilfiker observed in his essay, medical mistakes come in a subtly shaded spectrum, ranging from outright malpractice at one end to simple bad luck and bad timing at the other. Some errors occur because of a doctor's ignorance, some from lack of technical skill, some from carelessness, some from misjudgments, and some from what Hilfiker called "a failure of will"—situations

ples, which run the gamut from a heedless action with no repercussions to a disaster with life-or-death consequences:

• A woman goes to the drugstore with a prescription for blood-pressure medication. While filling the prescription, the pharmacist notices that instead of "catapres," the drug the woman has been taking for some time, the doctor has written "captopril," an entirely different blood-pressure drug. The pharmacist calls the doctor, who admits he wrote the wrong drug name on the prescription form. The correct medication is dispensed to the patient.

• A physician is called out of the office on a personal emergency— her elderly mother has fallen and broken her hip. She leaves a stack of lab reports from the morning's patients unread on her desk. When she returns the next day, she sees that one diabetic patient's test showed a dangerously high blood-sugar level. The lab is supposed to phone the office immediately when it discovers this kind of potentially serious problem, but it failed to do so. The doctor calls the patient only to discover that he was rushed to the hospital hours earlier in a diabetic coma.

• A man named Elias Simpson and an unrelated woman named Elisa Simpson both attend the same busy urban medical clinic. A blood test shows that Mr. Simpson is anemic; his doctor orders a series of additional tests to find out why. Several weeks later, when all the tests have returned negative, the doctor looks at Mr. Simpson's chart again and finds that the original blood assay has Elisa's name on it and was filed in Elias's chart by mistake. All the additional procedures Elias underwent were unnecessary.

Custom Medical Stock Photo

in which doctors know exactly what to do but fail to do it because they are distracted, pressured, or exhausted. Distinguishing between them all and meting out suitable measures of justice, compensation, support, and reassurance to all parties may require an authority with wisdom simply not to be had in our society. Consider the following examples,

• An infant is recovering from heart surgery in a pediatric intensive-care unit. When the doctor caring for the baby calculates the dose of the heart drug digoxin suitable for the baby's weight, he forgets to "carry the zero." Another doctor checks the numbers but fails to pick up the error, as do the pharmacist dispensing the drug and the intensive-care-unit nurse. The infant receives 10 times the correct dose and dies.

All of the above patients are victims of a medical error. Should any of them—or their survivors—be told of the mistake? How would they react? Would the patients or their families benefit unequivocally from knowing the truth? Would disclosure keep the error from being repeated?

In his eloquent 1997 book *Do We Still Need Doctors?*, John D. Lantos, a physician and medical ethicist at the University of Chicago, is as wary of full disclosure as he is of the secrecy of past generations. Lantos writes:

Mistakes cannot be properly assessed or categorized without some vision of the larger project of which they are a part....Full disclosure implies that someone else can judge, that the facts will speak for themselves. But facts are often morally mute....Doctors used to be empowered to judge their own mistakes, and this societal faith maintained a certain view of the medical profession. Today, it is unclear who should judge and by what criteria. Increases in disclosure or judgment will not restore lost faith in medicine as a profession.

IMPETUS FOR CHANGE

Despite these and other misgivings on the part of physicians, the trend

As many as three million injuries a year are caused by medical accidents in hospitals.

toward disclosure continues to gain momentum. Even the AMA, once the preeminent champion of the profession's privacy and autonomy, has changed its policy. In June 1997 the organization launched a new nonprofit enterprise, the National Patient Safety Foundation, to promote discussion, research, and solutions to the problem of medical errors. This step was prompted by growing public recognition of the problem: 42% of those questioned in a 1997 Harris Poll said that they had been witness to a medical error, either in their own personal care or in that of a friend or relative. According to AMA estimates, as many as three million injuries a year are caused by medical accidents in hospitals, at a cost approaching $200 billion. Serious injuries due to errors may occur in more than 17% of surgical and intensive-care-unit patients.

Legal, medical, and health care industry consultants have come to the conclusion that the first step in eliminating errors in medicine is to change the way the profession regards and reacts to them. Lucian Leape, a surgeon and faculty member at the Harvard School of Public Health who is an acknowledged expert on the subject of medical errors, has pointed out that despite the new dialogue about doctors'

J. Albert Diaz—The Miami Herald/KRT Photos

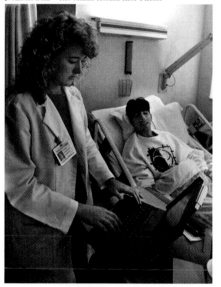

Hospitals, keenly aware of the potential dangers of medication errors, are developing safeguards to prevent such problems. (Above) A hospital pharmacist enters a patient's prescription information into a computer right at the bedside.

mistakes, physicians are still trained to think that they should be perfect. Errors are felt to result from defects in education or motivation and are punished "through social opprobrium and peer disapproval."

In contrast, in other high-risk enterprises errors are depersonalized in a number of ways. The aviation industry is a good example. First, industrywide systems are specifically designed to minimize errors; second, pilots are trained to willingly cede autonomy to an external authority (the air traffic controller) in high-risk situations (a busy airport); and finally, aviation safety has been institutionalized in independent regulatory agencies with government-mandated responsibilities.

Now medicine is slowly, creakily beginning to accept some of these same kinds of safeguards. Ironically, some changes in the medical profession's attitude are a direct response to the ad hominem ugliness of protracted court battles in malpractice claims.

In 1984, for example, Libby Zion, the teenage daughter of a well-known New York City journalist, died as a result of a tangle of errors subsequently unraveled only in an acrimonious trial. Libby was an emotionally troubled but otherwise healthy 18-year-old college freshman who was admitted to the hospital with a fever and a painful ear infection. The resident on call gave her a pain medication that should not have been combined with the powerful antidepressant drug she was also taking. When Libby's temperature reached more than 40.6° C (105° F) within a few hours of her admission to the hospital—possibly owing to the combination of the two drugs—the intern responsible for her case was too busy with other patients to evaluate her promptly, and her own family doctor did not go to the hospital. Libby died from hyperthermia (dangerously elevated body temperature) the following morning.

Prominent among the mistakes that led to Libby's death, the court concluded, were the misjudgments of an overtired and inexperienced medical resident. Subsequently, New York state enacted laws to limit the work hours and intensify the supervision of residents. Now, thanks to the Zion trial and verdict, young doctors staffing New York hospitals cannot legally work the kind of hours I was

To prepare themselves for a real-life emergency situation, physicians-in-training "practice" medicine on a lifelike mannikin with palpable pulses and audible heart sounds.

Jerome Yeats—Science Source/Photo Researchers

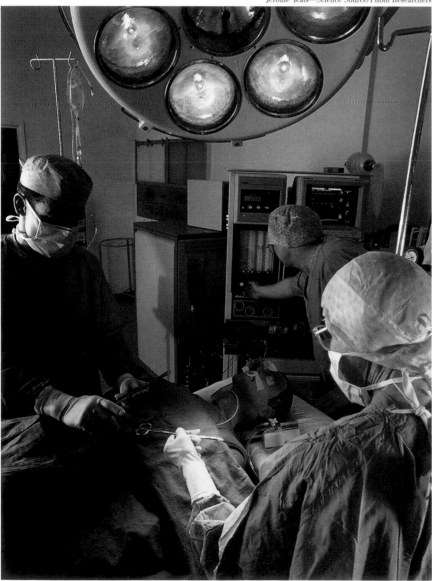

working when I shot José full of the wrong medication.

Some of the factors that enabled my own personal contribution to the statistics of medical error are also being slowly addressed. Among the measures being instituted are careful examinations of the dynamics of medication errors in hospitals. There is now general agreement that expert pharmacy personnel should control drug dispensing whenever possible and that the pharmaceutical industry should be strongly discouraged from giving drugs similar names and similar labels. Ultimately, computers may be pressed into service as the only "fail-safe" drug dispensers, ones that will always remember a patient's weight, height, and allergies and will never forget the correct dosage of a medication.

Computers are also being enlisted to help teach young doctors how to function in emergency situations. Sophisticated computer-animated dummies are now being used by some anesthesia, critical-care, and surgical-training programs to simulate the bodily processes of critically ill people, right down to falling blood pressure and declining urine output. Some of these artificial patients are even capable of emitting audible cries of pain when anesthetics and other medications are incorrectly administered. The premise is that physicians who learn the basics on dummies are likely to commit fewer errors of inexperience when they turn to real patients. No studies yet support this notion, but its intrinsic logic is hard to deny.

TO ERR IS...INEVITABLE

The innovators who are behind these changes realize that eliminating all error from medicine is impossible—

Guy Billout

as Leape put it, "Error is an inevitable accompaniment of the human condition." Instead, they envision a future in which medical errors are reduced to a minimum, and mistakes that do occur are caught by the system before—not after—a patient has been harmed.

The ironic consequence of their vision is that when it has been achieved, doctors will once again occupy a zone of grace and infallibility not unlike the one they inhabited in centuries past. They will be bolstered by computers, of course, and a cadre of other hardworking, highly trained professionals, but still medicine will become just about as infallible an enterprise as it once only pretended to be. How this will affect the relationship between doctors and their patients is hard to predict. Patients often have unpredictable reactions to medical mistakes, reactions that even computer programs might have difficulty simulating.

Take José, for instance, who, after our eventful introduction, spent a tumultuous three weeks under my care in the hospital intermittently bleeding from his throat. We became good friends during several long, panicky nights together— nights that, incidentally, New York state's new legislation would now forbid, legally obliging me to go home and hand José over to someone else's care, no matter how sick he might be.

José finally left the hospital in pretty good shape and came to see me in the medical clinic for several years afterward. He never tired of talking about the first 20 minutes of our acquaintance.

"I'm so sorry," I would say for the hundredth time. "It doesn't matter," he would say. "You didn't mean nothing by it. I felt real bad when that guy started yelling at you. I wanted to punch him out."

FOR FURTHER INFORMATION

Bosk, Charles L. *Forgive and Remember: Managing Medical Failure.* Chicago: University of Chicago Press, 1979.

Hilfiker, David. *Healing the Wounds: A Physician Looks at His Work.* New York: Pantheon Books, 1985.

Lantos, John D. *Do We Still Need Doctors?* New York: Routledge, 1997.

69

CHILDREN GASPING FOR BREATH IN THE INNER CITY

BY CHARLES-GENE MCDANIEL

Most of the time Sandra Biber and her husband, Rusty Callaway, can cope with the demands of caring for three children with asthma. "But occasionally," Biber says, "it just feels like we have several more variables to juggle than we have hands for. When one of the kids is sick, it is just overwhelming. There is no one to pick up the slack, no family nearby."

Biber estimates that she or her husband must miss half a day of work a month to take the younger two children to the doctor and a full day a month because

Stephen Shames—Matrix

of sickness in one or another of their children.

The oldest child, Bekki, 15, has only mild exercise-induced asthma and may have a handful of flare-ups a year. (This form of asthma is fairly common in youngsters; after a few minutes of strenuous exercise—running is the most common provoking activity—they become short of breath and may start wheezing or coughing. Often such attacks resolve spontaneously within 30 to 60 minutes, even if exercise is continued. Exercise-induced asthma, however, is easily prevented by taking appropriate medication just prior to the activity.) Jeremy, 11, and Benjamin, 3, however, have both had asthma since infancy, and their conditions require fairly constant attention. To keep their asthma under control, both must use medications daily and have their airflow monitored regularly on a peak flow meter (a simple, inexpensive device that can give an early warning of an imminent asthma flare-up).

Biber and Callaway note how challenging it can be to try to keep

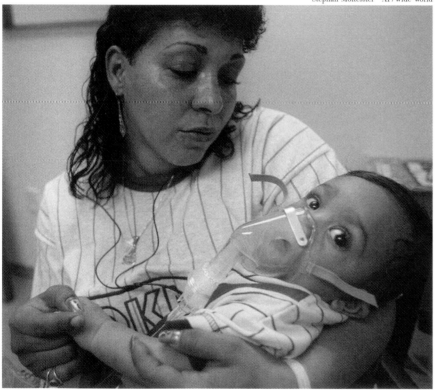

Stephan Moitessier—AP/Wide World

Elsa Santini of the South Bronx, New York, has five children with asthma; here she holds the youngest, Eric, as he receives treatment in an emergency room.

Charles-Gene McDaniel *is a freelance medical writer and Professor Emeritus of Journalism, Roosevelt University, Chicago.*

the asthma of an active toddler like Benjy in control. Still, the parents go out of their way to let their children live as normally as possible. Biber, a volunteer for the Allergy and Asthma Network/Mothers of Asthmatics, Inc., an organization that helps educate families about the prevention and treatment of asthma, does not want her boys to grow up feeling that they

The inflamed... airways act as a one-way valve...air is inspired but cannot be expired.

are "different" or less capable than other children. That means, among other things, that the Biber-Callaway children participate in sports (with their pediatrician's approval). It also means that the family has a dog, a recent acquisition, but they keep the pet out of the children's bedrooms to minimize their exposure to the animal's dander (dead skin scales), which, along with saliva and urine, carries an asthma-provoking allergen.

The Biber-Callaways, a middle-class couple living in Sharon, Massachusetts, share challenges faced by growing numbers of American parents. On the whole, their three children fare very well. Elsa Santini, who lives in the South Bronx, New York, has five young children with asthma; they are not so fortunate. Between the ages of six and nine months, the youngest Santini child, Eric, was treated for severe asthma 15 times in a hospital emergency room. Each time the doctor placed an oxygen mask over little Eric's mouth and nose—and he stopped gasping and screaming—his mother was able to breath a temporary sigh of relief, knowing it had been another close call.

Medical experts are duly alarmed about the rapid rise in the incidence of asthma—especially among children—worldwide. Globally the disease is now estimated to affect some 100 million–150 million people. Among the world's industrialized countries, the United States has seen one of the sharpest rises; since 1980 the prevalence of the disease has increased by 66%. According to the National Center for Health Statistics, between 1990 and 1995 (the latest year for which data have been analyzed) the number of cases of asthma in Americans rose from 10.4 million to 15 million; close to 5 million of those asthma sufferers are under age 18.

WAITING TO EXHALE

Asthma is a chronic inflammatory disorder of the bronchial tubes of the lungs in which the airways—the vital breathing passages—become obstructed. During normal breathing, inhaled air is carried from the mouth to the tiny air pockets (alveoli) in the lungs, where life-giving oxygen and the waste product carbon dioxide are exchanged. The air travels through two main channels (bronchi) that branch into smaller, narrower passages (bronchioles) within each lung.

In those with asthma, the very sensitive smooth muscles that surround the airways go into spasm when they are stimulated by an asthma "trigger"; this results in tightening and narrowing of the inner airway space (lumen), known as bronchoconstriction. At the same time, the inside lining of the airways becomes swollen and inflamed owing to fluid buildup (edema) and infiltration by immune system cells, and the membrane and glands that line the airways produce excessive quantities of thick, sticky mucus.

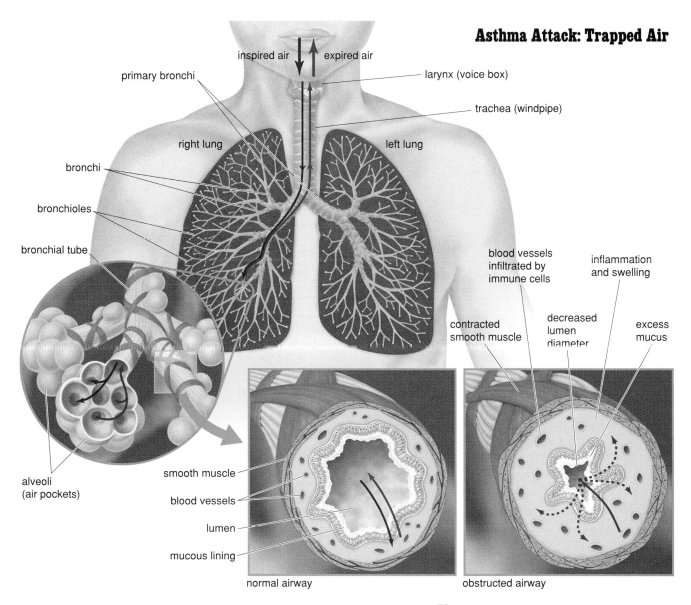

Asthma Attack: Trapped Air

inspired air expired air

primary bronchi

larynx (voice box)

trachea (windpipe)

right lung

left lung

bronchi

bronchioles

bronchial tube

blood vessels infiltrated by immune cells

inflammation and swelling

contracted smooth muscle

decreased lumen diameter

excess mucus

alveoli (air pockets)

smooth muscle

blood vessels

lumen

mucous lining

normal airway

obstructed airway

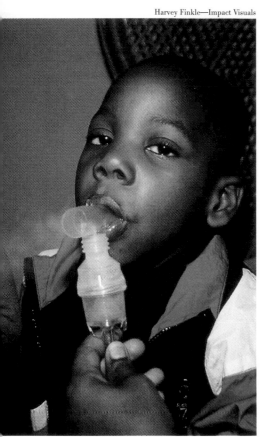

This five-year-old, who lives in Philadelphia's inner city, has severe asthma that requires almost constant attention.

The inflamed, mucus-clogged airways act as a one-way valve—*i.e.*, air is inspired but cannot be expired. Asthma specialist Michael A. Kaliner, medical director of the Institute for Asthma and Allergy in Washington, D.C., notes that a person with asthma "can trap as much as two liters of air in his or her lungs—enough to fill a basketball." Such trapped air is largely responsible for the discomfort of asthma. The characteristic high-pitched whistling sound, or wheezing, that accompanies asthma is caused by the patient's attempt to exhale through clogged passages. Other hallmark asthma symptoms are coughing, shortness of breath, and tightness of the chest.

Asthma-precipitating factors, or triggers, include allergens (*e.g.*, pollen, molds, animal dander, cockroaches, dust, foods, feathers); irritants (cigarette smoke, ozone, cleaning agents, chemical fumes, perfume, occupational dusts and vapors); exercise; respiratory infection (colds, flu); weather (abrupt changes in humidity, cold air); emotional stress and excitement; and drugs (aspirin, certain heart medications).

Though there is no cure, effective treatments are available to prevent and/or alleviate asthma attacks. Anti-inflammatory drugs (including corticosteroids) and a new class of nonsteroidal drugs, leukotriene receptor antagonists (introduced in the U.S. in late 1996), are effective in preventing asthma attacks. These medications are used on a regular basis to control the underlying inflammation. Bronchodilators are "rescue drugs" that relax the tight muscles surrounding the airways and thereby halt an attack in progress. Overreliance on bronchodilators, however, may mask the progression of the underlying disease.

A LOT OF SPECULATION

Reasons for the dramatic upsurge in asthma—particularly pediatric cases—are not entirely clear. Among the gamut of culprits that have been blamed for the increase are: the filth in the air we breathe; the thinning ozone layer; El Niño; crowded living conditions in an increasingly urbanized world; cigarette smoking (which is increasing among women and minority youth); exposure to second-hand (or passive) smoke; exposure to smoke in utero; inherited predisposi-

> Among racial and ethnic minorities... rates of asthma-related visits to hospital emergency rooms are about 8 to 10 times the national average.

tion; cockroaches; "sick buildings"; improved diagnosis and reporting; mobile telephones; and declines in the quality of medical care. But as Scott Schroeder, chief of pediatric pulmonology at Montefiore Medical Center in the Bronx, says, if you "talk to 10 doctors" you will "get 10 different opinions. We're just not that sophisticated yet."

Ironically, advances in medicine may have contributed to rising rates of asthma. Studies have shown that the incidence of allergies and asthma tends to rise in countries where childhood immunization rates are high. Theoretically this occurs because vaccines, though lifesaving, may disturb the normal development of the immune system. Certain naturally acquired childhood infections, like measles, are thought to trigger protective immune reactions. When a child is vaccinated and thereby protected from infection, immune-system cells presumably have less work to do. Having no viruses or parasites to attack, they become hyperresponsive (according to this theory) and may grossly overreact to normally harmless substances in the environment or to any of the aforementioned asthma triggers.

Antibiotics may also interfere with immune development. A recent study by Julian Hopkin, a respiratory disease specialist at Churchill Hospital in Oxford, England, found that children who are given broad-spectrum antibiotics (effective against multiple microorganisms) before age two are three times more likely to develop hay fever, asthma, and the allergic skin disorder eczema than are children who are not given antibiotics. Internationally, doctors—often under pressure from concerned parents—have become accustomed to prescribing antibiotics as a "quick fix" for minor ailments like sore throats and ear infections, even though they may be of viral origin (against which antibiotics are *not* effective). Asthma specialist John Warner, professor of child health at the University of Southampton, England, finds the asthma-antibiotic theory intriguing. He speculates that "the bugs we have in our bowels help our immune system to respond normally." If those bugs are knocked out by powerful antibiotic drugs, immune system functioning may become abnormal, or "more 'allergic,'" he says. But Warner emphasizes that the causative role of antibiotics in allergies and asthma needs to be considerably further investigated.

Another recently reported study from the U.K. revealed that especially frequent bathing may increase a young child's risk of developing allergies, including asthma. Researchers at the Institute of Child Health at the University of Bristol looked at 14,000 children born in the Avon area between 1991 and 1992 and found that those who bathed every day and washed their hands more than five times daily were 25% more likely to develop asthma than their less-hygienic peers. "The findings fit the hypothesis that the current increase in asthma could be attributed to improved standards of hygiene, which means that children experience fewer infections and that could leave them more vulnerable and sensitive to allergens," commented Jean Golding, one of the study's investigators.

DISPROPORTIONATE SUFFERING

In inner-city areas across the United States, there are very large populations of poor people who, like the five Santini children in the South Bronx, rely on hospital emergency rooms for crisis care but receive no ongoing care for asthma. Authorities are particularly concerned because even though asthma is a controllable disease, the number of asthma-related deaths in the U.S. rose from 2,891 in 1980 to 5,600 in 1995. Paradoxically, among all population groups, the age at which people die (from all causes) has been increasing, but it has been decreasing among people with asthma. The high death rate is most pronounced among racial and ethnic minorities living in inner cities, where rates of asthma-related visits to hospital emergency rooms are about 8 to 10 times the national average. More than one study has

Asthma on the Rise in the U.S.*

Category	1980		1987–89		1993–94	
Race	Number of cases	Rate per 1,000	Number of cases	Rate per 1,000	Number of cases	Rate per 1,000
White	5,790,000	30.4	8,270,000	41.1	10,700,000	50.8
Black	880,000	34.0	1,510,000	51.7	1,880,000	57.8
Other	100,000	22.5	280,000	32.7	540,000	48.6
Sex						
Male	3,350,000	32.0	4,910,000	43.0	6,150,000	51.1
Female	3,410,000	29.2	5,290,000	42.3	7,400,000	56.2
Age group						
0–4	360,000	22.2	620,000	33.9	1,280,000	57.8
5–14	1,520,000	42.8	2,130,000	60.7	2,790,000	74.4
15–34	2,160,000	27.7	3,210,000	40.1	4,050,000	51.8
35–64	1,960,000	28.1	2,980,000	36.8	4,090,000	44.6
≥65	770,000	30.7	1,260,000	42.1	1,480,000	44.6
Total	**6,770,000**	**30.7**	**10,200,000**	**42.9**	**13,690,000**	**53.8**

*Based on National Health Interview Surveys 1980–94 (most recent figures available).
Source: *Morbidity and Mortality Weekly Report*, Surveillance Summary, vol. 47, no. SS-1 (April 24, 1998), Centers for Disease Control and Prevention.

shown a very high correlation between low socioeconomic status and rates of hospitalization or death from asthma.

Especially alarming to public health experts is the disproportionate number of African-Americans affected by and dying from asthma. Data from the National Heart, Lung, and Blood Institute (NHLBI) indicated that in 1979 African-Americans of both sexes were about twice as likely as people from other racial groups to die from asthma; by 1994 their death rate from asthma was three times greater. Most studies indicate that asthma prevalence in blacks is twice that among whites, and asthma death rates are twofold to sixfold higher for

The bodies, feces, and saliva of cockroaches... constitute one of the most potent allergens to which inner-city children are exposed.

black children than for white children. African-Americans are hospitalized for asthma far more fre-

(Above) Underside of a cockroach, a pest that is prevalent in inner cities—and a major contributor to childhood asthma.
(Below) Latino children living in the Mission District of San Francisco.

76

(Above) David Butow—Saba; (top) Davies & Starr—Gamma/Liaison

barriers, and culturally based beliefs about illness, Hispanic children have a high prevalence of asthma and asthma-related hospitalizations. American Lung Association data indicate that children of Puerto Rican background have the highest rates of any minority population; about 20% of those aged 6 months to 11 years are affected.

A study by researchers at Dartmouth Medical School, Hanover, New Hampshire, recently found that asthma hospitalization rates in Maine, Vermont, New Hampshire, and New York had risen among black and Hispanic children living in poor neighborhoods in metropolitan areas, al-

quently (from two to five times more often) than their white counterparts.

As a result of poverty, a lack of access to medical care, language

though hospitalization rates for non-asthma causes fell substantially over the same period. There was no single reason for the increase, but the researchers speculated that the most vulnerable children may have had less-effective medical care than white children from higher-income families. Other studies have shown that poor children with asthma are generally sicker than their better-off counterparts—*e.g.*, they spend more time in bed and are frequently hospitalized as a result of their illness. Reporting their findings in the February 1998 issue of the journal *Pediatrics*, the Dartmouth investigators concluded: "Children hospitalized for asthma represent the failure of our social safety net as well as the failure of prospective disease management. Hospitalization for asthma is rarely inevitable."

Researchers from the Johns Hopkins University School of Medicine, Baltimore, Maryland, and the Howard University School of Medicine, Washington, D.C., found that children living in poor urban areas commonly receive inadequate or inappropriate medication, which leads to frequent emergency room visits and/or hospitalizations for asthma. Among these asthma sufferers, the use of anti-inflammatory medications (recommended by the NHLBI in its guidelines for the management of asthma) was less than half that in the

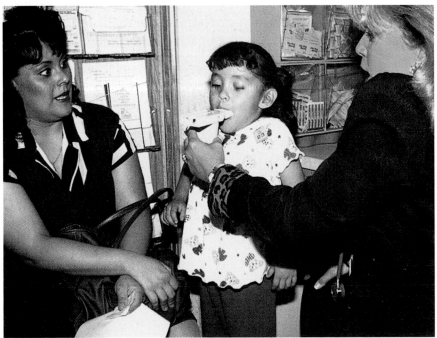

(Top) Kids playing outdoors in Berlin, New Hampshire, are exposed to pollutants from a local paper mill. (Left) A nurse in Los Angeles shows a child and her mother how to use a peak flow meter, an important device for monitoring asthma patients' airflow.

Outreach workers for the National Cooperative Inner-City Asthma Study visit the homes of young Chicago asthma sufferers and show them practical ways to reduce their exposure to indoor allergens.

Photo by Janice B. Terry, courtesy of the Inner-City Asthma Study of Children's Memorial Hospital, Chicago

use." Only 70 of the 392 participating families reported having problems paying for medications. Yet 19%

of 276 children whose health plans paid for prescribed drugs used no medication for asthma at all.

general pediatric population with asthma, whereas bronchodilators, which are meant for treatment of acute attacks, were fairly widely used.

Another disturbing finding from the same study was that more than half of the children who were nine years of age and older were responsible for their own medications, and a large number of them took no medication at all. Although some studies have suggested that higher asthma rates among poorer people are a reflection of their lack of access to medical care, the Johns Hopkins–Howard University investigators found that among their inner-city-dwelling subjects, "difficulties with access to care did not appear to be related to the pattern of medication

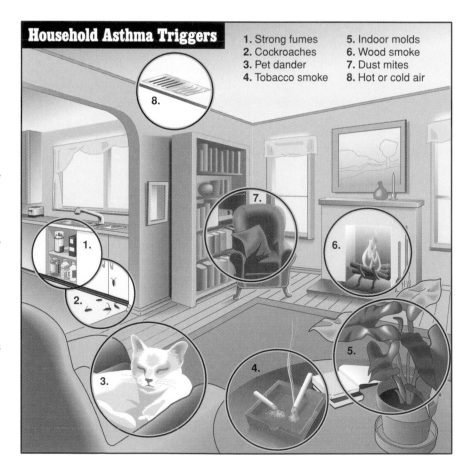

Household Asthma Triggers

1. Strong fumes
2. Cockroaches
3. Pet dander
4. Tobacco smoke
5. Indoor molds
6. Wood smoke
7. Dust mites
8. Hot or cold air

INNER-CITY FOCUS

In order to determine why poor children in inner cities suffer from asthma at such disproportionately high rates, the National Institute of Allergy and Infectious Diseases (NIAID) initiated the National Co-operative Inner-City Asthma Study. Medical and public health professionals are studying the problem in eight major inner-city areas—East Harlem, New York; the Bronx; Baltimore; Cleveland, Ohio; Chicago; Detroit; St. Louis, Missouri; and Washington, D.C. with the goal of finding ways to reduce this added burden on the poor, especially the hard-hit racial and ethnic minorities.

The first phase of the study (1991–94) enrolled more than 1,500 children aged 4 to 11 and their adult caretakers—of whom nearly 75% were African-American and 20% Hispanic. A number of factors were found to be associated with asthma severity. These included exposure to high levels of indoor allergens (especially cockroaches), to smoking among family members and caretak-

ers, and to nitrogen dioxide, a toxic atmospheric pollutant produced by the combustion of fossil fuels. Other environmental factors cited were dust mites, cat dander, ozone, sulfur dioxide, and particulates from diesel exhaust. More than half of the participants also had difficulty getting follow-up care for their asthma.

In the second phase of the study (1994–96), nurse practitioners acted as asthma counselors, working with more than 1,000 high-risk children and their families to manage the children's condition and reduce their exposure to environmental triggers of asthma. Initiating pest-control measures to rid homes of cockroach allergen was one of the key steps taken. Indeed, one of the most important findings of the first phase of the study was that the bodies, feces, and saliva of cockroaches, which collect in household dust, constitute one of the most potent allergens to which inner-city children are exposed—more potent than dust mites, molds, or cat dander.

The second phase of the study was tremendously successful; NIAID re-

ported that more than 90% of enrolled families complied with the intervention program, "which led to a striking reduction of asthma symptoms, an improved quality of life, better school attendance, and a 30 percent decrease in asthma-related hospitalizations and unscheduled physician and emergency visits for asthma."

Owing to the promising results of the first two phases, NIAID has funded a continuation of the research. Earlier investigation had shown that psychological adjustment in children and adults and stressful events in the family environment were "significant concerns" for inner-city dwellers. Investigators are now looking more closely at psychosocial factors; everything from living in crowded and run-down housing to the marital status of parents will be considered. And study teams around the country are looking for ways that stress can be mitigated in the lives of children with asthma—their goal being to reduce the number of days on which these youngsters experience symptoms.

George S. Malindzak, Jr., a psychologist at the National Institute of Environmental Health Sciences, Research Triangle Park, North Carolina, says that to ignore stress when trying to pin down asthma's causes in underserved populations "would be a mistake. There is no question that it is involved." Stress, he adds, is known to "release all kinds of mediators"—*i.e.*, chemicals that can trigger asthma symptoms.

REVERSING THE TREND

Prompted by the alarming magnitude of the problem of childhood asthma, a 15-member coalition of physicians, nurses, and representatives from lay groups organized the Asthma Zero Mortality Coalition. The coalition's goal is to reduce asthma deaths to zero by the year 2000. The efforts are focused on six cities: Atlanta, Georgia; Boston; Chicago; New York City; San Francisco; and Washington, D.C. A two-pronged campaign is directed at increasing awareness of asthma and its symptoms among the general population and educating physicians about the disease and its treatment.

The latter activity is crucial, says Michael LeNoir, chief of allergy at San Francisco General Hospital, who is chairman of the coalition. Doctors are "in the front line of any effort to deal with asthma," he says. Yet "a lot of physicians don't know how to treat the disease." The coalition conducted a survey of 990 primary care physicians who treated an average of 18 asthma patients a month. LeNoir was dismayed to find that a vast majority of doctors had a poor understanding of asthma's pathophysiology. Only one in 10 was aware of the NHLBI's asthma-management guidelines, and some 79% of doctors queried said they were likely to treat

only acute episodes of asthma, rarely its underlying causes. "We have a responsibility to reduce this morbidity and mortality," LeNoir insists. "Asthma can be controlled, deaths can be prevented."

FOR FURTHER INFORMATION

Books

DeSalvo, Louise. *Breathless: An Asthma Journal.* Boston: Beacon Press, 1998. A writer's scholarly exploration of her struggles with asthma and her search for its causes.

Edelman, Norman. *American Lung Association Family Guide to Asthma and Allergies.* Comprehensive and authoritative guide. Boston: Little, Brown and Co., 1998.

Gosselin, Kim. *Taking Asthma to School.* St. Louis, Mo.: JayJo Books, 1998. Written for children with asthma.

Lane, Donald J. *Asthma: The Facts.* New York: Oxford University Press, 1996. The third edition of this volume by a physician who has asthma himself; covers all aspects of treatment, including self-help and complementary therapies.

Sander, Nancy. *A Parent's Guide to Asthma.* New York: Plume Books, 1994. Practical handbook that focuses on the physical and emotional impact of asthma on the family.

Sander, Nancy. *Consumer Update on Asthma.* Fairfax, Va.: AAN•MA, 1993. Guide that addresses the diagnosis and treatment of asthma, from mild to life-threatening.

Weiss, Jonathan H. *Breathe Easy: Young People's Guide to Asthma.* New York: Magination Press, 1994. Practical patient-oriented guide written for children with asthma up to age 13.

Organizations

Allergy and Asthma Network•Mothers of Asthmatics, Inc. (AAN•MA)
Suite 150
2751 Prosperity Ave
Fairfax VA 22031
800-878-4403
703-641-9595
Web site: http://www.aanma.org

American Academy of Allergy, Asthma & Immunology (AAAAI)
611 E Wells St
Milwaukee WI 53202-3889
800-822-2762
Web site: http://www.aaaai.org

American Lung Association (ALA)
Call 800-LUNG USA to contact your local office.
800-586-4872
Web site: http://www.lungusa.org

Asthma and Allergy Foundation of America (AAFA)
Suite 502
1125 15th St NW
Washington DC 20005
202-466-7643
Web site: http://www.aafa.org

National Heart, Lung, and Blood Institute (NHLBI)
National Asthma Education and Prevention Program
NHLBI Information Center
PO Box 30105
Bethesda MD 20824-0105
Phone: 301-251-1222
Fax: 301-251-1223
Web sites:
    http://www.nhlbi.nih.gov/nhlbi/nhlbi.htm
    http://www.nhlbi.nih.gov/nhlbi/othcomp/opec/naepp/naeppage.htm

National Institute of Allergy and Infectious Diseases (NIAID)
NIAID Office of Communications
Building 31 Room 7A-50
31 Center Dr MSC 2520
Bethesda MD 20892-2520
301-402-1663
Web site: http://www.niaid.nih.gov

ASTHMA: A VIP LIST

Asthma and astonishing achievements are not mutually exclusive. That is the theme of a forthcoming book, *Asthma Among the Famous*, by asthma and allergy specialist Sheldon G. Cohen. Cohen, who holds the positions of scientific adviser at the National Institute of Allergy and Infectious Diseases and scholar in the History of Medicine Division at the National Library of Medicine, Bethesda, Maryland, has compiled a wealth of information about the impact of asthmatic illness on the lives and careers of nearly 100 historical personages. The majority of these famous figures lived at a time when truly effective asthma treatments were not yet available and state-of-the-art knowledge could offer little, if anything, in the way of symptom relief. Yet despite asthma's discomforts and disabilities, each of the individuals Cohen profiles achieved notable eminence in his or her respective field and time.

Covering a span of 20 centuries, the list that follows is from *Asthma Among the Famous*, OceanSide Publications, Providence, Rhode Island.

Erich Lessing—Art Resource

Portrait of a young John Calvin

- **Lucius Annaeus Seneca** (4 BC–AD 65)
  Roman orator, author, and statesman
- **Pliny the Elder** (AD 23–79)
  Roman historian and encyclopedist
- **Al-Afdal** (1169–1225)
  Arab sultan of Damascus and Egypt
- **Henri de Mondeville** (1260–1320)
  French surgeon
- **John Calvin** (1509–64)
  French theologian and religious reformer

- **Chu I-hai, prince of Lu** (1618–62)
  Last regent of the Chinese Ming dynasty
- **John Locke** (1632–1704)
  British physician and philosopher
- **William III** (1650–1702)
  Prince of Orange and king of Great Britain
- **John Arbuthnot** (1667–1735)
  Scottish physician and author
- **Peter I/Peter the Great** (1672–1725)
  Russian czar
- **Antonio Vivaldi** (1678–1741)
  Italian violin virtuoso, composer, and conductor
- **Samuel Johnson** (1709–84)
  British poet, critic, essayist, and lexicographer
- **Tobias G. Smollett** (1721–71)
  Scottish surgeon and novelist
- **Edmund Burke** (1729–97)
  Irish-born British statesman and political philosopher
- **John Paul Jones** (1747–92)
  American naval officer
- **William IV** (1765–1837)
  King of Great Britain, Ireland, and Hanover
- **Ludwig van Beethoven** (1770–1827)
  German composer
- **Sydney Smith** (1771–1845)
  British clergyman and journalist
- **John Bostock** (1773–1846)
  British physician
- **René-Théophile-Hyacinthe Laënnec** (1781–1826)
  French physician

British statesman Benjamin Disraeli

Culver Pictures

Prolific early-20th-century novelist Edith Wharton

- **Lemuel Shaw** (1781–1861)
  American jurist
- **Martin Van Buren** (1782–1862)
  Eighth president of the United States
- **Daniel Webster** (1782–1852)
  American lawyer, orator, and statesman
- **Giacomo Leopardi** (1798–1837)
  Italian writer and scholar
- **Benjamin Disraeli** (1804–81)
  British statesman and writer
- **Abdelkader** (1808–83)
  Founder of the Algerian state
- **Oliver Wendell Holmes** (1809–94)
  American physician, poet, novelist, and
  philosopher
- **Tseng Kuo-fan** (1811–72)
  Chinese scholar, statesman, and general
- **Charles Dickens** (1812–70)
  English novelist

- **Morrill Wyman** (1812–1903)
  American physician, discovered ragweed as a cause of
  hayfever
- **Henry Ward Beecher** (1813–87)
  American churchman and orator
- **Charles H. Blackley** (1820–1900)
  British homeopathic physician and hayfever
  investigator
- **William Tecumseh Sherman** (1820–91)
  U.S. Union Army general
- **Henry Hyde Salter** (1823–71)
  British pioneer asthma specialist
- **Antonio Guzmán Blanco** (1829–99)
  11th president of Venezuela
- **Ambrose Bierce** (1842–1914)
  American journalist and author
- **Marie-Bernarde Soubirous** (1844–79)
  French saint of the Catholic Church
- **Joseph Pulitzer (**1847–1911)
  American journalist and publisher
- **Olive E.A. Schreiner** (1855–1920)
  South African writer
- **Woodrow Wilson** (1856–1924)
  28th president of the United States
- **Juan Vicente Gómez** (1857–1935)
  18th president of Venezuela
- **Theodore Roosevelt** (1858–1919)
  26th president of the United States
- **Edith Wharton** (1862–1937)
  American novelist
- **Max Broedel** (1870–1941)
  American anatomist and medical illustrator
- **Marcel Proust** (1871–1922)
  French author
- **J. Calvin Coolidge** (1872–1933)
  30th president of the United States
- **Arnold Schoenberg** (1874–1951)
  Austrian-American composer and
  conductor
- **Padre Pio** (1887–1968)
  Italian Roman Catholic cleric
- **Graciliano Ramos** (1892–1953)
  Brazilian novelist

- **Djuna Barnes** (1892–1982) American novelist
- **Helen Hayes** (1900–93) American actress and author
- **Robert Donat** (1905–58) British actor
- **Francis Bacon** (1909–92) English artist
- **Elizabeth Bishop** (1911–79) American poet
- **Dylan Thomas** (1914–53) Welsh poet
- **Alyce King Clarke** (1915–95) American vocalist, member of the King Sisters
- **John F. Kennedy** (1917–63) 35th president of the United States

Stage and screen star Helen Hayes

Leftist rebel Che Guevara, 1961

Leonard Bernstein, conducting with passion, July 5, 1970

- **Leonard Bernstein** (1918–90) American composer and conductor
- **Che Guevara** (1928–67) Argentine physician and revolutionary
- **Ernest N. Morial** (1929–89) African-American political leader and mayor of New Orleans

- **Moses Gunn** (1929–93) American actor
- **Robert Joffrey** (1930–88) American dancer and choreographer
- **Teresa Teng** (1953–95) Taiwanese vocalist

PICTURING ASTHMA

Featured on this and the next three pages are artworks by individuals who accepted the challenge of Zeneca Pharmaceuticals to convey what it's like to live with asthma. Entrants to the "Inspiration in Asthma" art competition numbered over 600 and came from 13 countries.

Works by Bill Geldart,
United Kingdom (above),
and D. Parker, United States
(right).

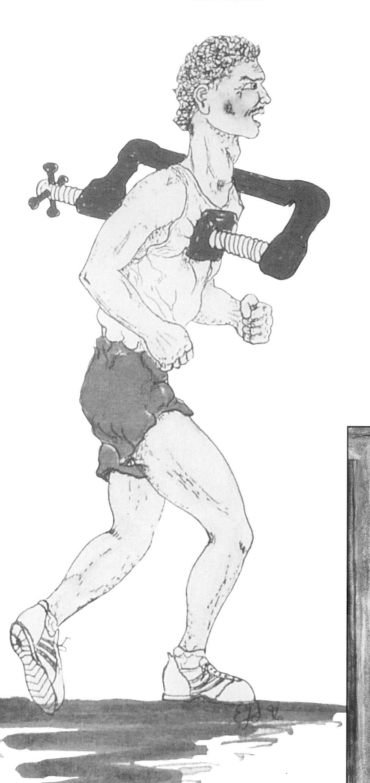

Works by Eric (left) and Dill
(below), both from the U.S.

86

Works by Jon (left) and Frances (below), both from the U.K.

87

A SANGUINE ATTACHMENT:
2,000 YEARS OF LEECHES IN MEDICINE

BY ROY T. SAWYER, PH.D.

My love of leeches began when I was six. As a child I spent countless hours immersed in the Carolina swamps, captivated by their plants and animals. It was not uncommon to come across a terrapin (a medium-sized turtle) covered with leeches or even to find a leech feeding on my leg after I had been swimming. Snakes and lizards, butterflies and birds—each took a turn for my attention, but leeches easily won me over. For all I knew at the time, I was the only person in the world fascinated by these curious little worms.

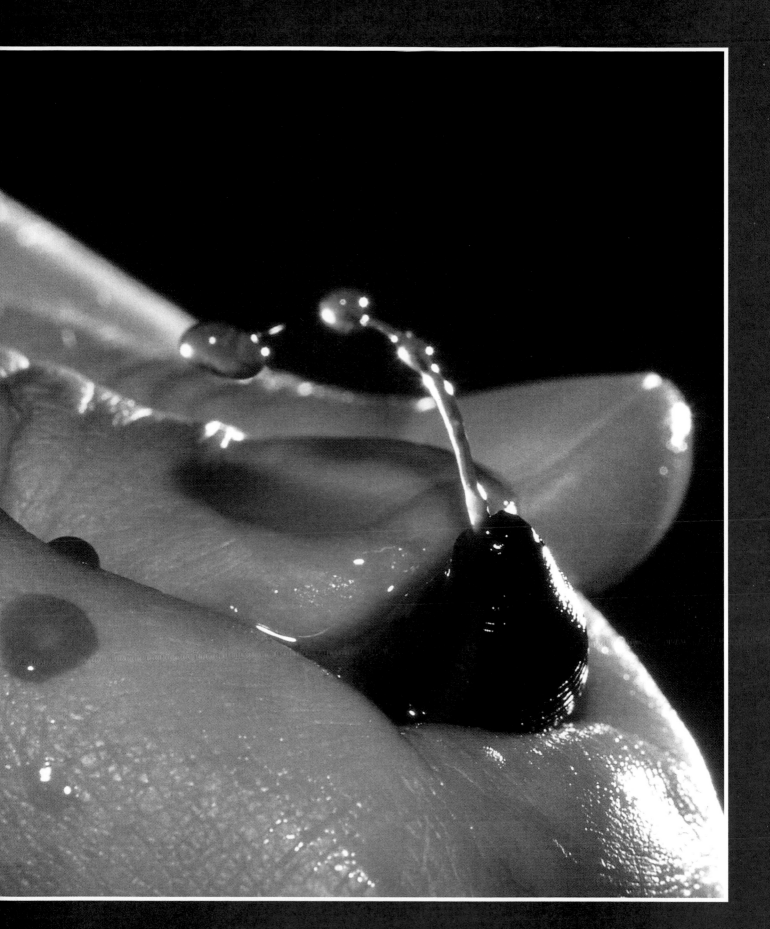

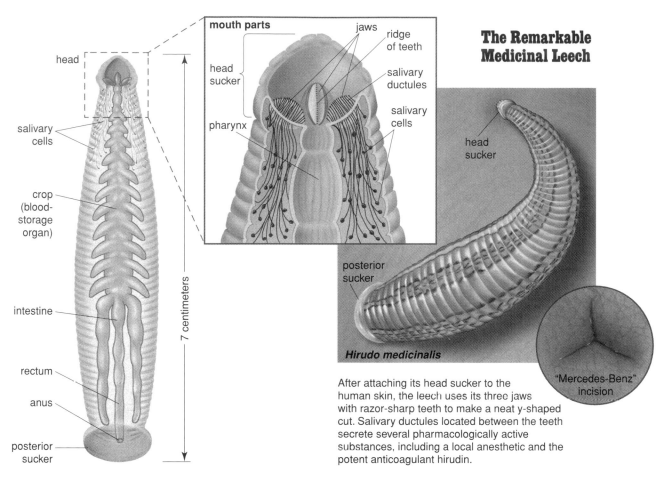

mouth parts

head sucker

jaws

ridge of teeth

salivary ductules

salivary cells

pharynx

7 centimeters

head

salivary cells

crop (blood-storage organ)

intestine

rectum

anus

posterior sucker

The Remarkable Medicinal Leech

head sucker

posterior sucker

Hirudo medicinalis

"Mercedes-Benz" incision

After attaching its head sucker to the human skin, the leech uses its three jaws with razor-sharp teeth to make a neat y-shaped cut. Salivary ductules located between the teeth secrete several pharmacologically active substances, including a local anesthetic and the potent anticoagulant hirudin.

(Overleaf) A medicinal leech (*Hirudo medicinalis*) is "milked" for the pharmacologically active substances in its saliva.

Roy T. Sawyer, Ph.D., is Founder and Director, Medical Leech Museum, Charleston, South Carolina; Founder and Managing Director, Biopharm (UK) Ltd., Hendy, Wales; and author of the three-volume textbook Leech Biology and Behaviour *(Oxford University Press, 1986).*

Who could have guessed that this naive obsession would grow into a career—or that one day the boy who loved leeches would contribute to the bloodsuckers' revival in modern medicine?

SLIMY WORMS

Most people have never seen a leech. They have only read or heard shocking accounts of leeches' use in bloodletting in times long past. Or they imagine horrific encounters with them in far-off tropical jungles, perhaps recalling scenes from *The African Queen* (1951) and Charlie Allnut's (Humphrey Bogart's) infamous pronouncement: "If there's anything in the world I hate, it's leeches—filthy little devils!"

As a leech biologist, I am continually surprised that the general public

is so unfamiliar with these common creatures. In fact, there are about 650 species of leeches in the world. At least one species, *Helobdella stagnalis*, is found on every continent on Earth (save Australia). Though leeches predominantly live in freshwater, some species inhabit oceans; still others live on land. In North America they are found not just in subtropical marshes and swamps of the South but in lakes, ponds, and streams in northern regions. They abound in the Great Lakes area. In such widely frequented places as New York City's Central Park and San Francisco's Golden Gate Park, the casual stroller is rarely more than a stone's throw from a leech-filled pond.

The nearest relative of the leech is the earthworm. These two types of annelids (segmented worms) share the distinction of being hermaphrodites (having functional reproductive organs of both sexes). Offspring are produced when eggs secreted by one leech are fertilized by sperm from another leech. The hatchlings (miniatures of the adults) develop in cocoons that are deposited either in water or on land.

A fundamental difference between leeches and earthworms is that the latter eat decaying plant matter, whereas leeches are invariably carnivorous—predaceous as well as often sanguivorous (feeding on blood), depending on the species. Because their primary method of feeding—for which they have gained considerable notoriety—is sucking blood, leeches must be a great deal more devious than their earthworm cousins just to stay alive. For the sake of survival, some leeches have become quite specialized, residing where they are sure to find good blood meals. For example, in the Sahara Desert one species dwells mainly in the noses of camels. Another leech lives in the anus of the hippopotamus! One type of leech inhabits caves in New Guinea, where it sucks the blood of bats. In Asian rain forests leeches find their prey in bushes; in Tibet they lurk along high mountain trails. Still other leeches live in the frigid polar seas, where they feast on the blood of arctic and antarctic fish.

The use of leeches in medicine has a long and colorful past, extending back at least 2,000 years of recorded history. As a youngster I was fairly

Most people have never seen a leech.

indifferent to the stories I'd heard about the medicinal use of leeches "in the olden days." I was far more interested in how the repulsive creatures lived than in any potential uses they might have. Eventually, however, I came to suspect that prior generations had learned to exploit the leech's bloodsucking proclivities for what must have been legitimate reasons. Still later my interest took a decidedly scientific turn; I became focused on their unique biochemistry and began to see leeches as a veritable "living pharmacy."

Even among bloodsucking leeches there are no species that feed exclusively on humans. In fact, there are only a few types of leeches that are so specialized in their ability to draw blood from humans that they have been used in medicine and can be rightfully called "medicinal." In Europe there is only one variety of medicinal leech, namely, *Hirudo medicinalis*. Though once prevalent across the continent, these freshwater leeches became an endangered species, mainly as a result of overcollecting during a period of "leech mania" in the 19th century.

The bloodsuckers that live in North America have relatively poorly developed mouth parts and consequently have not been useful in medicine. For this reason, the early colonists imported large numbers of *H. medicinalis* from Europe to satisfy domestic medical needs.

In this 1827 lithograph, "Les Sangsues" ("The Leeches") by Louis Boilly, a doctor carefully applies a leech to the neck of his ailing patient; the young boy in the foreground stands ready to assist with a jarful of additional leeches.

CHECKERED PAST

Ancient Sanskrit writings of the Indian physicians Caraka and Sushruta appear to be the first documented evidence of the use of leeches in medicine. The great treatise on medicine *Sushruta-Samhita* devotes a whole chapter to "Leeches: How and When to Use Them," describing the many medicinal applications of leeches in remarkable detail. Hippocrates, the father of Western medicine (460–377 BCE), made no mention of leeching, but the Greco-Roman physician and surgeon Galen (AD 129–c. 216) occasionally

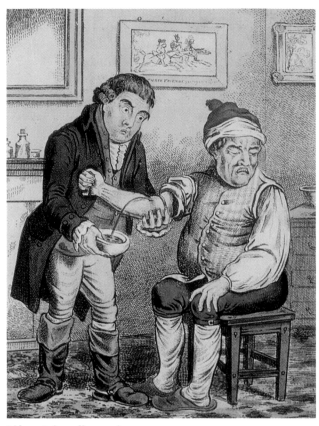

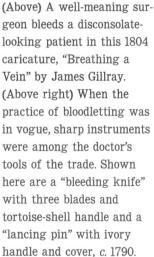

(Above) A well-meaning surgeon bleeds a disconsolate-looking patient in this 1804 caricature, "Breathing a Vein" by James Gillray. (Above right) When the practice of bloodletting was in vogue, sharp instruments were among the doctor's tools of the trade. Shown here are a "bleeding knife" with three blades and tortoise-shell handle and a "lancing pin" with ivory handle and cover, c. 1790.

advocated the bleeding of patients with leeches, a practice that persisted to some extent in various parts of the world for many centuries.

Then, toward the beginning of the 19th century, came the notorious period of leech mania. Peaking in France between about 1820 and 1845, this was a time during which enormous quantities of leeches—literally tens of millions—were used in the name of medical progress. The most illustrious advocate of leeching was François-Joseph-Victor Broussais (described by the historian of medicine Arturo Castiglioni as the "most sanguinary physician in history"). In Broussais's day as many as five million to six million leeches a year were used to purge more than 300,000 liters of patients' blood in Parisian hospitals alone. Broussais himself was alleged to have prescribed as many as 30 leeches for his patients—before even examining them. In some cases patients lost as much as 80% of their blood in a single purge.

It was during this manic period that *leeching* became incorporated into the pseudoscientific framework associated with *bloodletting*. A distinction needs to be made between the two terms. Leeching, along with *cupping* and *scarifying*, was a relatively minor method of initiating localized bleeding. (Cupping was a method of drawing blood to the surface of the body by application of a heated glass vessel that formed a partial vacuum against the skin; scarifying involved making small scratches on the skin. Of the three methods, leeching was purportedly the least painful.) Aside from the

Leeches offer a safe and effective way of relieving locally congested blood in delicate areas.

The European leech (*H. medicinalis*) lives in freshwater, is about 10 centimeters (4 inches) long, and has a dark exterior with greenish or brownish-yellowish markings. In the early to mid-1800s, it was not uncommon for Parisian physicians to treat patients with 30 or more leeches at a time. As a result of this "leech mania," *H. medicinalis* became an endangered species.

aberrant period of leech mania, throughout most of history leeches have generally been used *in moderation* to treat *appropriate* medical conditions. There is little question, for example, that leeches offer a safe and effective way of relieving locally congested blood in delicate areas, such as around a "black eye."

In contrast, bloodletting, also known as *venesection*, or *phlebotomy*, was a much more all-encompassing practice that involved the opening of a vein to remove some quantity of blood—usually a sizable one. For the most part, bloodletting (by incision into a vein or application of excessive numbers of leeches) was a gruesome practice, and for good historical reasons neither scientists nor laypeople today can be very objective about it. Though many would like to dismiss the subject altogether, it seems to me that two recurring claims for the validity of bloodletting deserve attention.

The prominent early American physician Benjamin Rush of Philadelphia was among the practitioners who believed in the first of these claims—that bloodletting was a valuable therapy if applied in the early stages of inflammation or fever. It was by such early intervention that Rush claimed to have saved thousands of lives during the devastating yellow fever epidemic of 1793. (Among other symptoms, yellow fever is marked by a rapidly rising fever.) Even though this treatment was highly controversial, Rush held to its validity throughout his lifetime.

Less obvious is why leeches were also used persistently to treat certain other medical conditions, most notably eye complaints such as glaucoma and chest infections like pneumonia. An extract from the autobiography of Sir Charles Forte, founder of the international Trusthouse Forte chain of hotels, is illuminating:

As soon as I was born [in a remote village in Italy in 1908] it was clear that I was having difficulty breathing, probably due to pneumonia, which was a recognized killer of babies in mountain villages....As it became clear I was getting worse, all the known conventional remedies having failed, in desperation the family doctor applied leeches. Appalling as it sounds to use this mediaeval remedy on a new-born baby, in my case it seems to have worked. Apparently the moment the leeches began to swell with my blood my condition improved and soon I was yelling lustily. I have good reason to be thankful to the leeches.

Should Forte's case and similar anecdotal evidence of the effectiveness of leech treatments be taken seriously? I think so. Doctors of the past may have been ignorant of the scientific mechanisms behind their treatments, but when they saw that a method that had been used for a couple of thousand years was often beneficial, they could hardly ignore it.

Even more intriguing to me is the ancient claim that regular bloodletting maintains health. In the

93

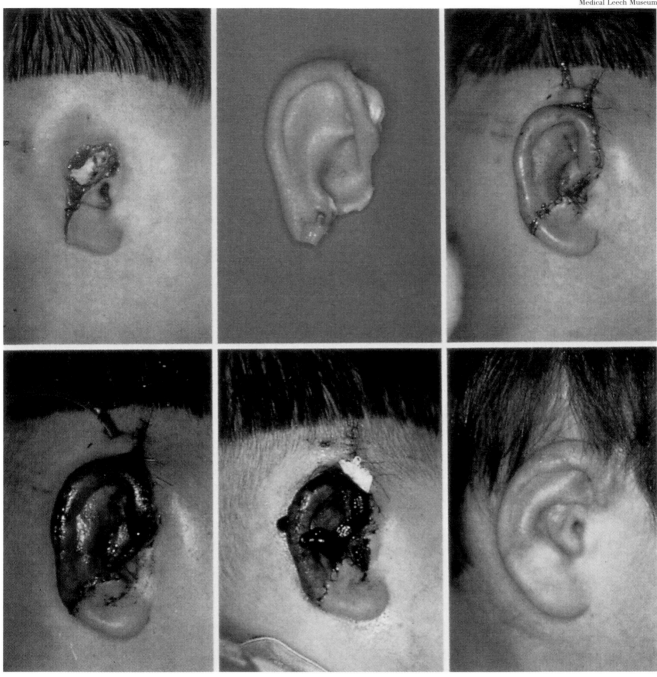

After a dog bit off Guy Condelli's right ear, Boston surgeon Joseph Upton re-attached it but couldn't get its blood supply going. A shipment of leeches from Wales saved the day. (Right) The fortunate five-year-old expressed his gratitude to the supplier of the leeches.

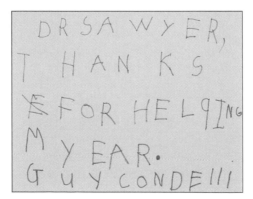

DR SAWYER,
THANKS
FOR HELPING
MY EAR.
GUY CONDELLI

Middle Ages, especially in monasteries, it was commonly believed that there were propitious times to have blood removed—for example, in the spring. In some cases it was prescribed on a monthly basis. This belief has not entirely vanished. One of my students recently looked into beliefs about bloodletting that are still current in the Middle East.

94

She found that it was a widespread practice for people in Tehran to visit a local "bleeder" faithfully every month for reasons that would seem vague or obscure to most Westerners. There are times when I cannot help but wonder whether such traditional bleeders, so highly respected and trusted within their own communities, perhaps know something that contemporary physicians do not. I was especially intrigued by a report that appeared in the *British Medical Journal* (March 15, 1997); Finnish investigators found that men who had voluntarily donated blood were less likely to have heart attacks than were their counterparts who did not give blood. Although the study was by no means conclusive about the connection between blood loss and cardiovascular health, it suggested a link that deserves further study.

TALES FROM THE LEECH-FARMING FRONT

In the early 1980s, having chosen to make a career as a leech biologist, I realized that with the serious decline of *H. medicinalis* in its natural European habitats, it was becoming increasingly difficult to obtain enough leeches (anywhere in the world) for study. Convinced as I was that there was much to be learned about medicinal applications of leeches, I began breeding them. In the process of writing a three-volume textbook on leeches, which took me about 12 years, I saw the potential for discovery of unique pharmaceuticals derived from leech saliva and became determined to set up a research company for this purpose.

Such a career move, I knew, would be personally and professionally tricky, requiring me to leave the security of academia. Nonetheless, in

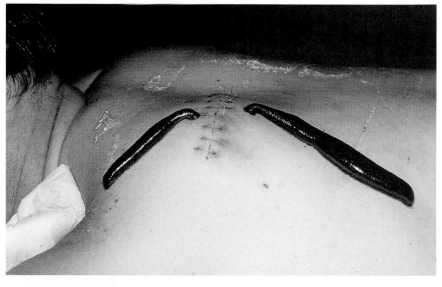

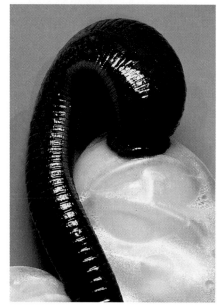

(Above) Leeches are applied to a patient's back to drain a hematoma, an accumulation of blood within the tissues (in this case, resulting from an injury). (Left) In order to suck blood, a leech must first attach its head sucker onto the skin of its host. In the middle of the sucker are its unique three jaws with razor-sharp teeth.

1984 I risked all to start the world's first leech-breeding farm. I was joined in this venture by my wife, Lorna, and my Welsh in-laws, Tom and Evelyn Jones. We started the company called Biopharm (UK) Ltd. in south Wales—much like an enterprising Italian family might open a restaurant. For a time, my wife supported us (by teaching school), but within a year or so she too joined the company as a full-time director. My mother-in-law helped with cleaning and maintaining the leech tanks, and my father-in-law (who had

learned typing and shorthand during World War II) served for a number of years as an unpaid secretary. For the first year most of our leech farming was carried out in the garden shed and garage of our home. Now our facilities are located on a large early Victorian country estate prominently overlooking a tidal river outside Swansea, Wales. In 1988 a second branch of Biopharm opened in Charleston, South Carolina.

It soon became evident that Biopharm's very existence had created an unforeseen market for leeches. A few weeks after the facility in Wales opened, I received a somewhat desperate phone call from a nearby hospital; doctors in the plastic surgery unit wanted leeches to

95

try to save a man's ear, which had been partially severed in an occupational accident. Because this was our first "customer," I drove the leeches to the hospital myself. To my surprise, I encountered an entourage of doctors, nurses, and ancillary staff who led me to the patient, expecting *me* to apply the leeches to a very sad-looking ear! The surgeons had reattached the ear but were unable to get the circulation going; heroic measures were called for. With the patient's wife looking on, I very hesitantly showed the clinicians how to apply a leech. Fortunately, the treatment worked; the blood supply to the reattached ear was restored.

Biopharm's most celebrated case came six months later. A five-year-old boy in the Boston area had been attacked by a dog, which had totally severed one of his ears. Biopharm shipped leeches to Boston Children's Hospital, where surgeon Joseph Upton succeeded in saving the youngster's ear. Three weeks later the youth's picture appeared on the front page of the *Boston Globe* with the headline "Doctors Use Hungry Leeches to Save Boy's Reattached Ear." Some months later Upton sent me before-and-after photographs, accompanied by a letter in a child's script that is one of my most prized possessions. It reads: "Dear Dr. Sawyer, Thanks for helping my ear. Guy Condelli." This single well-publicized case led to the enthusiastic use of leeches by surgeons across the United States.

In June 1989 an expatriate Englishman working in a diamond mine in Botswana had his hands inside an open industrial coil spring when it

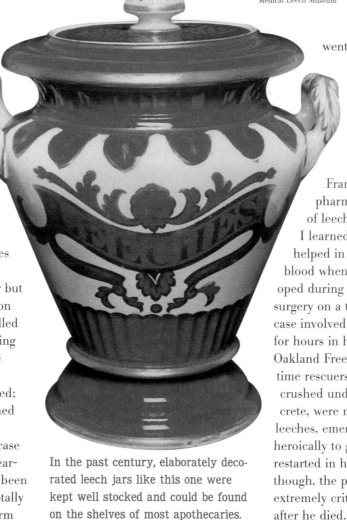

In the past century, elaborately decorated leech jars like this one were kept well stocked and could be found on the shelves of most apothecaries.

suddenly snapped shut. He lost all the fingers on his left hand and the thumb and middle finger on his right hand. Surgeons were able to save some of fingers and reconstruct a functional "thumb" on his right hand, but then a complication developed. The venous flow in the reattached index finger on one hand was poor, and the finger had become dangerously swollen. A doctor on the team knew that leeches might help. As one local newspaper reported, "A medical team with a fast car was waiting at Jan Smuts Airport [Johannesburg] early today for a jar of 30 deliberately starved bloodsucking leeches. The leeches' arrival may save an injured…worker…from a lifetime of discomfort." Indeed, soon after the application of leeches, the swelling

went down and the finger turned "a healthy pink." The grateful patient told a reporter that he could not "even feel [the leeches] feeding."

After the 1989 San Francisco earthquake, Biopharm had calls for hundreds of leeches. From later feedback I learned that leeches had helped in the decongestion of blood when complications developed during reconstructive facial surgery on a teenage girl. A second case involved a man who was trapped for hours in his car when the Oakland Freeway collapsed. By the time rescuers got him out, his legs, crushed under the weight of concrete, were nearly lifeless. Using leeches, emergency physicians tried heroically to get the circulation restarted in his legs; in this case, though, the patient's condition was extremely critical, and shortly thereafter he died.

In Maastricht, The Netherlands, an eight-year-old boy underwent reconstructive surgery to correct several congenital facial deformities. After the operation his tongue swelled so severely that it became life-threatening. Diuretics, steroids, and antibiotics were given over a period of five days but did not reduce the swelling. With the application of 27 leeches (rushed on demand from Wales to Holland), the swelling was markedly reduced, and the boy was out of danger. A write-up of this unusual case by the Dutch doctors who treated the boy was published in *The Journal of Laryngology and Otology* (May 1995).

From its breeding facilities in Wales and South Carolina, Biopharm ships leeches to hospitals throughout the world every day. I can attest that there is rarely a dull day in the leech business! On one occasion a courier van transporting Biopharm leeches was hijacked by a terrorist group in London. A particularly sad case from the early days—before leech-assisted microsurgery had "caught on"—was that of a young man in Queensland, Australia. Working in a sugarcane field, he got a hand caught in a harvesting machine and lost most of the fingers. He was taken to the hospital in Cairns, where an attempt was made to sew the severed fingers back onto the hand. After a short time, however, the fingers turned cold and blue, and the doctor said he would have to amputate in a day or so. The boy's mother had read about using leeches to save reattached fingers. (Apparently the doctor had not.) The mother somehow got my home phone number and rang me in the middle of the night. She explained the situation and begged me to contact the surgeon and attempt to persuade him to try leeches. I phoned the doctor in Australia and discussed the case with him, but he was adamant; the fingers were too far gone to be saved, and he intended to amputate them later that day.

LEECHES IN THE OPERATING ROOM

Thousands of patients owe the successful reattachment of body parts to miraculous technological advances in plastic and reconstructive surgery; at least some of those operations might have failed if leeches had not been reintroduced into the operating room. The appendages reattached include fingers, hands, toes, legs, ears, noses, scalps, and even penises. (Though they were not used in the widely publicized John Wayne Bobbit case, leeches, I am told, were on standby.)

The pioneering use of leeches in modern plastic and reconstructive surgery can be attributed to two Slovenian surgeons, M. Derganc and F. Zdravic from Ljubljana, who published a paper in the *British Journal of Plastic Surgery* in 1960 describing leech-assisted tissue flap surgery (in which a flap of skin is freed or rotated from an adjacent body area to cover a defect or injury). These surgeons credit their own use of leeches to a Parisian surgeon, one Philippe-Frédéric Blandin, who reported in 1836 that he had used leeches to restore circulation following reconstruction of a nose.

The rationale behind the use of leeches in surgical procedures is fairly straightforward; nonetheless, it is subject to misunderstanding, even by clinicians. The key to success is the exploitation of a unique property of the leech bite, namely, the creation of a puncture wound that bleeds literally for hours. The leech's saliva contains substances that anesthetize the wound area, dilate the blood vessels to increase blood flow, and prevent the blood from clotting.

Microsurgeons today are quite adept at reattaching severed body parts, such as fingers. They usually have little trouble attaching the two ends of arteries, because arteries are thick-walled and relatively easy to suture. The veins, however, are thin-walled and especially difficult to suture, particularly if the tissue is badly damaged. All too often the surgeon can get blood to flow in the reattached arteries but not in the veins. With the venous circulation severely compromised, the blood going to the reattached finger becomes congested, or stagnant; the reattached portion turns blue and lifeless and is at serious risk of being lost. It is precisely in such cases that leeches are summoned.

There is no drug in the modern arsenal that can duplicate the effects of a leech bite.

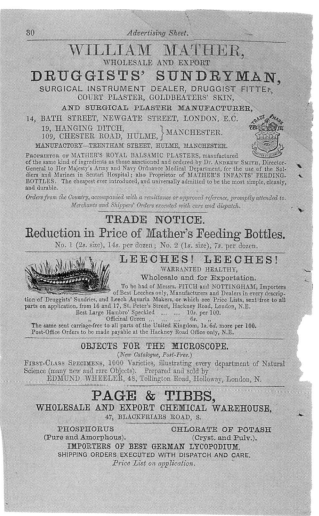

Advertisements for druggists' supplies in an 1868 issue of *Pharmaceutical Journal* included one for "LEECHES! LEECHES! WARRANTED HEALTHY, Wholesale and for Exportation. To be had of Messrs. FITCH and NOTTINGHAM, Importers of Best Leeches only."

The surgeon will apply one or two leeches to the part of the finger in which blood is congested. A typical three-gram medicinal leech feeds for approximately 30 minutes, during which time it ingests about 15 grams of blood. After feeding to repletion, the leech naturally detaches, but the wound continues to bleed for an average of 10 hours, which results in a total blood loss of approximately 120 grams. Such prolongation of bleeding is truly phenomenal and unique to leeches. There is no drug in the modern arsenal that can duplicate the effects of a leech bite. The microsurgeon has learned to encourage this bleeding rather than stop it, in order to facilitate circulation through a grafted appendage. When bleeding has almost ceased, another leech might be applied until the appendage is clearly out of danger. By using the leech, the surgeon borrows time, keeping the appendage alive until the body has reestablished its own circulation—usually within three to five days.

Rarely (about once in every 2,000 leech applications) a patient will develop a secondary infection from the bacteria that live in the leech gut. This appears to happen only when the patient's arterial circulation is poor or lacking. For this reason, the use of leeches on patients with inadequate blood flow in the arteries is considered inadvisable.

MERCEDES-BENZ BITE

To understand why the medicinal leech has proved so useful in modern reconstructive surgery, one needs to consider its mouth parts. Uniquely, the leech has three jaws that are exquisitely designed for the purpose of sucking the blood of humans. Each jaw is a muscular organ compressed into an arch with approximately 100 very sharp teeth on the outer rim. Owing to the tripartite arrangement of the jaws, the leech bite produces a neat cut (resembling the Mercedes-Benz emblem) that directly exposes the patient's underlying blood vessels. More than one microsurgeon has commented to me that in surgical terms this is the "perfect" skin entry. Because the mechanical stress is in three equal directions, there is minimal unwanted tearing of tissue, as can occur with a scalpel incision. The beauty of nature's design did not escape the ancients; the eminent 7th-century physician-surgeon Paul of Aegina advised "joining three equal lancets together, so that by one application it may produce three incisions."

The leech feeds by first attaching its head sucker onto the skin. The mouth, located in the middle of the sucker, opens to expose the razor-sharp teeth, which cut into the skin. Terminating between the teeth are individual salivary cell ductules that release pharmacologically active substances. One is a potent local anesthetic that renders the bite virtually painless (a clever trick of the trade for an animal that must escape detection to get a blood meal!).

Another substance is a so-called spreading factor (an enzyme that facilitates the spread of fluid through the tissues). The latter, which has been isolated and called Orgelase (Welsh for "from the leech"), quickly dissipates substances in the leech saliva—including the most powerful anticoagulant (inhibitor of clotting) known—away from the wound.

POTENT CARDIOVASCULAR DRUG

The absence of clotting associated with leeches was a well-known phenomenon that had long intrigued John Berry Haycraft, a 27-year-old physiologist who lived in Wales. In 1884 he identified the powerful anticoagulant in the saliva of *H. medicinalis*, later to be called hirudin. This was the first natural inhibitor of blood clotting to be discovered. Over three decades later, in 1916, a second important anticoagulant—heparin—was isolated from mast cells in connective tissues of vertebrates.

From the outset, the potency and specificity of hirudin were appreciated. Consequently, hirudin played a pivotal part in the formulation of the essentially correct model of blood coagulation (c. 1904) It also contributed to the scientific understanding of the safe storage of blood and had a role in the development of blood transfusions, which were both vitally important during the world wars. The full characterization of hirudin, however, had to wait for advances in the science of protein chemistry in the mid-1950s. It was then that Fritz Markwardt at the Institute of Pharmacology and Toxicology, Erfurt (Germany) Medical Academy, was able to isolate purified hirudin to modern standards.

(Opposite page and below) Photographs, Medical Leech Museum

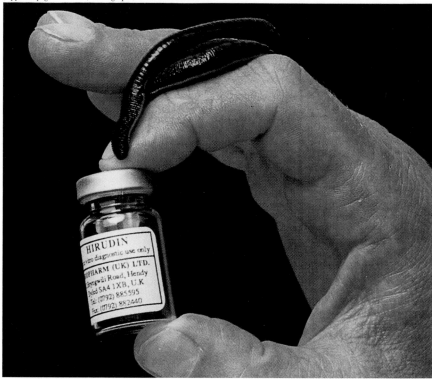

Hirudin, extracted from the saliva of medicinal leeches, is the most potent natural anticoagulant (*i.e.*, inhibitor of blood clotting) known. Medical scientists are just beginning to realize the clinical potential of this blood-modifying agent.

Markwardt found hirudin to be a low-molecular-weight polypeptide composed of 65 amino acids that was highly specific for inhibiting thrombin, the enzyme that facilitates the clotting of blood. The clinical potential of this potent inhibitor of thrombin was immediately recognized. As it was found only in the heads of leeches, however, there was no way to acquire adequate quantities for study. Finally in 1986, using the tools of biotechnology, hirudin was successfully cloned in several different European laboratories, and it became possible to produce unlimited quantities. Once it was available, genetically engineered hirudin showed remarkable promise in animal trials. Today it is clear that these hirudin derivatives are clinically valuable products of high efficacy and low toxicity.

For many years cardiologists relied on heparin for acute anticoagulation. Heparin, however, has important limitations. It does not inhibit thrombin that has already become bound to a growing clot. Nor does it stop thrombin from stimulating platelets, the small circulating cellular "marbles" in blood that normally aggregate and become sticky within seconds of tissue injury. (The resultant "platelet plug" keeps the injured patient from bleeding to death.)

Although hirudin is generally comparable to heparin in treating patients after heart attack, there are certain indications for which hirudin derivatives are demonstrably superior. For instance, it was reported in *The New England Journal of Medicine* (Nov. 6, 1997) that hirudin is highly effective in preventing deep-

Photographs, Geoff Tompkinson—Aspect Picture Library

collaboration with Roger Munro, a hematologist at Morriston Hospital, Swansea, Wales, showed that blood coming from a leech wound, in fact, clots in normal time, after about 15 minutes. During the first 15 minutes, the hirudin apparently washes out of the wound. How can it be that the blood clots normally but the wound continues to bleed for hours on end?

This enigma was solved by focusing on platelets. Munro showed that the platelets emerging from the leech-induced wound do *not* aggregate. Further research revealed the presence of a previously unsuspected

The author's love of leeches began when he was six. (Above) He displays two of the slimy creatures that continue to be the focus of his attention. (Right) Knee-deep in a pond in South Wales, the leech-gathering biologist is hard at work.

vein thromboses (blood clots in the legs) after total hip-replacement surgery. In clinical trials carried out at 31 medical centers in 10 European countries, patients who had received recombinant hirudin twice daily for at least eight days after hip replacement had a 40% lower risk of developing thromboses than did patients who were given heparin.

ENIGMA OF THE LEECH BITE

The leech was accepted in microsurgery well before the underlying mechanisms of its bite were understood. Most surgeons, even today, assume that the prolonged bleeding associated with a leech bite is due to the anticoagulant hirudin. Recently, however, Biopharm researchers, in

biochemical in leech saliva, subsequently given the name Calin (Welsh for "heart"). Calin binds to collagen, the most potent natural inducer of blood clotting. Biopharm researchers have proposed that Calin acts like a "collagen-coating paint," cleverly neutralizing collagen's capacity to induce blood clotting.

DISCOVERY IN THE AMAZON

The discussion of the medicinal uses of leeches thus far has applied only to the European leech *H. medicinalis*.

Because there are 650 species of leeches in the world, I began to wonder whether all leeches produced hirudin. Or might some leeches produce other anticoagulants? As an evolutionary biologist, I had reason to suspect that the leech's habit of bloodsucking—and the biochemistry associated with it—may have evolved more than once. (Substances in leech saliva do not occur by chance but are the result of millions of years of adaptation to feeding on the blood of mammals.)

Among the bloodsucking leeches there are two major groups with totally different mouth parts. As noted above, *H. medicinalis* relies on its tripartite jaws to feed. Members of the other group of bloodsucking leeches possess a proboscis (a narrow, tubular appendage resembling a drinking straw) and two salivary glands that secrete chemicals. The proboscis inserts into the victim's skin, penetrating deeply into the tissue, which enables the leech to feed in a manner similar to mosquitoes.

If a new anticoagulant was to be sought in leeches, the best place to look would be among the proboscis species. The perfect candidate would be a leech that feeds on mammals. As a rule, though, proboscis leeches feed on lower animals (*e.g.*, fish, frogs, and reptiles). There was one apparent exception; an obscure paper published in 1849 led me to have a keen interest in a gigantic leech—attaining a length of half a meter (about 18 inches)—discovered by Italian naturalist Vittore Ghiliani in the Amazon Basin. For me the exciting thing about this leech was not its size, impressive though that was, but the claim (undoubtedly exaggerated) that just a few such Amazonian leeches could kill a horse! In other words, here was a proboscis leech that fed on mammals—the ideal animal to answer the question about hirudin.

As far as I knew, the giant Amazon leech, *Haementeria ghilianii*, had not been seen by any member of the scientific community in the 20th century. Needless to say, the chances of finding it seemed remote. Nonetheless, in 1977, supported in part by the American Philosophical Society, I organized an expedition to the last place that *H. ghilianii* had been found, the coastal region of Amazonian French Guyana. With assistance from the Pasteur Institute—which was running a local antimalaria program—and French-speaking Indians, we eventually found the giant leech in massive swamps. We collected about 35 of the animals, which we took home for breeding. This original colony, which lived for more than 11 years, yielded several pharmacological surprises.

Once sufficient numbers of *H. ghilianii* had been bred and countless salivary glands dissected, we demonstrated, in collaboration with Andrei Budzinski at Temple University, Philadelphia, that the giant Amazon leech secretes an enzyme that cleaves (breaks apart) the blood-clotting factor fibrinogen; we named this enzyme hementin. Later we showed that hementin has a pharmacologically unique property—namely, it is able to break down a type of platelet-rich "white clot" that precipitates heart attacks and against which a commonly used class of drugs— known as fibrinolytics, thrombolytics, or "clot busters" (*e.g.*, tissue plasminogen activator, streptokinase, urokinase)—is not effective. The latter drugs are often given intravenously

following a suspected heart attack; if administered within six hours of initial symptoms, such therapy has the potential to minimize damage to the heart muscle by dissolving (or "busting") a recently formed clot that has lodged in a partially narrowed coronary artery.

Whereas European medicinal leeches produce hirudin, an inhibitor that prevents blood clots from forming in the first place, the giant Amazon leech produces the enzyme hementin, which dissolves clots after they have formed. Why did these two types of leech adopt such different biochemical strategies? I suspect the answer lies in *H. ghilianii*'s proboscis, an appendage that can measure 15 centimeters (about 6 inches) or more in length and, for all intents and purposes, can be considered a "blood vessel." In sucking blood through this long tube, the giant leech has to cope with hematologic circumstances faced by no other animal species on Earth. It takes about a minute for blood to pass along the length of the proboscis; this is slow enough for platelets to aggregate, which means a

platelet plug could form as the leech sucks blood. It would therefore be imperative that the plug be broken down quickly; otherwise, the proboscis would become totally blocked with a fibrin clot, and the leech would starve!

Subsequent to the discovery of hementin, Biopharm researchers found still another unique biochemical in the giant Amazon leech's saliva. Named tridegin (from the Welsh word for "thirteen"), this inhibitor of the blood-clotting factor XIII prevents blood clots from hardening. Working synergistically, hementin and tridegin keep the proboscis open long enough for *H. ghilianii* to ingest up to 25 grams of blood.

BLOODSUCKERS: A LIVING PHARMACY

Realizing that a whole new range of novel cardiovascular drugs might be derived from the leech, several pharmaceutical companies have been consulting with Biopharm scientists for a number of years. Several clinical trials with hirudin either have been completed or are under way. The clinical indications for the spreading factor Orgelase are manifold; it might, for example, aid in the deep penetration of tissues by a local anesthetic that is given prior to surgery. Calin, as a collagen neutralizer, would be of enormous benefit in most kinds of surgery; it too is being explored. Hementin is currently being developed by a European pharmaceutical company as a possible "clot-busting" drug—one that will rapidly dissolve clots that are not responsive to the current selection of thrombolytics. There are at least a dozen other pharmaceutically active substances that have been isolated from about 10 leech species that are

The Amazon Leech: Another Approach to Bloodsucking

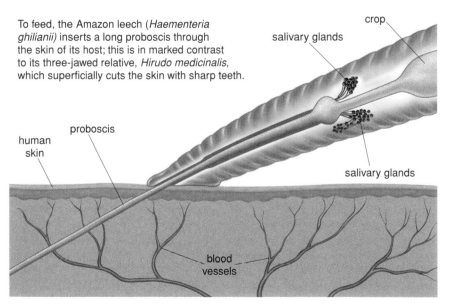

To feed, the Amazon leech (*Haementeria ghilianii*) inserts a long proboscis through the skin of its host; this is in marked contrast to its three-jawed relative, *Hirudo medicinalis*, which superficially cuts the skin with sharp teeth.

crop

salivary glands

salivary glands

human skin

proboscis

blood vessels

currently being (or soon will be) investigated.

Leeches are not the only blood-sucking creatures whose secretions could be the basis of cardiovascular drugs. In fact, there are about 40,000 such species, encompassing vampire bats, ticks, fleas, bedbugs, bloodsucking flies, and many others. I truly believe that each of these groups may have its own pharmacological story to tell. In fact, I would go so far as to say that in the future secretions from bloodsucking animals could be to cardiovascular diseases what penicillin was to infectious diseases in the past. Ironically, many of these bloodsuckers are also carriers of devastating diseases—*e.g.*, plague, typhus, malaria, yellow fever, sleeping sickness, and Lyme disease.

NOT FOR THE SQUEAMISH

The practical benefit of looking to the past with an open mind has been demonstrated several times in this article. Most significant is the debt owed by contemporary reconstructive surgeons and their thousands of patients to a little-known publication by a surgeon in Paris in 1836. For myself, I must credit an obscure Italian paper published in 1849 for leading me to the Amazonian wilds in search of a giant leech.

With all the truly remarkable advances there have been in Western medicine, the traditional methods of and clinical reasons for using leeches are rapidly being forgotten. With a sense of urgency, I believe this information should be conserved. Toward that end I established the Medical Leech Museum in Charleston in 1995. This small, privately owned facility is a repository for materia medica documenting leeching and bloodletting practices of the

"Oh Joy, the Leech Charmers!" by Max Ernst (*c.* 1930) is one of many artworks in the world's only leech museum.

past. Presently included in this one-of-a-kind collection are scientific papers and various other documents, a great many physical artifacts like "bleeding bowls," lancets, and exquisite 18th- and 19th-century leech jars, and even leeches themselves.

Not only does the museum have a wealth of scientific and clinical relics, it also has a collection of paintings and prints to attract any art lover. Here are works from the 16th to the 20th century with a common theme—bloodletting and leeching. Artists include Rembrandt, Cornelis Dusart, Romeyn de Hooghe, Egbert van Heemskerk, William Hogarth, the English caricaturists James Gillray and Thomas Rowlandson, and even the German surrealist Max Ernst. About these works the museum's Web site says, "Fine art at its best, but not for the squeamish!"

For me personally, the collecting of leech-related relics helps keep the past alive. Perhaps I am in a minority, but I strongly suspect that leeches and other bloodsucking animals have not yet had their heyday in medicine!

FOR FURTHER INFORMATION

The Medical Leech Museum
The Gadsden House
329 East Bay St
Charleston SC 29401
803-557-9143
Web site:
http://www.biopharm-leeches.com/museum.htm

TEENAGE TURBULENCE

If you've ever wondered what planet teenagers come from, you are not alone. Since the dawn of history, adults all over the world have been scratching their heads, asking, "Were we as foolish—and as impossible to comprehend—when we were young?" The answer, by and large, is yes.

BY MIHALY CSIKSZENTMIHALYI, PH.D.

Just having some fun! On a balmy July evening teenagers jump from the top of an old mill dam in Cedarville, Ohio.

Mihaly Csikszentmihalyi (pronounced "CHICK-sent-me-high-ee") is Professor of Human Development and Education in the Department of Psychology at the University of Chicago. For several decades he has been gathering data on adolescent behavior, the subject of two of his books: Being Adolescent, *with Reed Larson (1984), and* Talented Teenagers: The Roots of Success and Failure, *with Kevin Rathunde and Samuel Whalen (1993). He is probably best known for his research into states of optimal experience, or the condition he calls "flow." Among his most popular books are* Flow: The Psychology of Optimal Experience *(1990),* Creativity: Flow and the Psychology of Discovery and Invention *(1996), and his most recent,* Finding Flow: The Psychology of Engagement with Everyday Life *(1997).*

(continued from page 104)

On a cool summer night, an otherwise "perfectly normal" 15-year-old boy hung from the trestles of a railway bridge, trembling with a combination of terror and excitement as he waited for a freight train to rumble overhead a few inches above his fingers. Why was he doing this? Because, being a young man, he needed to prove to himself and his buddies that he had the "right stuff." Of course, there might have been other ways of proving this, but offhand he couldn't think of any.

That same summer evening, the eldest daughter of a respected suburban family, was spending the chilly night in a car parked in the garage at Chicago's O'Hare International Airport with a star athlete from her high school. It was their first date. They had been to a party, got drunk, and then piled into a friend's car. The next thing they knew, they were at the airport and the driver of the car had walked off somewhere, so the girl and her date were left alone. She was concerned: What would happen to her? She knew he had a reputation

for being "fast" and taking drugs. She was worried about unprotected sex and anxious about what her parents would do when they found out she hadn't returned from the party. Luckily, the boy passed out in the backseat, and the only unpleasant outcome for the young woman was a scolding when she finally got home.

There is nothing very unusual about these vignettes. They describe "typical" adolescents who are not *trying* to drive their elders crazy, nor are they stupid. Rather, like the 200,000 or so generations that preceded them on this Earth, they have been "programmed" to act in predictable ways from puberty into young adulthood. Today's teens are simply following a biological "script" that they have inherited over aeons of evolution. The problem is that the script wasn't written for young people who will reach adulthood in the 21st century, and owing to dramatic changes in cultural conditions over the last few hundred years, contemporary adolescents often have trouble fitting into society.

TROUBLESOME TRANSITION

Indeed, there are very good reasons for typical adolescents to be like they are so much of the time—rebellious, distracted, thoughtless, heedless of risk. Between the ages of 12 and 20, young people go through so many physical and social changes that it is difficult for them to know how they should behave. During puberty—a word that derives from the Latin for "to be covered with hair"—young bodies grow stronger and are infused with hormones that stimulate desires appropriate to ensuring the perpetuation of the species. If our pubescent forebears did not get on with the

serious tasks of earning a living and having a family at an early age, they were unlikely to live long enough to see their children grow up. Thus, boys (favored by natural selection for being, among other things, aggressive and adventuresome) started hunting as soon as they could heft a spear, and girls (solicitous and nurturant) began bearing babies after their first menses.

A seamless transition to adulthood has never been easy, but it seems to be getting harder. In the past virtually every society had formal ways for older individuals to help young people "find themselves" and take their place in the community. Initiations, spirit quests, the Hindu *samskara* life-cycle rituals, and other rites and ceremonies evolved to help young men and women make the transition from childhood to adulthood. An outstanding feature of such coming-of-age rites was their emphasis upon instruction in proper dress, deportment, morality, and other behaviors appropriate to adult status.

The Kumauni hill tribes of northern India offer a vivid example of a culture that maintains its traditional rituals celebrating distinct stages in every child's life. On these occasions women paint scenes from Hindu mythology on the bare, red-earth-colored floors and walls of their houses. The scene depicted corresponds to the child's age. Thus, when a girl reaches puberty, her home will be decorated with elaborate representations of a certain goddess's coming of age; wooed by a young god, she is escorted to the temple in a rich wedding procession. Anthropologist Lynn Hart, who has lived among the Kumauni, has noted that each child grows up at the center of the family's attention knowing that his or her life echoes the lives of the gods. No doubt Kumauni teenagers sometimes act in ways that seem wild to their elders, but what's important is that older family members help ease the passage through this stage of life, giving young people a sense of being connected to the community.

Xhosa youths in South Africa are covered with clay during a ceremony initiating them into manhood. At this critical juncture in their lives, the young men receive instruction from clan elders that will help them adjust to their new adult status.

James Nachtwey—Magnum

A seamless transition to adulthood has never been easy, but it seems to be getting harder.

107

(Above) Rapturous teens in Prague relish every second that their idol, Michael Jackson, is on stage. (Right) Young people do not have a lot of options when it comes to their schooling; if they did, probably few would choose to spend their time sitting in classrooms.

STIFLED IN THEIR PRIME?

From a biological perspective, adolescence should be the best time of life. Most physical and mental functions are at their peak during the teenage years—speed, strength, reaction time, and memory, for example. This is the time when body awareness is most intense, and it can feel so "right" to let loose and dance wildly. It is the time when foods taste best, appetite is heartiest, sleep is sweetest, and music is most seductive. Furthermore, it is in adolescence that new, radical, and divergent ideas often have their most profound impact on the imagination.

Perhaps more than anything else, teenagers have a remarkable built-in resiliency. Psychologists have noted that they manifest a unique ability to overcome crises and find a positive meaning in negative events. In studies that my colleagues and I have done, we found that teens fully recover from a really bad mood in about half the time it takes adults. All too often, however, despite this resilience, the teen years are *not* the most fulfilling but the most stressful. Many of the conditions society has imposed on teens stifle their natural instincts and inhibit their potential for positive experience. These conditions deserve special attention.

108

Restrictions on physical movement. Our bodies are our most basic possession, and most of us feel a need to control the location of our body—to determine where we want to be when. Teenagers spend countless hours sitting at desks processing information and concepts that often seem abstract or irrelevant to them. But few young people—no matter how academically inclined—would *choose* to spend the better part of a dozen years sitting in classrooms. Even straight-A students say that most of the time they are in school they would rather be "somewhere else." When Kevin Rathunde, Samuel Whalen, and I were doing the research for our book, *Talented Teenagers: The Roots of Success and Failure* (1993), the teenagers we interviewed overwhelmingly preferred to spend their time in places where they were least likely to be under adult supervision; public parks and malls ranked high among their choices.

The layout of contemporary communities presents another obstacle for adolescents, especially those living in suburbia. Some teens spend as many as four hours each day in transit, just getting to and from school, work, and friends' houses. Getting from place to place is not something most teens have control over until they obtain their own driver's license (an event that, not surprisingly, is the major rite of passage in contemporary adolescence). But even with access to a car, many teenagers lack appropriate places to go and rewarding activities in which to participate. In 1990 more than half of the respondents in a nationwide survey of U.S. high-school sophomores said that "just driving or riding around" was an activity they engaged in at least once or twice a week. Watching television and "just hanging out" were the two activities that occupied most of their free time.

Adolescents generally find that activities that involve physical movement are among the most pleasurable and gratifying. Yet the opportunities they have for participation in stimulating activities are dwindling. As schools across the United States face fiscal crises, nonacademic subjects such as physical education are often the first to be cut from the curriculum. In many public school systems, extracurricular activities—sports, dance, and drama, for example—no longer exist.

Absence of meaningful responsibility. Outside of school adolescents have a bewildering array of consumer choices. Just think of the number of television programs—no less TV channels—they can watch and the number of movies they can see at the local mall or rent at the local video outlet. Then there are the CDs, cosmetics, computers and computer paraphernalia, clothes, athletic shoes, and so on.

Although teenagers today have no end of material choices, they have few meaningful responsibilities, in

Alexander the Great took charge of his father's armies and began his celebrated career of conquest in his late adolescence.

sharp contrast to earlier generations. Alexander the Great (356–323 BCE) was still a teenager when he set out to conquer a large part of the known world at the head of his father's Macedonian armies. Lorenzo de' Medici (1449–92), known as Lorenzo the Magnificent, was a ripe adolescent when his father sent him to Paris to work out subtle financial

(Right) Forced to labor long hours in coal mines, youths growing up at the beginning of the 20th century were deprived of a childhood. (Opposite page) Youngsters growing up at the end of the 20th century are "deprived" of meaningful responsibilities that give them a sense of purpose.

Why would anyone choose to pierce his or her nose, tongue, nipples, or eyelids?

deals with the king of France. On a less exalted level, until a few generations ago, boys as young as five or six years old were expected to work in factories or mines for 70 or more hours a week. In almost all parts of the world, girls were expected to marry and take on the responsibilities for running a household as early as possible.

In 1950 the psychoanalyst Erik H. Erikson described adolescence in modern Western societies as a "moratorium," a period of freedom from responsibilities that allows young people to experiment with a number of options before committing themselves to a lifelong career. Such a moratorium may be both necessary and appropriate in a culture with so many rapidly changing occupational opportunities and such a diversity of lifestyles. Excluding young people from responsibilities for too long, however, can mean they never properly learn how to manage their own lives or care for those who depend on them.

There are, of course, exceptions to the rule; some adolescents manage to create astonishing opportunities for themselves. William Hewlett and David Packard were teens when they started experimenting with electronic machines in their parents' garages, and they founded their legendary Hewlett-Packard company when they were only in their mid-20s. As an adolescent, Microsoft Corp. co-founder Bill Gates was already formulating his business strategy that just a few years later would dumbfound the IBM colossus and make him one of the wealthiest men in the world.

By and large, however, most teens play a waiting game, expecting to start "really living" only after they leave school. This isolation of teens from "real" life, useful as it is for their preparation for future niches in society, can be enormously frustrating for them. It should not really be surprising that adolescents are torn between the urges that the past has programmed into their bodies and the restraints that the present asks of them. In the meantime, in order to feel alive and important, many of them act in ways that seem senseless to the rest of the populace.

Why would anyone choose to pierce his or her nose, tongue, nipples, or eyelids? Why would a teenager dye her pretty head of auburn hair shoe-polish black and cut it so it stands up in spikes? Why would another shave his head? What

Young women graduates of a school for pregnant teenagers in Albuquerque, New Mexico, "go out into the world" already saddled with child-rearing duties.

Parents are often incredulous when an intelligent, well-brought-up adolescent girl becomes pregnant.

drives a teenager to veer down steep cement stairs at top speed on a skateboard? Or spend a night huddled on a cold sidewalk in front of a Ticketmaster outlet to be sure of getting a ticket for a Verve concert? Or take illicit drugs purchased from a complete stranger on a street corner? Or have unprotected sex in the age of AIDS? Or "play" with guns? Such behaviors make sense only to people who are desperate for attention, who are unsure of themselves, who feel that no one trusts them or has much use for them. In other words, they make sense to a great many teenagers.

The worst consequence of adolescents' not having clear or real responsibilities is that they come to assume that what they *do* does not matter—and therefore that *they* do not matter. Although the excessively high expectations that some parents have for their children can be

overwhelming and oppressive, the opposite situation is more common—parents who have no expectations communicate an indifference that makes a child feel he or she has no self-worth. Low self-esteem borne of a lack of responsibility may be a factor in the high incidence of depression and suicide among today's teenagers.

Confusion about sexuality and intimacy. Parents are often incredulous when an intelligent, well-brought-up adolescent girl becomes pregnant. Doesn't she know any better? Didn't she think of the consequences? Adults who ask these questions do not understand that engaging in promiscuous sex can be a way for young people to exhibit their sophistication and prove themselves in a challenging context. Nor do adults appreciate that "safe sex" may not be a priority for adolescent girls. Rather, they want to prove they

are attractive and desirable; they want to act as adults; they want to control attention and power; and, on some level, they want the chance to show their nurturing capacity—by taking on the responsibility for another life.

During the sexual revolution of the 1960s and 1970s, it was widely assumed that progressive attitudes and the availability of oral contraceptives ("the Pill") would allow young people to be freer and happier than any previous generation in history, because they would be less repressed. Society has learned, somewhat belatedly, that sexual freedom is not necessarily conducive to health, personal growth, or social well-being. So much of the advertising that permeates young people's lives encourages them to think that sex is the be-all and end-all of life. Although contemporary culture encourages and indeed commodifies physical sexuality, it

provides few clues about how to express intimacy, show commitment, or handle responsibility. In part because of the blatant commercial exploitation of sexuality, many adolescents become so focused on the physical aspects of sex that they never come to appreciate the things that make human relationships truly valuable.

The enormous frequency of out-of-wedlock pregnancies in our times could be read to mean that teenagers are now sexually liberated, but in reality most such pregnancies severely limit the options of young parents and curtail their opportunities for growth. Saddled with premature duties, young parents typically have limited educational, occupational, and lifestyle choices.

Isolation from adults. In most U.S. grammar and high schools the student-teacher ratio is at least 20:1; classroom atmosphere is therefore

Despite their reputation for laziness, adolescents generally welcome challenges; they especially value opportunities that allow them to grow in competence.

influenced considerably more by peers than by teachers. At home, the average amount of time teens spend without parents or other adults present is about three and one-half hours each day. Moreover, during the little time when adolescents are at home with their parents, often all parties are exhausted from a hard day at school or work, and either the family watches television or the child disappears to study, listen to music, or talk to friends on the telephone.

Estrangement from parents has clear effects. Researcher Jeremy Hunter at the University of Chicago has shown that teens who do little and spend little time with their parents are likely to be bored, uninterested, and self-centered. In one study it was found that adolescents spent an average of only three minutes a day alone with their fathers, and often that time was spent in front of the television set. Even "quality time" cannot compensate for so little time. That isolation from adults—parents in particular—can have detrimental effects on a young person is well illustrated by the following case history.

Keith was a 14-year-old participating in a study that Reed Larson and I conducted a number of years ago. At the time, his parents were going through a divorce. Keith spent weekdays with his mother in the city, and on the weekends he stayed in the suburb where his father had moved. Because of this arrangement, he rarely saw his friends from school, and in the suburban neighborhood he felt isolated and alone. For the first few days of the study, staying at his mother's house, Keith reported that

Not all teenagers choose to spend their spare time "just hanging out." (Below) Dominic Penn of New Jersey, aged 13, enjoys sharing his computer savvy with senior citizen Clare Meadows.

all he did was listen to a Grateful Dead album from morning to night.

On one occasion he went into his father's closet to try on the shirts he had left behind. One in particular, a moss-green corduroy shirt that faintly smelled of campfire smoke, brought back strong memories. Keith remembered snuggling against that shirt on chilly summer nights when his father had taken him on camping trips. He put on the shirt and cut the sleeves to fit his arms. Then he took a bottle of aspirin from the bathroom cabinet, went to his room, and swallowed 70 pills. Before passing out, he wrote in his diary: "My mom wants me to hate my dad, and my dad wants me to hate my mom. Why are they doing this to me? I love them both."

Fortunately, his sister noticed the empty bottle. After having his stomach pumped in the emergency room and spending two days in the hospital, Keith was back in fine physical form. His act, desperate as it was, made his parents realize that a teenager needs attention and love as much as he needs food; they adjusted their living arrangements so that Keith was able to spend considerably more time with both his father and his mother—a situation that in the long run worked out well for everyone concerned.

The lack of meaningful and enjoyable cross-generational activities clearly contributes to the pathologies of adolescence. This situation is especially problematic in urban ghettoes, where until recently there existed a lively "street-corner society." Older African-American

men shared their own experiences with younger ones on a regular basis; the setting for this interchange was casual and relaxed and the repartee boisterous and jocular. As Elijah Anderson points out in his book *Streetwise: Race, Class, and Change in an Urban Community* (1990), this vital facet in the socialization of young black men is fast disappearing, to the detriment of individual lives and the viability of the community.

No power, no control. The obstacles to fulfillment already mentioned imply that young people have little control over their lives. Much of their day-to-day activity is mandated by parents, teachers, and various other elder "supervisors." Adolescents report that about half of their daily life is spent doing things that they "have to do" rather than things that they even remotely "want to do." In a recent study funded by the Alfred P. Sloan Foundation, my colleagues and I examined the productive activities of adolescents over a week—going to school, working at a job, doing homework, participating in sports, pursuing hobbies, making future plans—and found that about 80% of the time, the subjects felt they were doing things out of obligation rather than choice. Moreover, the activities that are presumed (by adults) to play the primary role in preparing youngsters for life are usually seen by the young people as "chores" that run counter to their own desires.

With no power and no control, teens often feel that they have marginal status. Young males in this situation may be driven to seek the respect that they feel they lack. According to experts, most gang fights and instances of juvenile homicide occur when teenage boys feel that they have been "dissed" (treated disrespectfully). Lacking clear roles, adolescents may establish

their own pecking order and spend their time pursuing deviant activities.

Such deviance can take many forms. Insecurity and rage often lead to vandalism, juvenile delinquency, and the indiscriminate use of drugs and alcohol. These activities are increasingly prevalent among teens of all social classes in all types of communities. In the past half century, most measures of teenage deviance have increased by about 300%. According to U.S. Department of Justice statistics, from 1983 to 1992 the rates of juvenile murder and nonnegligent manslaughter doubled. The same source estimated that in the early 1990s some 186,000 American children were taking guns to school. Violence and crime, of course, are as old as humankind; the eminent French historian Philippe Ariès, author of *Centuries of Childhood* (1962), noted that in the 12th century Parisian boys as young as seven years old carried daggers with them to school to defend themselves.

But most experts today would agree that juvenile violence has reached clearly frightening—indeed intolerable—proportions.

Juvenile violence is often driven by the boredom young people experience in a barren environment. Even the wealthiest suburbs with the most lavish amenities can be "barren" when viewed from the perspective of adolescents. Ironically, suburban life is meant to protect children from the dangers of the big city. Parents choose suburbia to raise their families with the best of intentions; they hope, of course, that their children will grow up happy and secure in the safe havens they have worked so hard to provide. But safety and homogeneity can be quite boring. When deprived of mean-

(Above) Teenagers duke it out on a New York City street, attracting a crowd of young watchers. (Below) A San Diego police officer arrests a teenage crime suspect. Boredom and a sense of powerlessness are often the forces that drive teens to commit delinquent acts.

(Above) Barbara Alper—Stock, Boston/PNI; (below) Stephen Shames—Matrix

These Liberian boy-soldiers have taken up arms well before reaching adolescence. (Opposite page, top) Kipland Kinkel, 15, of Springfield, Oregon, was arraigned on May 22, 1998, charged with murdering his parents and two students at his high school.

ingful things to do, many teens find that the only opportunities for "feeling alive" are stealing a car, breaking a school window, or ingesting a mind-altering drug. A middle-class adolescent caught red-handed with jewelry that he had stolen from a neighbor's house said, "If you could show me something else that is this much fun, I might try it." He was particularly proud that he had pulled

Corinne Dufka—Reuters

it off "without waking up the owners." Like other teenagers, by "fun" he meant something exciting and slightly dangerous that takes guts as well as skill.

All around the world there are restless young males who have been easily manipulated to serve evil ends. Roving bands of Asian and African rebels have conscripted bored teens who have found excitement and self-respect behind machine guns, and millions have died a premature death as a result. In the United States many urban dwellers now live in fear of being attacked by so-called super-predators—gangs of kids who are willing to beat up or kill for a pair of Nikes or an expensive gold watch.

On March 24, 1998, two gun-happy youngsters, aged 11 and 13, ambushed their Jonesboro, Arkansas, schoolhouse. In less than five min-

All around the world there are restless young males who have been easily manipulated to serve evil ends.

utes, they managed to fire 22 rounds of ammunition, killing 4 girls and 1 teacher and wounding 10 other people. About two months later a 15-year-old from Springfield, Oregon, killed both his parents and several hours later opened fire on his classmates in his high-school cafeteria; 2 youths died and 22 were wounded.

Fortunately, the situations just described are worst-case scenarios. The troubled youngsters from Jonesboro and Springfield were captured by police within minutes of committing their atrocities. Nonetheless, many criminal justice and public health professionals believe that strict law enforcement alone will not be effective against a mounting tide of disaffected youth.

IS TEENAGE TURMOIL INEVITABLE?

The majority of teenagers will survive the turbulence of adolescence. Early in this century child psychologists—Anna Freud, among them—concluded that the Sturm und Drang ("storm and stress") of adolescence was a normal feature of growing up, which allowed young people to break away from parental influences and establish their own individuality. More recent studies, done in the 1980s, cast doubt on the notion that stress at this stage of life is inevitable. For example, one large 10-country survey found that only a minority of adolescents (20%) reported having feelings of loneliness, emptiness, depression, or confusion. On the whole, however, it seems that in diverse cultures and in all historical periods stretching as far

back as written records, adolescence has been considered, variously, "a time of troubles," "the age of fire," "the years of burning," and "the shapeless age." It is unlikely that this consensus (which is both historical and cross-cultural) is based on a misapprehension.

The Sturm und Drang of adolescence will not go away on its own—and the situation could get worse. Fortunately, however, behavioral scientists have gained some valuable insights into the conditions that cause teenage conflict. Moreover, adults are in the position to alleviate some of the frictions that make intergenerational relations a lot more strained than they need to be. The facts suggest several courses of action.

BEYOND HEAD SCRATCHING

"I like math most when there is a hard problem and I can figure it out. When it's really hard at first and then I look at it and see the light," commented a highschool freshman.

"I enjoy drawing most when I know I've tried really hard and it's gone the way I wanted it to. It may start out bad, but if you keep at it then it just gets better, maybe better than what you thought it would be," said an aspiring artist.

"All my life I've always set goals, I mean one goal after the next," noted a young musician. *"I just work and work and work. It makes me feel good when I can reach goals. My whole life is goals."*

For some adolescents, like those quoted above, the challenges of learning are enough. Many young people, however, are not that fortunate. They find little interest and joy in the opportunities that the adult

A piccolo player tunes up before playing in a local parade with his Oakland, Maryland, marching band. Young people need stimulating activities to help them weather the storm and stress of adolescence.

117

One very telling study found that typical teens spend an average of only three minutes a day alone with their fathers. Yet, compassionate companionship is one of the greatest gifts a parent can give a young person weathering the storm of adolescence.

Jennie Woodcock—Reflections
Photolibrary/Corbis

world provides for them. To help them, community leaders and educators would do well to take adolescent needs into account when deciding on educational curricula, when establishing laws regarding work, and in urban planning and other matters that affect the quality of life of this vulnerable age group. While waiting for society to initiate constructive solutions in the areas just mentioned, parents can do a great deal to help their teenagers get involved with life.

Despite their reputation for laziness and passivity, teenagers seem to most value activities that present them with incremental challenges and make it possible for them to improve their skills. They are happiest when involved in sports and hobbies, music or art, and intimate friendships. My colleagues and I have found this again and again in studying adolescent behavior. These activities allow them to expand their skills, grow in competence, and consequently feel good about themselves. When they don't have situations that make them feel fully functioning and important, teenagers will often seek them out.

An African-American girl living in the inner city was just a junior in high school when her mother died and her father left her to take care of two younger siblings. She feared she would flunk out of school. A triumphal moment came when she presented a pie she had baked to the women's group of her church. The praise she received from these respected elders made her feel more appreciated and competent than at any other time of the week.

A 15-year-old boy living in an affluent suburb was bored almost continuously until he discovered that he had a knack for building decorative outdoor ponds for exotic fish. From then on he was busy researching the best pumps for recirculating water, the most interesting and beautiful rocks, and unusual species of freshwater fish. When he was designing and experimenting with new pond installations, he felt on top of the world.

Given that the leading causes of adolescent mortality are accidents, suicide, substance abuse, and violence, concerned adults must be on the lookout for signs of teens' dissatisfaction with life. A teenager who is generally bored or anxious, is either always alone or always in the company of peers, or lacks intense interests and seems to have few sources of joy may turn to more destructive forms of engagement.

118

Research indicates that those rare adolescents who have the opportunity to develop a relationship with an adult role model (parental or otherwise) are more successful than their peers in coping with the everyday stresses of life and are better able to recover from extreme adversity. Clearly a social environment that provides opportunities for more frequent intergenerational interaction on this level would go a long way toward setting young people on the path of optimal development.

The specific remedies for teenage boredom, loneliness, frustration, and anxiety will vary widely, depending on the individual and his or her strengths and opportunities, but the general principle is the same—healthy growth requires that the natural resilience of adolescents be allowed to assert itself. While allowing their teenagers plenty of freedom and independence, parents must also present them with meaningful challenges and—perhaps most important—*spend time with them*, listening, advising, questioning, laughing, playing, and sharing their anger and pain. Whatever adults can do to encourage young people's involvement with life is bound to be helpful. The best efforts of adults are likely to prevent teens from seeking refuge in passive entertainment, and they will almost certainly steer them away from self-destructive alternatives.

FOR FURTHER INFORMATION

Ariès, Philippe. *Centuries of Childhood.* Translated by Robert Baldick. London: Pimlico, 1996.

Benson, Peter L. *All Kids Are Our Kids: What Communities Must Do to Raise Caring and Responsible Children and Adolescents.* San Francisco: Jossey-Bass, 1997.

Bukowski, William M.; Newcomb, Andrew F.; and Hartup, Willard W., eds. *The Company They Keep: Friendship in Childhood and Adolescence.* New York: Cambridge University Press, 1996.

Csikszentmihalyi, Mihaly, and Larson, Reed. *Being Adolescent: Conflict and Growth in the Teenage Years.* New York: Basic Books, 1984.

Csikszentmihalyi, Mihaly; Rathunde, Kevin; and Whalen, Samuel. *Talented Teenagers: The Roots of Success and Failure.* New York: Cambridge University Press, 1993.

Dryfoos, Joy G. *Safe Passage: Making It Through Adolescence in a Risky Society.* New York: Oxford University Press, 1998.

Hersch, Patricia. *A Tribe Apart: A Journey into the Heart of American Adolescence.* New York: Fawcett Columbine, 1998.

Pollack, William S. *Real Boys: Rescuing Our Sons from the Myths of Boyhood.* New York: Random House, 1998.

119

FEMALE INCONTINENCE: THE SECRET IS OUT

BY JEAN S. GOTTLIEB, PH.D.

It was a bitterly cold but otherwise ordinary winter workday. Ordinary, that is, until I sneezed and felt a sudden, uncontrollable warm spurt of urine. I scurried to the bathroom, praying all the while that I wouldn't run into a colleague until I'd had time to conceal the telltale wet spot on the back of my skirt. Just an isolated event, I assured myself, as I tied my sweater around my waist to conceal the embarrassing evidence. But was it? What if it happened again? What if it happened on the train? At the grocery store? A mixture of shame, panic, and helplessness overwhelmed me.

Few of us remember when or how we were "toilet trained," "housebroken," or whatever euphemism was in vogue at the time we made it out of diapers. Learning to control our bodily functions

120

Of the 13 million Americans who suffer from incontinence, the vast majority—11 million—are women. The number one risk factor is vaginal childbirth.

Jean S. Gottlieb, Ph.D., is a historian of science, formerly with the University of Chicago Press, and currently working as a freelance writer, editor, and bibliographer.

is a genuine rite of passage, granting us not only the physical rewards of dryness and enhanced comfort but important social and psychological rewards as well.

Achieving continence is a natural developmental event and, in most cases, would eventually take place even without parental intervention. Still, most of us are introduced to the idea through the ordeal of toilet training, which instills in the childhood conscience a powerful inhibi-

tion against "accidents." No wonder, then, that even the coolest grown-up feels thoroughly humiliated by that first episode of adult incontinence. In fact, it was not until a couple of years after *I* experienced my first leaky sneeze that I was finally able to move past the guilt, embarrassment, and denial—indeed, the imperative to conceal my disgrace—and ask for help.

WHY A "FEMALE PROBLEM"?

Health professionals define urinary incontinence (UI) as "the socially unacceptable loss of urine that *the patient sees as a problem.*" It is not, in itself, a disorder but rather a symptom, an indication of another, underlying condition.

Incontinence may have a variety of causes, including urinary tract infection, kidney stones, stroke, spinal cord injury, cancer, neurological disease (*e.g.*, multiple sclerosis, Parkinson's disease), and nerve damage secondary to diabetes. Incontinence may also occur as a complication of surgery. It may be a side effect of some drugs, particularly diuretics (agents that stimulate the production of urine and, therefore, activity of the bladder). The drinking of coffee and alcoholic beverages can promote or exacerbate incontinence, as can obesity.

Sometimes it occurs even when the bladder itself is functioning normally; a person whose mobility is limited may find it hard to get to the toilet in time, for example, whereas an individual with dementia may not recognize when his or her bladder is full. Incontinence due to these latter conditions is commonest among the disabled and the elderly and accounts for a large proportion of nursing home admissions.

Thirteen million Americans, 85%—11 million—of them women, suffer from UI. (For the facts about male incontinence, *see* Sidebar: "The Men's Side of the Story," page 131.) Female sufferers are by no means all elderly: 10–30% of women between the ages of 15 and 64 have experienced urinary incontinence.

Why are women especially vulnerable? The number one risk factor is vaginal childbirth. As a result of the physical stresses of pregnancy, labor, and delivery, the bladder and its supporting tissues and nerves may lose some of their function. Bladder (and bowel) control may be compromised, and the ability of the supporting muscles to hold the bladder and other structures in their proper position may be impaired. For unknown reasons, smoking too compromises the tone of these muscles, as does the drop in estrogen levels associated with menopause. The anatomy of the female urinary tract also plays a part in women's vulnerability to UI (*see* below).

DENIAL AND DELAY

After that first "wet sneeze," I felt I could no longer count on my bladder. I spent the next two years feeling apprehensive about "accidents" and watching my life become increasingly circumscribed. Instead of talking to my doctor or confiding in a friend—or even my husband—I curtailed the activities that didn't include ready access to a toilet. During the winter months we spend in Florida, this meant giving up one of my favorite activities, leisurely fishing expeditions in our small, open boat. Finally, I began making trips to the bathroom even when I didn't really have to urinate. (This, I learned later, is exactly the wrong thing to do, because it doesn't give the bladder

Activities that were once enjoyable—like going to a play or concert—become fraught with anxiety for the woman who feels she can no longer "count on" her bladder.

the exercise it needs to stay strong and flexible, stretching as it fills and then squeezing and contracting as it empties.) I began carrying a flashlight in my purse and making sure I got the aisle seat at concerts, plays, and movies and on airplanes. On a weekend auto trip with a group of friends, I was the only one perpetually looking for the ladies' room, the only one whose thoughts were focused more on the next pit stop than on the scenery.

My "margin of safety"—the period of time when I was pretty confident that a cough, a sneeze, or a vigorous action like pulling up the anchor wouldn't precipitate a minor (or major!) leakage episode—shrank alarmingly. A business meeting that lasted more than 40 minutes became an uneasy trial. Needless to say, when coffee was passed around, I always declined. If this was "part of getting older" and my choice was either to wear "adult diapers" or stay home, both prospects were equally unthinkable. Torn between desperation over my predicament and embarrassment at the idea of discussing urination with anybody—including my doc-

Instead of talking to my doctor or confiding in a friend ... I curtailed the activities that didn't include ready access to a toilet.

123

Reluctant to confide in even their closest friends, many women who have a problem with continence suffer in silence.

tor—I finally managed, ever so casually, to mention my "little leakage problem" at my annual checkup.

Half of the women who suffer from UI never mention it to their doctors or anyone else; those who finally get up the courage to speak up and seek help have waited, on average, seven to eight years. The following case histories are fairly typical.

Martha A., 64, the wife of a physician and an urbane and enlightened woman, told me that though she no longer has confidence in her "retention capability," as she delicately put it, she would "never dream of mentioning this" to her doctor. "I'd like to try one of the in-office procedures I've heard about, but I simply can't bring myself to ask him about it," she remarked ruefully.

Anne F., a 50-year-old librarian, said that she began "dripping a little" four or five years ago. A sneeze or a cough would inevitably trigger a leak. "Every time I'd get a cold," she told me, "I'd be a nervous wreck." It took her three years to mention the condition to her doctor, who referred her to a local medical group that specializes in incontinence management. She had surgery for incontinence in January 1997 and no longer dreads the winter cold season.

Jane R., 70, an urban planner, had her first experience with incontinence six years ago. When she mentioned it to her doctor, he advised her to postpone treatment because of her other, more serious medical problems, particularly multiple sclerosis diagnosed some 20 years

124

earlier. She continued to press him for alternatives, in the meantime resorting to absorbent pads and moisture-proof undergarments, complaining all the while that she hated sitting at work "feeling like a baby" in wet pants. Finally, exasperated by recurrent urinary tract infections and unavoidable odor problems, she prevailed on her doctor to refer her to a urogynecologist, a physician who specializes in disorders of the female urinary and reproductive tracts. As a result of this consultation, she is now scheduled to have a collagen injection, an outpatient procedure (described in detail below) that should provide some relief.

Louise M., now in her early 70s, is one of the few women who were neither silent nor long-suffering. At the age of 36, after the birth of her sixth child, she began to experience stress incontinence, at first only occasionally when she coughed or sneezed and then pretty much every time. She consulted her doctor. "I had some sort of surgical procedure," she remembers, "and I haven't had a problem since. But in the hospital after surgery, I talked to the other patients, and these older women who were in their 50s or 60s told me they had had it [incontinence] for 20 or 30 years—and they had been putting up with it." She shakes her head in disbelief. "They told me they just coped."

"There are several reasons why women don't seek help for urinary incontinence," says Alan J. Wein, professor of urology at the University of Pennsylvania Medical Center in Philadelphia. Wein notes that in a recent survey, one-quarter of the women questioned admitted that they "felt embarrassed" about urinary incontinence and were "uncertain about dealing with the condition" in social situations. "Many women are unaware that a physician can help improve their condition or believe their problem isn't serious enough to consult a physician."

In fact, "any woman with this problem can be helped in some way—many nonsurgically," according to Renée Edwards, a urogynecologist at Rush-Presbyterian-St. Luke's Medical Center in Chicago. What's more, she adds, urinary incontinence should *not* be presumed to be a normal part of aging.

ANATOMY OF CONTINENCE

As soon as I said "leakage," my doctor nodded sympathetically. He seemed unsurprised. As a postmenopausal ex-smoker and mother of six (all delivered vaginally), I was, he said, a prime candidate for the condition known as stress incontinence. He suggested an evaluation by a urogynecologist. I took his advice and made an appointment.

The urogynecologist put me at ease right away, and before she took my history and examined me, she answered my questions about female anatomy and physiology and the nature of incontinence. She made UI seem less like a disgraceful lapse of propriety than a simple matter of anatomic wear and tear.

The human waste-disposal system consists of a group of organs, muscles, and nerves, all presided over by the brain. Some of the actions of this system are voluntary (under

Often women are unaware of the treatment options available—including a number that do not involve surgery.

"Any woman with this problem can be helped in some way—many nonsurgically."

The Urinary Tract

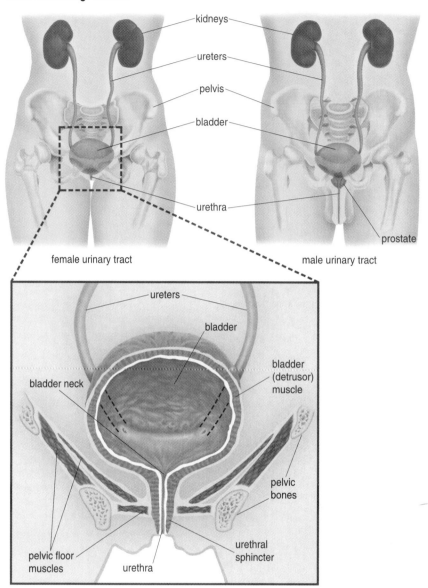

kidneys

ureters

pelvis

bladder

urethra

prostate

female urinary tract

male urinary tract

ureters

bladder

bladder neck

bladder
(detrusor)
muscle

pelvic
bones

pelvic floor
muscles

urethra

urethral
sphincter

the lower end of the bladder, blends into the urethral sphincter, a "gate-keeper muscle" that controls continence in both men and women.

Urine collects in the bladder and is stored until a person senses the need to void (urinate). At that time the bladder empties itself by means of muscular contractions that increase its pressure until this pressure is greater than that in the urethra, the tube through which urine is discharged from the body. It should be emphasized that the bladder is simply a "holding tank"; it plays no part in maintaining continence. It is the urethral sphincter—together with the support provided by the pelvic floor muscles (also called the pubo-coccygeus, or pc, muscles)—that is the continence mechanism.

The female urethra, which is approximately $3^{1}/_{2}$ cm ($1^{1}/_{3}$ in) long, is considerably shorter than its male counterpart (about 20 cm, or about $7^{3}/_{4}$ in). Since the degree of resistance provided by a tube depends in part on its length, men have more natural resistance against urine outflow than women do. The lower portion of the female urethra is embedded in the wall of the vagina, and its external opening is immediately in front of the vaginal opening.

Because the kidneys produce urine continually, it might seem logical that the need to void, or urinate, would also be constant. The bladder, however, has a built-in compensatory mechanism. Bladder pressure rises slowly as the first 100 ml of urine accumulate; having filled to that extent, the bladder has the ability to accommodate—to expand without increasing its pressure—until approximately 400 ml of urine have been collected. At this time a person with normal urinary function will experience the urge to void. If necessary, the urge can be suppressed and the

conscious control), and some are involuntary. Processing and storing of wastes are involuntary, whereas elimination is mostly a consciously willed process. Continence requires that the voluntary and involuntary systems work together.

Normal urinary function. Day and night, urine produced by the kidneys flows via the ureters, two 30-cm (approximately 12-in)-long ducts, or tubes, into the urinary bladder, a balloonlike muscular reservoir. The bladder neck, a narrowed section at

At birth a normal human infant possesses all the anatomic structures required for continence but lacks the ability to suppress the urge to urinate.

Female Urinary and Reproductive Organs

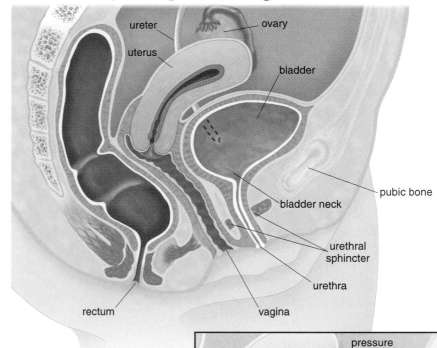

Weakened pelvic floor and sphincter muscles can be overwhelmed by an abrupt increase in intra-abdominal pressure—caused by coughing or sneezing, for example. The resulting sudden leakage of urine is called *stress incontinence*.

need to urinate deferred until the time and place are appropriate.

Although human infants are born with all the requisite anatomic structures—bladder, ureters, sphincters—their ability to suppress the urge to void is undeveloped, and they cannot control the need to empty the bladder once it has become full. It is because this control is voluntary that toddlers learn to keep their diapers dry during the day before they can do so at night. The key to normal voiding, then, lies in the control of the bladder, or detrusor, muscle through a complex feedback system of nerve impulses initiated as the bladder becomes distended. Once the bladder is full, nerves in the bladder signal the brain, triggering the urge

to urinate. When a person reaches the toilet, the brain signals the sphincter and pelvic floor muscles to relax and, at the same time, sends a message to the bladder to contract.

Kinds of incontinence. Most incontinence falls into one of three categories: stress incontinence, urge incontinence, or overflow incontinence. The sudden loss of urine caused by coughing, sneezing, jumping, or lifting a heavy weight is called *stress incontinence*. When the pelvic floor and sphincter muscles lose some of their strength and elasticity,

127

the stress of a sudden increase in bladder or intra-abdominal pressure can overwhelm them. Although rare in men, stress incontinence is the most common form of UI in women, which is not surprising, as it is also the form most commonly associated with childbirth.

People with *urge incontinence* find it difficult or impossible to keep from leaking, or even streaming, urine when approaching the toilet with the brain's "have to go" message. Spontaneous and involuntary contractions of the bladder override the "wait" command. Also called bladder, or detrusor, instability, urge incontinence may follow a stroke, or it may be the result of cognitive deficits

So-called adult diapers are one answer for people with bladder-control problems, but they are at best only a temporary solution. A variety of more permanent measures are now available.

associated with, for example, dementia, Parkinson's disease, or Alzheimer's disease. Often the contractions of urge incontinence occur in otherwise healthy women for unknown reasons. Bladder training (*see* below) can alleviate the bladder spasms. Stress and urge incontinence sometimes occur together; this condition is called *mixed incontinence.*

Overflow incontinence is the inability of the bladder to receive or read the signal to empty itself when full; as a result, urine simply spills out of the overfilled vessel. Due variously to nerve damage, cognitive problems, urethral obstruction, or an abnormally tight urethral sphincter, this type of incontinence often afflicts confused or not-very-mobile elderly people. A fairly common cause of obstruction leading to overflow incontinence is severe bladder or vaginal prolapse—the dislocation downward, or "dropping," of these organs.

Keith—Custom Medical Stock Photo

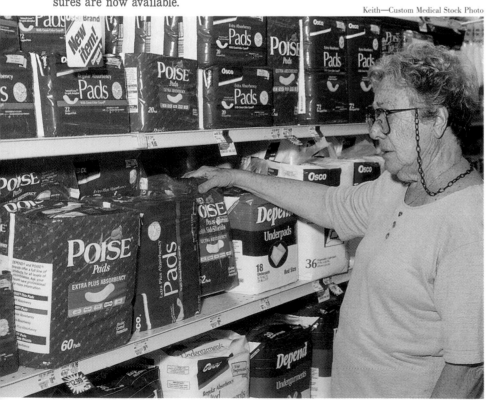

All those adult wetness-prevention products I'd seen on the drugstore and supermarket shelves now delivered a more immediate message to me.

TREATMENT: FIRST STEPS

My urogynecologist did a thorough medical history and evaluation. She asked me about my family history ("Did your mother or other female relatives have a problem with incontinence?"), reproductive history ("How many times have you been pregnant?" and "How were the babies delivered?"), lifestyle ("Do you participate in any sports? Do you smoke? Drink coffee?"), and the onset, frequency, and timing of my symptoms. She also asked about my general health and what medications I was taking. Then she performed pelvic and rectal exams to check the position of the bladder and other organs and rule out any obvious structural abnormalities. She also asked me to keep a "voiding diary" for a day or so, recording fluid intake, trips to the toilet, accidental leaks, and type of leak (urge, stress, or overflow).

The urogynecologist told me I had stress incontinence, the commonest type. All those adult wetness-prevention products I'd seen on the drugstore and supermarket shelves now delivered a more immediate message to me: you aren't the only one—there are a lot of people out there who have bladder-control problems. But before resorting to one of these temporary measures, I was determined to see if there might not be a permanent solution.

There are many kinds of treatment for urinary incontinence. Though alternative medicine may offer some useful procedures, such as acupuncture, it is wisest to consult a medical doctor first for a complete evaluation. This step will help a woman decide what sort of treatment is most likely to be successful in her particular case.

Treatment usually starts with the simplest and most obvious measure: changing any habits that may be exacerbating the problem. Since caffeine and alcohol heighten bladder activity, it is best to limit their

intake or avoid them altogether. Other foods and beverages—among them spicy foods, chocolate, acidic fruits and juices (*e.g.*, citrus, tomato), and artificially sweetened foods—can also irritate the bladder.

Many who have a problem with incontinence mistakenly believe that cutting down on their consumption of fluids will help prevent wetness episodes. In fact, an adequate intake of fluids, and especially water, is vital to health. It prevents dehydration and keeps the urine from becoming so concentrated that it irritates the bladder. Dehydration can actually increase bladder instability and problems associated with urge incontinence.

Bladder training. Many women, myself included, develop the habit of "preemptive toileting"—voiding early and often in an attempt to prevent accidents. A form of behavior therapy called bladder training is one way to overcome the anxiety that leads to

this self-defeating behavior. Bladder training is a matter of "timed voiding," establishing regular intervals for trips to the toilet and then gradually extending these intervals until the bladder has developed a retention time of two to four hours. Half of those who try bladder training report significant improvement, and 16% are cured. Incontinence in the elderly in particular can be helped by regularly scheduled trips to the toilet. This technique is especially useful for controlling urge incontinence.

Mary Rose S., a 42-year-old professional writer who suffered from unpredictable bladder spasms, is one patient who used this method suc-

> Treatment starts with simple measures like changing any habits that may contribute to the problem. Eliminating alcohol—which, like caffeine, stimulates bladder activity—is a first step.

cessfully. At first she tried coping with the problem by voiding every half hour. Anxiety about her need to be near a toilet made it impossible for her to pursue her career, which involved frequent travel to and from interviews, often on public transportation. When she finally consulted a physician, he recommended supervised bladder training and pelvic floor exercises (*see* below). Within months her "holding time" had doubled, and two years later she was enjoying the normal three-to-four-hour span between trips to the toilet. She adheres to the four-hour time interval (too long an interval can cause overstretching of the detrusor muscle, with resultant loss of elasticity) and does the exercises as part of her daily routine, "like brushing my teeth," she says.

Pelvic floor, or Kegel, exercises. Pelvic floor exercises, also known as pc exercises or, more commonly, Kegel exercises (after the U.S. physician Arnold Kegel, who developed the technique in the late 1940s), are the least-invasive treatment for (and protection from) UI. On my doctor's advice, I started my treatment with this technique. Pelvic floor exercises tone and strengthen the muscles that support the bladder and urethra. Isolating the correct muscles is fairly simple: while urinating, one simply attempts purposely to stop the flow. (This should be tried only as an experiment; to contract the urethral sphincter against the urine flow as a regular exercise can actually weaken that muscle.) At the same time, one tries to lift and tighten the pelvic floor muscles without contracting the abdominal muscles.

I was to do three sets of 10 squeezes each, contracting all of the muscles simultaneously, every day for the rest of my life. It takes a couple of months at least, depending on

muscle tone at the outset, to notice any difference, but three-quarters of those who consistently do these exercises notice less leakage, and 12% are cured. Pelvic floor exercises are recommended for everyone— young and old, male and female.

Weight training. Weight training using "vaginal cones" offers more intensive muscle toning than is afforded by pelvic floor exercises. The set of five plastic cones comes in graduated weights, from 20 to 70 g (0.706 to 2.5 oz). The patient starts by inserting the lightest cone into the vagina, contracting the pelvic floor muscles, and holding the cone in place for up to 15 minutes while standing and walking. As muscle strength increases, progressively heavier cones are used.

Biofeedback. Biofeedback is a technique for augmenting natural bodily "feedback" mechanisms— most of them entirely automatic—in order to produce a beneficial change in a physiological function. In the case of incontinence, biofeedback helps the patient isolate the correct muscles for the pelvic floor exercises and provides a measure of her progress in muscle strengthening. While the patient performs the exercise routine, a small probe inserted into the vagina sends signals generated by the muscle activity to a computer, which translates them into a pattern displayed on a video screen (much like the reading from an electrocardiogram). Biofeedback training is offered in most metropolitan areas, usually under the guidance of a psychologist. Lack of standardization among devices and training of personnel makes evaluation of the success of this technique difficult. Another potential drawback is that some insurance plans do not routinely cover it.

(*continued on page 132*)

THE MEN'S SIDE OF THE STORY

BY CHARLES-GENE MCDANIEL

Although far more women than men suffer from urinary incontinence (UI), it is not exclusively a "female" problem. Among men aged 15–64, 1.5–5% are incontinent, and among men over age 60 living at home, some 5–15% lack bladder control. The percentage is still higher for elderly men in nursing homes.

Types and causes

Men experience the same types of UI as women, although the causes may be different. Males have the unique problem of incontinence due to conditions affecting the prostate gland, the walnut-sized structure that produces fluid for semen. The prostate surrounds the urethra, the tube that not only transports ejaculate but also carries urine from the bladder to the penis. As men age, they often develop a nonmalignant condition known as benign prostatic hyperplasia (BPH)—enlargement of the prostate. Half of all men have BPH by age 60 and about 80% by age 80; however, only 40–50% ever experience symptoms as a result of it.

BPH first affects the inner part of the gland. As the tissue proliferates, pressure is exerted on the urethra where it passes through the prostate, restricting urinary flow (but generally not affecting sexual functioning). If the enlargement progresses to the point that the urethra becomes completely blocked, urine remains in the bladder until the bladder becomes so full that it simply overflows—i.e., overflow incontinence. The result is frequent leakage (dribbling) of urine. In extreme cases BPH must be treated surgically, and the surgery itself may result in incontinence of a temporary nature, usually lasting only until the prostate has healed. Incontinence of varying duration is also associated with prostatectomy (removal of the gland), a treatment for cancer of the prostate.

Treatment options

Paradoxically, although women are more likely to develop UI, men are more likely to seek treatment. Doctors say that women tend to accept incontinence as their personal burden, whereas men recognize it as something abnormal that should be remedied. Depending upon the type of incontinence, many of the same treatments used in women are recommended for men—for example, dietary changes, elimination of caffeine and alcohol, Kegel exercises, biofeedback, and behavior modification. Collagen injections and artificial sphincter implantation have had high success rates in the relief of male stress incontinence.

Incontinence due to BPH often can be remedied with medication, which, though not as effective as surgery, carries fewer risks. In recent years two classes of drugs in particular have been used. The first, called alpha-blockers, includes such drugs as doxazosin (Cardura) and terazosin (Hytrin). These drugs usually work fairly quickly if they are going to work at all. In patients who benefit, the improvement is likely to persist for at least two years. The second type of medication for BPH is finasteride (Proscar), an agent that partially shrinks the enlarged prostate by lowering the level of the major male hormone inside the gland. In those men who benefit from finasteride, the improvement appears to continue for at least five years. Reduction in size of the prostate may take six months or more. Studies show that the drug works best in cases of extreme enlargement.

Two minimally invasive medical procedures have been introduced recently for the treatment of BPH when medication does not work: transurethral microwave thermotherapy, in which a small probe is introduced via the urethra to heat and destroy prostate tissue, and transurethral needle ablation, in which two small needles deliver heat to the prostate, again destroying tissue. These techniques, which do not require hospital admission, appear to relieve symptoms more effectively than medication but less so than surgery. They have few side effects.

More invasive surgical procedures may be required for relieving BPH symptoms for some men. These include transurethral resection of the prostate, in which the innermost core of the gland is removed through the urethra, and transurethral incision of the prostate, in which cuts are made in the gland to relieve pressure around the urethra. UI may follow these procedures while the prostate heals, but complete incontinence is a rare complication, occurring in about one out of 100 men.

Charles-Gene McDaniel, *currently a freelance medical writer, is Professor Emeritus of Journalism, Roosevelt University, Chicago.*

In biofeedback training, the activity of a patient's pelvic floor muscles is translated into a visible pattern on a video screen, which allows her to monitor her progress in a program of muscle-strengthening exercises.

(*continued from page 130*)

Electrical stimulation. This painless in-office procedure employs a probe that emits a weak electric current. When the probe is inserted into the patient's vagina, the electricity stimulates the nerves communicating with the muscles of the pelvic floor, bladder, and urethral sphincter, which results in contractions of those muscles. Stimulating the nerves that activate these muscles actually calms the involuntary spasms associated with urge incontinence. Treatment sessions are generally scheduled for once or twice a week. Depending on patient response, the treatment can take anywhere from a few weeks to three months. Electrical stimulation is used in conjunction with other behavior modification techniques, such as timed voiding. The Agency for Health Care Policy and Research, a federal agency that systematically

evaluates the effectiveness of medical treatments, recommends electrical stimulation for UI, and many health care plans cover it.

Drug therapy. In postmenopausal women estrogen replacement has been shown to improve muscle tone and relieve symptoms of stress incontinence. Estrogen may increase the risk of breast cancer, however, and most doctors advise women who have had breast cancer or who have family histories of the disease to forgo hormone replacement.

Some new drugs are being developed and tested for treatment of urge incontinence (*e.g.*, oxybutynin, hyoscyamine, and tolterodine), but these may have unpleasant side effects as well as dangerous interactions with other medications and must be closely monitored by a physician. They also become less effective with regular use.

A class of drugs known as alpha-blockers (or alpha-agonists), which were developed for other medical conditions unrelated to UI, have the side effect of tightening the sphincter muscles and alleviating stress incontinence by improving muscle tone. They include tricyclic antidepressants like imipramine (Tofranil), some appetite suppressants (*e.g.*, sibutramine, phentermine), and some antihistamines and decongestants (*e.g.*, pseudoephedrine, phenylpropanolamine). These medications may have other side effects, however, including elevated blood pressure, anxiety, appetite loss, blurred vision, constipation, and heart rhythm irregularities.

SURGERY: AN OPTION TO CONSIDER

After about a month of doing pelvic floor exercises, I progressed to weight training with vaginal cones to speed up muscle strengthening. I performed the exercises three times a day for three months. Though the strength of my pelvic floor muscles increased measurably, urinary leakage continued. Having a coughing and sneezing cold was still an incontinence nightmare for me. The next step was a diagnostic test.

There are simple and complex diagnostic tests for UI. Urodynamics, the procedure I underwent, is one of the more complex. Urodynamics tests the bladder's capacity and function. It is an in-office procedure, and although unpleasant, it is not painful.

This is how it is done. The patient is seated in a birthing chair, and a catheter is gently inserted into the urethra to fill the bladder slowly with sterile water. When the patient indicates that her bladder is full, the amount of water infused is recorded. Then the patient is asked to cough,

My bladder was definitely not doing its job satisfactorily.

and the amount of fluid lost is also measured. Finally, the patient empties her bladder, and the quantity of fluid voided is recorded to determine if the bladder is emptying completely. The data are fed into a computer, and the resultant analysis of the bladder's efficiency at filling, storing, and emptying guides the doctor in recommending treatment.

I flunked the test. I had stress incontinence symptoms and postvoid retention—*i.e.*, there was still some urine in the bladder even after emptying. My bladder was definitely not doing its job satisfactorily. Would surgery work for me? The doctor told me that in cases like mine, the probability of success was 90%. My age, general health, and lifestyle suggested that I would benefit.

I decided to have surgery. Given the high probability of a lasting cure and low rate of postoperative complications, I felt I could endure the requisite three months of restrictions: showers but no baths, no lifting of anything heavier than five pounds, no vacuuming, no sex, and no aerobic exercises or stress of any kind on the abdominal muscles.

Surgery is the only relatively permanent way to reposition a prolapsed bladder, repair sagging vaginal and rectal tissue, and support the bladder and urethra against stress. Correcting or alleviating stress incontinence involves simply repositioning the bladder neck, but when these other repairs are necessary,

they are generally made at the same time. Studies indicate that for stress incontinence *retropubic surgery* (performed through an incision in the lower abdomen) and *sling procedures* (performed through the vagina with only a small abdominal incision) have higher cure rates—80%—but also longer recovery times than other surgical procedures for UI.

A woman who is a candidate for surgery should take into account, among other factors, the safety of the recommended procedure, its success rate, the surgeon's expertise, the experience of others with similar symptoms who chose a similar procedure, her own age and general health, how long the beneficial effects are predicted to last, and the likelihood of postoperative complications such as infection and bleeding.

In some patients—and I was one of them—the repositioned bladder

133

neck needs time to adjust to its new situation. The surgery had stunned my bladder into relative inaction, and it would void only small quantities of urine. I left the hospital with a suprapubic catheter, a small tube inserted into the bladder through a tiny incision in the lower abdomen just above the pubic bone. The tube was equipped with a small valve I could open and shut. When urinating normally, I kept the valve shut and measured the output from my bladder. Then I opened the valve so that whatever my bladder had not voided could empty into a measuring container. Within four or five days, my bladder was emptying normally, and the doctor simply slid the tube out of my body and put a piece of tape over the opening. She assured me that the incision would close up within a few days. It did.

OTHER ALTERNATIVES: THE LIST GROWS

A variety of procedures and devices—both long-term and temporary, surgical and nonsurgical—are providing help for women with UI. Several of these options are discussed below.

Artificial sphincter. Developed in the 1960s, the artificial sphincter has been used far more often in men than in women. The device consists of an inflatable ring-shaped sac similar to a blood pressure cuff, which encircles the urethra. It is implanted in a surgical procedure. The sac is filled with a fluid that keeps it inflated and thus squeezes the urethra closed. When the patient presses a valve (implanted, in women, in the labia), the sac deflates; this allows the urethra to open and urine to pass out of the body. The implantation procedure is difficult to

No longer did I spend my days furtively searching for the ladies' room.

perform in women, and because the female urethra is short, the device tends to deteriorate.

Implantable bladder stimulator. Implantable bladder stimulators may be especially useful for cognitively impaired persons with urge incontinence, although research studies on these products are incomplete. In the fall of 1997, the U.S. Food and Drug Administration approved one such device for use in adults with urge incontinence who have not been helped by other therapies. The device consists of a programmable generator, implanted in the abdominal wall, and a lead wire that carries electrical impulses from the generator to the sacral nerves. Stimulation of these nerves helps control bladder contractions. The cost of each implant has been estimated at $10,000, which will certainly limit its use.

Bulking substances. Injections of bulking substances can add supportive padding around a weakened sphincter or urethra and thus relieve stress incontinence. The most commonly used substances are bovine collagen, a natural protein derived from cow tissues, and fat from the patient's own body. The procedure can be performed in the doctor's office under local anesthesia. Injections are generally given in at least two stages so that the amount of bulk

added is enough to control, but not block, urine flow. Since collagen is gradually absorbed into the tissues, the treatment may have to be repeated. In 50% of patients the collagen implant holds for about two years; results for the other 50% have been disappointing. This is the treatment that Jane R., mentioned earlier, was anticipating.

Internal devices and patches. A pessary is a ringlike object that is inserted into the vagina in much the same way as a diaphragm. Also like a diaphragm, the newer pessaries can be removed by the patient. Pessaries function by holding the pelvic organs in their anatomically proper positions.

Similar to a pessary, the bladder neck support prosthesis is specifically designed to relieve incontinence by supporting and repositioning the bladder. It is reusable, but it must be removed, cleaned, and reinserted daily.

To help a woman make it through an evening at the theater or endure a long bus ride, there are tiny disposable catheters that the patient herself can insert into the urethra. After insertion, a balloon at the tip of the catheter inflates and prevents the escape of urine. When the woman wants to urinate, she pulls a thread that deflates the balloon and allows the device to be removed. It must then be replaced with a new insert.

Another recently developed temporary solution to UI consists of a foam patch that can be placed over the urethral opening and removed when the woman needs to urinate. It too must be discarded and replaced after each use. For women with persistent light leakage caused by a weakened sphincter, or for those needing temporary control of incontinence, these new disposable devices promise a new day.

Bob Winsett—Corbis

A LIFE RESTORED

Six weeks after my surgery, I sneezed while on my way to the toilet. No leak! I found that once again I could sit through a concert or drink coffee at a meeting without anxiety. Fishing trips were back on my agenda. No longer did I spend my days furtively searching for the ladies' room.

A year later I had a follow-up urodynamics test. I did not need to be told I'd passed with flying colors. Improvement came imperceptibly but steadily, and today, four years later, I realize that I didn't reap the full benefits of the surgery in terms of bladder endurance and general well-being for almost two years. Now I revel in the freedom from anxiety and shame. But most of all I delight in the restored function that has given me back a normal active life.

FOR FURTHER INFORMATION

Publications
Newman, Diane Kaschak, R.N.C., M.S.N., C.R.N.P., F.A.A.N., with Dzurinko, Mary K. *The Urinary Incontinence Sourcebook.* Los Angeles: Lowell House, 1997.

"Understanding Incontinence," consumer version of clinical practice guidelines established by the Agency for Health Care Policy and Research (publication number 96-0685) 800-358-9295 Web site: http://www.ahcpr.gov:80/ consumer/

Organizations
Bladder Health Council
c/o American Foundation for Urologic Disease
Suite 401
300 W Pratt St
Baltimore MD 21201
800-242-2383

National Association for Continence (NAFC)
PO Box 8310
Spartanburg SC 29305-8310
800-BLADDER

The Simon Foundation for Continence
PO Box 835
Wilmette IL 60091
800-23-SIMON
Web site:
http://www.simonfoundation.org

Web site
National Kidney and Urologic Disease Clearinghouse
http://www.niddk.nih.gov/health/ urolog/urolog.htm

MAKING A DIFFERENCE

BY ELLEN L. BASSUK, M.D.

The path one takes in life is rarely preordained, and a career path can seem a lot more tidy in retrospect than it ever was in fact. I often muse upon the chain of events that led me to stray from my chosen profession—clinical psychiatry—to become an advocate for homeless people.

When I entered Tufts University School of Medicine in Boston in 1964 at the age of 19, I already knew I wanted to specialize in psychiatry. My goal at that time was eventually to join the psychotherapy staff of a teaching hospital in a large urban center, probably New York City.

137

Confronted by the sight of this tiny infant and its desperate young parents, I understood clearly that homelessness was changing in the U.S.

Ellen L. Bassuk is President of the Better Homes Fund, a Newton, Massachusetts-based national non-profit organization dedicated to helping homeless families. She is also Associate Professor of Psychiatry, Harvard Medical School, and Editor in Chief, American Journal of Orthopsychiatry. *She edited the 1996 book* The Doctor-Activist: Physicians Fighting for Social Change.

After graduation from medical school in 1968, I still seemed to be headed in that direction. I became a resident in psychiatry, first at Boston University Medical Center and later at Beth Israel Hospital in Boston. Then from 1974 to 1982, I practiced psychiatry at Beth Israel Hospital and supervised the hospital's psychiatric emergency services. Most of my patients were individuals with serious mental illness, most commonly schizophrenia. Many were in a state of crisis and had little or no family support.

In the early 1980s life in the United States had become increasingly precarious for low-income people who were seriously mentally ill. For some years state mental hospitals had been closing their doors, discharging patients into "the community," where, in theory, they were to live with their families and receive outpatient treatment at local clinics. In practice, however, treatment never became as widely available as was necessary to serve the needs of those discharged from institutions, and many former patients had no families.

Around this time, single-room-occupancy hotels, which provided housing for large numbers of mentally ill people, were shutting their doors, and the residents of these facilities were being forced into shelters and onto the streets. Many communities lacked alternative housing for people unable to live independently. Also at this time, the benefits paid to the poor were being drastically cut.

In 1985, as part of a community task force on the needs of homeless people, I paid a visit to Boston's Long Island shelter. In those days the shelter primarily served homeless men, many with severe mental illness and substance-abuse problems. During this visit I noticed a teenaged couple sitting on a bench, their eyes fixed on a cardboard box balanced across their knees. Moving closer, I was able to see what the box held: a wrinkled, pink, week-old baby, curled up under a thin blanket.

This proved to be a defining moment of my life. Confronted by the sight of this tiny infant and its desperate young parents, I understood clearly that homelessness was changing in the U.S.—that whole families were now at risk of being turned out onto the nation's streets. My thoughts went immediately to my own children—to their innocence and vulnerability and to my hopes for them. I resolved then and there to refocus my professional life on finding solutions to the disturbing social problem of family homelessness.

Today the Better Homes Fund, a national nonprofit organization I founded along with David Jordan, then the editor in chief of *Better Homes and Gardens* magazine, is working in communities across the U.S. to provide services to struggling families, conduct research into homelessness, and arouse public awareness of this national disgrace. Without ever intending to, I became one of a long line of "doctor-activists," physicians who have devoted their careers not to ministering to the needs of individual patients but to improving the well-being of broader groups of people and, I hope, humankind in general.

THE "FAMILY DOCTOR": MAKING A COMEBACK

In the closing years of the 20th century, the role of the physician is undergoing dramatic changes. In the United States, the advent of managed care has meant that health services are available to more people than ever before—but, some authorities contend, at a profound price. Decisions about patient care are no longer made solely by the physician, and the patient's best interest is no longer the sole consideration guiding these decisions. In short, the healing art is being transformed into a cold business.

But not all of the changes taking place in medicine are for the worse. Traditional fee-for-service medicine encouraged aspiring doctors to pursue careers in narrow, highly specialized, and extremely lucrative fields like anesthesiology and radiology. Today, largely at the instigation of managed-care organizations, medical school graduates in increasing numbers are opting for careers as "generalists," choosing fields such as family practice, internal medicine, and pediatrics. Resurrection of the old-fashioned "family doctor" may, in fact, be an unintended—although highly desirable—consequence of managed care.

Regardless of the model of care, however, dedicated individuals will continue to be drawn to the medical profession out of a desire to alleviate human suffering on a broad scale. Throughout history dedicated practitioners have risked their careers—and sometimes even their lives—in the pursuit of social and humanitarian goals. There is no reason to believe this long tradition of concern for the disadvantaged will end any time soon—even in a health care system increasingly dominated by administrators and accountants.

A chronicle of doctors' contributions to the health and welfare of those most in need would, of course, require volumes. The following brief survey, however, should provide some idea of what doctor-activists are all about.

NOBLE TRADITION

The tradition of physicians' working to improve the living conditions of the masses originated in ancient Greece and Rome. Even in the earliest days of the Roman Empire, state-sponsored physicians tended to the poor, and public hospitals served the general population. Doctors also provided the impetus for public sanitation measures that allowed the citizens of Rome a level of hygiene superior to that enjoyed in some cities today.

It was during the Renaissance that the practice of medicine began what would prove to be a 400-year shift from arcane art to modern science. Many individuals stand out as having made seminal contributions to the public health in the intervening centuries. Edward Jenner (1749–1823), an English country doctor, developed the principle of vaccination. Although his discovery could have made him rich, Jenner chose instead to share it freely, vaccinating the poor in his rural garden after having rejected a prosperous London medical practice. Another English physician, John Snow (1813–58), sometimes called the "father of epidemiology," recognized that cholera is a waterborne disease and traced an outbreak in a London neighborhood to the local water supply. In the process he stopped one of the worst epidemics of a lethal disease ever to occur in Great Britain.

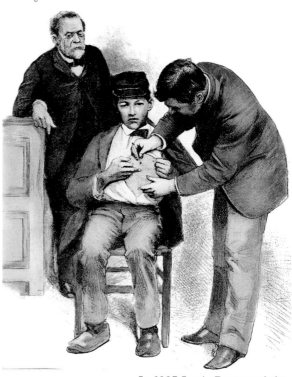

In 1885 Louis Pasteur (left), a respected scientist credited with many valuable discoveries, risked his reputation in order to save the life of a nine-year-old boy who had been bitten by a rabid dog. (An assistant gives the boy the first rabies inoculation.)

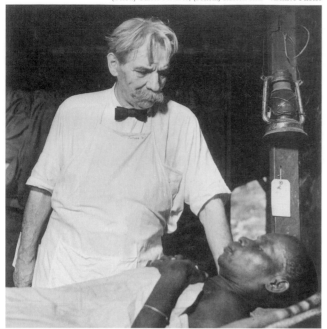

(Above) The German-born physician Albert Schweitzer attends a patient at the hospital he established in 1913 in Lambaréné, Gabon. (Below) American pediatrician Benjamin Spock participates in a peace rally in New York City (1971).

In France Louis Pasteur (1822–95), a scientist seeking the cause of rabies in animals, was called upon to treat a young boy badly mauled by a rabid dog. Knowing that the child faced almost certain death, Pasteur risked his reputation and ordered a series of experimental inoculations. When the treatment proved successful, he set up facilities for mass inoculations and even found lodgings for the poor who came to be inoculated.

The German pathologist Rudolf Virchow (1821–1902) is credited by many as the founder of modern public health advocacy. Virchow was among the first to recognize the connection between health and social conditions and to pronounce health care a fundamental human right. Carrying on the social activist tradition in the 20th century have been such physicians as the German medical missionary and humanitarian Albert Schweitzer; Helen Caldicott, a leader of the U.S. antinuclear movement; and the influential pediatrician Benjamin Spock, an outspoken opponent of the Vietnam War.

THE TRADITION LIVES ON

One of the greatest rewards afforded by my career as a physician-activist has been the opportunity to cross paths with extraordinary doctors who have made the choice to fight for social change. Not many of these people would claim that their vocation was clear to them from the start. Rather, the events and experiences of their lives shaped their views and forged their destinies. The following brief profiles illustrate the way deeply held principles and serendipitous events can converge to change the course of an individual's life and the lives of those he or she touches.

Service is "a privilege." Louis Fazen's father and grandfather were general surgeons in southeastern Wisconsin. His own early life, in what he described as "one of those 'Leave It to Beaver' families of the 1950s," was comfortable and secure. Then in the late 1960s, while on a medical school exchange program in Pakistan, Fazen witnessed the death of a

young girl who was waiting in line with her parents to see a doctor. The girl had cholera, a treatable condition, and probably could have been saved if she had received appropriate care. In that instant Fazen decided to become a pediatrician and to focus his energies on public health and preventive medicine.

Today Fazen treats an ever-growing clientele of low-income African-American and Latino families in inner-city Boston:

When I arrive at the clinic each day, I try to maintain a sense of service as well as a sense of humor. I chuckle as children and parents comment on my similarities to Mr. Rogers—his manners, appearance, and even voice. But this is not Mr. Rogers' neighborhood.

Dealing every day with medical needs made more urgent by grinding poverty, Fazen is continually inspired by the dedication of his colleagues—doctors, nurses, and other clinic staff members—who have devoted their lives to the care of disadvantaged people. As for himself, he considers it "a privilege" to work with people living in poverty.

Wearing others' shoes. In the late 1960s, shortly after their graduation from the University of Pittsburgh (Pennsylvania) School of Medicine, Tom and Edith Welty traveled to Tuba City, Arizona, where Tom planned to spend two years with the Indian Health Service (IHS) as an alternative to military service in Vietnam. This initial commitment, made

three decades ago, turned into a lifetime of service. In Tuba City the Weltys worked in a 75-bed hospital, performing virtually every kind of clinical service. About half of their adult patients spoke no English; tuberculosis was rampant, and malnutrition contributed to high rates of infectious disease among children. The work was hard but fulfilling. Both Weltys felt that their lives and the lives of their children were enriched by contact with the Navajo and Hopi cultures. In 1985, after a three-year interval at the Epidemic Intelligence Service (EIS) of the Centers for Disease Control and Prevention (CDC), they took up new posts with the IHS, this time in Rapid City, South Dakota. Today the couple live in Flagstaff, Arizona, but spend some time each year providing care to villagers in the African country of Cameroon.

The Weltys devoted the greater part of their professional lives to providing comprehensive health care to one of the nation's most underserved populations. Their research

One of [my] greatest rewards … has been the opportunity to cross paths with extraordinary doctors who have made the choice to fight for social change.

One of Tom Welty's patients on a recent visit to Cameroon was a 75-year-old village chief who complained of aches and pains—after a 16-kilometer (10-mile) walk!

Courtesy of Thomas and Edith Welty

Helen Davis—Sygma

Don Francis has been involved in the battle against AIDS since the disease first appeared in the early 1980s. He presently heads a company working to develop a vaccine against HIV.

and fieldwork transformed the quality and scope of medical treatment available to American Indian people. Among his many achievements, Tom developed standards of care for treating tuberculosis in the IHS; Edie started a much-needed obstetrics and gynecology program at the Rapid City IHS hospital.

The Weltys believe that being immersed in another culture taught them to be particularly receptive to new ideas. As they have written:

There are many lessons to be learned from the successes and failures of the past and from older cultures and traditional healers. If we are to work toward a better world, we must learn to respect the customs and beliefs of others. We must put on other people's shoes and view the world from their perspective.

Speaking out. As a student at Northwestern University School of Medicine in the 1960s, Donald

Francis was already an activist, working at a free clinic on the west side of Chicago, organizing protests against the Vietnam War, and counseling draft evaders. He learned early on the perils of challenging authority. A letter he wrote to his fellow medical students in his senior year, exhorting them to become involved with impoverished members of society and to resist the draft, earned him the enmity of the dean, who called him "a disgrace to the medical profession."

In 1969 Francis began a pediatric internship in Los Angeles. While caring for an inner-city youngster desperately ill with whooping cough—a highly preventable disease—he was struck by the utter needlessness of such suffering. That event strengthened his commitment to the field of preventive medicine. To avoid military service in a war he opposed, Francis joined the EIS,

[Francis's] plans for a program to prevent the spread of [AIDS] were ignored and undermined by politicians, scientists, and religious leaders.

142

where he began his training in infectious disease. Working at the CDC in the 1970s, he participated in the global campaign to eradicate smallpox. After three years of studying virology at Harvard University, he returned to the CDC uniquely qualified to investigate a baffling new disease then emerging among gay men in the U.S. Within a short time the disease was given a name, AIDS, and its cause, the virus designated HIV, was identified.

As gay men across the nation fell ill and died, Francis felt certain that his agency would meet this epidemic with full force. Instead, his plans for a program to prevent the spread of the disease were ignored and undermined by politicians, scientists, and religious leaders. In 1992, refusing to be muzzled, Francis gave dramatic testimony before Congress, charging the federal government with failure to respond to the AIDS crisis:

I spoke the truth about how America's public health had been jeopardized by the Reagan and Bush Administrations. I described how the CDC was prevented from doing its job by political extremism and a loss of understanding of the federal government's responsibility for epidemic control.

Jeopardizing his job and possibly even his career, he challenged prejudice and ignorance on behalf of the public's health. Retired from the

CDC in 1992, Francis is now working full time on the development of a vaccine against HIV.

Standing up to the tobacco companies. Judith MacKay grew up in a small village on the northeastern coast of England. She studied medicine at the University of Edinburgh, a school renowned for training women physicians. In 1967 she married a Scottish doctor home on leave from Hong Kong and returned there with him. Her life changed abruptly when she applied for a position in Hong Kong and discovered that the advertised salary was for a male doctor; government policy mandated that because she was a woman, her salary would be 25% less. Outraged, she embarked on a crusade against sexual discrimination in health care that provoked the ire of the Hong Kong medical establishment; in the process she became a controversial but highly effective public figure. Through writing a series of articles on women's health issues for a leading Hong Kong English-language

Undeterred by enmity, insults, and even a death threat, Judith MacKay persists in her criticism of tobacco companies' marketing efforts in Asia.

Inspired by the success of community health centers in South Africa, H. Jack Geiger (left) proposed that similar facilities be established in underserved areas of the U.S. Photo shows Geiger (with physician John Hatch) in 1966 at the site of the first American center, in Mound Bayou, Mississippi.

Photo by Dan Bernstein, courtesy of H. Jack Geiger

newspaper, she became acutely aware of the magnitude of the health threat smoking poses to women and of the aggressive recruitment of women by tobacco advertisers. Eventually, MacKay abandoned hospital medicine to focus all of her energies on exposing tobacco as a public health threat. Almost single-handedly, she has begun to turn public and political opinion against tobacco in Hong Kong and throughout Asia. For her efforts she has been reviled by tobacco companies and smokers' rights groups and labeled as "psychotic," "hysterical," "puritanical," and "sexually frustrated." She has even received a death threat. Still she continues to travel the world training governments and health organizations to combat tobacco use.

A few years ago I came to realize that tobacco [is] only a vehicle, albeit a very legitimate vehicle, for

me to empower individuals, organizations, and governments. Through my work I...help people recognize their ability to make decisions in the interest of their own or their country's health and to realize that they can stand up to vested commercial interests.

Champion of community medicine. Although H. Jack Geiger graduated from high school when he was 14, he did not enter medical school until he was almost 30. In between he was a newspaper copyboy, journalist, sailor in the merchant marine, and civil rights activist.

One night during his third year at Case Western Reserve School of Medicine, Geiger looked out over the darkened Cleveland, Ohio, skyline and had a revelation:

It occurred to me that...who got sick and who did not, what

144

happened to them next, and their interactions with the medical care system were all social as well as biological phenomena....If (as I had begun to realize) the social and physical environments, not medical care, were the real determinants of the health of any population, why couldn't that equation be run backwards? Why couldn't medical care be used to intervene in those environments? Why not make medicine an instrument of social change?

His thoughts that night launched him on a lifetime career in social medicine that would take him from community health centers in South Africa to towns in rural Mississippi and the streets of New York City's Harlem neighborhood. As an advocate of the concept of community health centers, Geiger inaugurated a national movement that has brought comprehensive care to countless low-income families. Along the way he was instrumental in establishing two organizations, Physicians for Social Responsibility and Physicians for Human Rights, as potent international voices against nuclear war and political oppression. Today he heads the department of community medicine at City University of New York Medical School.

A SHARED VISION

Reflecting on the nature of the doctor-activist, Julius Richmond—a dedicated pediatrician, one of the founders of the Head Start program, and former U.S. surgeon general—notes that despite the diversity of their interests, many of these individuals share certain core attributes:

- a well-developed social conscience rooted in an early and deeply held commitment to helping others

- inventiveness in developing ways to provide more and better medical services to a larger number of people
- courage to persevere in the face of opposition and criticism, even when told that "it can't be done"
- a high energy level, enabling the extraordinary personal effort required for implementing challenging programs
- resourcefulness in bringing people and programs together in innovative ways

Those who possess these qualities have the capacity to recognize an opportunity when it presents itself and the initiative to seize it.

Many physicians provide care only reluctantly to people who are members of minority groups, be they racial, ethnic, or economic minorities, or individuals whose sexual preference or mental status distinguishes them from the majority—those who, in Fazen's words, do not fit into the mainstream but dwell instead "in the slipstream of society." The doctor-activists seem to have a particular affinity for such people. Perhaps this is because they see the future prospects of the disadvantaged as inextricably tied to their own, a vision that implies a belief in the interconnectedness of all of humankind.

As the Tibetan Buddhist master Soygal Rinpoche explains it:

When you think of a tree, you tend to think of a distinctly defined object...but when you look more closely at the tree, you will see that ultimately it has no independent existence. The rain that falls on its leaves, the wind that sways it, the soil that nourishes and sustains it, all the seasons and the weather, moonlight and starlight and sunlight—all form part of the

Despite the diversity of their activities and interests, many of these [doctor-activists] share certain core attributes.

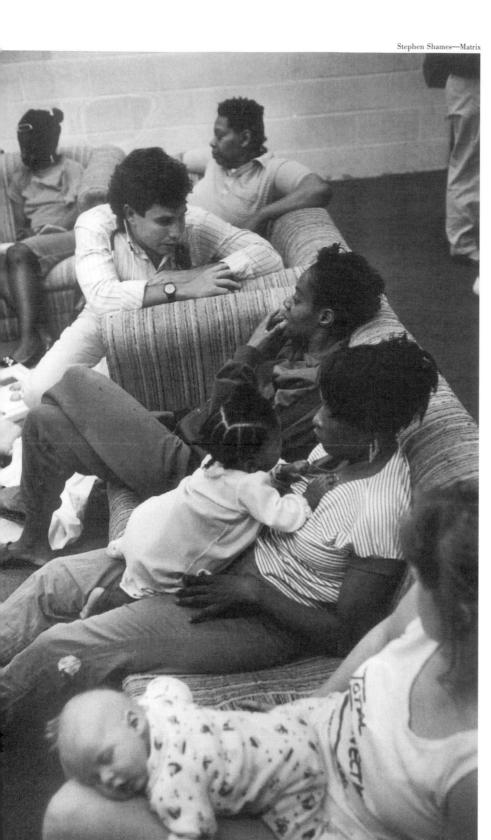

tree....Everything in the universe helps to make the tree what it is...it cannot at any moment be isolated from anything else.

Like rain, wind, and sunlight, the social, economic, and political circumstances of an individual's life constitute an environment that has inevitable consequences for the health of that person. To those in the medical profession who share this view of the world, trying to separate health from these other factors is, at the very least, counterproductive.

SEIZE THE MOMENT

The prospect of confronting huge issues like famine, nuclear war,

"We...never perceived our work as requiring major sacrifices."

homelessness, or the AIDS epidemic would cause many people to throw up their hands in despair. Although this is an understandable reaction, antismoking activist MacKay has warned that one must simply refuse to be overwhelmed: "You cannot allow the enormity of a problem to paralyze you, or you get absolutely nowhere."

Nor is it necessary to have a comprehensive plan of action in

A young physician from the Children's Hospital of Philadelphia volunteers his time at an inner-city shelter for recovering drug addicts and their families.

146

order to make a difference. Describing his own serendipitous path, Donald Francis recalled: "There was no plan. In grammar school, I wanted to be a garbage man—I liked their boots—or a mechanic—I liked their tools. I went to [the University of California at] Berkeley because my girlfriend went there. I went to Harvard because another girlfriend went there. I went to CDC for two years to avoid participating in the Vietnam War. And it all worked out."

Some who would do good are made cautious by the prospect of hardship. Yet the Weltys, who have

House call in rural Missouri, 1942: serving the disadvantaged has always brought its own rewards.

spent their lives in remote locations and in what was, at the beginning, an unfamiliar culture, have emphatically declared, "We…never perceived our work as requiring major sacrifices."

Making the choice to devote one's life to helping disadvantaged people is not "all give and no take." Reflecting on his daily work wrestling with "the inequities of health," Fazen concludes: "There is a great opportunity here for me to use my best clinical skills to help others….Each life fulfills a purpose."

For those who may be wondering just where and how to apply themselves to the work of addressing society's ills, Geiger offers this simple advice: "Watch for the moment—the

opportunity—that reflects your values. Seize it."

FOR FURTHER INFORMATION

Bassuk, Ellen L., ed., with Carman, Rebecca W. *The Doctor-Activist: Physicians Fighting for Social Change.* New York: Plenum Press, 1996.

Bateson, Mary Catherine. *Composing a Life.* New York: Penguin Books, 1990.

Colby, Anne, and Damon, William. *Some Do Care: Contemporary Lives of Moral Commitment.* New York: The Free Press, 1994.

Ryan, Frank. *The Forgotten Plague: How the Battle Against Tuberculosis Was Won—and Lost.* Boston: Little, Brown and Co., 1993.

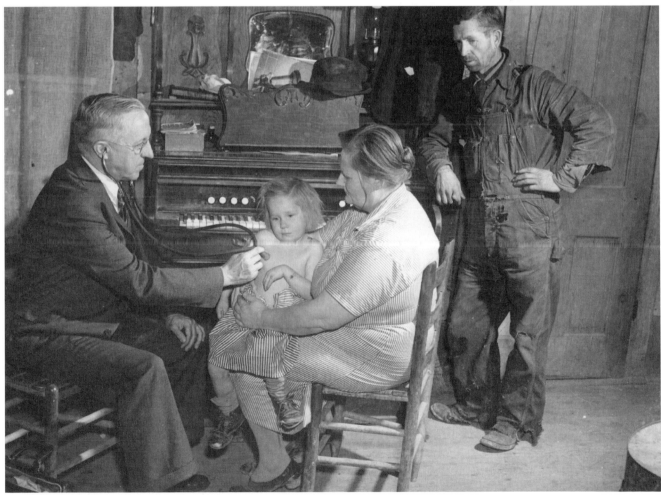

147

UNCIVIL WAR ON AMERICA'S HIGHWAYS

BY MARC DAVIS

Illustration by Tim Hussey

Furious because a van was blocking the roadway, a female motorist in Seattle, Washington, drove up onto the sidewalk, hitting and killing a pedestrian.

A Maryland state legislator driving to the hospital to visit his sick father bumped into the car in front of him when it stopped unexpectedly. When the driver of the other vehicle got out and

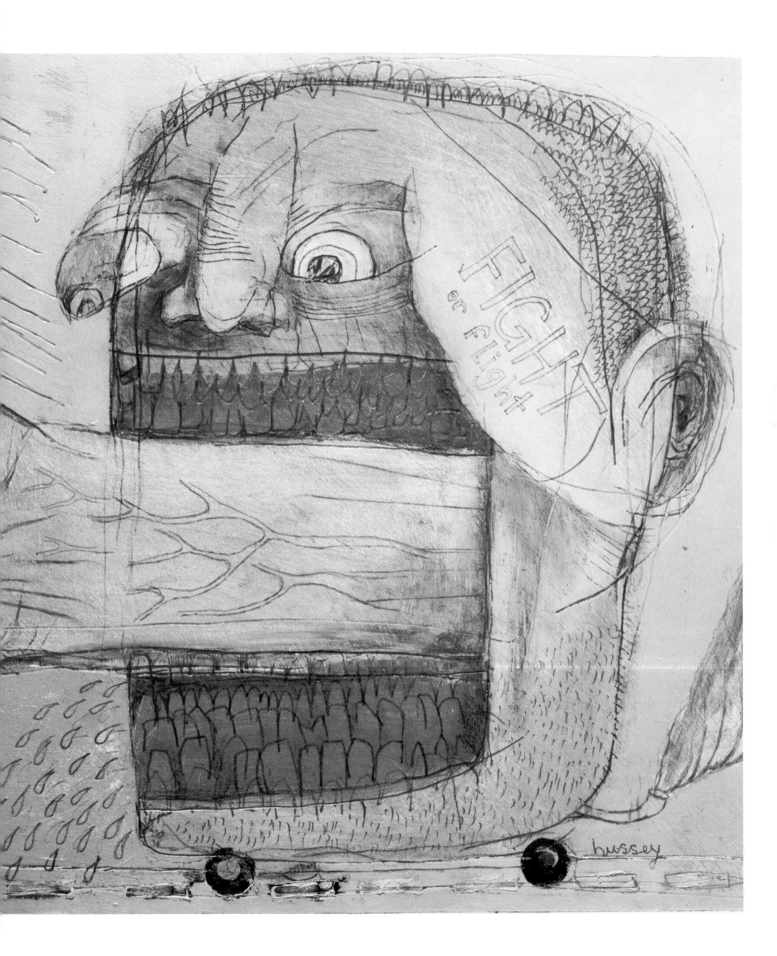

*A writer in Gurnee, Illinois, **Marc Davis** has contributed to the John Marshall Law School magazine, Britannica's Medical and Health Annual, and The Male Body: An Owner's Manual (Rodale Press). He also writes a weekly history column for the Chicago Tribune and has published several works of fiction.*

(Above) In an Ohio court in May 1997, a tearful Tracie Alfieri, right, is sentenced to 18 months in prison for causing an automobile accident in which another driver, Rene Andrews (below), pregnant at the time, suffered a miscarriage.

approached him, the lawmaker struck her face, breaking her sunglasses and blackening one of her eyes.

In Bedford, Massachusetts, an angry church deacon used a crossbow to shoot and kill a driver who cut in front of him.

In Los Angeles actor Jack Nicholson got into an altercation with another driver, who he believed had cut him off in traffic. When both cars stopped for a red light, Nicholson pulled a golf club out of his car and struck the windshield and roof of the other vehicle.

A Cincinnati, Ohio, woman slammed on her brakes in order to teach the tailgater behind her a lesson. In the accident that resulted, the other driver, who was pregnant, lost her baby.

Behind the wheel of almost any car on American highways, an otherwise civilized person may be seconds away from becoming a raving lunatic. These Jekyll and Hydes suffer from an increasingly widespread affliction known as "road rage."

Probably everyone who drives a car loses his or her temper once in a

while. The triggering incident may be an act of blatant discourtesy on the part of another motorist—relentless tailgating or a horn-blasting ultimatum to get out of the way—or merely the careless failure of a fellow driver to follow the rules of the road—neglecting to signal a lane change, for example. The term *aggressive driving* encompasses a broad spectrum of behaviors, from muttering an expletive or making a rude gesture to deliberately ramming an offending driver's vehicle or, at the farthest extreme, assaulting another motorist with a knife or a gun—full-blown road rage. So if *you've* ever let out a streak of swear words or impatiently tailgated a too-slow driver, you too have indulged in aggressive driving. Moreover, you are in the majority. One recent survey found that 80% of drivers are angry and frustrated much of the time behind the wheel.

THE HIGH COST OF "GETTING EVEN"

Although there is no universally accepted definition of aggressive driving, some local law-enforcement agencies have developed their own criteria. In Fairfax county, Virginia, the police department has established a working definition that sums the problem up neatly. Lieut. Robert Wall, a traffic-safety specialist with the department, says, "Aggressive driving is a combination of unsafe and unlawful driving actions that show a disregard for safety."

Some authorities make no distinction between aggressive driving and road rage. (In this article the terms are used interchangeably.) The American Automobile Association (AAA) Foundation for Traffic Safety defines aggressive driving as "an incident in which an angry or impatient motorist or passenger intentionally injures or kills another motorist, passenger, or pedestrian, or attempts to injure or kill another motorist, passenger, or pedestrian, in response to a traffic dispute, altercation, or grievance." It is also considered aggressive driving when a motorist "intentionally drives his or her vehicle into a building or other structure or property."

A particularly insidious characteristic of road rage is the tendency of incidents to escalate. Thus, one driver's misconduct, real or perceived, triggers aggressive behavior in another, which is then mimicked by the first driver in an effort to "get even"—an impulse that motivates many a road rager. All too often an on-the-road duel between drivers ensues, which ends in collision, injury, or even death.

Appearing before the congressional Subcommittee on Surface Transportation in July 1997, Ricardo Martinez, administrator of the National Highway Traffic Safety Administration, testified that rage was a factor in a substantial percentage of car crashes. Martinez estimated that aggressive driving had been involved in some 28,000 highway deaths and 3,000,000 injuries in the previous year alone. The cost to the nation of these outbursts of temper: $150.5 billion.

RAGE AROUND THE WORLD

Aggressive driving in the U.S. is reportedly increasing at an annual rate of almost 7%. In 1996 the

The wreckage from a disastrous multivehicle crash on the M4 near London is strewn across several lanes. Incidents of road rage are being reported with increasing frequency in the U.K., and lorry (truck) drivers are said to be among the worst offenders.

the Automobile Association of Great Britain, 90% of the respondents reported having been involved in road rage incidents, either as perpetrators or as victims, in the previous 12 months. More than half of them admitted having become infuriated by another driver; 1% reported that they had been physically attacked in a driving-related altercation. Another British study found that lorry (truck) drivers were among the worst offenders. Nearly 100,000 truckers admitted having aggressively pursued another vehicle within the previous 12 months, and 60,000 said they had climbed out of their cabs and physically threatened other drivers.

A few especially ugly incidents have shocked the British public into acknowledging that road rage is indeed a serious matter. In one of these an unemployed Worcestershire bus driver and his girlfriend driving on a rural highway got into a dispute with the teenage driver of another vehicle and his two passengers. After a chase both vehicles pulled off the road, and the drivers confronted each other. A passenger from the teen's car pulled a knife and fatally stabbed the bus driver.

In Germany, where there is a long tradition of aggressive driving, motorists may be fined for their antisocial behavior. The amount of the fine is based on the offender's income. The penalty for sticking out one's tongue at a fellow driver, for example, is a sixth of one month's salary. Police do not have to be present at the episode; a report, substantiated by a single witness, is sufficient.

Canadians too are attempting to come to terms with the problem. In March 1998, after two particularly violent incidents, the Ontario Provincial Police Department launched a pilot program to curb road rage.

(continued on page 156)

(Top) Law-enforcement agencies in several U.S. states are cracking down on aggressive drivers. (Opposite page) In a pilot program in Ontario, police officers distributed a two-sided educational card to motorists who appeared on the brink of losing their temper.

Washington, D.C.-based AAA Foundation for Traffic Safety commissioned Maryland security specialist Louis R. Mizell, Jr., whose company collects crime statistics, to compile a report on all traffic altercations involving violence over a nearly seven-year period. Mizell's data showed that between January 1990 and August 1996, police-reported road rage incidents rose 51%. His study identified 10,037 road rage episodes during that period, in which at least 218 people were killed as a direct result and 12,610 were injured. In more than 4,000 of these incidents, the perpetrator used a weapon—gun, knife, club, tire iron, cane—or his or her fists or feet. In some 2,300 cases, the aggressive driver used his or her vehicle as the means of attack. At least 94 enraged motorists, men and women, crashed their cars into buildings or other stationary targets.

The U.S. doesn't have a monopoly on road rage. The problem has also been recognized in Canada, the U.K., and Germany. In a 1995 survey by

Test Your Road Rage!

T **F**

A
1. I often mutter to myself about other drivers.   T   F
2. I get irritated a lot while driving.   T   F
3. When I'm in a traffic jam I tend to get angry or frustrated.   T   F

Add 1 point for each question in Section A above marked "true"

A. Total_____

B
4. When I'm in a hurry I sometimes tailgate.   T   F
5. I often honk at other vehicles to express my anger.   T   F
6. When I'm angry, I sometimes drive in a rude manner.   T   F
7. I often give "the finger" to others when driving.   T   F

Add 2 points for each question in Section B above marked "true"

B. Total_____

C
8. I often take risks on the road when I am angry.   T   F
9. When I get mad all rules "go out the window."   T   F
10. I have fought with another motorist.   T   F

Add 4 points for each question in Section C above marked "true"

C. Total_____

Now add Totals A, B, & C:_____ this is your road rage score.

What is Your Road Rage Score?

Score 0
BLUE: You are a sea of tranquility.

Score 1-2
GREEN: You are cool and collected most of the time.

Score 3-5
YELLOW: Caution! Your rising anger affects safety and health.

Score 6 and higher
RED: Danger! Your anger threatens lives. Reduce your stress!

See tips for reducing your Road Rage on reverse side

see
other
side

Reduce Your Stress: Advice for Aggressive Drivers

1. Do not assume that other motorists intend their actions.
2. Be forgiving of other motorists' mistakes. Think of a time when you committed a similar act.
3. Try to relax while driving. Take deep breaths when you feel angry or stressed.
4. Run a verbal "play-by-play" of roadway incidents as they occur. Say aloud what happened, what you think, and how you feel.
5. Act generously and be forgiving even when you don't feel that way.
6. Make yourself comfortable in your vehicle. Play relaxing music.
7. Choose not to express your anger. You have nothing to gain by acting out.

Be Safe: Tips for Avoiding Road Rage Incidents

1. Do not escalate roadway conflicts. You never know who you are dealing with in the other vehicle, and you have absolutely nothing to gain.
2. Avoid obscene gestures.
3. Avoid eye contact with aggressive drivers.
4. Communicate apologies with a raised palm, shrugged shoulders, and by mouthing "sorry."
5. When in a hostile situation, remain in your vehicle. Lock your doors and close your windows.
6. When driving, stay behind hostile drivers if possible. If necessary, drive to a police station or to a busy area to seek assistance. If required, use your horn to attract attention.

A Division of the Addiction and Mental Health Services Corporation

For Police assistance on Ontario highways
call 1-888-310-1122

(Below and opposite page, bottom) Photographs, Culver Pictures; (opposite page, top) Reed Saxon—AP/Wide World

(Left and bottom) Commuting on California's freeways used to be a breeze! Today those same highways (below) look more like parking lots. Increased traffic congestion has been a major factor in the rise of road rage.

(continued from page 152)
In this program police officers, alert to signs of fraying tempers in drivers, stop motorists who appear agitated and present them with a yellow card that poses 10 questions about their driving habits and scores their chances of being involved in a serious incident. The reverse side offers tips for avoiding anger and confrontation.

How do U.S. authorities account for the dramatic increase in aggressive driving? As Martinez told the subcommittee members, the causes

> "One of the best countermeasures to aggressive driving is the cop in the rearview mirror."

of road rage are complex, and experts are not entirely in agreement. Psychiatrists tend to attribute the behavior to personal problems and stress, whereas social scientists blame societal problems. Martinez himself cited three factors as indisputably linked to the rise in aggressive driving. One is the "me first" attitude of many drivers. They forget, he said, that driving is a privilege, not a right, and that the privilege requires responsible behavior. A second factor is lower levels of law enforcement than in the past, in many cases due to budget cutbacks. "One of the best countermeasures to aggressive driving," Martinez noted, "is the cop in

the rearview mirror." A third factor is increased congestion on the roads and highways, especially in urban areas. Although building new roads or adding lanes to existing ones would help, these are not practical solutions in many parts of the country. Instead, Martinez suggested, answers will have to be found in improved engineering of roads and better methods of traffic control.

Many other contributing factors are invoked by those trying to explain the emergence of road rage. Most of these come under the basic heading of pressures of modern life—hectic schedules, long work hours, the need of many families to have two incomes, etc. Some people also blame the deterioration in standards of behavior so often remarked upon by members of the "older generation," as well as the general decline in civility in daily interactions.

TRIGGERS

In his study for the AAA Foundation for Traffic Safety, Mizell assembled a list of the most common precipitators of road rage. Each of the following "reasons" for rage was associated with multiple incidents in which deaths and/or injuries occurred:
- "She wouldn't let me pass."
- "He was driving too slowly."
- "He kept honking his horn."
- "They were tailgating me."
- "He wouldn't turn off his high beams."

Other often-cited triggers included erratic driving—speeding up and slowing down for no apparent reason, excessive lane-changing—and obscene gestures. Several drivers, when questioned, admitted that they may have overreacted, although some thought that their action might at least have taught the other guy a lesson.

In some cases of aggressive driving, the car serves only as a means of venting anger over a stressful situation completely unrelated to perceived misconduct by another driver—for example, a man intentionally rams the vehicle of his ex-wife and her boyfriend, or a woman outraged at being stopped for a traffic violation uses her car to assault the officer who pulled her over. Sometimes the target is a stationary object. In one such incident in California, a man in his 20s tried to purchase beer at a convenience store but was turned away because he had no identification. Infuriated, he crashed his car into the store's gas pump, causing $500,000 worth of damage.

And if you think road rage happens only on the road, think again. In one Chicago suburb, shoppers competing for parking spaces at a crowded suburban mall have been observed exchanging obscene gestures, yelling at each other, and vandalizing the cars of those who outmaneuvered them in the race to claim coveted parking spots. At least one of these parking-lot ragers has been arrested for disorderly conduct.

PROFILE OF A "RAGER"

On the basis of his own driving behavior while in his 20s, when he was a self-avowed "tail-gating, blind-siding,…fist-shaking, oath-spitting" road rager, the British novelist Martin Amis writes, "The existence of the motor car lends strong support to the view that all men should be locked up from the ages of 15 to 35 inclusive." According to U.S. data, the vast majority of offenders are indeed youthful males in their late teens and early 20s. Many have criminal records or histories of violence and drug or alcohol prob-

lems. Generally, they are poorly educated, lack both affluence and influence, and have a history of emotional problems. Many are individuals who have recently lost a job or been involved in a divorce or domestic dispute.

This profile does not describe all road ragers. In Mizell's study, perpetrators ranged in age from 18 to 75. Women were responsible for slightly more than 400 of the 10,000-plus incidents. About 80 episodes were instigated by people over 50. Clinical

psychologist Arnold Nerenberg of Whittier, California, who describes himself as "America's road rage therapist," emphasizes that road rage may appear in a reasonable male or female, young or old, of any race—even in one who is generally a courteous, unexcitable person when not behind the wheel. Nerenberg says that family history may play a part in determining which individuals are likely to exhibit this kind of aggressive behavior: "Most people who suffer from road rage—about 60% according to a study I made last year among 585 people—had parents who

A family outing, c. 1904. Driving is no longer the genteel pastime it once was; today the gloves are off— in every sense!

were also aggressive drivers. So road rage may be learned behavior, or there may also be a genetic factor."

GETTING AHEAD

Some psychologists say that the need to "get ahead" on the highway is simply an extension of the competitiveness that pervades our entire culture. Thus, road ragers are likely to be people who feel that their self-esteem is on the line when they're on the road. When another driver cuts them off, they regard it as a personal affront that requires an immediate and appropriate redress. Or as Amis succinctly put it, "Men's lives are all about rivalry, competition, preferment; put a man in a car and he thinks he is being tested."

By its very nature the automobile is the perfect "vehicle" for these aggressive impulses. First, it confers on the driver an empowering sense of anonymity. Second, its steel shell, 1,360-kilogram (3,000-pound) mass, and capacity for a quick getaway confer upon him—or her—a false sense of invulnerability. And then, says Nerenberg, there's human nature: "Within the human psyche is an urge to release aggression on an anonymous other when we feel justified. It happens in warfare when we kill people we don't know." This impulse works in two ways on the road, he says: "I can flip you off because I'll never see you again," and "You're not a person like myself, with feelings."

FATAL INSTINCT

At the psychological heart of road rage, Nerenberg finds, is the driver's sense that he or she is physically endangered by other cars and their drivers. Like all humans facing a physical threat, these motorists are likely to react involuntarily in one of two ways: confront the opponent or flee the scene—the classic reaction known as the fight-or-flight response.

Herbert Benson, a psychiatrist at Harvard Medical School and a pioneer in the study of the mind-body connection, has described the fight-or-flight response as an instant, reflexive physiological and psychological reaction common to humans (and other animals) when confronted by sudden danger or stress. For the extra physical effort required for combat or a quick escape, the body flushes itself with adrenaline and other hormones, which in turn raise the blood pressure, speed the pulse and respiration rates, and increase blood flow to the muscles that will do the work of either fighting or running. These same changes, governed by the autonomic (involuntary) nervous system, can be observed in angry, frightened people on or off the road.

Scientists theorize that the body's ability to gear up for action in times of danger was an important evolutionary adaptation. The more successful an individual is in mobilizing these physiological resources, the

> ## "Men's lives are all about rivalry...;put a man in a car and he thinks he is being tested."

more likely he or she is to survive. But like some other adaptations that promoted survival in prehistoric times—the ability to store fat in times of famine, for example—this natural physiological response has to some extent outlived its usefulness. Just as most human beings in developed countries probably will never know famine (and, in fact, regularly eat too much), most are also unlikely to be suddenly confronted by a hungry tiger or a murderous rival from another clan. Nowadays, the fight-or-flight response is apt to be triggered by psychologically stressful situations in which neither "fight" nor "flight" is really an option. But then, try telling that to your autonomic nervous system.

ANGER = DEATH

Data accumulated over the past several decades indicate that the physiological changes that accompany surges of fear and anger and prepare the body to fight or flee ultimately have a harmful effect on the heart and blood vessels. Road ragers then are doubly endangered— not only are they at risk from collisions and driving-related violence, but they are also more likely than their calmer, less-confrontational counterparts to experience heart attacks and strokes.

The people who are most disposed to being road ragers—and who are also at increased risk of cardiovascular disease—have what psychologists call type A personalities. The term *type A* was coined in the late 1950s by two San Francisco cardiologists, Meyer Friedman and Ray Rosenman. In their type A patients, Friedman and Rosenman observed three notable characteristics: (1) a sense of time urgency—they were always in a hurry, (2) ambitious striving for success, and (3) a lot of "free-floating" hostility. In a long-term study of healthy middle-aged men, Friedman and Rosenman found that type A behavior was an independent risk factor for heart disease. Compared with men who were less competitive and less anger-prone, who were dubbed type B's, the men identified at the outset of the study as type A's were twice as likely to suffer a heart attack, die of disease of the coronary arteries, or develop angina pectoris, the characteristic chest pain associated with insufficient blood flow to the heart muscle. Further, type A's tended to have elevated levels of serum cholesterol and high blood pressure.

The hypothesis linking type A personality and heart attacks spawned an era of research into the relationship between personality and cardiovascular disease. Over time, other characteristics were ascribed to type A's, including cynicism, suspiciousness, and a quickness to anger. During the 1980s psychiatrist Redford B. Williams, Jr., at Duke University, Durham, North Carolina, and others began to focus their investigations on a single component of type A personality, hostility, which they deemed to be the most "toxic" type A trait.

The study of specific behaviors and personality characteristics that put people at risk of heart attack and stroke continues today, as does research into the physiological mechanisms involved. Although questions remain, it is now well accepted that mental and emotional stress—and a person's reaction to them—adversely affect blood pressure, cholesterol levels, and other cardiovascular risk factors. Clearly, then, it is in everyone's best interest to learn how to keep cool behind the wheel.

STEERING CLEAR

Road rage *can* be controlled, says John Larson, a Norwalk, Connecticut, psychiatrist. Larson, the author of *Steering Clear of Highway Madness* (1996), has been treating heart attack patients since 1963 and regularly holds one-day seminars for aggressive drivers. "Many of my heart patients are also quick to anger while driving," Larson notes. "My seminar helps them to prevent stress and anger on the road."

Larson offers five basic rules of the road:

• Don't plan your schedule in such a way that you are always rushing to get to your destination; leave enough time to enjoy the experience of driving. In other words, take some time to smell the roses.

• Don't compete with other drivers. Driving is not a sport. Let other drivers get ahead of you or go faster if they want.

• Show the same courtesy to other drivers that you'd show to a guest in your home.

• If you find yourself instantly disliking another driver for whatever reason, take a moment to realize that diversity is what makes life rich and interesting.

Thanks to the ubiquitous pressures of life in the late 20th century, a large segment of society is always in a rush. Put these harried, anxious people behind the wheel, and you have a recipe for disaster.

Rick Gerharter—Impact Visuals/PNI

• Don't take it upon yourself to teach bad or discourteous drivers a lesson. Forget about revenge and leave the punishment of other motorists to the police.

Okay, let's say that having taken Larson's tips to heart, you're now a calm, courteous driver. Suddenly a road rager is on your tail, honking his horn and flashing his headlights. How do you avoid confrontation and protect yourself against the wrath of this out-of-control driver? The following is what the National Safety Council advises:

• Keep cool and get out of the tailgater's way. Signal and change lanes.

• In general, be aware of triggers that can set off an aggressive driver. These are horn honking, loud radio playing, improper passing, failing to use a turn signal, and failing to obey the rules of safe driving.

• Keep away from aggressive or erratic drivers. Avoid eye contact with them. Stay calm and relaxed.

• If you have a cellular phone in the car, call the police if you believe that your safety and the safety of other drivers are threatened.

• Don't get drawn into the game with aggressive drivers. Immediately create some space between yourself and the road rager. Let him or her get ahead of you. Get out of the fast lane if you're driving too slowly.

• Exercise self-control. Don't let the actions of a reckless driver determine your behavior or elicit a response from you. Any response may escalate the situation. Don't do anything to antagonize the road rager.

• Ask yourself if it is worth your life and the lives of your passengers to teach a bad driver a lesson. Again, leave the lessons and punishment to law enforcement.

(*continued on page 162*)

FROM ANN LANDERS'S MAILBAG: OUTRAGE ABOUT ROAD RAGE

Tuesday—July 15, 1997

Dear Ann Landers: I would like your help in improving some of our nation's driving habits. I just read an article that said the top concern of most drivers is the angry motorist. The article described some aggressive driving behavior, such as weaving in and out of traffic, tailgating, blowing the horn, running red lights, making obscene gestures, passing on the right, flashing the headlights, and screaming at other drivers.

The article said we should be slow to react to such behavior and urged us to be calm and cautious when other drivers behave aggressively. I would like to add one more suggestion. Please tell the driving public to use their turn signals properly. Signaling one's intention to turn allows the driver behind you to slow down or move to another lane so traffic can flow smoothly.

Simple, everyday courtesy on the city streets and highways would help reduce driver aggression and prevent accidents. It would also allow everyone to return home feeling less stressed and in a better mood.

Retired U.S. Air Force Lt. Col. in Calif.

Dear Lt. Col.: It seems to me if someone is screaming, honking, flashing lights, and tailgating, the best thing to do is move over and let the other guy pass. If I were driving, that's what I'd do.

Tuesday—September 30, 1997

Dear Ann Landers: A while back, someone wrote to you about aggressive drivers. Your advice was simply to pull over and let them go by. That was sound advice because it can be dangerous to fight it out on the road. It does not, however, solve the problem of aggressive drivers, who are mostly men.

People are ever so polite to each other when they are face to face, but they let out their real feelings when they get on the turnpike, where driving is crazy. Thousands of people are cooped up all day in office buildings, and there is usually only one turnpike going out of the city. This means horrendous traffic jams. These nice, sane folks are half nuts by the time they get out of downtown.

Workers in a capitalist system like ours are hotly competitive because there are only a limited number of slots high up in the hierarchy of any business. When people are at work, they must be fairly polite to each other, but that doesn't mean they aren't secretly competitive. Is it possible for them to be less competitive on the highway? I doubt it. About the only time they can express their real feelings is when they get behind the wheel of the car.

The bosses in this society can afford to express themselves overtly. The rest of us have to keep our anger and hostility pent-up inside. The "battles" on the highway, where we let it all hang out, are symptomatic of the American way of life.

J.P. in Burlington, Conn.

Dear Burlington: How people behave when they get behind the wheel of a car tells us a great deal about their temperament, degree of maturity, and ability to handle frustration.

Drunken drivers can be arrested, but unfortunately, we have no protection against angry drivers who may be just as dangerous. There are no easy answers to this one. Your best bet is to drive defensively. Anticipate, and be prepared for the goofy and angry driver.

Reprinted by permission of Ann Landers and Creators Syndicate.

Courtesy of Ann Landers

Road rage is a matter of considerable concern to the readers of Ann Landers's syndicated column, which appears in more than 1,200 newspapers.

(*continued from page 160*)

Many ugly confrontations wouldn't happen if drivers didn't feel the need to teach other drivers a lesson. Law enforcement should be left to the professionals.

EDUCATION AND ENFORCEMENT

Law-enforcement agencies around the U.S. now recognize the problem of road rage, and some have initiated strict enforcement campaigns as countermeasures. In Fairfax county, for example, police issued more than 60,000 traffic tickets for aggressive driving between May 1997 and February 1998 in a concerted campaign against road rage. Supplementing the county's zero-tolerance policy—no warnings are given prior to issuing a ticket—are public service messages in the local media, which alert citizens to the dangers of road rage and advise them of upcoming police crackdown periods. The Fairfax county campaign is being conducted in concert with programs in 20 other jurisdictions in Virginia, Maryland, and Washington, D.C., in the densely populated region around the capital known as the "beltway." "There's been some reduction of road rage incidents, but not enough," says Lieutenant Wall, who introduced the program in his area in 1997.

Education is especially important because so many road ragers are unaware of their own behavior. Wall notes that a majority of the motorists ticketed in Fairfax county didn't believe they were aggressive drivers. Nerenberg, too, stresses that acknowledging the problem is a necessary step in overcoming it.

In February 1998 David Willis, president of the AAA Foundation for

Traffic Safety, announced plans for an ambitious nationwide campaign of public service announcements to be broadcast on radio. The messages will be aimed at drivers in their cars. The foundation has also distributed several hundred thousand copies of the brochure *Road Rage: How to Avoid Aggressive Driving*. (Single copies of the brochure are available from the foundation at no cost; *see* "For Further Information.")

In Illlinois legislation has been proposed that would make aggressive driving illegal and subject to strict penalties. Other states are expected to follow suit. Nerenberg goes so far as to suggest that motorists applying for or renewing driver's licenses be tested on their ability to identify and avoid potential road rage situations.

DRIVEN TO SELF-DESTRUCTION?

"Even if we can't reach every angry driver," says Willis, people need to

> ## "It takes two to tango—or in this case, two to tangle."

keep in mind that "it takes two to tango—or in this case, two to tangle. If we can convince millions of calm, mature motorists not to get sucked into encounters with angry drivers, many lives can be saved and injuries reduced on our nation's roads."

Perhaps the best way to defuse a potentially explosive encounter with a road rager who thinks he or she has been wronged is a simple signal saying, "I'm sorry." "Sixty-four percent of those I studied said an apology sign of some kind would dissipate their anger," says Nerenberg. In *The Handbook for Overcoming Road Rage* (1996), he advises

drivers to have compassion for themselves. "Rage and anger will destroy our health," he writes. "If another driver upsets us we don't want to waste emotional energy. It's not worth it."

FOR FURTHER INFORMATION

Books
AAA Foundation for Traffic Safety. *Aggressive Driving: Three Studies*. Washington, D.C.: 1997.

Larson, John A., M.D. *Steering Clear of Highway Madness*. Wilsonville, Oregon: BookPartners, Inc., 1996.

Nerenberg, Arnold, Ph.D. *The Handbook for Overcoming Road Rage*. Los Angeles: Seed-Thought Publishers, 1996.

Organization
AAA Foundation for Traffic Safety
1440 New York Ave NW
Washington DC 20005
202-638-5944
Web site: http://www.aaafts.org

163

ALICE IN MIGRAINELAND

**BY RICHARD M.
RESTAK, M.D.**

In 1952 the American headache specialist Caro Lippman described some unusual symptoms shared by several of his migraine patients. Instead of headaches—the most common manifestation of migraine—these individuals complained of bizarre sensations of bodily alteration and distortion. As one patient described to Lippman:

I felt that I was very tall. When walking down the street I would think I would be able to look down on the tops of others' heads, and it was very frightening and annoying not to see as I was feeling. The sensation was so real that when I would see myself in a window or full-length mirror, it was quite a shock to realize that I was still my normal height of under five feet.

Illustrations from *Alice's Adventures in Wonderland* (below and on following pages) by Sir John Tenniel.

Color illustrations from The Granger Collection

Another patient experienced his body "as if someone had drawn a vertical line separating two halves. The right half seems to be twice the size of the left half." One woman had the sensation of her left ear "ballooning out six inches or more." Some of the patients also reported distortions of time and space: "I felt as if I was going fast," or "It seemed as if everyone was talking and moving too fast."

Fearful of being thought insane, the patients tended to keep their strange experiences to themselves. Only with cautious questioning and reassurance was Lippman able to induce them to tell their stories. These migraineurs (migraine sufferers) were not, of course, insane; unlike people with schizophrenia and other psychoses, who cannot distinguish between hallucination and reality, Lippman's patients clearly recognized the unreality of their experiences. They did not believe that they were growing

larger or that parts of their bodies were changing in proportion to the rest; it only seemed that such weird transformations were taking place.

Lippman was the first to notice the similarity between these unusual migraine symptoms and some of the fictional occurrences in *Alice's Adventures in Wonderland* (1865) and its sequel, *Through the Looking Glass* (1871), by the English writer Lewis Carroll. In chapter 4 of *Alice's Adventures*, for instance, after drinking from a mysterious little bottle, Alice begins to grow; soon her head is "pressing against the ceiling," and she must stoop "to save her neck from being broken." Ultimately, just to fit into the room, she must lie down "with one elbow against the door, and the other arm curled round her head." This passage reminded Lippman of the description given by one of his migraine patients, who said that during an attack she felt as if her body were "growing larger and larger until it seems to occupy the whole room." Another patient described his sensations of bodily distortion as "this…feeling of being short and wide…a Tweedle-Dum or Tweedle-Dee feeling."

In a paper he wrote on these atypical manifestations of migraine, Lippman stated, "I would hesitate to report these hallucinations which I have recorded in my notes on migraine had not, more than 80 years ago, a great and famous writer set them down in immortal fiction form. *Alice in Wonderland* contains a record of these and many other migraine hallucinations." Further,

> ## "Alice trod the paths of a wonderland well known to her creator."

Richard M. Restak *is a neurologist in private practice in Washington, D.C., and the author of 11 books on the brain, including* The Brain Has a Mind of Its Own *(1991) and* The Modular Brain *(1994). His most recent works are* Older and Wiser: How to Maintain Peak Mental Ability for As Long as You Live *(1997) and* The Longevity Strategy *(1998; with David Mahoney).*

Lippman suggested that the writer's migraines had provided the raw data for Alice's bizarre and otherwise inexplicable experiences: "Lewis Carroll…was himself a sufferer from classic migraine headaches….Alice trod the paths of a wonderland well known to her creator."

WONDERLAND'S CREATOR

Lewis Carroll was the pen name of Charles Lutwidge Dodgson, who was born in Daresbury, Cheshire, England, in 1832. His father was a country curate who eventually became an archdeacon and a canon of Ripon Cathedral. Charles was the third of 11 children in the Dodgson family. He began early in his life to create games and entertainments for his younger siblings; at the age of 12, he undertook one of his first literary efforts, a series of publications called the *Rectory Magazines*, created for the amusement of the family.

He excelled in mathematics. After four years at the prestigious Rugby School, he earned a degree in mathematics at Christ Church College, Oxford, and from 1855 to 1881, he held the post of lecturer in mathematics there. He was ordained a deacon in the Church of England in 1861 but never took holy orders.

In his adult life Carroll continued to make up games, puzzles, stories, and impromptu amusements for children, especially the youngsters of his university colleagues. Prominent among his youthful audience were the three daughters of Henry George Liddell, the dean of Christ Church. It was for the Liddell girls, one of whom was named Alice, that Carroll made up a tale he originally called "Alice's Adventures Underground," loosely based on his ramblings with the children in the countryside around Oxford.

Alice Liddell was delighted with the story and begged him to write it down. A novelist visiting the dean's home subsequently read it and urged the reluctant author to seek a publisher. By the time of Carroll's death in 1898, the two *Alice* books were the most popular children's books in England. And, of course, they continue to be enjoyed by young and old readers the world over.

Carroll the man and his fictional works (as opposed to his rather unremarkable writings on mathematics) have been subjected to endless analysis and interpretation over the past century. One article, for example, held that the *Alice* stories were an elaborate allegory of the religious controversies that raged in Victorian England. In his introduction to *The Annotated Alice* (1960), Martin Gardner (a noted expert on mathematical puzzles) summarily dismissed this and other "learned commentaries" on Carroll's creations: "Like Homer, the Bible, and all other great works of fantasy," he observed, "the ALICE books lend themselves readily to any type of symbolic interpretation— political, metaphysical, or Freudian." Most scholars today agree with Gardner that the books have neither veiled meaning nor profound message.

Nevertheless, ever since Lippman first suggested that Carroll was a migraineur, Carroll scholars, some of them physicians, have continued to debate the existence of a link between the hallucination-like imagery of the *Alice* books and the physical health of their author. Among the questions they have pondered: Did Carroll (as Lippman contended) *truly* suffer from migraine? To what extent did mi-

graine—or some other neurological condition—influence his writings? Does an understanding of migraine's manifestations help in appreciating his oftentimes bizarre characters and situations? And finally, was Carroll indebted to migraine as the source of his literary inspiration? The 100th anniversary of his death seems an appropriate occasion to examine the evidence.

STRANGE SENSATIONS

One thing is certain—the experiences described by Carroll in the *Alice* books are encountered fairly regularly by neurologists who specialize in the treatment of migraine. About 15% of people with this condition tell of strange or abnormal sensations similar to those described by Alice. These occurrences range from phantom odors or tastes to sensory distortions and even to detailed, lifelike hallucinations. Time may seem to be accelerated, or

Alice Liddell, pictured at age six, was the real-life inspiration for Carroll's intrepid fictional heroine.

sounds seem louder than they should be. Sometimes the migraineur may be oppressed by vague feelings of disconnection from his or her surroundings. Changes in mood, usually depression and irritability, may accompany any of these alterations.

Some migraine sufferers experience curious visual disturbances. What the patient sees may be perceived incorrectly (illusion), or the visual system may produce images of things not really there (hallucination). Some patients describe an impression of flashing lights, popping flashbulbs, spots before their eyes, or other visual sensations involving color, shape, or brightness. Moments later they may experience temporary blindness in the same or a different part of their visual field. Others have visual hallucinations of the type neurologists label *formed,* or *complex;* these hallucinations typically involve people or animals that appear off to one side, materializing out of thin air in much the same way as the Cheshire Cat did in *Alice's Adventures.*

Finally, as so vividly described by Carroll, people and things may seem to the migraineur to grow larger (a phenomenon neurologists term *macropsia*) or smaller (*micropsia*). In some cases the size of objects and persons remains unchanged, but bizarre distortions seem to occur (*metamorphopsia*). For instance, one side of another person's face (or of the patient's own face in a mirror) may appear blurred or smudged. In several of the classic illustrations for the *Alice* books, the artist Sir John Tenniel uncannily depicts the experience of metamorphopsia just as it is described by people suffering from migraine. Tenniel's picture of Alice with her neck curiously elongated seems to match this description of a migraine episode by a sufferer: "I get

all tired out from pulling my head down from the ceiling. My head feels like a balloon, my neck stretches and my head goes to the ceiling. I've been pulling it down all night long." It is worth noting that Carroll reportedly gave Tenniel detailed instructions about the drawings.

As noted above, the visual illusions and hallucinations associated with migraine frequently are accompanied by depression or irritability. A sense of foreboding or a vague, poorly

defined anxiety sometimes precedes the visual changes or the headache. As the wife of one patient put it, "I can always tell—even before he can—when my husband is going to have one of his headaches, because for a few hours beforehand he's cranky and anxious."

CARROLL: SUFFERER OR STUDENT?

Several arguments have been advanced to disprove the hypothesis that Carroll incorporated his own migraine experiences into his stories. One of these objections can be dismissed rather easily: that Carroll himself did not have migraine because he rarely complained of headaches. While it is true that headaches usually occur during migraine attacks, they are not an invariable accompaniment. In a 1952 article in *Science Digest,* Lippman wrote, "The headache itself is one of the least important facets of the whole picture....[It] just happens to be the most common symptom."

Some migraine sufferers experience, without headache, a loss of vision on one side of the visual field, flashing lights, spots before the eyes,

Migraine patients tend to hide, deny, or at least minimize their auras.

fully formed visual hallucinations, bizarre visual distortions, word-finding difficulties, depersonalization, sudden unexplained fears, mood fluctuations, even outbursts of temper. On some occasions these experiences occur prior to the pain of a typical migraine headache, but in other instances the pain never comes. The rarity of headache complaints from Alice and the other characters does not, therefore, eliminate migraine as inspiration for events in Carroll's books.

The other objection to migraine as an important element in Carroll's creations is less easily dismissed. It was not until 1888, when he was 56 years old, that the author recorded in his journal his first migraine episode. More than 25 years had passed since the writing of *Alice in Wonderland*. Since Carroll kept a detailed diary throughout his life, it seems likely he would have recorded earlier episodes if they had occurred. But before accepting this argument, one should consider the intriguing diary entry from 1888:

This morning on getting up, I experienced a curious optic effect—of seeing "fortifications"— discussed in Dr. Lathan's book on "bilious headache." In this instance it affected the right eye only, at the outer edge and there was no headache.

The Lathan book to which Carroll referred was not popular science but a medical textbook. Carroll was fascinated by medicine and owned a large library of works on anatomy, medical diagnosis and treatment, and pathology. He also had a human skull and the skeletal remains of a hand and a foot. Indeed, for a person with no formal medical training, Carroll possessed a keen interest in the science of medicine. Given his sophisticated medical knowledge and the above diary entry, it seems reasonable to conclude that he was aware that migraine, then known as "bilious headache," can occur in the absence of head pain. Further, he knew that migraine can involve visual "fortifications," a medical term meaning shimmering lights sometimes described as resembling battlements. But if this was a first migraine attack at age 56—a rare circumstance among migraine sufferers—then how could it provide the basis for stories written so many years earlier?

One possible explanation is that Carroll heard these descriptions from a child, perhaps one of the many he befriended and entertained. One can easily imagine him drawing one of these youngsters out on the subject of her headaches and associated symptoms. Indeed, visual distortions of the type described in the *Alice* tales occur more commonly in child and adolescent migraine sufferers than in adults. In one clinical study of children with acephalic migraine—i.e., migraine without headache—conducted at McGill University, Montreal, two of the youthful patients experienced micropsia, one experienced temporal distortion (time seemingly speeded up), and one reported a vague sense of disconnection from her surroundings. Nonetheless, if a child's description of a migraine attack was the origin of

Alice's experiences of bodily distortion, Carroll left no written record of the fact.

An intriguing speculation comes from the Norwegian neurologist Jill Gordon Klee, who has suggested that although Carroll did not have migraine headaches until late in life, he may have experienced auras—the visual and other sensory manifestations that often precede the headache—from an early age. Further, she proposes, "Although Lewis Carroll may, in fact, have been among those who experienced these aura symptoms, he did not dare record these manifestations." Perhaps he too feared being thought insane. But hesitancy to disclose his symptoms would not have prevented him from giving them fictional form.

My own clinical observations confirm that migraine patients tend to hide, deny, or at least minimize their auras. This is especially true when the aura involves disturbances in identity, feeling, thinking, or perception. For instance, one of my patients, while paying for her purchases at a department store, suddenly experienced the salesclerk's face as a "distorted blur." Frightened and embarrassed, she fled the store and, while driving home, had to pull over to the side of the road because of the onset of an intense headache. Later, after treatment for her headaches, she spoke reluctantly—and only after considerable reassurance that her experiences did not suggest mental instability—about the visual distortions.

OF MERCURY AND MADNESS

Was Carroll an attentive student of the medical literature or simply an attentive observer of life? Or was he, perhaps, both? Some clues may lie in

another memorable character from the *Alice* stories, the Hatter. Traditional interpretation holds that the Hatter's eccentric behavior was modeled after the neurological symptoms typically observed in victims of mercury poisoning, or mercurialism—including anxiety, irritability, tremors, and memory loss. When he is called to give testimony before the King and Queen of Hearts in chapter 11 of *Alice's Adventures*, the Hatter, who has been interrupted while at his tea, is pale, anxious, trembling, and forgetful. "In his confusion," wrote Carroll, the Hatter "bit a large piece out of his teacup instead of the bread-and-butter."

In the 19th century, mercurialism was not uncommon in hatmakers, who were exposed to mercury salts in the manufacture of felt—hence the expression "mad as a hatter." The first description of the condition in the medical literature appeared in an obscure American journal, *Transactions of the Medical Society of New Jersey*, in 1860, five years before the publication of *Alice's Adventures in Wonderland*. The author, J. Addison Freeman, was equally obscure. Despite his fascination with medical matters, it is unlikely that Carroll read this article. But he may well have read a piece entitled "Mad as a Hatter" in the English magazine *Punch* (which often featured cartoons by Tenniel) in 1862.

If he was not acquainted with Freeman's paper or other scientific works on the subject, where did Carroll get his specific and medically sophisticated information? The pathological shyness sometimes seen in mercurialism—and evidenced by the Hatter's maneuvering away from Alice at the tea table and his timidity at the trial—was first noted in a medical article in 1912. No mention of mercurialism appears in any of

Complex hallucinations are never normal;…they always imply… a brain disturbance.

Carroll's journal entries. The author may have based his characterization on the popular wisdom about hatters or his own observations rather than on clinical descriptions of mercury poisoning. The same might be true of his descriptions of the bodily distortions accompanying migraine.

FOCUS ON HALLUCINATIONS

A basic understanding of the nature of visual illusions and hallucinations may perhaps help one to appreciate all of this speculation about Carroll and the state of his health. Although most people think of hallucinations as quite bizarre, they can occur to anyone under the proper conditions. Pressing on one's eyeballs, for example, can induce the illusion of spots before one's eyes. (It may also induce a migraine attack in some who are predisposed to the condition.) Or, when half closing one's eyes or staring off into the distance during moments of reverie, it is not unusual to see so-called floaters (tiny dark specks) or other normal entoptic phenomena—*i.e.*, visual images that originate within the eye.

The visual illusions and hallucinations generated within the brain itself are different in that they are more complex and fully developed. No matter how detailed and convincing, however, they always represent an abnormal perception of the nonexistent. It may be helpful to think of these kinds of hallucinations as internally generated images that are interpreted by the brain as if they were coming from the outside. Depending on their complexity, they may be the result of an overactive imagination or an impairment of brain function. At their simplest, they are like the animated shadows temporarily cast on a wall near a roaring fire. In complex hallucinations, by comparison, the figures are more permanent and lifelike.

Complex hallucinations are never normal; rather, they always imply the existence of a brain disturbance. The exact location of the disturbance is suggested by the nature of the hallucination—visual, auditory, etc.— and is marked by increased metabolic activity in those parts of the brain generating the illusion. (The site of brain activity can be pinpointed by means of sophisticated imaging techniques such as positron emission tomography and functional magnetic resonance imaging.) Dreams, for instance, are associated with an increase in blood flow in certain parts of the brain's visual areas.

The source of hallucinations, whatever their type, can be similarly identified:
- Visual hallucinations originate in the visual (also known as optic, or occipital) cortex.
- Auditory hallucinations—the sensation of hearing voices—originate in the auditory cortex.

- Phantom tastes and smells have their origin in the temporal lobe and its connections with the olfactory and gustatory cortex.
- Sensations of bizarre bodily distortions (*e.g.*, micropsia and macropsia) result from disturbances in the parietal lobe and other brain areas responsible for the sense of body image.

Nonpsychiatric causes of hallucinations include brain-altering drugs such as cocaine, ecstasy, and LSD; stroke or impending stroke; blood-vessel abnormalities involving the brain's visual-processing areas; and the form of epilepsy known as temporal lobe epilepsy (TLE). It is psychiatric disorders, however—and, in particular, schizophrenia—that are the most common cause of hallucina-

tions. Auditory hallucinations are the most common type experienced in schizophrenia. Typically, these voices criticize or demean the subject or command him or her to commit actions harmful to self or others. Whether visual or auditory, the hallucinations of schizophrenia are distinguished from those occurring in other disorders in that they are never amusing, whimsical, or appealing to the affected persons or those around them.

EPILEPSY AND MIGRAINE: CURIOUS CONNECTION

On the surface, a person suffering an epileptic attack would seem to have little in common with someone experiencing a migraine headache. Nonetheless, neurologists have noted some curious similarities in these seemingly disparate disorders. For one thing, both the migraineur and the person with epilepsy frequently describe an aura, which may take the form of odd smells or tastes or feelings of sudden fear or, more rarely, elation. Epilepsy patients have described visual distortions that, occurring in the absence of a seizure, would be indistinguishable from similar experiences in migraine. All of these strange experiences, which are common to both migraine and TLE, originate in the temporal lobes of the brain and the limbic system (deep-brain structures that are essential to emotion and motivation).

A connection between the disturbances in self-perception in epilepsy and electrical disturbances in these brain regions has been recognized by neurologists for more than a century. In the 1940s and '50s, the Canadian neurosurgeon Wilder Penfield was able to induce some of these strange feelings and perceptions in epilepsy

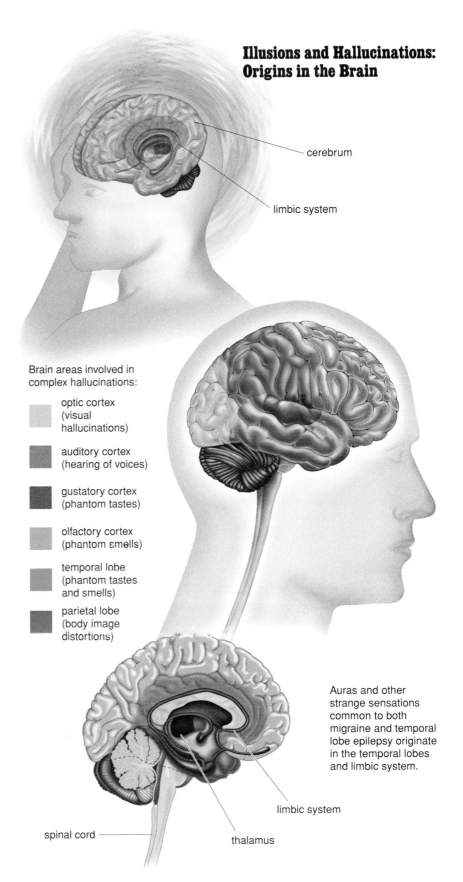

Illusions and Hallucinations: Origins in the Brain

cerebrum

limbic system

Brain areas involved in complex hallucinations:

- optic cortex (visual hallucinations)
- auditory cortex (hearing of voices)
- gustatory cortex (phantom tastes)
- olfactory cortex (phantom smells)
- temporal lobe (phantom tastes and smells)
- parietal lobe (body image distortions)

Auras and other strange sensations common to both migraine and temporal lobe epilepsy originate in the temporal lobes and limbic system.

spinal cord

thalamus

limbic system

patients during surgery by electrically stimulating the temporal lobes or limbic structures. Patients' descriptions of their experiences during the procedure led Penfield to label them "experiential illusions." For instance, a patient might describe a vivid visual hallucination of being at a distant place or encountering someone last seen many years previously. Penfield referred to the experiences as "illusions" because the patients never lost contact with reality, never for a moment doubted that they were anywhere but in an operating room in Montreal. Still, the experiences were quite real to them.

Not surprisingly then, some students of Carroll's works theorize that he may have been an epileptic rather then a migraineur. If so, his symptoms most likely originated in the temporal lobes of the brain. In the 1993 book *Seized: Temporal Lobe Epilepsy as a Medical, Historical, and Artistic Phenomenon*, the writer Eve LaPlante observed that in addition to "bizarre hallucinations, strange feelings, and involuntary actions," TLE is also linked to characteristic personality changes: "Between seizures many people with TLE are intensely emotional, deeply religious, and compelled to write or draw." Carroll

---

People with epilepsy are almost three times more likely than others to develop migraine.

---

displayed all three of the personality characteristics mentioned by LaPlante. His compulsion to write was especially remarkable. "One third of my life seems to go in receiving letters, and the other two-thirds in answering them," he once commented about the more than 98,000 letters he wrote during his lifetime. But his personality did not include other features that frequently accompany TLE—humorlessness, paranoia, guilt, and aggression, for instance.

There is another reason why a minority of Carroll scholars favor epilepsy over migraine as the source of his imagery. On occasion TLE occurs without any bizarre perceptual twists but rather consists merely in the sudden, unheralded loss of consciousness. Carroll experienced just such a loss of consciousness during morning chapel at Oxford in 1891. He described the incident in a letter:

I woke one morning from an uneasy dream, saying to myself "how very uncomfortable the pillow is!" & found myself lying on the floor up in the stalls of the cathedral. I wouldn't believe it at first, but thought I was still dreaming: but in a few moments I was broad awake, & found it really was so.

After sleeping off the attack, which he characterized as "epileptic, no doubt," Carroll described "a great deal of headache." Certainly his description and explanation of the episode are consistent with the diagnosis of epilepsy. He later wrote, "It is of course possible it may have been epilepsy, and not fainting."

Alternative diagnoses are possible but unlikely. He may, for example, have had a transient ischemic attack,

---

or TIA (a temporary, reversible loss of blood supply to an area of the brain), a harbinger of stroke. But TIAs almost always involve weakness in the face or limbs, loss of sensation, language difficulties, or problems with balance and coordination, none of which Carroll reported.

Further confusing the issue is evidence of a link between epilepsy and migraine; people with epilepsy are almost three times more likely than others to develop migraine. Conversely, a person with migraine is more vulnerable to certain experiences common to epilepsy, especially "dreamy" states marked by vivid, memory-like hallucinations or the sense of having previously lived through exactly the same situation (déjà vu) or, even more disturbing, the feeling of unfamiliarity when around familiar people and surroundings (jamais vu). The migraineur may also be susceptible to the sense of mystic or cosmic grandiosity sometimes described by those with epilepsy or to feelings of bemused puzzlement—things becoming "curiouser and curiouser" (in Alice's words in chapter 2 of *Wonderland*).

Carroll biographer Morton Cohen is one of those who reject the epilepsy theory. In researching a 1969 paper, "Lewis Carroll's Loss of Consciousness" (written with Roger Lancelyn Green, the editor of Carroll's diaries), Cohen sent all available information about Carroll's health to seven prominent neurologists. Not one of them was willing to label the author's loss of consciousness certain epilepsy. Fainting was the diagnosis most favored.

"Some recent attempts have been made to include the name of Lewis Carroll in history's long list of geniuses who suffered from temporal lobe epilepsy. For such efforts the documentary evidence is thin or sorely lacking," said another scholar, August A. Imholtz, Jr., of the Lewis Carroll Society of North America. Epilepsy is also considered unlikely by Sandor Burstein, who is both a physician and an internationally recognized authority on Carroll. In a personal letter to this author early in 1998, he wrote: "Based on my re-reading of the accounts of Carroll's loss of consciousness, I note that each was accompanied by a headache. I am now convinced that nothing more than migraine is needed to account for these episodes. Migraine answers all." In support of this contention, Burstein quoted from a 1996 paper on migraine: "Conventionally regarded as a specific type of headache with a small set of associated neurological symptoms, migraine can cause seizures, transient global amnesia, visual disturbances, vestibular dysfunction [inner-ear problems resulting in dizziness and loss of balance], and syncope [fainting]."

NOTHING BUT GENIUS

Like other long-standing controversies about Carroll, this is one that may never be settled. Since he never formally consulted a doctor about headaches—and certainly not about any sensory or perceptual distortions—it cannot be absolutely proved that migraine played a role in his literary works. But even assuming that Carroll suffered from migraine, the question remains: Can the fantastic imagery of *Alice's Adventures in Wonderland* and *Through the Looking Glass* be explained as nothing more than a by-product of an illness? In other words, does Carroll's creativity fall into the category the novelist Arthur Koestler once described as "nothing but-tery"—*i.e.*, love is noth-

ing but sublimated sexuality, patriotism is nothing but glorified chauvinism, and creative genius can be dismissed as nothing but a manifestation of mental or emotional turmoil? On this question there is general agreement among experts: Such a suggestion is nonsense.

Lewis Carroll was one of the world's uniquely creative geniuses. Indeed, it was only because of his genius that he was able to parlay migraine, a not-uncommon yet inconvenient and potentially disabling disorder, into inspired works of art that have entertained and fascinated generations of readers.

Hulton Getty/Liaison

Charles Lutwidge Dodgson, age 31, in a photograph taken two years before he would become known to his delighted readers as Lewis Carroll, author of *Alice's Adventures in Wonderland*.

FOR FURTHER INFORMATION

Books

Amor, Anne Clark. *Lewis Carroll: A Biography*. New York: Schocken Books, 1979.

Cohen, Morton N. *Lewis Carroll: A Biography*. Hardcover, New York: Knopf, 1995; paperback, New York: Vintage Books, 1996.

Cohen, Morton N., and Green, Roger Lancelyn, eds. *The Letters of Lewis Carroll*. New York: Macmillan, 1979.

Hudson, Derek. *Lewis Carroll*. Folcroft, Pennsylvania: Folcroft Library Editions, 1976.

LaPlante, Eve. *Seized: Temporal Lobe Epilepsy as a Medical, Historical, and Artistic Phenomenon*. New York: HarperCollins, 1993.

Sacks, Oliver. *Migraine*. Enl. rev. ed. Berkeley: University of California Press, 1992.

Organizations

Lewis Carroll Birthplace Trust
John Wilcox-Baker
Coombe Bank Cottage
Snatts Road
Uckfield
East Sussex TN22 2AN
England
Alice in Wonderland Collectors Network
Joel Birenbaum
2765 Shellingham Dr
Lisle IL 60532
Lewis Carroll Society of North America
18 Fitzharding Pl
Owings Mill MD 21117
Web site:
http://www.lewiscarroll.org
The Lewis Carroll Society of the U.K.
Web site:
http://ourworld.compuserve.com/homepages/Aztec/LCS.htm

DIABETES:
AN "EPIDEMIC" FOR THE 21ST CENTURY?

BY ANDREW KEEGAN

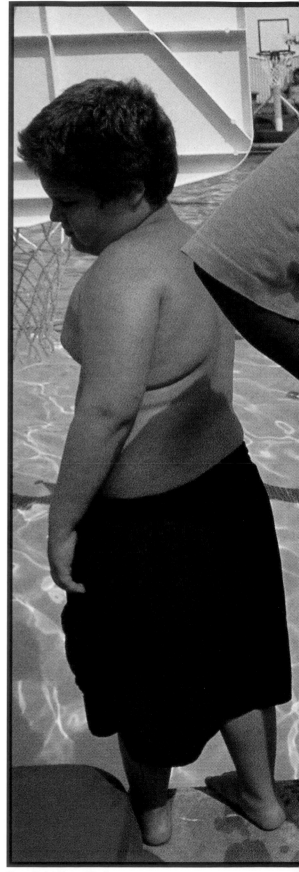

Donna Binder—Impact Visuals

With the approach of the new millennium, the list of looming threats to the public health grows longer by the day. The experts warn of the dangers of global warming, emerging infections, environmental pollution, and overpopulation. Yet hardly anyone is raising the alarm about diabetes.

Perhaps someone should. Worldwide, the number of people with diabetes has tripled since 1985. More than 135 million now have the disease and, according to the International Diabetes Federation, that number will more than double by 2025.

Worldwide Diabetes Prevalence

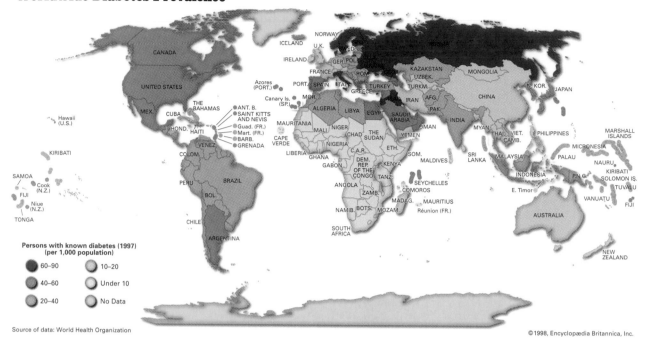

**Persons with known diabetes (1997)
(per 1,000 population)**

- 60–90
- 40–60
- 20–40
- 10–20
- Under 10
- No Data

Source of data: World Health Organization

©1998, Encyclopædia Britannica, Inc.

Andrew Keegan is an editor and writer in Alexandria, Virginia. For more than seven years, he has been Managing Editor of Diabetes Forecast, *the American Diabetes Association's flagship publication for people with diabetes.*

The 10,000 scientists and health care workers who gathered in Helsinki, Finland, in July 1997 for the federation's 16th international congress heard a bleak prediction: Diabetes is currently on track to become one of the major global public health challenges of the 21st century.

Most of the new cases of diabetes are expected to develop in the Third World—on the Indian subcontinent and in China and Africa. Still, it is unlikely that the United States will manage to escape the ravages of a disease now well on its way to assuming epidemic proportions. Diabetes incidence—that is, the number of new cases that are reported annually—is rising steadily in the U.S. (*see* graph, opposite page), and if current trends continue, some groups of Americans—in particular, ethnic minorities and the poor of all races—could experience increases as large as those being predicted for the populations of Calcutta, Shanghai, and Kinshasa.

IMPACT OF AN ILLNESS

Nearly 6% of the U.S. population— 15.7 million people—have diabetes mellitus, a condition that exacts a terrible toll in death and disability. Compared with people who do not have the disease, adults with diabetes have more than double the rate of high blood pressure, are at higher risk of stroke, and are two to four times more likely to die of heart disease. Diabetes is responsible for the majority of cases of blindness diagnosed in people aged 20–74, is the leading cause of end-stage kidney disease, and is the underlying cause of more than half of all lower-limb amputations. Women who develop diabetes during pregnancy are more likely than others to have complications. Poorly controlled diabetes also contributes to dental disease.

Although no racial or ethnic group is immune, African-Americans, Hispanic Americans, and American Indians have higher rates of diabetes than whites. Among African-Americans over age 20, for example, 10.8% have diabetes, compared with only 7.8% of whites in the same age group. Hispanic Americans over 20 are twice as likely to have the disease as their white counterparts, and among some Native American tribes, such as New Mexico's San Felipe Pueblo tribe and the Pima of Arizona, nearly 50% of the adult population is affected.

Type 1 diabetes: insulin essential. Nearly 10% of Americans with diabetes have the form of the disease known as type 1 diabetes (formerly known as insulin-dependent diabetes mellitus [IDDM], or juvenile-onset diabetes), in which, most often, the immune system attacks and gradually destroys the insulin-producing cells of the pancreas. (Insulin is the hormone that regulates the cells' use of glucose, or sugar.) Since the human body requires insulin, people with type 1 diabetes must have daily injections of the hormone in order to survive. Type 1 is most frequently diagnosed in puberty, although it is not uncommon in young children and even in babies. Adults can also develop this form of the disease.

The signs of type 1 diabetes include any or all of the following: extreme thirst, unexplained weight loss, frequent urination, extreme hunger or fatigue, and irritability. This condition requires urgent treatment.

Type 2 diabetes: first in prevalence. More than 90% of Americans with diabetes have type 2 diabetes (formerly known as non-insulin-dependent diabetes mellitus [NIDDM], or maturity-onset diabetes). Type 2 is characterized by cellular resistance to the action of insulin—*i.e.*, insulin resistance. When cells become resistant to insulin, or when insulin production by the pancreas is reduced, as is common in later stages of type 2, blood glucose levels rise. If these levels remain elevated over time, the eyes, kidneys,

> # It is unlikely that the U.S. will... escape the ravages of a disease now...assuming epidemic proportions.

and nerves can be irreparably damaged. Type 2 diabetes usually strikes in adulthood, typically after 45.

Type 2 may be virtually symptomless while it is developing. (The disorder often goes undiagnosed for as long as seven years before symptoms manifest themselves.) When symptoms finally do occur, they can include any of those listed above for type 1 plus blurred vision, tingling or numbness of the hands and feet, slow-to-heal cuts and bruises, and recurring skin, gum, or bladder infections. Even though type 2 is often symptomless as it develops, it *can* be detected by routine blood tests.

Other types. A small percentage of those with diabetes do not fit either the type 1 or the type 2 model. Gestational diabetes is a temporary form of insulin resistance that occurs halfway through pregnancy, causing high blood glucose levels. Although gestational diabetes generally disappears after childbirth, women who develop it are at increased risk of developing diabetes (especially type 2 diabetes) later in life.

Maturity-onset diabetes of the young, or MODY, is an atypical form of type 2 that affects young people. Other varieties of diabetes result

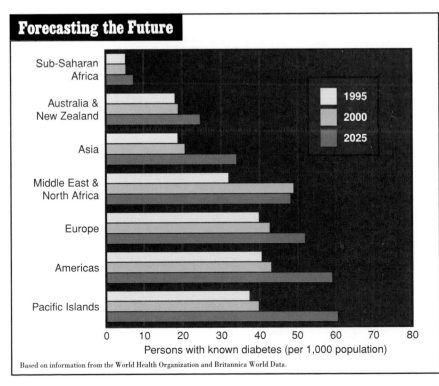

Forecasting the Future

Legend: 1995, 2000, 2025

Persons with known diabetes (per 1,000 population)

Categories: Sub-Saharan Africa, Australia & New Zealand, Asia, Middle East & North Africa, Europe, Americas, Pacific Islands

Based on information from the World Health Organization and Britannica World Data.

This six-year-old is one of the approximately 10% of Americans with diabetes who have type 1, the insulin-dependent form of the disease.

Diabetes in the U.S.: Past, Present, Future

Number of people with known diabetes (millions)

50, 30, 20, 12, 10, 8, 6, 4, 2

1960, 1970, 1980, 1990, 2000, 2020, 2050

Year

Sources: National Institutes of Health and Centers for Disease Control and Prevention, 1997.

from rare genetic syndromes, surgery of the pancreas, chemical exposures, drugs, malnutrition, or infections.

WHY HERE, WHY NOW?

The Bureau of the Census projects that the U.S. population will reach 393.9 million by the year 2050—nearly 50% larger than it is today. Even if the prevalence of diabetes (*i.e.*, the proportion of the population that is affected at any time) were to remain steady at 6%, by the middle of the next century the number of Americans with the disease would number roughly 23 million–25 million.

But incidence and prevalence rates are *not* holding steady. In 1997 approximately 798,000 new cases were diagnosed—the greatest number ever recorded in a single year, according to the Centers for Disease Control and Prevention (CDC). If this rate continues into the 21st century, another 39.9 million Americans will have been diagnosed by the year 2050. And since diabetes often goes undiagnosed, the actual number of cases could be even higher. (Efforts to identify people with unrecognized diabetes are now being intensified.)

Why is diabetes increasing so dramatically? After all, it is not a communicable disease that spreads from person to person like a cold or the flu. Instead, diabetes, like heart disease and cancer, develops over time as a result of a complex interplay of factors that influence an individual's risk of becoming ill.

Americans' waistlines and the nation's incidence of type 2 diabetes have been expanding in tandem. Today more than half of all adults in the U.S. are overweight.

Among these "risk factors" are a sedentary lifestyle, a high-fat diet, and genetics.

The "curse of progress." There is one overriding factor driving this rise in diabetes cases, and it's one few people would ever suspect of causing an epidemic: the rising standard of living. With improved living standards come reduced rates of infant and child deaths, improved access to medical care, and longer life spans. In 1900, for example, the average life expectancy for an American male

Diabetes, like heart disease and cancer, develops...as a result of a complex interplay of factors.

was 46.3 years. Females could expect to live to the ripe age of 48.3 years. About 4% of the total population was over 65. (Today, by comparison, life expectancy for men is just over 72 years and for women 78.8; the over-65 group constitutes close to 15% of the population.) In the early 20th century, therefore, a considerably smaller percentage of Americans lived long enough to develop type 2 diabetes and its complications. Like-

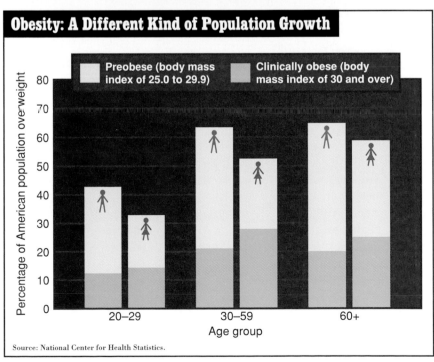

Obesity: A Different Kind of Population Growth

Preobese (body mass index of 25.0 to 29.9)

Clinically obese (body mass index of 30 and over)

Percentage of American population overweight

Age group

Source: National Center for Health Statistics.

181

The vast majority of Americans spend most of their time sitting—at the computer, in the car, or in front of the television set. A sedentary lifestyle is a well-recognized risk factor for type 2 diabetes.

wise, the prevalence of type 1 diabetes was limited by the shortened life expectancy of those with the disease, a situation that was to change dramatically with the discovery of insulin in 1921. Without insulin treatment, 5–10% of Americans who now have diabetes would have perished in childhood or adolescence.

When living standards in a country or community improve, other changes in lifestyle invariably follow. Generally, the diet is transformed as people have increased access to foods high in fat, salt, and sugar. At the same time, jobs that involve physical labor tend to be replaced by sedentary occupations, which means that people's need for energy (calories) actually declines. Finally, tobacco and alcohol also become more readily available. These changes, in turn, set the stage for the "curse of progress"—obesity—which has been linked not only to the development of type 2 diabetes but also to high blood pressure and heart disease.

Demography and disease. Changes in the ethnic and racial composition of the U.S. population are contributing to the increase in diabetes. For example, Hispanics, who currently make up approximately 11% of the population, are the fastest-growing minority group.

The census bureau estimates that by 2050, persons of Hispanic origin will constitute 24% of the population, and, as noted earlier, Hispanic Americans have approximately double the rate of diabetes of non-Hispanic whites.

The aging of the population is another demographic factor with a predictable impact on U.S. diabetes rates. Among Americans aged 20 or older, slightly more than 8% have diabetes. But among those 65 or older, the diabetes rate is 18.4%, or

Jobs that involve physical labor tend to be replaced by sedentary occupations.

almost one person in five. As the "baby boomers"—more than 76 million strong—approach retirement age in 2011, the percentage of the population 65 and over will increase and, along with it, the number of older people with diabetes.

Interplay of genetics and lifestyle. That genes—particularly ones located on chromosome 6—play a part in diabetes is certain. What is unclear is how genes that predispose people to developing diabetes interact with factors—like diet—that promote the disease in susceptible individuals. In the case of type 1 diabetes, scientists have suggested a number of possible triggers, including viruses or a protein in cow's milk. Among the factors suspected of contributing to type 2 diabetes are a sedentary lifestyle, a high-fat diet, obesity, and the aging process.

THE GOOD NEWS

If there is any good news, it is that diabetes is an eminently treatable disease. A landmark 10-year study of people with type 1 diabetes, which ended in 1993, showed that the microvascular (small blood vessel) complications that affect the eyes, kidneys, and nerves are not an inevitable consequence of diabetes but rather a result of failure to control the disease. The study demonstrated that these complications can be prevented if patients closely monitor and stringently control their blood glucose levels. As Frank Vinicor, director of the Division of Diabetes Translation at the CDC, explains it, this improved treatment regimen "can go a long way toward improving the quality of life of people with diabetes." And, notes Vinicor, intensive control of blood sugar, if combined with smoking

cessation and control of blood pressure and cholesterol, also promises to reduce the macrovascular (large blood vessel) complications, such as heart disease, which are responsible for the large majority of diabetes deaths.

Making life easier. The tools for diabetes control grow more sophisticated and effective with each passing decade. By using home blood glucose meters, which became available only in the early 1980s, people with diabetes can now get accurate readings of their blood sugar levels in less than a minute. Insulin pumps not much bigger than a pack of playing cards, worn on a belt or attached to the clothing, can be programmed to provide a steady dose of insulin and extra doses at mealtime, mimicking much more closely than injections the actions of a fully functioning pancreas. And in just the past few years, four new drugs for type 2

The members of this Hispanic American family are more likely than their non-Hispanic neighbors to develop diabetes. Ethnic and racial differences in the prevalence of the disease indicate that genetic factors must play a part.

Complications of Diabetes: From Disabling to Deadly

- Heart disease
- Stroke
- High blood pressure
- Blindness
- Kidney disease
- Nerve damage
- Amputations
- Dental disease
- Problems in pregnancy and childbirth
- Diabetic coma
- Increased susceptibility to certain diseases

A scientist at the University of Pennsylvania examines islet cells under the microscope. Innovative treatments for diabetes are on the horizon, but strategies for preventing or delaying the disease will determine whether the looming "epidemic" can be averted.

diabetes—Glucophage (metformin), Precose (acarbose), Rezulin (troglitazone), and Prandin (repaglinide)—have become available in the U.S. New "designer" insulins, such as rapid-acting Humalog (lispro), are also being introduced.

On the horizon. Further breakthroughs are anticipated in the near future. Wristwatchlike devices that provide an estimate of blood glucose levels without drawing blood, using a painless laser beam or a virtually painless probe into fluid in the tissue just beneath the skin, are already being tested on humans. Implantable sensors may soon be able to monitor blood glucose levels continuously. If such sensors could be made to work in tandem with implanted insulin pumps, the two devices could function virtually as an artificial pancreas. Investigation also continues into alternative ways of delivering insulin orally and via nasal sprays; an insulin-inhalation system for type 1 diabetes has recently been shown effective in clinical trials and may become available in as little as two to five years. Still another promising line of research involves transplanting healthy, insulin-producing pancreatic (islet) cells into people with diabetes. The transplanted cells may be encapsulated to shelter them from the recipient's immune system, or

Could You Have Diabetes and Not Know It?

		At-Risk Weight Chart	
		Height without shoes (feet/inches)	**Weight** without clothing (pounds)
1. My weight is equal to or above that listed in the chart.	Yes = 5 No = 0 _____		
2. I am under 65 years of age, *and* I get little or no exercise during a usual day.	Yes = 5 No = 0 _____	4' 10"	129
		4' 11"	133
		5' 0"	138
3. I am between 45 and 64 years of age.	Yes = 5 No = 0 _____	5' 1"	143
		5' 2"	147
		5' 3"	152
4. I am 65 years old or older.	Yes = 9 No = 0 _____	5' 4"	157
		5' 5"	162
5. I am a woman who has had a baby weighing more than nine pounds at birth.	Yes = 1 No = 0 _____	5' 6"	167
		5' 7"	172
		5' 8"	177
6. I have a sister or a brother with diabetes.	Yes = 1 No = 0 _____	5' 9"	182
		5' 10"	188
		5' 11"	193
7. I have a parent with diabetes.	Yes = 1 No = 0 _____	6' 0"	199
		6' 1"	204
Total		6' 2"	210
		6' 3"	216
		6' 4"	221

Scoring: 3–9 points

You are probably at low risk now, but you may be at higher risk in the future. New guidelines recommend that everyone age 45 and over be tested for the disease every three years. (People at high risk should consider being tested at a younger age.)

Scoring: 10 or more points

You could be at high risk for diabetes. See your doctor soon and be tested.

©1998, American Diabetes Association.

If you weigh the same as or more than the amount listed for your height, you may be at risk for diabetes. The chart shows unhealthy weights for men and women age 35 or older at the listed heights. At-risk weights are lower for individuals under age 35.

immunosuppressant drugs may be used to prevent rejection.

Prevention: the goal. Despite the promise of these new treatment approaches, costly and complex therapies like transplants and implants are likely to benefit only the most affluent patients and those capable of understanding and following complicated treatment regimens. Of potentially greater consequence to millions are efforts to determine whether the disease can be prevented or delayed. Two important clinical trials, both sponsored by the National Institutes of Health, are testing prevention strategies for the two types of diabetes. The first is examining whether the use of insulin by people at greatest risk of type 1 diabetes—but not yet diagnosed with the disease—can prevent it from developing. The second trial is exploring whether intensive lifestyle modification (diet and exercise) or metformin can prevent or delay type 2 diabetes in highly susceptible individuals.

IGNORANCE *ISN'T* BLISS

Of the 15.7 million Americans who have diabetes today, 5.4 million are unaware that they have the disease. But ignorance, in this case, is not bliss; even when undiagnosed, diabetes can harm the eyes, kidneys, nerves, blood vessels, and heart. Because type 2 disease may be symptomless in its early stages, a person can have blood sugar levels in a diabetic range for many years before medical problems prompt him or her to visit the doctor. In the meantime, vital body systems are undergoing hidden damage.

Clearly then, public awareness is one of the keys to preventing a diabetes "epidemic." Public education campaigns and screening programs can reach the most vulnerable members of the population—people in susceptible minority groups, overweight individuals, those with a family history of diabetes, the elderly,

Nearly one person in five in the fast-growing over-65 age group has diabetes—and many may not even know it. Identifying those not yet diagnosed is a clear priority.

Of the 15.7 million Americans who have diabetes today, 5.4 million are unaware that they have the disease.

Too much food and too little physical activity—the party can't go on forever.

Michael S. Green—AP/Wide World

and women who have given birth to babies weighing more than 4.1 kilograms (9 pounds). (The birth of a larger-than-normal infant is often a sign of maternal high blood glucose levels.) By finding undiagnosed cases and identifying people at risk, such initiatives could save millions of lives.

In addition to its cost in human suffering, diabetes care alone now costs the American economy $98 billion annually. Some 15% of U.S. health care resources are spent on persons with diabetes each year, and diabetes care accounts for roughly 27% of the Medicare budget. Not surprisingly, given the current pressures to control health care costs, these numbers are beginning to attract the attention of policy makers. In 1997 the balanced-budget agreement included $2.4 billion to fight diabetes. On July 1, 1998, Medicare began, for the first time, to cover the costs of supplies for blood sugar monitoring (lancets, glucose meters, and test strips) for all eligible individuals, as well as paying for outpatient training in diabetes self-management. Awareness is growing on Capitol Hill that these expenditures not only improve quality of life but also make good fiscal sense.

AN AVOIDABLE EPIDEMIC

If current trends continue, at some point in the next century more than a million Americans a year could be developing diabetes. By 2050 more than 50 million could have the disease.

What can each of us do? "We can't control our family history, we can't control our genes, we can't control our aging," says Vinicor. "But if we control our weight and our physical activity levels, the evidence is increasingly convincing—although we have to await the results of the trials—that we might be able to prevent type 2 diabetes. Likewise, through clinical trials, we may learn how to prevent type 1."

So the die is not yet cast. New technologies and medications, public education campaigns, population screening programs, trials of prevention strategies, and basic scientific research all offer hope that diabetes can be controlled and a potential "epidemic" averted.

FOR FURTHER INFORMATION

Books

American Diabetes Association Complete Guide to Diabetes. New York: American Diabetes Association/Bantam Books, 1996.

Beaser, Richard S., M.D., with Hill, Joan V.C., R.D., and the Joslin Education Committee. *The Joslin Guide to Diabetes: A Program for Managing Your Treatment.* New York: Fireside, 1995.

Organizations

American Diabetes Association
http://www.diabetes.org
CDC Division of Diabetes Translation
http://www.cdc.gov/diabetes
Department of Veterans Affairs
http://www.va.gov/health/diabetes

NO MAN IS AN ISLAND

BY PETER HARRIGAN

© 1998, EB, Inc.

Picture a tropical island in the Pacific. The sun is shining; coconut palms sway in the breeze. The average daily temperature hovers around 26.7° C (80° F). The lifestyle is carefree and relaxed. The inhabitants are members of close, caring extended families that have lived in this same familiar place for generations. Now imagine that nearly half of these people are suffering from a disease that will eventually cause severe disability or early death, and many are already either blind or missing a foot as a result of complications of that disease.

Such is life on Nauru, a 21-square kilometer (8.1-square mile) island republic in the southwestern Pacific with a population of just over 10,000. And Nauru is not alone in having an exceptionally high rate of diabetes and its often deadly complications. For as-yet-unknown reasons, the indigenous peoples of the Polynesian and Micronesian regions seem to be especially prone to diabetes, a disorder that is strongly influenced by genetic predisposition but is helped along by diet and other lifestyle factors. In some populations in the Western Pacific, 40–50% of adults have type 2 diabetes.

What is special about the people of Nauru is that they are now in a unique position to contribute to the scientific understanding of the disease and, perhaps, to improve the lives of people everywhere who suffer from it. The Nauruan government and the International Diabetes Institute (IDI), based in Melbourne, Australia, have agreed to cooperate in a genetic study that may provide valuable information about the specific role of genes in diabetes.

Lush tropical vegetation surrounds the Buada Lagoon, a shallow, inland body of water some 1,600 meters (about one mile) from the western coast of Nauru. The interior of the island is now largely deforested.

Bryan and Cherry Alexander

Nauruan women after Sunday church services. Since the 1950s the population of this tiny island has experienced soaring rates of diabetes.

Nauru: a brief history

For centuries Nauru was isolated both geographically and culturally. The inhabitants enjoyed the kind of idyllic existence dreamed about by dwellers in less-hospitable climes. Their isolation ended, however, with the "discovery" of the island by Europeans in 1798. Extensive contact with outsiders did not begin until the 1830s, when Nauru became a port of call for whaling ships. Missionaries and traders followed soon after, which led to an increasingly sedentary lifestyle for many of the islanders, who became clerks, salespeople, and teachers. In 1888, with German commercial interests growing, Nauru became part of Germany's Marshall Islands protectorate. In the 20th century the island was a mandate first of the League of Nations and later of the United Nations. It became independent in 1968.

The traditional Nauruan diet consisted largely of fish like tuna, bonita, and Spanish mackerel; black noddies, quail, and other birds; coconuts; and fruit. A trend toward dependence on nontraditional foods began around 1920, when German traders began to import canned salmon, sugar, rice, ships' biscuits (a sort of hard, dry cracker), beer, and tobacco. Conducting medical research on the island in the mid-1920s, C.W. Bray, an Australian physician, noted a high infant mortality rate, a lack of stamina in adults, and an unusual susceptibility of Nauruans to disease, all of which he attributed to abandonment of the native diet.

The event that was forever to change Nauru's physical environment and social fabric was the discovery of abundant deposits of phosphates, valuable as fertilizer. A British firm began strip mining in 1907, and the mining, processing, and export of phosphates have been the mainstay of the island's economy ever since. As a result of phosphate wealth, the per capita income of Nauru is among the highest in the world. This economic success has been tempered, however, by the destruction of the island's natural vegetation and other kinds of intrusions into traditional ways. Today more than 80% of Nauruans' food is imported, and, on average, 56% of the people are overweight.

Legacy of "Coca-colonization"?

Studies of the disproportionate rate of diabetes in the indigenous peoples of the Pacific have implicated "Coca-colonization"—the Westernization of lifestyle and, especially, diet—as the chief cause. In one long-term study, scientists from the IDI and the health department of Western Samoa (now Samoa) sought to discover the reason for the increasing incidence of diabetes in that island nation. (Samoa is about 3,200 kilometers [2,000 miles] southeast of Nauru and has a population of about 169,000.) They concluded that a single overarching factor—obesity—was responsible, especially in the more rural areas of the country. Increased consumption of fat, refined carbohydrates, alcohol, and total calories all played a part in the Samoans' weight gain, the researchers found, as did declining levels of physical activity.

Difficult as it may be for most Americans to comprehend, obesity was traditionally encouraged in many Pacific island cultures. Paul Hambruch, a German ethnologist who visited Nauru in the early 20th century, wrote, "Corpulence was fostered as it was exquisite to be big and fat." Nonetheless, diabetes was virtually nonexistent there prior to 1954. By the late 1980s, however, 32% of Nauruans 20 years of age or older had diabetes—nearly eight times the prevalence in Europe and Australia.

Despite decades of research into the causes of diabetes, the relative influence of genes and lifestyle remains a matter of debate. Paul Zimmet, director of the IDI, believes that genetics plays the bigger part in the development of diabetes in indigenous peoples but that environmental factors act as a precipitating cause. "If Pacific islanders have a proven genetic predisposition but lead a natural, traditional lifestyle," he says, "they won't get diabetes." It is only when these people make the transition to an urbanized environment, he explains, that lifestyle changes trigger their genetic susceptibility to the disease. In Zimmet's view, though, the important question is not the degree to which genetics is involved but rather which genes are functioning abnormally—and in what way—to cause diabetes. Answering these questions will be a complex process—a matter, he says, of "sorting out about 40 or 50 different genetic causes."

A unique study

The ideal "laboratory" in which to investigate the contribution of genetic factors would be a geographically discrete population with a disproportionately high incidence of diabetes—in other words, a population like that of Nauru. In 1997 Zimmet and his colleagues at the IDI concluded an agreement with the government of Nauru that will allow them to conduct a genetic analysis of the islanders. (At the time of this writing, negotiations were also under way to launch similar studies in Samoa and its neighbor to the south, Tonga.)

Zimmet, who has been medical adviser to the Nauruan government since 1975, has already collected blood samples from more than 1,000 people. These samples will provide the genetic material to be used in the study. The analysis will be conducted by him and others at the IDI, possibly with assistance from geneticists at the University of Melbourne. The results of this research are expected to be available in about five years.

This forbidding, stony landscape is all that remains on much of the island after a century of strip mining.

Who stands to benefit? If specific genes are identified as responsible for the high incidence of diabetes in Nauruans, a screening test could be developed and used to identify those islanders at greatest risk. And if the study were to yield a method for altering the diabetes-causing genes, the Nauruan government would receive royalties from the sale of the therapy. The knowledge acquired might even have universal application, enabling scientists to determine whether an individual is genetically predisposed to diabetes and, possibly, to prevent the disease from developing. If the study yields the results scientists hope for, it will be a win-win situation for all involved.

Peter Harrigan *is a freelance medical and science writer in Pennant Hills, New South Wales, Australia, and a regular contributor to the "News" section of the British journal* The Lancet. *He is also a registered clinical psychologist.*

A KIWIFRUIT A DAY . . .

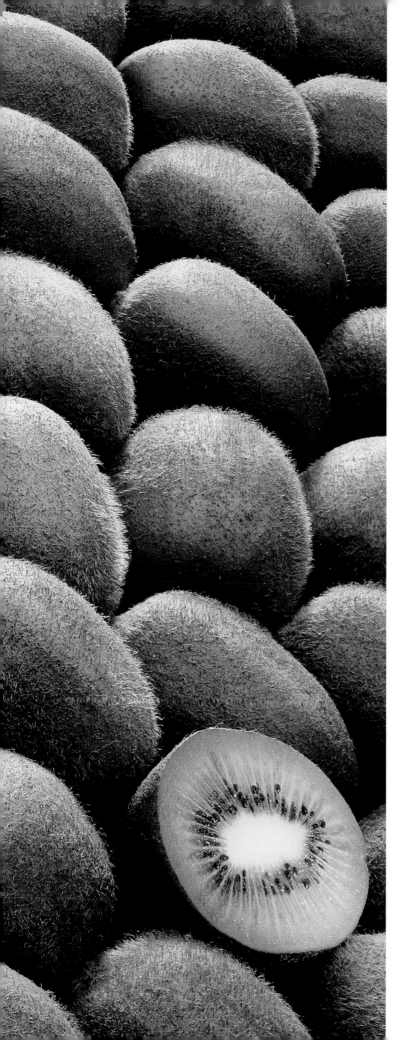

BY SUSAN M. KLEINER, PH.D., R.D., C.N.S., F.A.C.N.

When the oranges are golden, physicians' faces grow pale.
—Japanese proverb

Fruits are the most spiritually beneficial of all foods.
—Paramahansa Yogananda (1893–1952), Indian yogi and founder of the Self-Realization Fellowship

How often does someone (besides your mother) tell you that you need to eat *more* of anything? Whereas the message to *eliminate* or *decrease* saturated fat, calories, sugar, salt, alcohol, and caffeine has become firmly embedded in the public consciousness, the advice to *add* more fruits to our daily intake doesn't seem to have reached us.

191

Plump, dark-purple, California-grown table grapes are covered with a whitish natural bloom that keeps moisture in and protects them from decay. Grapes are among the many fruits believed to contain substances that may protect against cancer.

Susan M. Kleiner is a registered dietitian; owner of High Performance Nutrition, Mercer Island, Washington, a firm that provides private-practice nutritional consulting to athletes, sports teams, media, and industry; a health and nutrition writer and columnist for medical journals, newsletters, and trade publications; and Affiliate Assistant Professor, Nutrition Science Program, University of Washington, Seattle.

In fact, fruit—ideally four to five servings a day—may be the best medicine money can buy.

In the fall of 1991, the National Cancer Institute and the Produce for Better Health Foundation initiated the 5 A Day for Better Health Program, recommending a minimum of five servings of fruits and vegetables every day. That advice is echoed in most international and national dietary guidelines. Why, then, doesn't fruit play a more important role in most people's diets? Recent surveys suggest that barely 23% of American adults meet the five-a-day fruit and vegetable standard, with most eating only three and a half servings each day, only one of which consists of fruit. Likewise, the majority of children consume less than a serving a day; only one in 14 youngsters aged 2–18 consumes two or more servings.

CORNUCOPIA OF BENEFITS

Fruit is generally characterized as the edible product of a plant or tree that includes the seed and its envelope.

Along with being sweet and tasty, fruits are packed with substances that enhance health. More than any other food group, fruits offer a dense package of nutrients with few calories and virtually no fat. The average fruit serving has only 60 calories, and most fruits contain less than 1% fat (avocados, with a whopping 30 grams of fat in a medium-sized fruit, are a notable exception).

The greater-than-70% water content of most fruits makes them juicy and refreshing; the natural sugar in fruit, fructose, gives these low-calorie foods a degree of sweetness that most of us desire. Fruits, which are typically high in carbohydrates (although this varies with the type of fruit and its maturity), are excellent sources of vitamin C (ascorbic acid). (Citrus fruits are the best-known sources of vitamin C, but there are many other good sources, including kiwifruit, papaya, and strawberries.) Other important micronutrients found abundantly in fruit are beta-carotene (a chemical that converts to vitamin A in the body), folate, vitamin E, potassium, and magnesium. Each of these nutrients plays a critical role in the promotion of health and the prevention of disease.

Fruits also contain substantial amounts of the important nonnutritive food factors fiber and phytochemicals. Fiber enhances the digestive process, stimulates bowel movements, lowers cholesterol, and has a positive influence on blood sugar levels. Phytochemicals (*phyto* comes from the Greek word for "plant") have been shown to influence the body's biochemistry in numerous subtle but health-protective ways. In the race to find ways to reduce the risk of chronic diseases like heart disease and cancer, both fiber and phytochemicals are receiving major research attention.

FRUIT AND OBESITY

That fruit is an important component of any diet is increasingly clear. It seems intuitive that fruit should be especially important in diets for losing or controlling weight. Research indeed bears this out. To better understand the impact of diet on weight and body mass, investigators in Spain looked at the differences between the diets of elderly individuals who were overweight and elderly people of normal weight. Their surprising finding was that there was

Most fruits contain less than 1% fat.

no difference in caloric intake between the two groups. Those in the overweight/obese group, however, ate more of their calories as protein and less as carbohydrates compared with those in the normal-weight group. In food terms meat was a primary staple

in the diets of the overweight, whereas fruits figured substantially in the diets of normal-weight Spaniards.

Pectin: natural weight-loss aid. Aside from its role as a nutrient-dense, low-calorie food, fruit includes a component that appears to have a role in promoting weight loss. Pectin, a type of fiber in complex carbohydrates that is found in the cell walls of many fruits, has long been used by the food industry as a thickening and gelling agent, a texturizer, an emulsifier, and a stabilizer. Those who make their own fresh-fruit jams and jellies also use pectin (a variety that has sugar added to it).

In 1997 researchers published the results of a study that found that significant amounts of pectin in the diet, which is not absorbed by the human digestive tract, can have a number of desirable physiological effects. These include: decreasing serum cholesterol levels, moderating the natural rise in blood sugar following a meal (in both diabetic and normal subjects), delaying the rate at which the stomach empties, and increasing satiety levels in obese persons.

A fruit stall in Barcelona. A study of the diets of elderly people in Spain found that normal-weight individuals ate substantially more fruit than did their overweight counterparts.

Because of its apparent impact on blood glucose levels, stomach-emptying time, and satiety, pectin makes the eater feel full longer and therefore seems to diminish appetite. Food manufacturers have begun to use this natural food constituent as a fat or sugar replacer in processed low-calorie foods such as salad dressing and frozen desserts. Pure pectin powder (available at health-food stores) mixed with orange juice appears to be a useful complement to a sound weight-loss program that includes exercise and a reduced-calorie diet. Apple pomace (pulp from which the juice has been extracted) and citrus peels are the main sources of commercially available pectins. Good dietary sources are bananas, beets, lemon pulp, passion fruit rind, papaya, and guava.

Too much of a good thing. Even though fruits and fruit juices play an

Fruit juices are a highly concentrated source of calories; one cup of orange juice has about the same number of calories as two whole oranges. Most young children would be better off eating more whole fruit and drinking fruit juices only in very limited amounts.

important role in the diets of children as well as adults, too much of a good thing can be harmful. Recent studies have linked the consumption of large amounts of fruit juice by preschool-aged children to obesity (as well as short stature). Fruit juices are a concentrated source of calories. One cup of orange juice or apple juice contains about 120 calories, whereas one whole orange or apple contains just 60 calories. And though fruits are excellent sources of certain nutrients, their juices do not contain the same array of nutrients available in milk, another essential food in the diets of children. Youngsters who

drink large quantities of juice, and do so in place of milk, tend to get limited amounts of the important substances that are found in milk and are essential for growth—namely, calcium, phosphorus, riboflavin, vitamins A and D, and protein.

As a general rule, the American College of Nutrition recommends that toddlers and young children drink less than one and one-half cups (12 fluid ounces) of juice per day. They should also be encouraged to consume two to three one-cup servings of milk daily—fat-free (at 80 calories per cup) or low-fat (at 120 calories). To quench thirst throughout the rest of the day, kids, like adults, should drink water.

FRUIT AND DISEASE

There is a reason we are being told to eat more fruits and vegetables. Study after study has shown that apples—as well as oranges, melons, berries, and virtually every other fruit—*do* keep the doctor away!

Citrus fruits are especially important protectors against disease. Their high vitamin-C content may help protect cell membranes and DNA from oxidative damage. (Oxidation is a normal metabolic process that can lead to cancerous changes, accelerate the aging process, and contribute to heart disease and degenerative diseases like arthritis.) In addition to acting as an antioxidant, vitamin C may help prevent cancer through its ability to scavenge nitrites and

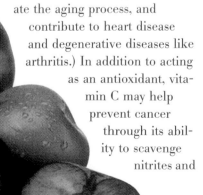

block the formation of nitrosamine, a potentially carcinogenic substance. (Nitrites are chemical additives commonly used as curing agents in meats; during cooking at high temperatures, nitrites combine with amines to form nitrosamines, which are known to cause cancer in laboratory animals.) One of the well-established functions of vitamin C is collagen synthesis; collagen is an insoluble fibrous protein that is the chief constituent of connective tissue and is also found in bones. In promoting collagen synthesis, vitamin C may hinder tumor formation and growth.

Citrus fruits also contain coumarin and D-limonene, phytochemicals that have been shown to increase the activity of glutathione transferase, an enzyme that enables the body to rid itself of toxic substances. There are about 20 carotenoids, another type of phytochemical, in citrus fruits. Carotenoids are the pigments that give certain fruits and vegetables their red, yellow, or orange color and are associated with a reduced risk of cancer, heart disease, and age-related macular degeneration, a leading cause of blindness in people over the age of 65. Pink grapefruit contains a high level of the carotenoid lycopene, the reddish pigment abundant in tomatoes, which has shown significant antitumor activity (particularly against prostate cancer).

Cancer. Does just eating more fruit reduce the risk of developing cancer? Yes! An analysis of 156 dietary studies published in the *Journal of the American Dietetic Association* in 1996 found that fruit and vegetable consumption provided significant protection against many cancers (at least 25 types). In fact, people who ate greater amounts of fruits and vegetables had about one-half the risk of getting cancer of those who

Before they are packed for commercial distribution, grapefruits are sprayed with wax and yeast, which helps maintain freshness. The antioxidants in citrus fruits reduce the risk of heart disease and stroke.

ate little fruit. Numerous studies have shown that a high fruit intake is associated with a reduced risk of lung cancer, the most common cause of cancer death in the United States in both men and women. There is also especially convincing evidence showing that fruit eaters are better protected against stomach cancer than non-fruit eaters. Citrus fruits in particular have been consistently shown to be protective against cancers of the stomach, esophagus, mouth, and pharynx. Against breast cancer, which strikes one in nine women, the data clearly show that high fruit consumption is protective. A study of 2,400 Greek women showed that those with the highest intakes of fruit (six servings per day) had a 35% lower risk of breast cancer than women who ate the least fruit (fewer than two servings per day).

Cardiovascular disease. The disease-prevention power of fruit does not stop with cancer. As noted above, people with high levels of carotenoids in their blood have a reduced risk of heart disease. Several studies have shown that the risk of heart disease decreases with increasing consumption of vitamin C, carotenoids, and citrus fruits. One study

showed that men with a low intake of vitamin C and beta-carotene were two to four times as likely to develop heart disease and stroke as those whose antioxidant consumption from fruits and vegetables was adequate. Anthocyanins—water-soluble orange-red, crimson, and blue pigments found in many fruits, such as strawberries, cherries, cranberries, raspberries, blueberries, grapes, and black currants—inhibit cholesterol synthesis and thereby protect against

Citrus fruits are especially important protectors against disease.

cardiovascular disease. Epidemiological studies suggest that disease risk is lowest in people eating an average of at least 5 kilograms (11 pounds) of citrus fruit per year.

Hypertension. Potassium, magnesium, and calcium have all been credited with having potential blood-

An orange grove in California's San Joaquin Valley. Fruit-farm workers who eat large amounts of the crops they pick (especially citrus fruits) have a lower incidence of gum disease than workers on grain farms, who eat little fruit.

blood pressure significantly within two weeks (without the use of any blood-pressure-lowering medications). The DASH "combination diet" basically doubled the 5-a-day goal, so subjects ate at least 10 servings of fruits and vegetables every day.

Diabetes. People often think that because persons with diabetes have trouble controlling their blood sugar, they should not eat fruit, a source of sugar. This is entirely wrong. In fact, the natural sugars in fruit and fruit juices raise blood sugar levels less than many refined, starchy carbohydrate foods. Clinical studies have shown that fructose consumption by those with type 2 (non-insulin-dependent) diabetes results in either improved or unchanged metabolic control of blood sugar. The combination of fructose, a sugar that is metabolized slowly, and pectin, which slows digestion and absorption of food, makes whole fresh fruit an ideal component of the diabetic diet.

Gum disease. Eating fruit also affects dental health. A study that compared the periodontal (gum) status of workers on fruit farms, who ate lots of fruit on a regular basis, with that of workers on grain farms (who ate relatively little fruit) found that fruit consumption had a decid-

pressure-lowering effects; fruit is a rich source of the first two minerals. A landmark study published in *The New England Journal of Medicine* (April 17, 1997) showed that eating the right foods can lower blood pressure as efficiently as drugs. Known as Dietary Approaches to Stop Hypertension (DASH), this clinical trial enrolled 459 men and

women volunteers of various ethnic backgrounds with normal, high-normal, or high blood pressure. Subjects within all blood-pressure ranges who consumed a diet containing twice the amounts of fruits, vegetables, and low-fat dairy products in the typical American diet and less than half the saturated fat eaten by most Americans were able to lower

edly beneficial effect on oral tissues. Those who consumed large amounts of a variety of fruits had a low incidence of periodontal disease, whereas farm workers who consumed especially large amounts of mainly citrus fruits had by far the lowest incidence. The highest incidence of gum disease was seen in the grain-farm workers eating the least fruit.

WINNERS AND LOSERS

Who's eating enough fruit? Who's not? Certain groups of people tend to fare considerably better than others when it comes to fruit consumption.

Vegetarians. Just because a person is a vegetarian does not mean that he or she eats the recommended number of servings of fruit every day. Nonetheless, vegetarians appear to have the best fruit-consumption record. A British study followed the diets and lifestyles of 11,000 health-conscious people over a 17-year period. Forty-three percent of the subjects were vegetarian; 38% ate nuts or dried fruit daily; and 77% ate fresh fruit daily. Most of the subjects also ate whole-grain bread and salad daily, and only 19% smoked. This highly health-conscious group had a death rate that was about half that of the general population. When all the variables were considered statistically, the single most influential factor was daily fruit consumption! Low death rates from heart disease, cerebro-vascular disease, and indeed "all causes" correlated highly with eating fresh fruit on a daily basis.

Highly active people. Athletes and those who are extremely physically active are usually able to eat significantly more than their sedentary counterparts without gaining weight. But being an athlete does not mean that a person will make the right nutritional choices. In the 3rd century AD, Diogenes Laertius wrote that Greek athletes trained on "dried figs, moist cheese, and wheat," and other records suggest that the earliest Greek and Roman Olympians included plenty of fruit in their training diets.

Today experts in the science of sports nutrition recommend that competitive athletes eat diets high in carbohydrate, moderate in protein, and low in fat and including lots of fresh fruits and vegetables. At the 1997 Olympic Games in Atlanta, Georgia, more than five million meals that fit that bill were served to competitors. The menus included an abundance of fruit at every meal.

Whole fresh fruit [is] an ideal component of the diabetic diet.

Adolescents. Since chronic diseases usually take many years to develop, it is important that youngsters, as well as adults, eat diets rich in fruits and vegetables. Surveys of high-school students in the United States show that just like their parents, adolescents are eating inadequate amounts of fruits and vegetables. A study published in 1996 in the journal *Preventive Medicine* found that between one-third and one-half of high-school students reported that they did not eat *any* fruit on the day preceding the survey. Nearly twice as many students from lower socioeconomic backgrounds reported inadequate fruit consumption as did those of higher socioeconomic status.

Cultural background. Culture and upbringing can have considerable influence on our diets. Among the adolescents surveyed in the study referred to above, fruit and vegetable consumption varied widely according to ethnic group. African-Americans on the whole had the poorest vegetable consumption but ate plenty of fruit. Native Americans had the lowest fruit consumption. Asian Americans fared the best of any ethnic group, consuming adequate amounts of both fruits and vegetables. Gender and age differences appeared to play little or no role in the adolescents' consumption patterns; however, other factors that were associated with better fruit and vegetable intake were high academic achievement and greater family connectedness.

Europeans. When European diets are studied, distinct northern and southern eating patterns emerge. The southern (Mediterranean) diet appears to be the most healthful and in closest agreement with current dietary guidelines. The diets of people from the southern regions of France, Italy, Portugal, and Spain contain adequate but not excessive calories and are rich in grains, vegetables, fruits, lean meat, and olive oil. On the whole, southern Europeans have a low intake of animal products, saturated fat, and "luxury" breads (primarily those made with refined flour). By contrast, the food pattern in northern Europe resembles that of younger and older adults in most industrialized countries, consisting of a fair but not especially high intake of vegetables and fruits but a relatively high consumption of animal products, which results in a diet that is high in fat content.

PRACTICAL ADVICE FOR THE CONFUSED

Most people these days are concerned about the safety of the food that they serve to others and eat themselves. Fruits are a special concern. Where were the fruits grown? Under what conditions? What pesticides were used, and how safe or potentially harmful are they? Has fruit juice been pasteurized or refrigerated to eliminate the risks of bacterial contamination? And finally, is organic fruit better?

Fear of chemicals. Most of the fruits consumed by the general population are not organic—*i.e.*, they are grown in chemically fertilized soil

Comparing Apples and Oranges: A Nutrient Scorecard

Fresh fruit serving: 100 grams (3.2 ounces)	Nutrient index (Daily Value per 100 grams)	Calories per nutrient
Kiwifruit	16	3.8
Papaya	14	2.8
Cantaloupe	13	2.6
Strawberries	12	2.5
Mango	11	5.9
Lemon	11	2.5
Orange (Florida)	11	4.2
Red currants	10	5.7
Mandarin orange	9	5.1
Avocado	8	20.9
Tangerine	8	5.2
Grapefruit	7	4.3
Lime	7	4.3
Apricot	7	7.3
Raspberries	7	6.4
Honeydew melon	6	6.0
Pineapple	5	10.2
Persimmon	5	14.6
Grapes (Empress)	4	17.9
Blueberries	4	14.0
Plum	4	13.4
Banana	4	22.4
Watermelon	3	9.4
Peach	3	13.4
Nectarine	3	15.3
Cherries	3	21.0
Pear	2	32.8
Apple with peel	2	32.8

Source: Paul A. Lachance and A. Elizabeth Sloan, "A Nutritional Assessment of Major Fruits."

198

Photographs, Agricultural Research Service/USDA

and treated with approved pesticides. Organic produce, by contrast, is grown in chemical-free animal manure or compost, and synthetic chemical pesticides are not used. In the U.S. the use of chemicals for growing food is closely regulated on today's farms. New pesticides undergo strict testing over many years before they are used in mass produce production. Whereas there is some reason to be concerned about older chemicals registered before 1970, when less-stringent testing conditions were permitted, studies assessing pesticide residues in produce grown in the U.S. show that the levels are virtually always well below the maximum allowable levels for adults established by the Department of Agriculture (USDA).

On the other hand, there had long been unanswered questions regarding the appropriate levels of chemicals in foods consumed by children. The Food Quality Protection Act of 1996, however, placed strict limits on the amounts of pesticide residues allowed in foods consumed by infants and children. "If a pesticide poses a danger to our children," said Pres. Bill Clinton upon signing the bill into law, "then it won't be in our food."

As to the nutrient content of organic versus nonorganic fruit, there is no difference. In the end, the

Most of the fruits consumed by the general population are not organic.

consumer must make his or her own choice. Organic products are less widely available than nonorganic and often are more expensive. Populations that eat large amounts of fruits and vegetables grown in the standard way—with chemicals—have lower rates of cancers and other chronic diseases. All things considered, fruits, regardless of the farming method, should be a major component of everyone's diet.

When one purchases traditionally grown produce, it is wise to follow these guidelines for reducing pesticide residues:

- Wash fresh produce (including citrus fruits and melons) with a scrub brush, and rinse thoroughly under running water.
- Use a knife to peel oranges and grapefruits; do not bite into the peel.
- Peel waxed fruit; waxes don't wash off and can seal in pesticide residues.
- Peel fruits such as apples, when appropriate. (Peeling removes pesticides that remain in or on the peel; on the other hand, it also removes fiber, vitamins, and minerals.)

Food-poisoning fears. Contrary to popular belief, animal products are not the only source of food poisoning. Recently, there have been several well-publicized outbreaks of food poisoning from bacterially contaminated fruit juices, raspberries, and strawberries. These outbreaks spurred considerable debate over regulatory issues.

An outbreak of *Escherichia coli* O157:H7 in late 1996 was traced to unpasteurized organic apple juice. It is clear that pathogens can survive in fruit juices, and there is no doubt that the process of pasteurization virtually eliminates the risk of bacterial contamination. Although nonpasteurized fruit juices may taste

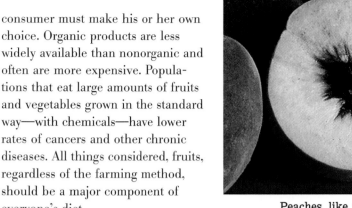

Peaches, like most fruits, should be scrubbed with a brush and rinsed under running water to remove pesticide residues.

Not All Fruits Are Created Equal

Best Sources of Nutrients and Fiber

Vitamin C	Potassium
Kiwifruit[1]	Avocado[1]
Papaya[1]	Banana[2]
Strawberries[1]	Kiwifruit[2]
Lemon[1]	Cantaloupe[2]
Orange[1]	Apricot[2]

Vitamin A	Vitamin E
Mango[1]	Avocado[1]
Cantaloupe[1]	Mango[2]
Apricot[1]	Kiwifruit[2]
Persimmon[1]	Cherries[2]
Tangerine[2]	Apricot[2]
Mandarin orange[2]	Nectarine[2]

Folate	Magnesium
Avocado[1]	Avocado[2]
Papaya[2]	Kiwifruit[2]
Honeydew melon[2]	Banana[2]

Dietary fiber
Raspberries[1]
Red currants[1]
Avocado[1]
Persimmon[1]
Kiwifruit[2]

[1] Fruit meets Food and Drug Administration (FDA) definition for "excellent source" based on 140-gram (5-ounce) reference serving.

[2] Fruit meets FDA definition for "good source" based on 140-gram reference serving

Source: Paul A. Lachance and A. Elizabeth Sloan, "A Nutritional Assessment of Major Fruits."

slightly better, the difference is not worth the risk. Before purchasing or drinking apple cider, it is always wise to ascertain that it has been pasteurized. Health officials in the U.S. are now considering legislation requiring the pasteurization of all fresh fruit and vegetable juices.

Produce grown outside the U.S. is not required to meet USDA standards. And though some imported produce from Central and South America is checked for contamination at the border, this is not always the case; moreover, border checks are not foolproof. In 1996, 900 people in 11 states and Canada fell victim to a gastrointestinal disorder attributed to what was then a little-known organism, *Cyclospora cayetanensis;* investigators traced the infection to raspberries grown in Guatemala. In April and May 1997, raspberries from Guatemala and Chile were implicated in a series of cyclosporiasis outbreaks in New York, California, Nevada, and Texas.

Many of these issues and concerns are only partially within our control. But one very important one—how food is handled once it has reached our kitchens—is completely in our hands. The most common source of food poisoning is poor sanitation on the part of the preparer. In addition to washing hands before preparing any kind of food, one should follow several other safe-food-handling guidelines:

- Store partially used canned goods, including juices, in glass or plastic containers.
- Keep hot foods hot and cold foods cold.
- The "danger zone" of 15.6°–51.7° C (60°–125° F) allows rapid growth of bacteria and production of toxins. Foods should never be kept in this

zone for more than two or three hours.
- Throw out foods that show signs of mold.
- When traveling in less-industrialized countries, always peel raw fruits and vegetables and avoid any

Nutritionally, one can get the most bang for the buck by choosing a variety of fruits.

kind of raw vegetable salads, since the water used to wash the vegetables may be contaminated. The safest practice for travelers is to consume only cooked foods.

Potent combinations. Far too few people taking prescription drugs for common conditions know about possible interactions between the medications they take and the foods they eat. Interactions between drugs and foods, however, are by no means uncommon. Pharmacists are the most likely to know about them; often the doctors who prescribe the medications do not. Citrus juices in general and grapefruit juice in particular are notorious for causing

Water-soluble reddish pigments called anthocyanins, found in cherries and virtually all berries, may help protect against cardiovascular disease.

inadvertent drug overdoses. Numerous studies have shown that grapefruit juice greatly enhances the body's ability to absorb certain drugs. The drugs known to interact in this way with grapefruit juice include amlodipine, caffeine, cortisol, coumarin, cyclosporine, diltiazem, 17B-estradiol, felodipine, midazolam, nimodipine, nifedipine, nitrendipine, nisoldipine, terfenadine, theophylline, triazolam, and verapamil. In 1998 researchers identified compounds called furanocoumarins in grapefruit, which they suspect are responsible for the adverse drug reactions.

Among the symptoms that have been attributed to the so-called grapefruit juice effect are dizziness, facial flushing, accelerated heart rate, headache, and drowsiness. People taking any of the above medications should avoid doing so with citrus juice. Because at least one study suggested that grapefruit juice consumed as long as 24 hours before taking a medication may enhance the drug's effect, it would be wise for these people to avoid citrus juices altogether.

IT BEATS A TWINKIE

Although eating any fruit is better than eating no fruit, fruits are not all created equal. The five-a-day program and the USDA's Food Guide Pyramid consistently advise two to four servings of fruit each day, but these recommendations do not specify which fruits to eat. To help people select the most nutritious fruits, Paul

Lachance, professor of food science, Cook College–Rutgers University, New Brunswick, New Jersey, and A. Elizabeth Sloan, president of Applied Biometrics, Stuart, Florida, developed a rating system for 28 popular fresh fruits. They based their ratings on two parameters of nutrient density: (1) a Daily Value per 100 grams (DV/100g) of nine nutritional factors (namely, protein, total vitamin A, thiamine, riboflavin, niacin, folate, vitamin C, calcium, and iron) and (2) calories per nutrient (the "cost" in calories to deliver 1% of each of the nine nutrients). Kiwifruit was number one on their list, followed by papayas, cantaloupes, strawberries, mangoes, oranges, lemons, red currants, Mandarin oranges, and avocados. (*See* table, page 198, for entire list.)

The Center for Science in the Public Interest (CSPI) recently did its own evaluation of fruits, including fresh, canned, dried, and frozen varieties, which was published in the *Nutrition Action Healthletter*, May 1998. To arrive at its scores for 47 fruits, the CSPI added up the percentage of the DV of seven dietary constituents (vitamin C, folate, potassium, calcium, iron, fiber, and carotenoids). The top 10 fruits on its list were: guavas, watermelons, pink or red grapefruit, kiwifruit, papayas, cantaloupes, dried apricots, oranges, strawberries, and fresh apricots. At the bottom of the list were raisins, fruit cocktail, canned pears, sweetened cranberry sauce, and unsweetened applesauce. Despite its precise ratings for fruits, the CSPI's "bottom line" message was that "*any* fruit is better than no fruit....Even the lowest-scoring fruit beats a Low Fat Twinkie, hands down."

> # The more fruit we eat, the greater our chances are of staying healthy and fit for a lifetime.

GETTING THE MOST FROM FRUIT

Storing fruits correctly will make a huge difference in how long they stay fresh and how good they taste. Since most fruit is shipped unripe, it needs to stay out of the refrigerator until it has ripened. To speed ripening, fruit can be placed in a closed paper bag on a kitchen counter (and checked for ripening progress daily); the gases that collect in the bag promote ripening. Once ripe, fruits (bananas excepted) should be refrigerated.

Loss of nutrients can be minimized by following these simple rules:

- Always purchase fresh produce.
- Store fruit whole rather than cut up.
- Never soak fruit in water for extended periods of time.
- When peeling and paring a piece of fruit, remove as little as possible.
- Refrigerate precut fruit (*e.g.*, a quarter or half a melon), and make

sure it is stored in an airtight wrapper or container.

- Defrost frozen fruit in a microwave oven to minimize the loss of water-soluble nutrients.
- To minimize the amount of surface area exposed to water, cook fruit in large pieces and use just enough water to prevent scorching. When not stirring, keep the pan covered.

There is no question that raw whole fruit is the most nutritious form. But fresh fruit may not always be available, or it might not be a practical choice. Some people may not like eating apples, but they relish applesauce. Others need to avoid hard, crisp fruits for dental reasons. Moreover, some people may consider seeds in fruit a bother. Here are some things to keep in mind:

- Fresh-squeezed juices have all or most of the nutrients in fruit but eliminate much of the fiber.
- Processed juices lose some nutrients through heat processing and pasteurization.
- Freezing retains more nutrients than any other storage method. In fact, frozen fruits may have a better nutrient profile than some fresh fruits, especially if the latter are stored improperly or kept too long.
- Canning, drying, and cooking fruits all cause a loss of vitamin C as a result of heating or evaporation.

Nutritionally, one can get the most bang for the buck by choosing a variety of fruits, in a variety of forms, prepared in different ways. The more fruit we eat, the greater our chances are of staying healthy and fit for a lifetime. It's not worth fretting over the nutritional differences between a kiwifruit and pink grapefruit. Don't worry that cantaloupe has more carotenoids than honeydew melon if honeydew is what you fancy. Quite simply, eat lots of fruits and enjoy the sweet rewards!

FOR FURTHER INFORMATION

Books

Duyff, Roberta Larson. *The American Dietetic Association's Complete Food & Nutrition Guide.* Minneapolis, Minnesota: Chronimed Publishing, 1998.

Greene, Karen, and Dufy, Raoul. *Fast! Fresh! Fruity!: Delicious Low Fat Foods with Fruit.* New Hope, Pennsylvania: New Hope Press, 1994.

Kleiner, Susan M., and Friedman-Kester, Karen. *The Be Healthier Feel Stronger Vegetarian Cookbook.* New York: Macmillan General Reference USA, 1997.

Netzer, Corinne T. *The Complete Book of Food Counts.* New York: Dell Books, 1997.

Pennington, Jean A.T. *Bowes & Church's Food Values of Portions Commonly Used* (17th edition). Philadelphia: Lippincott-Raven, 1997.

Robinson, Kathleen, and Luckett, Pete. *Vegetarian's A to Z Guide to Fruits & Vegetables.* Tucson, Arizona: Fisher Books, 1996.

Rosso, Julee. *Fresh Start for Fruit.* New York: Ivy Books, 1998.

Schlesinger, Sarah. *500 Low-Fat Fruit and Vegetable Recipes: The One-Stop Source for Healthful, Great-Tasting Meals.* New York: Villard Books, 1995.

Smith, M.J. *The Miracle Foods Cookbook: Easy, Low-Cost Recipes and Menus with Antioxidant-Rich Vegetables and Fruits That Help You Lose Weight, Fight Disease, and Slow the Aging Process.* Minneapolis, Minnesota: Chronimed Publishing, 1995.

Tantillo, Tony, and Gugino, Sam. *Eat Fresh, Stay Healthy.* New York: Macmillan General Reference USA, 1997.

Periodicals

Food & Nutrition Letter
Rodale Press
33 E Minor St
Emmaus PA 18098
215-967-5171
Fax: 215-967-6263

Nutrition Action Healthletter
Suite 300
1875 Connecticut Ave NW
Washington DC 20009
202-265-4954
Web site:
http://www.cspinet.org/nah

Tufts University Health & Nutrition Letter
8th Floor
53 Park Place
New York NY 10007
800-274-7581
Web site:
http://www.healthletter.tufts.edu

Organizations

National Center for Nutrition and Dietetics
The American Dietetic Association (ADA)
216 W Jackson Blvd
Chicago IL 60606-6995
312-899-0040
Fax: 312-899-1979
Web site:
http://www.eatright.org

U.S. Department of Agriculture (USDA)
14th & Independence Ave SW
Washington DC 20250
202-720-2791
Web site:
http://www.usda.gov

U.S. Food and Drug Administration (FDA) Center for Food Safety & Applied Nutrition
200 C Street SW
Washington DC 20204
202-456-7035
Web site:
http://vm.cfsan.fda.gov/list.html

LAUGHTER: TIME TO

TAKE IT SERIOUSLY

BY KEVIN DAVIS

It's no joke—laughter really is good medicine. During the past two decades, studies have shown that laughter triggers physiological changes in the body that can stimulate the immune system and prompt the brain to produce potent natural painkillers. In addition, researchers have found that laughter is effective in reducing stress, which is known to contribute to a range of health problems from heart disease to digestive and skin disorders. As a result of this growing body of data, health care professionals, clinical researchers, and other scientists are finally starting to take laughter seriously, recognizing that tickling the funny bone can have profound effects on the mind, body, and spirit.

205

(Above) Buster Keaton, hapless hero of silent films, in *The General* (1927); (overleaf) the Three Stooges, masters of slapstick comedy, in *Have Rocket, Will Travel* (1959).

NO ADVERSE EFFECTS

Neurologist and researcher Barry Bittman is one of the many physicians who are convinced of laughter's benefits. "I believe there are some substantial and phenomenal breakthroughs in medicine that support the value of laughter and humor," says Bittman, who is also the CEO of

Kevin Davis is a freelance writer and journalist in Chicago. He recently attended the 10th annual convention of the American Association for Therapeutic Humor.

TouchStar Productions, Meadville, Pennsylvania, a company that produces and distributes books, audiotapes, and videotapes on healing and the mind-body connection. "Treating the mind and spirit has become an integral part of the healing process, and laughter is part of that," he observes.

The American Association for Therapeutic Humor, whose members include doctors, nurses, psychologists, and other health care professionals, has been promoting the healing powers of humor since 1987. The group, which now has a membership of more than 600 people, holds conferences and workshops around the United States, encouraging health care providers to embrace laughter and humor as a valuable healing tool.

"This is the only treatment that benefits the doctor as well as the

patient. And it has very few side effects," notes Ed Dunkelblau, a Chicago-area clinical psychologist who is also the president of the association. The advocates of therapeutic humor do not view it as a form of alternative medicine, according to Dunkelblau. Rather, they see humor as complementary, supporting and augmenting conventional medical treatment.

Joel Goodman, founder of the Humor Project, a resource center and consulting business based in Saratoga Springs, New York, has been investigating the health effects of laughter for more than 20 years. "There are many physiological [and] mental health benefits. I think everyone has had the experience of a hearty laugh, and feeling good and relaxed from it. Thankfully, the research seems to be confirming that it's good for us."

The zany Marx Brothers in *A Day at the Races* (1937).

THE NO-SWEAT WORKOUT

Laughter, simply defined, is a physical response to humor, an anatomic and physiological reaction to something perceived by the lauger as funny. So-called mirthful laughter, a more pronounced and sustained reaction than a simple giggle or chuckle, is the most intense response and is associated with a host of bodily changes—respiratory, cardiovascular, musculoskeletal, and biochemical.

Laughter disrupts the normal breathing rhythm, causing the individual to inhale more deeply and exhale more forcefully than usual; the vigorous exhalation expels from the lungs residual air left behind in normal breathing and provides a more complete exchange of air. A person's heart rate increases during laughter but then briefly drops below the original baseline level. The degree of increase varies with the intensity and duration of the laughter.

Muscle activity also varies according to the laughter's intensity, ranging from modest activation of the facial, neck, scalp, and shoulder muscles to more substantial activation that involves the muscles of the diaphragm and abdomen; "convulsive" laughter involves most of the body's skeletal muscles as well. Like the increase in heart rate, the effect on the muscles is temporary and is closely followed by a brief period of considerable muscle relaxation with the cessation of laughter. Right after a good laugh, most people feel light and invigorated, a sensation much like the "runner's high." This euphoria has been attributed to the release of substances known as endorphins—natural painkillers—into the bloodstream.

One of the pioneering experts in the study of laughter and health is William F. Fry, Jr., a psychiatrist and professor emeritus of clinical psychiatry at the Stanford University School

> ## "[Humor] is the only treatment that benefits the doctor as well as the patient."

207

Lucy (Lucille Ball) and Ethel (Vivian Vance) out on a limb in "I Love Lucy" (1952).

HUMOR AS A HEALING FORCE

A merry heart doeth good like a medicine.

—Proverbs 14:10

Long before the link between humor and health became a subject of scientific scrutiny, physicians and philosophers alike recognized that optimism and a positive outlook have a salutary effect—and a melancholy, pessimistic disposition, just the opposite. In the early 1950s Caro Lippman, a San Francisco headache specialist, wrote that he advised his migraine patients, "Maintain your

of Medicine, who began his work in this field in the 1950s. Fry has found that laughter and aerobic exercise have much in common. A good belly laugh, he maintains, is the aerobic equivalent of exercising 10 minutes on a rowing machine or pedaling 15 minutes on a stationary cycle. His research suggests that the physiological mechanisms of laughter, which stimulate the blood circulation and activate the muscles in much the same way as aerobic exercise, may have a similar beneficial effect on the body.

sense of humor. A good belly-laugh is first-rate therapy." Around the same time, the influential clergyman Norman Vincent Peale published his inspirational best-seller *The Power of Positive Thinking* (1952).

It was not until the publication in 1979 of Norman Cousins's book *Anatomy of an Illness as Perceived by the Patient*, however, that the notion of humor as a healing force captured the popular imagination and the attention of the medical community. Cousins, longtime editor of the *Saturday Review*, had been diagnosed with ankylosing spondylitis, a life-threatening and extremely painful disease that involved severe inflammation of his spine. Upon learning that he had an illness for which medicine had little to offer, Cousins checked himself out of the hospital and into a nearby hotel, where he watched tapes of old Marx Brothers and Three Stooges movies and "Candid Camera" television shows. He later wrote that for every 10 minutes of hearty belly laughter, he was able to get about two hours of pain-free sleep.

Cousins also reported another, more concrete benefit of his laughter therapy—one that his doctor confirmed: his sedimentation rate dropped measurably after he watched comedy videos and enjoyed a few minutes of hearty laughter. Sedimentation rate is a measure of the rate at which blood cells settle out of the plasma; an elevated sedimentation rate is an indication of infection or inflammation in the body.

Though Cousins eventually recovered, it is hard to say whether laughter—along with the unwaveringly positive outlook he maintained throughout the ordeal—cured him. *He*, at least, was convinced that it played a *significant* part. "Laughter serves as a blocking agent," he wrote.

"Like a bullet-proof vest, it may help protect you against the ravages of negative emotions that can assault you in disease."

After the publication of *Anatomy of an Illness*, Cousins became an adjunct professor at the University of California, Los Angeles, School of Medicine and, until his death in 1990, was the leading U.S. proponent of therapeutic humor. It was largely at his urging that biomedical scientists began to pay serious attention to the effects of laughter on the mind and body.

HOW STRESS HURTS

In the 1960s and '70s, medical science first began to appreciate the role of negative emotions in heart disease. Since that time scientists have begun to confirm the long-suspected link between emotions and body chemistry, demonstrating that the mind and the body are intimately intertwined. This research has led to the establishment of an entirely new discipline, psychoneuroimmunology—the study of the intricate relationship between the nervous system and the immune system. That negative emotions can be detrimental to health has now been been well documented, and the mechanisms involved are finally starting to yield their secrets.

Stressful situations trigger a cascade of physiological changes that prepare the body to take action. In the early 20th century, the pioneering American physiologist Walter B.

Lily Tomlin as the meddlesome operator Ernestine on "Laugh-In" (1970).

"A good belly-laugh is first-rate therapy."

Cannon coined the term *fight-or-flight response* to describe these changes, which include, among others, the secretion of hormones that trigger a sudden surge in heart rate and blood pressure. Although this physiological response is useful in the face of a physical threat, it serves little purpose when the trigger is psychological, an emotion of, say, anxiety or rage. Over the long term, repeated exposure to psychological stresses and repeated triggering of the fight-or-flight response can have adverse effects on health, particularly on the heart and blood vessels and the immune system.

Numerous experiments conducted during the past two decades have focused on the health consequences of psychological stressors like anxiety, loneliness, and bereavement. In the early 1980s, for example, immunologist Ronald Glaser and psychologist Janice Kiecolt-Glaser at Ohio State University—two researchers who have been in the vanguard of the investigation of mind-body links—measured levels of stress-related hormones and disease-fighting immune-system cells in medical students before and during final exams. They found that at exam time the students had higher-than-normal levels of stress-related hormones and

Jane Curtin (right) looks ill as Roseanne Roseanna-danna (played by the late Gilda Radner) holds forth on "Saturday Night Live."

decreased levels of an important immune-system component known as natural killer cells, which combat viruses and cancer.

In a similar vein, in the early 1990s a team of British and American medical researchers investigated the purported link between stress and susceptibility to infection. First, they asked a group of volunteers to fill out a questionnaire about the frequency with which they had experienced stressful life events and negative emotions; on the basis of the subjects' answers, the researchers divided them into four subgroups, ranked by degree of stress. Next, the subjects received nasal drops containing respiratory viruses. The data showed that the subsequent incidence of respiratory infections and colds correlated with the subjects' stress levels.

A JOKE A DAY...

Advocates of therapeutic humor believe that laughter can have the opposite effect of negative emotions, suppressing the ill effects of stress and enhancing health. In the past 10–15 years, considerable research has been conducted to test this hypothesis.

Many studies of laughter's effects on stress and the immune system have focused on immunoglobulin A, or IgA, an antibody that helps fight upper respiratory tract infections. In the 1980s, for example, Kathleen Dillon and Brian Minchoff, at Western New England College, Spring-

No one has shown that laughter does any harm.

field, Massachusetts, measured the concentrations of IgA in the saliva of two groups of volunteers. One group then viewed a humorous video. The researchers recorded significant increases in the concentration of IgA in subjects who watched the video and unchanged levels in the others.

In 1987 Arthur Stone, a psychologist at the State University of New York at Stony Brook, monitored salivary IgA levels in a group of 100 men for three months. He found that positive and negative life events—a pleasant day's fishing, an acrimonious argument with the boss—had a clear impact on antibody levels. In a 1990 study Herbert Lefcourt at the University of Waterloo, Ontario, gave a group of volunteers a test that scored their sense of humor. Then he showed them funny videos. Subjects whose test scores indicated a highly developed sense of humor exhibited a larger increase in IgA concentration after viewing the videos.

Some of the most promising research on the effects of laughter on

Katharine Hepburn cracks up her host on "The Dick Cavett Show" (1979).

the immune system comes from psychoneuroimmunologists Lee Berk and Stanley Tan at Loma Linda (California) University Medical Center. Their preliminary findings suggest that mirthful laughter increases immune-system activity and decreases the hormones associated with stress. Berk and Tan showed a comedy video to one group of medical students, and a control group simply sat quietly in a room. Blood samples revealed that those who watched the video had significant increases in several indicators of immune activity, including natural killer cells; IgA; activated T cells, which battle infections; and gamma interferon, an immune-system messenger. The video viewers also had lower levels of cortisol, a stress-related hormone that suppresses the immune system. The control group showed no significant changes in their blood levels of these substances.

Berk and Tan describe laughter as a state of "eustress"—i.e., the opposite of stress. Recognizing that stress is linked to suppression of immune-system activity, they believe that eustress may have the opposite effect. Their work has also demonstrated that laughing lowers blood pressure and triggers the release of a flood of endorphins. Tan believes that humor provides a safety valve that shuts off the flow of stress hormones.

Sol Klotz and Susan Hunter, immunologists at the University of Central Florida, have examined the immunologic effects of humor on people with cancer and AIDS. Their preliminary results show that IgA is secreted profusely when patients laugh, a sign that the immune system responds quickly to humor.

Although all these data are encouraging, experts in the field caution that much work remains to be done. The long-term immune-system effects of humor have not been documented, and the possible influence of outside factors has not been ruled out. On the positive side, however, no one one has shown that laughter does any harm.

BRING IN THE CLOWNS

Even though further research needs to be done, cancer centers and AIDS clinics are increasingly employing humor in the treatment of patients. Humorous books and funny movies and tapes are being provided by many institutions as part of their own "humor programs." Since 1986 the Big Apple Circus in New York City has been sending clowns into hospitals. They work mostly in pediatric wards to cheer children and help ease their fears.

Judy Goldblum-Carlton, a professional humor therapist in the department of pediatrics at the University of Maryland School of Medicine, often dresses up as a clown called "Dr. Lollipops" and roams the hospital corridors looking for anyone in need of cheering up. She carries a host of gags and tricks up her sleeve,

211

White House hilarity: Pres.
Jimmy Carter with pianist
Vladimir Horowitz and his
wife, Wanda (1978).

including a compact mirror that, when opened, lets out a scream.

Goldblum-Carlton recognizes that there are times when her services are not welcome. "I try to be appropriate with what I do," she says. "I know how to stand there and blend in with the wall, and I know when to disappear. You have to be sensitive when using humor." She sees her role as beneficial for everyone in the hospital. "My job is to evoke hearty laughter from children, their family, and the staff. I believe the recovery rate of patients is faster. I don't have a scientific study to prove it, but I see it. And it's cost effective health care if you can get somebody out of the hospital one day earlier."

Bob ("Dr. Bucket") Bleiler is not a doctor, but he plays one on the hospital ward—a clown doctor, to be

exact. A retired insurance-claims superintendent, Bleiler visits hospitals in Camden, New Jersey, carrying with him an assortment of props that may include rubber chickens, plastic bones, bulbous foam noses, and thick Coke-bottle glasses. He and another clown friend often work as a team.

They especially enjoy working with patients who are about to undergo surgery. "We'll give them a silly sticker to put on their surgical bonnet. And when we can, we do a nose transplant," Bleiler says. "We have three sizes of noses and let them 'pick' their own nose." He adds, "A clown becomes a comforter in hard times."

Karen Peterson, a clinical psychologist who has worked with AIDS patients in Miami, Florida, has found that the positive mental and physical effects of humor make it a valuable part of any treatment program. Peterson is coauthor of *AIDS Prevention and Treatment: Hope, Humor,*

and Healing (1992), a textbook aimed at both health professionals and laypersons. She believes that humor offers patients a renewed outlook on life and helps with the symptoms of depression. "You have to make sure it's used at the right time with the right person and the right way or it can be devastatingly negative," Peterson said. "You have to have an established rapport; you should never use humor too early on in the therapy." She adds, "You have to be careful that you don't use humor that in any way is derogatory."

One of Peterson's close friends managed to maintain a remarkable sense of humor even while in the late stages of AIDS. "He would have me laughing about the most painful things, and I saw how effectively he used humor to cope," she said. "When you look at people who are HIV positive, the ability to laugh in the face of death is incredibly empowering."

UPI/Corbis-Bettmann

Sometimes the queen is also a joker: Elizabeth II and Pres. Ronald Reagan (1983).

THE FUNNY SIDE OF CANCER

Cancer is no laughing matter, but for a number of cancer patients humor has proved to be an invaluable tool for helping them cope. Some think it has also boosted their body's ability to battle the disease. Ricki Carroll, a businesswoman and single mother in Ashfield, Massachusetts, learned in 1995 that she had breast cancer. "I thought my life would be over by the morning," said Carroll, who was 43 at the time of her diagnosis. "I even started planning my own funeral." But something told her that she should try to lighten up. She painted her chest and upper body with a rainbow, hearts, and daisies. Her friends baked breast-shaped cookies. Her boyfriend visited her at the hospital wearing a rainbow-colored wig and red clown nose.

Carroll believes humor and positive thinking were the key to her survival. "Nobody needs to paint their body to get through surgery, but everybody should find what feeds their soul," Carroll says. "Anything that a patient can do to get to the other side of the fear is going to help. Whether it helped me get rid of or cure my cancer, I have no idea. But it did help me get through the fear."

Christine Clifford, another survivor of breast cancer, is the founder of the Cancer Club, a support group and resource center based in Edina, Minnesota. She also is the author of a humorous account of her own illness, *Not Now...I'm Having a No Hair Day*. Clifford, also a mom and businesswoman, said she learned early on how serious the medical profession is and how grimly people react to the disease. "Cancer is a very difficult subject for most people to discuss," she notes.

After her diagnosis Clifford cried for three days. The treatments were depressing. Her hair fell out. Seeing her bald head for the first time, a friend commented that she resembled Captain Picard, the commander of the spaceship on the "Star Trek" television series. "I laughed hard," Clifford said. "And I realized it was the first time I had laughed since this all happened." She was amazed at how good it felt. After that, she made an effort to have more laughter and humor in her life.

Clifford's friends gave a "chemotherapy shower." The guests were asked to bring hats to cover their friend's hairless head. At first the guests were somewhat solemn. Then someone offered Clifford, an ex-smoker, a cigarette. She responded, "No thanks, I already have cancer." There was stunned silence—followed by hearty laughter. "After that, the party began, and we all laughed really hard," Clifford recalls. "I

213

Romanian villagers speak a
universal language.

realized how important laughter was
going to be in my recovery process.
Because chronic illness has touched
so many of us, it's up to all of us to
help the patients and survivors get
back into the mainstream of life. And
I think the way to do that is through
laughter and humor. Laughter flings
open the shutters and lets the light of
life come in."

RX: SMILE!

Will doctors soon be prescribing
humor? Bittman, for one, hopes so.
He's a member of a group of humor
researchers who helped develop a
software program that allows physicians to create customized laughter
"prescriptions." (If this trend catches
on, it may not be long before your
doctor instructs you to watch two
"Seinfelds" and call him in the
morning.) The computer program is
called SMILE, an acronym for

Subjective Multi-media Integrated
Laughter Evaluation. By asking patients what makes them laugh, which
movies, books, or comedians they
enjoy, doctors can create individual-
ized humor profiles.

Bittman envisions the program's
someday being used in hospitals,
clinics, rehabilitation centers, support
groups, and doctors' offices. "It's
basically a menu," Bittman says.
"When patients go to the hospital,
they have a choice of what they want
to have for breakfast or lunch. Well,
here we give them a choice of what
kind of humor they'd like."

One of the leading advocates of
humor for healing is Patty Wooten, a
registered nurse in Santa Cruz,
California, and the author of several
books on the subject. She hopes to
see the humor-for-healing movement
continue to grow. "We want to give
people permission to laugh. We want
to say it's okay."

For the medical establishment to
take laughter even more seriously,

Wooten believes, there must be
further research. "I think we need to
see the research going on in hospitals, nursing homes, and health care
centers and out of the laboratory.
And hopefully we can prove some
kind of cost effectiveness, a way to
show that it will affect the bottom
line, that it will decrease the
[hospital] stay, improve symptom
management, increase compliance,
motivate someone to a healthy
lifestyle, enhance learning." Wooten
is encouraged by current trends. "I
think health care is changing rapidly;
the old way is being destroyed and a
new way is being built."

William Fry agrees. "We have
reason enough to believe that mirth
is good for us. The individual
physiologic effects have been identified in a scientifically sound fashion,
and those effects, generally speaking,
are beneficial…in the sense of
enhancing certain functions that
could be considered to be compatible
with survival."

Joel Goodman of the Humor Project also predicts a bright future for therapeutic humor. "Certainly in the last 20 years, I've seen a lot of people come on board....It has shown up in a variety of ways. We've given grants to over 250 hospitals, human service agencies, and non-profit organizations to help them develop positive projects and tap the power of humor. So people are actually putting their money where our mouths have been." With the evidence of the health benefits of humor growing every day, the movement to "tap the power" of this potent force is likely to continue to attract adherents.

FOR FURTHER INFORMATION

Jeffry W. Myers—Corbis

A giggle a day...

Books

Clifford, Christine. *Not Now...I'm Having a No Hair Day.* Duluth, Minnesota: Pfeifer-Hamilton Publishers, 1996.

Cousins, Norman. *Anatomy of an Illness as Perceived by the Patient.* New York: Norton, 1979.

Cousins, Norman. *Head First: The Biology of Hope.* New York: Dutton, 1989.

Klein, Allen. *The Healing Power of Humor.* Los Angeles: J.P. Tarcher, 1989.

McGhee, Paul. *Health, Healing and the Amuse System.* 2nd ed. Dubuque, Iowa: Kendall/Hunt Publishing Co., 1996.

Nelson, Donna Enoch. *One Life to Laugh.* Glendale, California: Potentials, 1990.

Radner, Gilda. *It's Always Something.* New York: Simon & Schuster, 1989.

Wooten, Patty. *Compassionate Laughter: Jest for Your Health.* Salt Lake City, Utah: Commune-A-Key Publishing, 1996.

Organizations

American Association for Therapeutic Humor
Suite 303
222 S Meramec
St Louis MO 63105
314-863-6232
Web site:
http://www.ideanurse.com/aath

Journal of Nursing Jocularity
PO Box 40416
Mesa AZ 85274
602-835-6165
Web site:
http://www.jocularity.com

International Society for Humor Studies
Don Nilsen
Arizona State University
Department of English
Tempe AZ 85287-0302
602-965-7592

Other resources

The Cancer Club
Christine Clifford
6533 Limerick Dr
Edina MN 55439
612-944-0639
Web site:
http://www.cancerclub.com

The Humor Project Inc
Suite 210
480 Broadway
Saratoga Springs NY 12866-2288
518-587-8770
Web site:
http://www.wizvax.net/humor

Jest for the Health of It
Patty Wooten
PO Box 8484
Santa Cruz CA 95061
408-460-1600
Web site:
http://www.jesthealth.com

TouchStar Productions
522 Jackson Park Dr
Meadville PA 16335
800-861-3296
Web site:
http://www.touchstarpro.com

ATTENTION DEFICIT DISORDER:

THE LURE OF A LABEL

BY WADE ROUSH

Len was a man who rarely finished anything he started. A talented painter with a remarkable eye for detail, he typically lost interest in a painting long before completing it. He was also a writer, filling notebook after notebook with keen observations on the world around him. He often talked of someday publishing a book. His notes were jumbled and unreadable, however, and he could never bring himself to organize them.

Tom had a different problem. It wasn't that he couldn't finish things. Instead, the demons of ambition drove him so relentlessly that he had dozens of projects going at once. He found them so absorbing that he

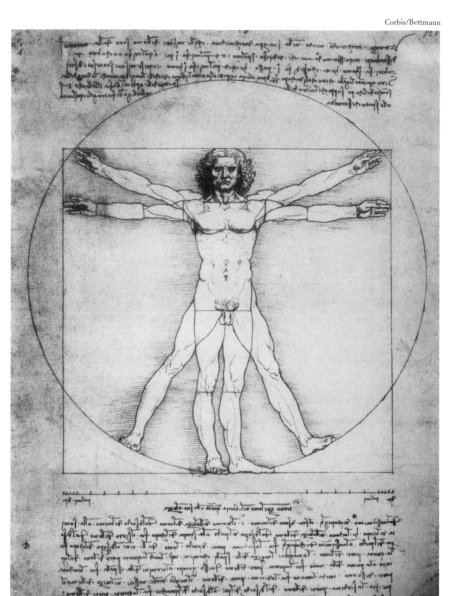

sound hauntingly familiar. Len's restlessness and distractibility and Tom's impulsiveness and tendency to "hyperfocus" at times are among the characteristics that make both school and work an ordeal for millions who have ADD. Then, too, both men seem to be missing out on some of life's greatest pleasures—in Len's case, the satisfaction that comes with accomplishment, and in Tom's, the rewards of friendship and intimacy. Could they be helped by a drug like Ritalin (methylphenidate)? Reading their case histories, many physicians and psychiatrists would probably say yes.

But would the experts really be justified in labeling Len and Tom as "disordered"? Likewise, is it reasonable to presume that medication could offer them fuller lives? The history books certainly indicate otherwise. For "Len" is none other than Leonardo da Vinci, and "Tom" is the brilliant inventor Thomas Edison. Were they alive today, some experts have speculated, both Edison and Leonardo would probably be diagnosed as suffering from ADD. Yet had either of these men been less eccentric or less spontaneous, more disciplined or more practical, or had they sought medicines to calm their flights of fancy, the Italian Renaissance of the 15th century and the technological revolution of the late 19th century would have been without two of their guiding geniuses.

WHAT'S IN A NAME?

It was not until the 1950s that doctors began to classify as "mentally deficient" individuals who had difficulty paying attention on demand. Various ominous-sounding terms were coined to describe this behavior, among them *minimal brain damage* and *hyperkinesis*. In 1980

slept only four hours a night and could spare little time for anybody. On the afternoon of his wedding, in fact, he told his new bride he needed to go to his office for an hour. Once there, he became completely lost in his work and didn't think about the time—or his waiting wife—until midnight.

❧   ❧   ❧

To the parent of a child with attention deficit disorder (ADD) or to an adult with the condition, the problems of these two men probably

Wade Roush is a freelance science writer in the San Francisco area and a former staff writer at Science *magazine.*

218

the American Psychiatric Association (APA) replaced these labels with a new one—*attention deficit disorder.* Then in 1987, revising its criteria for the diagnosis of mental disorders, the APA linked ADD with hyperactivity, a condition that sometimes goes hand-in-hand with attention disorders but may exist independently. The new syndrome was officially named *attention-deficit/hyperactivity disorder,* or *ADHD.* (The terms *ADD* and *ADHD* are often used interchangeably; for the sake of simplicity, *ADD* is used henceforth in this article.)

Although these labels are relatively new, the hallmarks of ADD—impulsivity and distractibility—are as old as humanity itself; think of mischievous mythological characters like the classical gods Eros and Cupid, the Mesopotamian god Enki, and the trickster figures of Native American folklore. Many of history's transforming events have been brought about by castle-in-the-air-building daydreamers and restless, fidgety fortune seekers: the great explorers, the Leonardos and Edisons, so many of the immigrants who left Europe in search of a new world. The list of historical figures who might have been diagnosed with ADD had the concept been invented includes the mathematician Albert Einstein, the British statesman Winston Churchill, and at least one U.S. president, John F. Kennedy.

Today, however, people who have been diagnosed with ADD—some of them psychiatrists and psychologists—are challenging the notion that personality traits like inattentiveness, impulsivity, and distractibility deserve the label "symptoms." This vocal minority argues that these characteristics are often merely the flip sides of valuable attributes like insightfulness, originality, and inventiveness.

Corbis/Bettmann

They contend that many people labeled as having ADD are neither "deficient" nor "disordered"—that, in fact, the issues of attention and distractibility need to be completely rethought.

ILLNESS OR STIGMA?

ADD is no stranger to controversy and debate. Anyone who has picked up a newspaper or magazine in the last six months has undoubtedly seen at least one article alleging that ADD is grossly overdiagnosed and overtreated. Or they may have seen an article proclaiming that ADD is not a true, biologically based illness but rather an excuse for disruptive behavior, bad grades, inability to hold a job, or just plain laziness.

Those calling for a fundamental reevaluation of the thinking about ADD hold that overdiagnosis is not an issue; plenty of people, they say, fit the diagnosis of ADD. Nor do they wish to argue the issue of a

Although the label "ADD" may be recent, the behaviors it describes are age-old. A psychologist looking at a scribbled page from Leonardo da Vinci's notebooks (opposite page) or the poor school reports of the young Winston Churchill, who grew up to become England's greatest statesman (above), might see in both clear symptoms of attention deficit disorder.

legitimate medical illness versus one that is imagined or fabricated. The real problem, as they see it, is that ADD is not a mental disorder at all but simply a different state of mind. It is because of this difference that people with ADD often do not function well in standard learning or work environments. And it is because of this difference that such people frequently show enormous originality and creativity. Like other "minorities," say the adherents of this view, people with ADD meet constantly with ignorance and intolerance, and it is these attitudes—*not* the attributes of ADD itself—that are largely to blame for the academic and career failures of individuals with the diagnosis. It is society and its expectations that need to change, they claim, not those with short attention spans and high energy.

The emerging scientific evidence about the causes and consequences of ADD lends some plausibility to this radical viewpoint. Neurologists are finding, for example, that the anatomic and physiological differences underlying ADD appear to be mere variations in the timing of brain development rather than outright defects. Other researchers have suggested that the behaviors characteristic of ADD may once have conferred an evolutionary advantage, which would explain why their underlying genetic components have been conserved in the human gene pool. In her book *A.D.D. and Creativity*, Lynn Weiss, a psychotherapist who has ADD, says simply, "Attention Deficit Disorder is a total misnomer."

NO EASY DIAGNOSIS

ADD has never been a clear-cut medical condition like ulcers or cataracts, with easily recognizable symptoms or definitive diagnostic tests. Since 1980, however, psychiatrists and psychologists in the U.S. have agreed that children and adults merit the label if they persistently show a combination of traits including, among others, forgetfulness, distractibility, fidgeting, restlessness, impatience, difficulty sustaining attention in work, play, or conversation, or difficulty following instructions and completing tasks. According to the diagnostic criteria in the APA's *Diagnostic and Statistical Manual of Mental Disorders, Fourth Edition (DSM-IV)*, at least six of these must be present "to a degree that is maladaptive," and these behaviors must cause "impairment" in two or more settings—*e.g.*, at school or work and at home. Inattention predominates in some cases, hyperactivity in others, and in a "combined type" of ADD, the two are present together.

ADD is now the most commonly diagnosed childhood psychiatric disorder, affecting an estimated 3–6% of American schoolchildren. And whereas it was believed for many years that most children with ADD eventually outgrew it, more and more adults are now being diagnosed with the condition. Psychiatrist John Ratey, the author of several books on the subject, has said that 40–60% of children with ADD "do not leave their problems behind; they simply become less visibly restless."

But long before psychiatrists defined the disorder, an effective treatment was at hand. The class of drugs known as amphetamines increases the amount and activity of the neurotransmitter norepinephrine (noradrenaline) in the brain. (Neurotransmitters are chemicals that carry nerve impulses from one neuron to another.) Although they act as a stimulant in most people, amphetamines were found in the 1930s to have the paradoxical effect of calming or "slowing down" hyperactive children. Methylphenidate—probably better known by the brand name Ritalin—a milder cousin of the amphetamines, was developed in 1955, and the number of hyperactive and inattentive children taking this and related drugs has increased steadily ever since. Between 1990 and 1996 alone, the number of American children regularly taking Ritalin grew from 500,000 to 1,300,000, according to one study. Another found that Ritalin prescriptions for adults rose from 217,000 in 1992 to 729,000 in 1997.

Why a stimulant medication should have the effect of diminishing hyperactivity is just one of several conundrums surrounding ADD. Also unknown is why boys with the condition outnumber girls by a ratio of three to one. Even the cause of ADD, though extensively investigated, remains a puzzle. Over the years many theories have been advanced only to be abandoned for lack of evidence. The suspects have included bad parenting, brain damage due to head trauma, brain damage secondary to bacterial or viral infection, brain damage due to exposure to substances such as alcohol (prenatally) or lead (postnatally), and food allergy. After studies in the late 1980s linked sugar and food additives with hyperactive behavior, many parents scoured the kitchen cupboards, throwing out sugary cereals and other popular kids' foods over howls of protest from their offspring. This research too has now been largely discredited.

About one thing, however, the majority of medical professionals seem certain: that ADD is a disorder and *not* a difference. Indeed, experts such as Edward Hallowell, coauthor with Ratey of the 1994 best-seller *Driven to Distraction*, argue that the

categorization of ADD as a neurobiological disorder was an important step forward, since it clearly distinguished the ability to pay attention or control one's impulses from other mental capacities such as innate intelligence. Once ADD was acknowledged as a disorder, it could be expected that impulsive or inattentive people would no longer be dismissed as "slow" or "stupid."

But the medicalization of ADD has not stopped doctors from evaluating people with the condition according to their shortcomings rather than their strengths. The criteria for ADD in *DSM-IV* clearly state that the diagnosis can be applied only when

The number of hyperactive and inattentive children taking [Ritalin] and related drugs has increased steadily.

A Florida middle-school secretary prepares to dispense the day's doses of Ritalin to the 40 students at her school whose doctors have prescribed the stimulant drug for them.

Children with short attention spans and high energy may also be enormously creative. Too often, however, they are categorized according to their shortcomings rather than their strengths.

there is "clear evidence of...significant impairment in social, academic, or occupational functioning."

THE BRAIN IN ADD

No one is denying that people diagnosed with ADD often have a tough time negotiating their way through life. Studies have shown that more than a quarter of children with ADD are held back a grade in school, and a third fail to graduate from high school. Young people with ADD are more likely than others to experience social rejection by their peers and, as they grow up, to have higher rates of felony arrests and criminal convictions, addictive disorders such as substance abuse and compulsive gambling, psychiatric problems such as anxiety and depression, and even traffic injuries and cardiovascular disease.

The fact that many people diagnosed with ADD experience fewer problems once they start taking stimulants like Ritalin would seem to confirm a neurobiological basis for the condition. Still, it may be premature to conclude that the difficulties experienced by people with ADD originate exclusively in their brains.

Behind the old label "minimal brain damage" was the assumption that attention problems and hyperactivity resulted from physical injuries to the brain, perhaps traceable to complications during childbirth. Fifty years ago, however, when this terminology was introduced, there was no reliable way to test the assumption. Today, using imaging technologies like positron emission tomography and functional magnetic resonance imaging, neurobiologists are able to compare the structure and function of the brains of people with and

> It may be premature to conclude that the difficulties experienced by people with ADD originate exclusively in their brains.

without ADD. And they have indeed found some differences. But the differences are subtle and rather mysterious, having to do with the physical size of various brain regions or the levels of blood flow or glucose metabolism. In no way do they resemble the effects of birth injuries such as brain hemorrhage or oxygen deprivation.

A study published in 1991, for example, which compared the brains of boys with and without ADD, found that the corpus callosum, the band of nerve fibers that connects the brain's two hemispheres and is thought to help suppress automatic impulses, contained slightly less tissue in those with ADD. Nonetheless, the brains of all of the boys in the study were judged to be clinically normal. A similar study in 1994 discovered small size discrepancies in the brain structures known as the caudate nuclei. In boys without ADD, the right caudate nucleus was normally about 3% larger than the left caudate nucleus; this asymmetry was absent in boys with ADD. The significance of this discrepancy is unclear.

223

Other studies have detected not just anatomic but functional differences between ADD and non-ADD brains. One research team recently observed decreased blood flow through the right caudate nucleus in adults with ADD. A 1993 study showed that an area of the prefrontal cortex known as the left anterior frontal lobe metabolizes less glucose in adults with ADD, an indication that this area may be less active. Still other research showed higher levels of norepinephrine throughout the brains of people with ADD, and lower levels of another substance that inhibits norepinephrine's release. Metabolites, or breakdown products, of another neurotransmitter, dopamine, have also been found in elevated concentrations in the cerebrospinal fluid of hyperactive boys.

According to some authorities, 3% to 6% of American children have ADD. For unknown reasons, boys with the condition outnumber girls by a ratio of three to one.

A DEVELOPMENTAL HYPOTHESIS

If these anatomic and physiological variations are not associated with injury, what exactly do they indicate? Xavier Castellanos of the Child Psychiatry Branch of the National Institute of Mental Health proposes that they all involve a sort of "braking system" in the brain. At any waking moment, the brain is coursing with many overlapping thoughts, emotions, impulses, and sensory stimuli. Attention can be defined as the ability to focus on one stimulus or task while resisting extraneous impulses; people with ADD, Castellanos and other researchers speculate, have lower-than-average control over such impulses, with the result that their train of thought is repeatedly "derailed."

The cortical-striatal-thalamic-cortical circuit, a chain of neurons in the brain that connects the prefrontal cortex, the basal ganglia, and the thalamus in one continuous loop, is thought to be one of the main structures responsible for impulse inhibition. The size and activity differences found in the prefrontal cortex and basal ganglia of people with ADD, Castellano believes, are evidence of a delay in the normal growth and development of this inhibitory circuit.

If this supposition is correct, it would help to explain why the symptoms of ADD sometimes subside with age. The cortical-striatal-thalamic-cortical circuit in the brains of people with ADD may fully mature—providing more nearly "normal" levels of impulse inhibition—only in the third decade of life, and never in some people. This develop-

mental-lag hypothesis might also explain how stimulant medications work to enhance attention. In one study, treatment with Ritalin restored average levels of blood flow through the caudate nucleus; and in other trials dopamine levels, which normally decrease with age but remain high in people with ADD, fell after treatment with Ritalin. The hypothesis would coincide, finally, with recent observations that the social development of children with ADD progresses at the same rate as that of their peers but with a lag of two to three years. (Even larger variations in the timing of some other developmental processes, it should be noted, are accepted as quite healthy; girls, for example, may experience the onset of menstruation as early as age 9 or as late as 16.)

Adding to the new view of ADD as a difference rather than a disorder are recent findings and speculations from the world of genetics. ADD is now thought to be at least partly hereditary. About 40% of children with the condition have a parent who has ADD, and 35% have a sibling who is affected. Among identical twins, if one twin has ADD, there is an 80–92% likelihood that the other will as well. Since 1996, moreover, three reports of genes possibly linked to ADD have surfaced.

PRESERVED BY NATURAL SELECTION?

The above-mentioned findings are unsurprising in light of Castellano's hypothesis, given that growth and development are regulated by the interplay of thousands of genes. Common variations in the brain's developmental schedule would almost certainly have genetic antecedents. But whether ADD reflects a

Recent research indicates that genetic factors probably play a part in ADD. If one identical twin has the condition, the chances that the other is also affected are greater than 80%.

developmental lag or not, the discovery that its behaviors are apparently genetically rooted suggests that it is not an aberration but rather belongs to the normal spectrum of human behavior, just like other complex traits that have recently been associated with specific genes—from novelty seeking to homosexuality to certain violent behaviors. "After all," wrote journalist Claudia Wallis in a 1994 *Time* magazine article on ADD, "it is just as likely that researchers will someday discover a gene for a hot temper, which also runs in families. But that doesn't mean that having a short fuse is a disease requiring medical intervention."

Distractibility and impulsiveness would have been advantageous for hunters in early human societies.

Indeed, some researchers assert that the genes contributing to ADD exist for good reason—they confer an evolutionary advantage and thus have been preserved by natural selection. In his 1993 book *Attention Deficit Disorder: A Different Perception*, Thom Hartmann suggested that extreme distractibility and impulsiveness would have been advantageous for hunters in early human societies, who would have needed to be acutely sensitive to movement around them and ready to spring into action at any moment.

Other authorities, such as John Shelley-Tremblay and Lee Rosen, dispute the particulars of Hartmann's theory, arguing that even before the invention of agriculture, few humans relied on hunting for sustenance. They suggest an alternative explanation. Unlike other primates, they note, adult humans have little body hair for their infants to cling to and must instead carry or lead their young everywhere. In early human groups noisy, squirming youngsters would have been more likely to attract parental attention and would therefore have been better protected from the perils of the jungle, forest, tidal pond, or savanna. "What is viewed today as maladaptive, because it often leads to negative responses from peers and teachers, would have provided a distinct advantage," wrote Shelley-Tremblay and Rosen in a 1996 article in *The Journal of Genetic Psychology*.

CROSS-CULTURAL COMPARISONS

If restless, disruptive behavior posed less of a problem at other times in human history, could this also be true in other cultures in the present

When the behavior of presumably normal Taiwanese children was evaluated according to an American rating scale, nearly 10% of the youngsters qualified for a diagnosis of ADD.

day? A brief survey of diagnostic practices outside North America reveals that the notion of ADD as a disorder requiring medical intervention is highly culture-bound and largely peculiar to the United States and Canada. This is not to say that the behaviors characteristic of ADD are absent from children in other nations. In 1993 researchers using an American-devised rating scale tested more than 4,000 Taiwanese primary-school students. They found that close to 10% of the youngsters could be classified as having ADD.

The larger question, of course, is not how children score on a test but rather whether they are identified by their own parents, teachers, and doctors as having a problem. In Great Britain and France, only about 1% of children are diagnosed with hyperkinetic disorder, the closest equivalent to ADD in the World Health Organization's International Classification of Diseases (the diagnostic system used by most medical professionals outside North America). And many in the British medical establishment hope this number will remain comparatively low. The British Psychological Society (BPS) suggested in a 1997 report that physicians and psychiatrists should resist the American example of applying medical labels to a wide variety of attention-related problems: "The idea that children who don't attend or don't sit still in school have a mental disorder is not entertained by most British clinicians."

WHAT'S "NORMAL"?

Neurobiology, genetics, and anthropology, then, all seem to argue for a more expansive view of what constitutes "normal" variation in people's ability to pay attention and stifle impulses. Many experts and people with ADD have already embraced this broader view and are working hard to promote it. Their zeal is understandable; the attitudes of parents, educators, and physicians toward difficult, underachieving children will ultimately determine whether these children are provided with suitable learning environments that capitalize on their skills or are simply pressured to conform and offered medication as an aid.

It is precisely this pressure to conform, some experts argue, that is the underlying cause of many of the problems experienced by children and adults with ADD. Because they are unusually receptive to stray thoughts, connections, and stimuli, people with ADD have difficulty following classroom lectures, completing assignments on time, or behaving docilely at home or in public. As a result, they often fail to meet expectations and are informed of this over and over again by their elders and peers, with inevitable and powerful effects on their self-esteem. ADD's documented "comorbidity"— that is, the greatly increased rate of medical and behavioral problems such as depression, addictive disorders, and criminality among people with the condition—is almost entirely attributable to this cycle of negative reinforcement, many researchers argue. "In my own experience, many [children diagnosed with ADD] are energetic, creative and independent youngsters struggling with the constraints of an inattentive, conflicted or stressed adult environment," writes psychiatrist Peter Breggin, a well-known opponent of drug treatment for psychiatric and psychological conditions.

In their 1997 book *Shadow Syndromes*, Ratey and coauthor

Catherine Johnson argue that many people who have ADD or a milder "shadow" version of the condition reap the advantages of "high energy, high enthusiasm, and the ability to hyperfocus, all of which can take a

(Above) Some authorities suggest that instead of treating hyperactive kids with drugs, parents and teachers should provide more opportunities for them to channel their excess energy into sports and other constructive activities. (Left) Sometimes ADD persists into adulthood. The person who thrives on chaos may have difficulty coping in settings where linear thinking and organization are prized above all.

227

These high-spirited British youngsters are less likely than their American counterparts to be diagnosed with ADD—for the simple reason that British psychiatrists and psychologists have resisted labeling attention-related problems as mental disorders.

person to great heights in some realms." Some teenagers and adults say they are actually glad to have the condition, since their lives would be less interesting otherwise. Indeed, Weiss jokes that if people with ADD had written the APA's diagnostic manual, countless individuals now considered "normal" would be diagnosed with "CDD (Creativity Deficit Disorder)" or "IDD (Intuition Deficit Disorder)."

Weiss and other experts believe that ADD can work as an asset. Yet to people with the disorder, typical classrooms and workplaces seem designed expressly to reward people who think linearly and follow instruc-

tions to the letter while thwarting those who thrive on chaos, unpredictability, and imagination. The latter group needs a combination of structure and variety to succeed, experts say. Filing systems, appointment books, and alarm clocks, for example, could help people with ADD stay "in sync" with the rest of the world. Teachers could hold the attention of ADD students with lessons that are briefer and faster-paced than usual. Parents could channel the energy of kids with ADD by encouraging them to participate in high-energy activities like sports.

Implementing changes in the educational process is difficult, of course. It is far easier to prescribe a focus-enhancing medication such as Ritalin. In a 1995 survey reported in the *Archives of Pediatrics & Adolescent Medicine*, a majority of pediatricians acknowledged that drugs are usually the only treatment option they recommend for children with ADD.

Medication, it is important to repeat, usually works. People who take Ritalin and similar medicines say the drugs help them concentrate, which helps them get more work done and, in turn, reduces frustration and increases self-confidence. This is surely a great boon. Yet as the report from the BPS put it, it is important "to separate questions about the effectiveness of medication from arguments about whether to use medications. The former questions are empirical, the latter ethical and sociological."

WHO NEEDS TO CHANGE?

In the long run, the popularity of drug therapies for ADD raises a knotty ethical question: Is it more desirable for millions of people to have their thinking processes pharmaceutically adjusted to fit the requirements of society than for society to accommodate different ways of thinking? In other, roughly equivalent realms of social policy, the answer to this question has seemed obvious. The Americans with Disabilities Act of 1990, for example, acknowledged the rights and needs of people with physical disabilities and mandated that the physical environment be modified where necessary to assist them. Differences in sexual orientation, too, are protected by antidiscrimination laws in many cities and states.

The parallel with homosexuality is instructive. Same-sex attraction, like impulsivity, has always been a part of the human condition, but it came under the scrutiny of the medical profession only in the 1890s, when a German psychologist coined the term *homosexuality*. For the next three-quarters of a century, medical professionals classified it as a form of mental illness and attempted to treat it through psychotherapy and other methods. Finally, in 1973, the APA was persuaded to eliminate homosexuality from its official roster of mental disorders. Today most members of the gay community—and their friends, families, and physicians—see it simply as a way of being, no more pathological than left-handedness. (Left-handedness, incidentally, was also thought at one time to be abnormal and a condition that needed to be "corrected.")

The advocates of the new view of ADD seem to be sending a similar message to society: those labeled with ADD are not "sick"; they're different. It is society's attitude toward them that needs to change. Whether society will accept this view and what part science will play in the process remain to be seen.

FOR FURTHER INFORMATION

Books

Barkley, Russell. *Attention-Deficit Hyperactivity Disorder: A Handbook for Diagnosis and Treatment.* New York: Guilford Press, 1990.

Hallowell, Edward M., and Ratey, John J. *Driven to Distraction: Recognizing and Coping with Attention Deficit Disorder from Childhood through Adulthood.* New York: Pantheon Books, 1994.

Hallowell, Edward M., and Ratey, John J. *Answers to Distraction.* New York: Pantheon Books, 1994.

Ratey, John J., and Johnson, Catherine. *Shadow Syndromes.* New York: Pantheon Books, 1997.

U.S. National Institute of Mental Health. *Attention Deficit Hyperactivity Disorder.* NIH Publication no. 94-3572. Washington, D.C.: U.S. Government Printing Office, 1994.

Weiss, Lynn. *A.D.D. and Creativity.* Dallas: Taylor Publishing, 1997.

Web sites

"Attention-Deficit Hyperactivity Disorder," Internet Mental Health, http://www.mentalhealth.com

Attention! magazine, published by Children and Adults with Attention Deficit Disorders (CHADD), http://www.chadd.org/atten

"ADD/ADHD," from LD OnLine: The Interactive Guide to Learning Disabilities for Parents, Teachers, and Children, http://www.ldonline.org/ld_indepth/add_adhd/add-adhd.html

The Mining Company Guide to Attention Deficit Disorder, http://add.miningco.com/

HYPERICUM:
A HUMBLE HERB WORTHY OF THE HYPE?

BY MADY HORNIG, M.D.

The clamor for St. John's wort—the latest trendy herbal remedy, hailed as a cure for depression and other ailments, including anxiety and chronic fatigue syndrome—is a clear reflection of the public's growing infatuation with alternative medicine. Americans are turning to herbal products and alternative therapies like acupuncture in increasing numbers. In fact, a study published in *The New England Journal of Medicine* in 1993 found that slightly more than one-third of U.S. adults had used at least one unconventional form of health care—from herbs to homeopathy—in the preceding year.

Why are so many people eager to embrace these unconventional therapies? Certainly, one reason is disenchantment with a system of medical care that is seen by many as becoming increasingly technological and impersonal. Another factor is

230

In Germany, where St. John's wort is well accepted by the medical establishment, patients can fill prescriptions for this herbal antidepressant at their local pharmacies.

Mady Hornig is Visiting Researcher, Laboratory for Neurovirology and Microbial Pathogenesis, University of California, Irvine.

a growing distrust of conventional drugs, based at least in part on the publicity that has surrounded several medications recently withdrawn from the market because of serious, sometimes even life-threatening, side effects. On a more personal level, virtually anyone who regularly takes medication has probably experienced an unpleasant side effect of some sort.

Herbal remedies, by comparison, are perceived by the public as "natural" and therefore safe. They offer the advantage of being readily available and requiring no visit to the doctor. And, of course, they are usually less expensive than comparable prescription products. Some—St. John's wort among them—have been used by millions of people with very few serious adverse effects.

But American scientists still have their doubts about herbal remedies in general and St. John's wort in particular. Is it safe? What of the potential for interactions with other drugs, especially in people not under a physician's care? Does the remedy work, and if so, how? Is it better than the antidepressant drugs already in use? Consumers may have said "yes" to this popular herbal treatment, but many scientists are still saying, "Where's the proof?"

PHARMACY IN A PLANT

St. John's wort, or *Hypericum perforatum*—also known as goatweed, Klamath weed, and, in Chinese medicine, *qian ceng lou*—is a perennial plant that has been used medicinally since the time of Hippocrates. The word *wort* derives from the old English word *wyrt*, meaning "plant." The popular name comes from the fact that the star-shaped golden flowers are in peak bloom

around June 24, when the birth of St. John the Baptist is celebrated.

The plant and its extracts have traditionally been made into teas for the treatment of nervous disorders and applied locally in the form of an oil to promote wound healing. In Germany, where herbal remedies are well accepted by the medical establishment and covered by health insurance, standardized extracts of *H. perforatum* are more widely prescribed than the popular antidepressant drug fluoxetine (Prozac).

St. John's wort contains a wide variety of substances—most of them unfamiliar to the public at large—that have an equally wide variety of effects in the body. These include:

- naphthodianthrones (including hypericin and pseudohypericin—the former traditionally presumed to be responsible for the herb's antidepressant effect)
- flavonoids (including amentoflavone, which has both sedative and anti-inflammatory effects and is now thought by many to be the primary antidepressant ingredient)
- phloroglucinols (substances thought to have antibiotic properties)
- proanthocyanidins and procyanidins (a chemical class with antioxidant, antiviral, and vasorelaxant [blood-vessel-dilating] properties)
- tannins
- coumarins
- epoxyxanthrophylls

Herbal remedies ... are perceived by the public as "natural" and therefore safe.

- essential oils (some with sedative properties)
- amino acids (including gamma-aminobutyric acid, or GABA, a neurotransmitter [nerve-impulse-transmitting chemical] that enhances sedation)
- betasitosterol (a plant estrogen)

Depending on the method by which the herbal agent is prepared, the concentrations of these different substances vary. Likewise, different preparations of St. John's wort vary greatly in both efficacy and potential toxicity. In this article, to avoid confusion, the whole plant will henceforth be referred to as St. John's wort; *Hypericum* or *H. perforatum* will refer to alcohol extracts of the whole plant (*i.e.*, preparations made by dissolving the herb in an alcohol such as methanol, a process that causes certain ingredients to become more concentrated); and hypericin will refer specifically to that particular component of the whole plant.

A LOOK AT THE EVIDENCE

Like most other herbal remedies, St. John's wort has not yet been scientifically studied in the U.S. The first American clinical trial of the herb was scheduled to begin in 1998. (*See* Sidebar, "Herbal Remedies Under Official Scrutiny," page 238.) At present, most of the data on the effectiveness of the herb in treating depression come from research conducted in Europe, particularly in Germany. Since most of these studies involved relatively small numbers of patients, usually fewer than 100, their results have not been considered conclusive. To overcome this limitation, researchers in Munich and San Antonio, Texas, collaborated on a meta-analysis of 23 trials of St.

John's wort. (Meta-analysis is a technique for pooling the data from a number of studies in order to derive more meaningful results than are provided by any one of them individually.) Their findings were published in the *British Medical Journal* in August 1996.

All of the trials included in the analysis were conducted in Germany; the results of most had already appeared in German medical journals. Fifteen of these studies were double-blind, placebo-controlled trials—*i.e.*, patients treated with *H. perforatum* were compared with another group who received an inactive substance, and neither the subjects nor the researchers knew who had received what. In the other eight trials, patients who received *Hypericum* were compared with controls who took conventional antidepressant drugs (in most cases, agents belonging to the category known as tricyclic antidepressants, such as imipramine and amitriptyline). Slightly more than 1,700 patients were represented in the pooled studies; all were individuals diagnosed with mild to moderate depression, and all were treated on an outpatient basis.

The meta-analysis showed that *Hypericum* extracts are significantly more effective than placebos and equally as effective as the standard antidepressant drugs with which they were compared. Slightly more than 60% of those treated with a low daily dose of *Hypericum* (containing no more than 1.2 milligrams of the hypericin component) improved; higher dosages (up to 2.7 milligrams of the hypericin component) yielded a 75% improvement rate. Side effects of *Hypericum* (*e.g.*, dizziness, dry mouth) were typically mild, and patients taking the herbal extract experienced less-frequent side effects than those treated with antidepres-

A page from a German medieval manuscript (*c.* 1200) shows physicians gathering herbs for medicinal use. These traditional remedies have been trusted by generations of healers and their patients.

sant drugs; only 0.8% of patients taking the herb discontinued treatment because of adverse effects, compared with 3% of patients taking prescription antidepressants.

This study received a great deal of publicity, and its results have been widely cited as confirming the value of St. John's wort in treating depression. But it is by no means the last word. Even the researchers themselves emphasized the preliminary nature of their findings. "Current evidence is inadequate to establish whether hypericum is as effective as other antidepressants," they wrote. "Additional trials should be conducted to compare hypericum with other antidepressants in well-defined groups of patients; to investigate long-term side effects; and to evaluate the relative efficacy of different preparations and doses."

Who's helped? So far, most of the clinical trials of St. John's wort have involved people with relatively mild chronic depression. Patients with somatic symptoms associated with their depression (*e.g.*, aches and pains, lack of energy, sleep problems) may be particularly responsive; in one small study, after only four weeks patients taking St. John's wort reported dramatic improvement of symptoms such as lethargy, fatigue, and sleep disturbances. Similarly, *Hypericum* extract has been shown to help people suffering from seasonal affective disorder (SAD), depressed mood associated with the short daylight hours of winter. The typical symptoms of SAD—fatigue, increased craving for carbohydrate foods, and hypersomnia (excessive need for sleep)—were as responsive to *Hypericum* extract as to therapeutic exposure to bright light, an accepted treatment for SAD. It appears, then, that patients with particular types of depression may benefit more than others from this type of treatment.

Although the herb has been less widely studied in people suffering from severe depression, the evidence thus far indicates that this group too may benefit. Some authorities also speculate that elderly people, who are more sensitive than their younger counterparts to drug side effects, may tolerate St. John's wort better than standard antidepressants.

Determining dosage. Higher doses of *Hypericum* than those used in the trials referred to above—in the range of 0.9 milligram of the hypericin component three times a day—appear to yield a greater therapeutic response without an appreciable increase in side effects. (This dosage is roughly equivalent to 300 milligrams of most standardized *Hypericum* preparations taken three times a day.) Most European doctors recommend a dosage in this range for depressed individuals being treated on an outpatient basis.

Given the wide variability in the contents of different St. John's wort preparations, however, and the variation in the relative concentration of each ingredient in each prepared dose, it is exceedingly difficult to standardize doses. As the scientists who conducted the meta-analysis acknowledged, much more research must be done before safe doses can be determined. Specifically, studies need to be done comparing the clinical effects of different preparations with different concentrations of ingredients, single and combined, in different patient populations.

Safety. Several million people in Germany have used *Hypericum* extracts without any apparent serious adverse effects. The side effects that have been reported are mostly mild and few in number. In the 23 studies included in the meta-analysis, for example, the overall incidence of side effects was 19.8% for *Hypericum*, compared with 35.9% for standard antidepressant therapy. The most commonly reported side effects of the herb include dry mouth, dizziness, gastrointestinal complaints (especially constipation), and confusion. There have also been a few reports of allergic reactions.

Whether St. John's wort can be taken safely by women who are pregnant or breast-feeding is not known. Likewise, little is known about the risks of overdose. When cattle and sheep ingest the plant in large quantities, some of the animals develop hypersensitivity to sunlight, and there have been reports of increased photosensitivity in humans taking the herb; in the controlled trials, however, this side effect was also reported by a comparable percentage of people taking a placebo.

HOW IT WORKS: A MYSTERY

As noted above, St. John's wort contains at least 10 constituents thought to be pharmacologically active. Its mood-elevating properties may be due to the actions of several of these, either individually or in combination. The St. John's wort preparations available at health-food stores are usually standardized to the hypericin content—that is, they contain approximately 0.9 milligram of hypericin in each 300-milligram tablet of *Hypericum* extract.

Although all of the known chemical constituents of *H. perforatum* have been analyzed and studied, scientists still do not know exactly which ones are responsible for the herb's therapeutic effects—or, for that matter, how these effects are achieved. One hypothesis is that St. John's wort acts on anxiety and depression by changing the availability or activity of certain neurotransmitters, especially serotonin and GABA. Then again, some scientists have proposed that, at least in certain cases of depression, the antidepressant properties of the herb are due not to mood-elevating chemicals but rather to constituents that fight viruses. Yet another hypothesis suggests that the antidepressant action of *Hypericum* may be due to the effect of certain constituents on immune function. And although hypericin was traditionally assumed to be the active ingredient in St. John's wort, other components of the plant also have the potential for psychoactive effects.

Psychoactive properties. Hypericin was initially believed to act by inhibiting monoamine oxidase (MAO)—an enzyme that is responsible primarily for breaking down the neurotransmitters serotonin and norepinephrine, both of which have pronounced effects on mood. An MAO inhibitor, as the name implies, is any substance that inhibits, or prevents, the normal action of the enzyme. The result is an increase in the amount of neurotransmitter available to the cells. One class of antidepressant drugs—usually referred to simply as the MAO inhibitors (*e.g.*, isocarboxazid [Marplan], phenelzine [Nardil])—functions on this very principle.

It would seem logical to presume, then, that the MAO-inhibiting property of St. John's wort accounts for its antidepressant effect. But the actions of the herb are not this simple. For one thing, pure hypericin is not an MAO inhibitor. Certain flavonoid constituents of the herb do have potent MAO-inhibiting capabilities, but most scientists contend that the amount of flavonoids present in properly prepared extracts of *H. perforatum* is not sufficient to produce this effect.

The theory that hypericin acts by altering neurotransmitter levels is further complicated by the fact that it is one of many substances incapable of crossing the blood-brain barrier, a sheath of cells surrounding the capillaries of the brain that selectively prevents many types of molecules from entering the brain's circulation. The blood-brain barrier allows oxygen, caffeine, nicotine, and alcohol, for example, to penetrate the brain but screens out most drugs. If hypericin is indeed unable to penetrate the brain, then it must be assumed either that its primary site of action lies outside the central nervous system (the brain and spinal cord) or that it enters the central nervous system via certain brain regions where there is no blood-brain barrier. Another alternative is that it is allowed to traverse a "leaky," or defective, blood-brain barrier com-

promised by infection, increased body temperature, stress, or other factors.

Antiviral effects. Hypericin and certain substances derived from it are known to be active against herpes simplex virus type 1 (the virus associated with cold sores) and possibly retroviruses, including HIV (the virus that causes AIDS). The fact that depression resistant to standard antidepressant therapy is occasionally associated with viral infection raises the intriguing possibility that it is the antiviral properties of St. John's wort—rather than its actions on the nervous system—that are responsible for the antidepressant effects. Further, in the laboratory *Hypericum* preparations appear to inhibit production of the immune system regulators known as cytokines, which are involved in fighting viral infections. Overproduction of cytokines has been associated with a depression-like sense of malaise.

Influence on the immune system. Hypericin's ability to inhibit the production of immuno-modulators (substances that regulate immune responses) could result in a reduction of the activity of the body's primary "stress hormone" system, the hypothalamic-pituitary-adrenal (HPA) axis, by decreasing production of stress-related hormones. Because depression is associated with both hyperactivity of the HPA axis and increases in certain immunomodulators, hypericin's effects on these could

Yvonne Hemsey—Gamma/Liaison

> ## Several million people in Germany have used *Hypericum* extracts without any apparent serious adverse effects.

American consumers have embraced this latest "hot" herbal remedy with enthusiasm, spending some $200 million on *Hypericum*-containing products (including lipsticks!) in 1997 alone.

Depression can be a serious, even life-threatening, condition. When severely depressed people treat themselves with nonprescription herbal medications, they may not get much-needed professional help.

be responsible for some of the herb's therapeutic benefits. Interestingly, chronic fatigue syndrome is also associated with altered activity of the HPA axis, which could account for the benefits of St. John's wort to individuals with this condition.

HIDDEN HAZARDS OF SELF-MEDICATION

Up to 50% of people with major depression attempt at least once to take their own life, and as many as 25% eventually succeed in killing themselves. Half of those who commit suicide have never sought professional help. Moreover, up to 70% of people treated with antidepressant drugs fail to respond to the first drug they take. Clearly, these findings show that depression can be a life-threatening illness, and treating it may require time, patience, and professional expertise.

As mentioned above, St. John's wort has the advantage of being

available without a prescription, but this very feature may also be a disadvantage. Some who decide to try the herb—including some who suffer from severe depression—may not get the results they anticipated. After taking it for a few weeks, they may feel no better; they may even feel worse. Unaware that there are other drugs available and that it may take time to find the right one, self-medicating individuals could become increasingly despondent, perhaps even suicidal.

Still another hazard of self-medication is lack of awareness of dangerous, or even lethal, interactions that may occur with prescription medications, over-the-counter products, and even foods. Although St. John's wort has so far been shown to have a low incidence of side effects, it is not wholly without dangers.

One particularly serious adverse effect is the so-called serotonin syndrome, a potentially lethal condi-

tion marked by confusion, fever, chills, sweating, flushing, speech difficulties, unstable gait, muscle contractions, and hyperactive reflexes. Untreated, it can progress to unstable blood pressure, delirium, and in some cases even death. In the past year at least two cases of apparent classic serotonin syndrome have been reported in individuals taking St. John's wort. In one case the patient was taking the herbal remedy alone; in the other case the patient began to take St. John's wort within six days of discontinuing trazodone, an antidepressant with serotonin-system activity. Fortunately, both patients survived.

The risk of serotonin syndrome is not confined to those taking St. John's wort; the condition can occur in any individual combining medications that increase production or availability of serotonin, including the selective serotonin reuptake inhibitors, or SSRIs (the class of antidepressants that includes Prozac),

236

the MAO inhibitor antidepressants, venlafaxine (Effexor; a chemically unique antidepressant), some other new antidepressant drugs, and the amino acid supplement L-tryptophan (no longer sold in the U.S. but available in Canada and elsewhere). What makes the risk associated with St. John's wort especially noteworthy is the unquestioning assumption of so many consumers that "natural" remedies can do no harm.

The possibility that the whole herb or one or more of its components may inhibit MAO is particularly important when considering potential interactions with other substances. Compounds that inhibit MAO—including the antidepressants and other drugs whose therapeutic effect depends on this property—have one extremely dangerous side effect: they can interact with tyramine, a component of many fermented foods, among them wine, beer, and aged cheeses, causing a sudden and drastic rise in blood pressure. In extreme cases a stroke may result. MAO inhibitors may also interact with certain sympathetic nervous system enhancers, including psychostimulants like amphetamine and methylphenidate (Ritalin); ephedrine and pseudoephedrine (constituents of many cough and cold remedies); and other MAO inhibitors. If St. John's

Up to 50% of people with major depression attempt at least once to take their own life.

wort acts as an MAO inhibitor, it too may interact with these other compounds. In 1997, for example, an elderly Minnesota woman was reported to have suffered a hypertensive crisis (blood pressure of 260/140) resulting in a paralyzing stroke while using St. John's wort in combination with a sympathetic nervous system stimulant she was taking for bladder spasms.

The promotion of St. John's wort as an herbal alternative to the diet drug combination "fen-phen" (fenfluramine plus phentermine) raises similar concerns, especially since most consumers who take these over-the-counter remedies are not under medical supervision, and many are unaware of the potential for drug interactions. Depending on the preparation of St. John's wort that is used, diet regimens that combine the herb with ephedrine could have enough MAO inhibitory activity to dangerously increase blood pressure.

TO TAKE—OR NOT?

From the evidence thus far, *Hypericum* extract appears to be a promising herbal antidepressant that is well tolerated by most who take it. Much remains to be learned, however. Scientists are uncertain, for example, whether the herb is more effective for certain types of depression than for others. Patients with what is termed *anergic* depression—characterized by symptoms like fatigue, sleepiness, and mental sluggishness—seem to be more responsive than others, but the effects of the herb in people with different subtypes of depression have not yet been studied in controlled clinical trials. Also unknown is the quality of different commercially available preparations of *Hypericum*. And more work must be done to determine the

overall toxicity of the herb and the hazards of overdose.

It is important that anyone who is considering the use of St. John's wort for depression understand just exactly what *is* and *is not* known—especially about the potential for interaction with other substances and the possibility of previously unrecognized adverse events. When taken by informed individuals under medical supervision, this humble weed may indeed prove to be an effective alternative to antidepressant drugs.

FOR FURTHER INFORMATION

Publication
HerbalGram (quarterly), published by the American Botanical Council and the Herb Research Foundation (*see* below).

Organizations
American Botanical Council
PO Box 144345
Austin TX 78714-4345
512-926-4900
Web site:
http://www.herbalgram.org
Herb Research Foundation
Suite 200
1007 Pearl St
Boulder CO 80302
303-449-2265
Web site:
http://www.herbs.org/
OAM (Office of Alternative Medicine)
Clearinghouse
PO Box 8218
Silver Spring MD 20907-8218
888-644-6226
Web site:
http://altmed.od.nih.gov/oam/clearinghouse/

Web site
http://www.primenet.com/~camilla/STJOHNS.FAQ

HERBAL REMEDIES UNDER OFFICIAL SCRUTINY

BY SANDRA LANGENECKERT

Echinacea *(Echinacea purpurea)*

Ginkgo...kava...ginseng...echinacea...black cohosh...saw palmetto—these exotic-sounding botanical names are now familiar to millions of Americans who have turned to herbal remedies for relief of everything from colds and flu to hot flashes and prostate problems. In 1997 alone, American consumers spent almost $2 billion on herbal products. Yet the medical establishment on the whole has been reluctant to endorse such therapies, on the grounds that the evidence of their benefits is largely "anecdotal"—that is, based on nothing more than the subjective reports of people who have tried them. Medical scientists in the U.S. and many other developed countries typically demand more rigorous proof of efficacy, based not on personal accounts but on objective data gathered in a kind of study known as a controlled clinical trial. In such a trial, a remedy under scrutiny—whether an herbal extract or a sophisticated new drug—is compared with an inactive substance, or placebo, under a strict research protocol.

Now, with public interest in herbal medicine at an all-time high, controlled clinical trials of these long-used remedies are finally being initiated in the U.S. Many of the trials are being conducted in cooperation with the Office of Alternative Medicine (OAM), an agency established by Congress in 1992 with a specific mandate to rigorously review therapies that have otherwise been considered unorthodox or on the "fringe." Within a few years scientists should have data on the safety and effectiveness of a number of popular herbal remedies. The following is a sample of trials of specific herbs that are in various stages of completion.

Echinacea

Traditionally used by American Indians as a treatment for burns and snake and insect bites, echinacea is believed by many modern authorities to boost immune function. Echinacea-containing products are widely touted as a cure for colds and flu. Researchers at Bastyr University Research Institute, Bothell, Washington, have enrolled 160 volunteers in a 16-month trial to determine whether the

Sandra Langeneckert is a freelance writer and a copy editor at Encyclopædia Britannica, Inc., in Chicago.

pressed juice of the plant *E. purpurea* effectively reduces the incidence and severity of respiratory tract infections.

Ginkgo

Ginkgo biloba has been an essential component of Chinese medicine for thousands of years. Current interest focuses on its purported ability to enhance mental acuity and improve memory. A highly publicized yearlong multicenter study, reported in the Oct. 22/29, 1997, issue of the *Journal of the American Medical Association*, concluded that an extract of the herb had favorable, albeit modest, effects on the mental function of people diagnosed with dementia. In an ongoing trial, researchers at the Kessler Institute for Rehabilitation, West Orange, New Jersey, are studying ginkgo's impact on cognition, cardiovascular regulation, mood, and daily functioning in people who have suffered a stroke or other brain injury.

Kava

A member of the pepper family, kava (*Piper methysticum*) has long been believed to possess calming properties. In 1997 scientists at Virginia Commonwealth University conducted a double-blind study of the ability of kava to alleviate the stress and tension associated with everyday life. They reported in the March 1998 *Alternative Therapies in Health and Medicine* that kava, administered in the form of the supplement Kavatrol, was more effective than a placebo in reducing nonclinical levels of anxiety.

Lavender

Lavender (*Lavandula* species), prized for centuries for its fragrance, has also been used medicinally as an antiseptic

Fan-shaped leaves of the ginkgo tree (*Ginkgo biloba*)   French lavender (*Lavandula stoechas*)

and to relieve digestive problems. Today it is being investigated as a cancer therapy. In an ongoing study at the University of Wisconsin Medical School at Madison, researchers are using perillyl alcohol, one of the main components of lavender oil, to treat breast, prostate, and ovarian cancers. Future trials may involve the use of the substance as a treatment for colon cancer and chronic leukemia.

Saw palmetto

An extract from the berries of the saw palmetto (*Sabal serrulata*), a small palm tree native to the southeastern U.S. and the West Indies, has been widely used in Europe to relieve symptoms of benign prostatic hyperplasia (BPH), or enlargement of the prostate gland. The condition is common in men over age 50 and can cause troublesome urinary symptoms—in particular, frequent urination. A study now under way at medical centers in California, Wisconsin, Connecticut, and Florida is investigating the use of a drug made from saw palmetto for relief of symptoms associated with BPH. There is especially keen interest in the herb because it is believed to provide relief without causing impotence or decreased sex drive, both of which are not uncommon side effects of the drugs now being used to treat BPH.

St. John's wort

In November 1997 scientists at the National Institutes of Health announced plans for the first American clinical trial of St. John's wort (*Hypericum perforatum*). The herb will be the subject of a three-year investigation assessing its role in the treatment of clinical depression. Some 330 patients will be randomly assigned to treatment with either St. John's wort, a selective serotonin reuptake inhibitor (the class of antidepressant drugs that includes Prozac), or a placebo. The study is being sponsored jointly by the OAM, the National Institute of Mental Health, and the Office of Dietary Supplements.

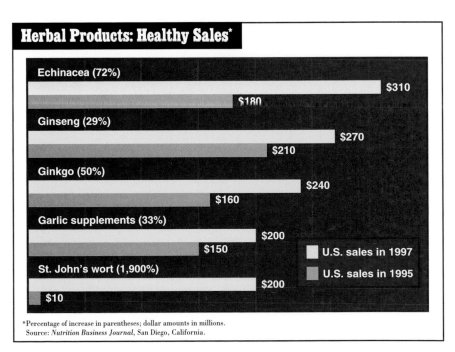

Herbal Products: Healthy Sales*

Echinacea (72%) — $310 / $180
Ginseng (29%) — $270 / $210
Ginkgo (50%) — $240 / $160
Garlic supplements (33%) — $200 / $150
St. John's wort (1,900%) — $200 / $10

■ U.S. sales in 1997
■ U.S. sales in 1995

*Percentage of increase in parentheses; dollar amounts in millions.
Source: *Nutrition Business Journal*, San Diego, California.

IT'S PROBABLY SOMETHING

YOU ATE...

Back in 1950, if public health authorities had been asked to predict the most serious challenges that would face them in the year 2000, it's unlikely that many would have put food poisoning near the top of their lists. At that time antibiotics were just coming into

BY ADRIENNE A. HARKAVY

The true extent
of foodborne
illness can only
be estimated.

common use against diseases like tuberculosis, and summer epidemics of infantile paralysis—polio—still terrorized the nation. The safety of the food sold in U.S. markets and served up in American homes and eating establishments was one thing the public could rely on.

Not any longer. Today, outbreaks of foodborne disease regularly make headlines, and second-graders who've never heard of polio know that the potentially deadly bacterium *Escherichia coli* may lurk in undercooked hamburgers. The number of Americans affected by foodborne diseases each year is staggering: as many as 81 million by some estimates. Each year, some 9,000 deaths are attributed to these ailments. And since the reported cases of foodborne illness represent only a small fraction of the total, these numbers may be only the tip of the iceberg.

People who come down with an upset stomach often assume—usually rightly—that the problem will go away without treatment. Most shrug off their symptoms as "just a little bout of stomach flu" and never see a doctor. (Actually, the term *stomach flu* is a misnomer; influenza, or "flu," is a respiratory illness caused exclusively by viruses. Foodborne illness is most commonly bacterial.) Still others who become ill may lack access to medical care. Thus, a number of people in a community may contract a foodborne disease without the health authorities' ever being informed. Moreover, local and state health agencies often lack the resources to investigate outbreaks thoroughly. As a result, the true extent of foodborne illness can only be estimated.

If the public health community has been taken unawares by the recent rise in foodborne disease, it has wasted no time analyzing the factors responsible. Certainly Americans' increasing reliance on imported foods is a critical one, as are changes in domestic food production and distribution. Altered eating habits have played a part, as have the emergence of new foodborne "bugs" and the evolution of more virulent strains of familiar organisms. But these developments need to be put into perspective. First, it is necessary to understand something about the nature of foodborne disease.

GUESS WHO'S COMING TO DINNER?

The unappetizing truth about the spread of foodborne illness is that virtually any food can be a vehicle for pathogens (disease-causing agents) responsible for a wide range

Adrienne A. Harkavy is a medical writer based in Maine.

(Overleaf) "Voluptas Carnis" by Pieter Aertsen (1508/09–75). (Right) A field-worker harvests raspberries at a farm just outside Guatemala City. In 1996 tainted berries from Guatemala were implicated in an outbreak of cyclosporiasis that affected more than 1,400 consumers in North America. Increasing American reliance on imported produce is a major factor in the rising incidence of foodborne disease.

Moises Castillo—AP/Wide World

Virtually any food can be a vehicle for disease-causing microorganisms. Uncooked items like these salad-bar offerings are particularly likely culprits.

of unpleasant symptoms. Although a visit to the doctor is the only way to know for sure if you have a foodborne infection, common symptoms include nausea and vomiting, severe abdominal cramps, diarrhea (often bloody), dry mouth, double vision, difficulty swallowing, and flulike symptoms such as fever, chills, headache, and backache. Symptoms may occur within hours after eating a suspect food or as long as 10 days afterward. As the epidemiologist for the state of Maine, Kathleen Gensheimer, observes, "People always think it's their last meal, but—depending on the bug—it can take days before symptoms appear."

The risky business of eating. All foodborne diseases begin in the same way—with the ingestion of a food substance that contains an infectious agent. Though any food can be a potential hazard (especially when handled improperly), high-protein foods of animal origin—meat, poultry, seafood, and dairy and egg products—are implicated more frequently than others. Moreover, food can be contaminated at any of the many points in its journey from farm or processing plant to table. *Salmonella*, for example, may colonize the digestive tracts of live chickens and

can remain in butchered birds throughout processing. Likewise, the bacterium can be transferred from contaminated poultry parts or carcasses to wholesome ones during processing. Finally, although food may reach home and restaurant kitchens in a fresh, untainted state, it may then be contaminated by poor handling or storage practices.

Pathogens may reproduce in the food itself or in the diner's digestive system. Whether illness develops depends primarily on two factors: the quantity of the disease-causing organism ingested and the susceptibility of the person who ingested it. Susceptibility varies widely; some people are more vulnerable than others to infection in general and to certain pathogens in particular. Whereas foodborne diseases are self-limiting—*i.e.*, they go away on their own—in most healthy adults, some segments of the population are at greater risk than others for severe illness or life-threatening complications like hemolytic uremic syndrome, the potentially fatal kidney disorder caused by the deadly strain of *E. coli* designated O157:H7.

The vulnerable. Not only are the elderly the fastest-growing segment of the U.S. population; they are also the

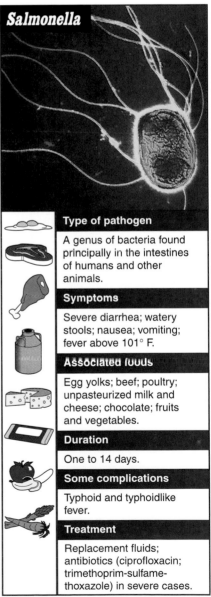

Salmonella

Type of pathogen

A genus of bacteria found principally in the intestines of humans and other animals.

Symptoms

Severe diarrhea; watery stools; nausea; vomiting; fever above 101° F.

Associated foods

Egg yolks; beef; poultry; unpasteurized milk and cheese; chocolate; fruits and vegetables.

Duration

One to 14 days.

Some complications

Typhoid and typhoidlike fever.

Treatment

Replacement fluids; antibiotics (ciprofloxacin; trimethoprim-sulfame-thoxazole) in severe cases.

largest group at risk for foodborne disease. Older people are particularly vulnerable because advancing age is associated with both a decline in immune competence (the ability of the immune system to successfully combat disease) and the onset of chronic diseases such as diabetes, heart disease, and cancer. Moreover, with aging the stomach produces less bacteria-destroying acid, and the kidneys may become less efficient in filtering bacteria from the blood.

Others especially vulnerable to foodborne illness are those whose immune systems have been weakened by diseases such as diabetes, cancer, and AIDS. Foodborne illnesses can be extremely difficult to treat in people suffering from chronic diseases. And in some cases the treatments for chronic conditions are themselves responsible for the increased susceptibility. For example, although medical advances such as radiation treatment and chemotherapy have increased life expectancy for many with cancer, these therapies are associated with a reduction in the ability to ward off infection.

Pregnant women are also at high risk, as some foodborne illnesses can bring about miscarriage or stillbirth. Infants and young children are particularly vulnerable because their immune systems are not fully developed until several years after birth. Certain foodborne pathogens have been associated with the development of urinary tract infections, meningitis, and kidney failure in infants and children. In fact, *E. coli* O157:H7 is now the leading cause of acute kidney failure in children in the U.S. Another potent bacterium, *Listeria monocytogenes*—which is spread through certain dairy products and triggers the disease known as listeriosis—may cause miscarriage or infect the blood of a fetus.

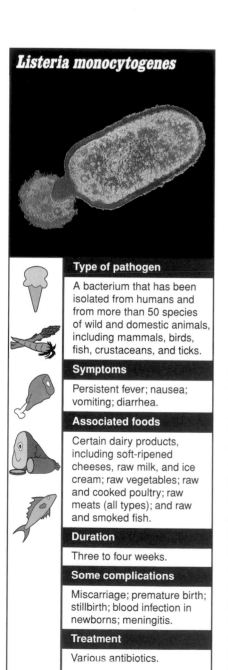

Listeria monocytogenes

Type of pathogen

A bacterium that has been isolated from humans and from more than 50 species of wild and domestic animals, including mammals, birds, fish, crustaceans, and ticks.

Symptoms

Persistent fever; nausea; vomiting; diarrhea.

Associated foods

Certain dairy products, including soft-ripened cheeses, raw milk, and ice cream; raw vegetables; raw and cooked poultry; raw meats (all types); and raw and smoked fish.

Duration

Three to four weeks.

Some complications

Miscarriage; premature birth; stillbirth; blood infection in newborns; meningitis.

Treatment

Various antibiotics.

Photo by Kari Lounatmaa—
Science Source/Photo Researchers

WHAT'S "BUGGING" YOU?

Although bacteria cause the most commonly reported foodborne illnesses, they are not the only agents of such disease. There are at least five categories of foodborne pathogens: bacteria, viruses, parasites, food toxins, and "unknown."

Bacteria: varied and versatile. Bacteria inhabit virtually all environments, including soil, water, organic matter, and the bodies of multicellular animals. They are an essential part of the Earth's ecology. Some are beneficial to humans and are even used in food processing; most do not cause disease. On the other hand, bacteria are responsible for more than two-thirds of all outbreaks of foodborne illness in the U.S. There are literally thousands of different strains of bacteria that can cause foodborne illness, and that makes it difficult to generalize about their characteristics and effects. For example, though most bacteria prefer warm temperatures, a few, like the highly virulent *E. coli* O157:H7, are able to multiply even when the food they reside in is refrigerated. Though cooking destroys most species of bacteria, some can survive boiling. And some, like *Clostridium perfringens*, which causes enteritis (intestinal inflammation) and diarrhea, thrive in environments where there is little or no oxygen. Such bacteria are termed anaerobic because they can survive in an oxygen-poor atmosphere.

The bacteria associated with foodborne illness spread easily and rapidly because their needs are simple: sufficient moisture and nutrients, a favorable temperature, and time to reproduce. Animal protein foods such as meat, eggs, poultry, and (continued on page 246)

BATTLING BACTERIA: THE PROBLEM OF ANTIBIOTIC RESISTANCE

BY ADRIENNE A. HARKAVY

Not only are bacteria now responsible for more than two-thirds of all outbreaks of foodborne illness in the U.S., but a growing number of species can defy virtually all existing antibiotics. Like other living things, bacteria require certain conditions—sufficient food, suitable moisture and temperature—for survival, growth, and multiplication. These conditions vary widely from one species to another. When conditions are favorable, bacteria reproduce rapidly, which means that mutations (changes in the genetic material) can arise in a relatively brief period of time. In fact, the speed with which bacteria can reproduce and mutate is one factor that helps them develop resistance to antibiotics.

Stuart B. Levy, a professor of microbiology at the Tufts University School of Medicine, Boston, and president of the Alliance for the Prudent Use of Antibiotics, was one of the first scientists to warn of the public health threat posed by the emergence of drug-resistant organisms. As Levy explained in an article entitled "The Challenge of Antibiotic Resistance" (*Scientific American*, March 1998), bacteria acquire resistance in a variety of ways. Some bacteria may inherit resistance genes; others acquire them as a result of spontaneous mutations or through the strengthening of an already existing resistance trait. Still others acquire a defense against a given antibiotic from an adjacent bacterial cell by means of plasmids—tiny rings of DNA capable of transporting genes from one bacterial cell to the next. Viruses may also pluck a resistance gene from one bacterium and inject it into another. Moreover, when dead bacterial cells disintegrate, other bacteria may acquire the newly released genetic material.

Ironically, the use of antibiotics may actually contribute to the emergence of resistant strains. Bacterial cells that are susceptible to antibiotics are eradicated by these drugs, but cells that have developed resistance survive and, facing reduced competition, go on to proliferate. Subsequent generations of organisms resistant to one agent may or may not be susceptible to others. To date, strains of at least three potentially deadly bacteria that do not respond to any drugs—*Enterococcus faecalis*, *Mycobacterium tuberculosis*, and *Pseudomonas aeruginosa*—have been identified.

Many authorities now agree with Levy that overuse of antibiotics has played a major part in the recent increase in drug-resistant strains. According to his estimates, only half of the roughly 50 million pounds of antibiotics produced yearly in the U.S. are prescribed for use by humans—and, he claims, only half that use is appropriate. The other 25 million pounds of antibiotics are used agriculturally—as growth promoters for poultry and livestock and as aerosols for treatment of fruit trees. The antibiotic treatment of both animals and trees, like that of humans, has been associated with the emergence of resistant strains.

Levy and other health experts are also concerned about the recent proliferation of household antimicrobial products. During the past few years, the number of germ-fighting consumer products has increased steadily to include such diverse items as antimicrobial soaps and cleansers and various objects—toys, underwear, sponges, cutting boards, toothbrush holders—impregnated with germ-fighting chemicals. Levy contends that the use of such products could result in the emergence of resistant strains of common household bacteria that would otherwise be washed away with conventional soaps and detergents.

Moreover, a number of health experts maintain that the effectiveness of these new germ-fighting products is questionable. "The awareness that's being created about the need to be more conscientious in the home with respect to germs is important and well justified," observes Gail H. Cassell, chair of the department of microbiology at the University of Alabama at Birmingham, "but I think with the [antimicrobial] products, we have a long way to go before we can claim efficacy." As Cassell further explains, "Just because a toy has this component in it, doesn't mean it's going to maintain efficacy when dropped on the floor or on a dirty diaper. Organisms could still be viable."

Levy says that routine housecleaning can be accomplished effectively with standard soaps and detergents and with tried-and-true disinfectants such as chlorine bleach, alcohol, ammonia, and hydrogen peroxide. He warns that if we attempt to create a sterile household environment, we may find instead that we have created "bugs" resistant to just about everything.

(*continued from page 244*)

fish often provide just these conditions. Further, items such as knives and other utensils, cutting boards, and human hands can transmit bacteria and other contaminants to food. The home kitchen provides many environments—sponges, dish towels, countertops, sinks, wooden utensils—where bacteria can flourish. Water also can be a source of bacteria and other pathogens.

Bacteria possess two properties that enable them to develop resistance to the very agents that were developed specifically to kill them—antibiotics. The first is their ability to mutate, or undergo genetic change, very rapidly. The second is the speed with which they can multiply. Bacterial cells, which are constantly evolving, can exchange genetic material not only with cells of the same species but with cells of other species. This happened during an outbreak of dysentery in Central America in the 1970s. Scientists suspect that a virus carried a toxin-producing gene from *Shigella*, the bacterium that caused the outbreak, to an *E. coli* cell. (*See* diagram below.) The result was a nasty and

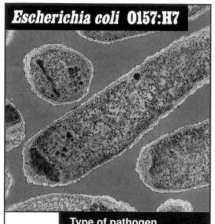

Escherichia coli O157:H7

Type of pathogen	A particularly virulent strain of the bacterium *E. coli* (a normal inhabitant of the intestines of all animals, including humans).
Symptoms	Watery and/or bloody diarrhea; abdominal pain; nausea; occasional vomiting; fever (in some but not all cases).
Associated foods	Raw or undercooked ground meat; unpasteurized milk.
Duration	Five to eight days.
Some complications	Gastroenteritis (intestinal inflammation); hemolytic uremic syndrome (a life-threatening kidney condition).
Treatment	Replacement fluids; antibiotics not usually needed; antidiarrheal medication should not be used.

E. coli O157:H7: How a "Superbug" May Have Evolved

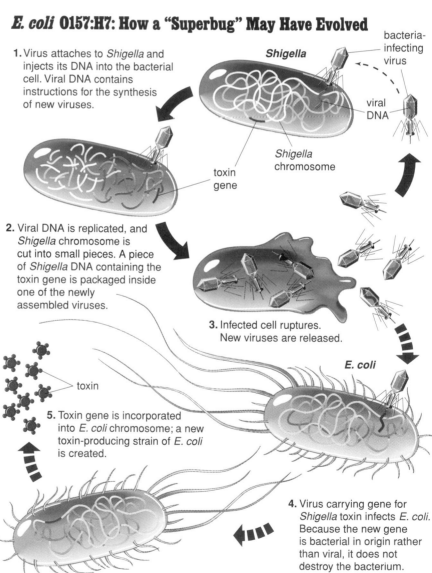

1. Virus attaches to *Shigella* and injects its DNA into the bacterial cell. Viral DNA contains instructions for the synthesis of new viruses.

2. Viral DNA is replicated, and *Shigella* chromosome is cut into small pieces. A piece of *Shigella* DNA containing the toxin gene is packaged inside one of the newly assembled viruses.

3. Infected cell ruptures. New viruses are released.

4. Virus carrying gene for *Shigella* toxin infects *E. coli*. Because the new gene is bacterial in origin rather than viral, it does not destroy the bacterium.

5. Toxin gene is incorporated into *E. coli* chromosome; a new toxin-producing strain of *E. coli* is created.

Shigella

bacteria-infecting virus

viral DNA

Shigella chromosome

toxin gene

E. coli

toxin

E. coli O157:H7

The great majority of food-borne illnesses in the U.S. are attributed to meals eaten away from home. The restaurant kitchen is an ideal setting for the transmission of foodborne pathogens.

sometimes deadly new bug, *E. coli* O157:H7.

Viruses: tiny but deadly. Like bacteria, viruses—tiny infectious agents too small to be seen with an ordinary microscope—can mutate in response to environmental challenges. This explains why viruses, too, readily become resistant to drugs. Unlike bacteria, however, viruses lack an independent metabolism and can grow or multiply only within living "host" cells.

Viruses cause infection in three ways: (1) they replicate (reproduce themselves) in sufficient numbers to damage inhabited cells; (2) they cause inhabited cells to release toxic substances; and (3) they trigger the body's immune system—after it recognizes viral markers on the cells of an infected organ, which signal the invader's presence—to launch an immune response that damages the organ. Viruses that cause foodborne illness, such as the hepatitis A virus, are usually transmitted by the fecal-oral route through contaminated water and food. For example, a virus may be transmitted from human

feces to food by a restaurant worker who neglects to wash his hands after using the toilet or by a mother who fails to wash after changing her baby's diapers. Viruses are also frequently contracted by people who drink sewage-contaminated water.

Foodborne viruses are found worldwide. One of the largest recorded outbreaks of foodborne viral disease occurred in 1997 when some 260 students and teachers in Michigan were sickened by hepatitis A. The outbreak was linked to contaminated Mexican strawberries that had been served in school lunches.

Parasites: particularly dangerous. Food and water are also vehicles for parasites. The parasites that cause foodborne illness include tapeworms, roundworms, and certain protozoans. Trichinosis, a disease caused by the small roundworm *Trichinella spiralis*, is transmitted to humans who eat undercooked pork that harbors encapsulated larvae of the parasite.

In recent years outbreaks of cyclosporiasis, a foodborne illness caused by a little-known protozoan, *Cyclospora cayetanensis*, have been

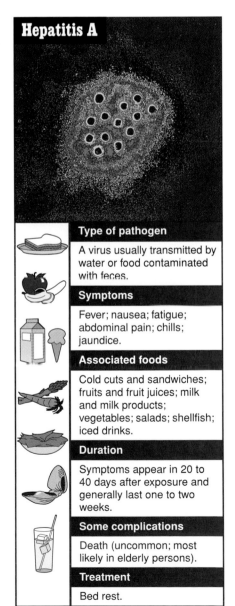

Hepatitis A

Type of pathogen	
	A virus usually transmitted by water or food contaminated with feces.
Symptoms	
	Fever; nausea; fatigue; abdominal pain; chills; jaundice.
Associated foods	
	Cold cuts and sandwiches; fruits and fruit juices; milk and milk products; vegetables; salads; shellfish; iced drinks.
Duration	
	Symptoms appear in 20 to 40 days after exposure and generally last one to two weeks.
Some complications	
	Death (uncommon; most likely in elderly persons).
Treatment	
	Bed rest.

> For the first time in history, some countries have begun to grow crops specifically to meet the demand of consumers halfway around the world.

reported with increasing frequency. The first known outbreak of *C. cayetanensis* infection in the U.S. occurred in 1990 when 21 staff members at a Chicago hospital were infected after drinking contaminated water. Among foodborne pathogens, parasites are particularly dangerous; about 5 of every 1,000 persons who contract a parasitic foodborne illness die from that illness.

Food toxins: potent poisons. Toxins, often associated with seafood, can cause neurological or allergic symptoms as well as gastrointestinal upset. Like parasitic diseases, illnesses due to food toxins have a high mortality rate, killing 5.4 of every 1,000 victims. The most dramatic of these illnesses is triggered by tetrodotoxin and is acquired by eating improperly prepared pufferfish. Neurological symptoms occur 20 minutes to three hours following ingestion, and death usually occurs within four to six hours. Another well-known potent food toxin is ciguatoxin, found in tropical marine fish that have eaten a particular alga. A major outbreak of ciguatoxin poisoning occurred in Florida in 1991; 20 people became ill after eating contaminated amberjack at the same seafood restaurant.

Still to be identified. One of the most alarming facts about foodborne illness is that a very high number of pathogens have yet to be identified. Statistically, in fact, most cases of foodborne disease are classified as "cause unknown," since, except in the case of large outbreaks, tests to determine the identity of the infectious agent are not conducted.

FOOD: GLOBAL TRAVELER

With fresh peaches for sale at the supermarket in January and apples abundant in July, many people have forgotten that fresh fruits and vegetables were once seasonal and limited in availability. Until the 1940s or '50s, most fresh foods were consumed in the general vicinity of where they were grown or raised. Poultry, for example, might have come from a chicken farm in a nearby town or even from one's own coop; fruits and vegetables, too, tended to be home- or locally grown. In winter, people in northern regions relied on root vegetables like potatoes and turnips and stored fruits such as apples as well as home-canned or store-bought produce. One-stop shopping hadn't been invented—the homemaker purchased meat and poultry from the butcher, produce from the greengrocer, and packaged goods from yet another store. In many cases the shop owners knew the growers and producers who supplied foods to their businesses.

The food supply is vastly different today. Depending upon the season, anywhere from 30% to 70% of produce sold in the U.S. has been grown outside the country's borders. Food imports have doubled since the 1980s, and imported food is here to stay.

Jeremy Sobel, a medical epidemiologist at the Centers for Disease Control and Prevention (CDC) in Atlanta, Georgia, points out that for the first time in history, some countries have begun to grow crops specifically to meet the demand of consumers halfway around the world. Guatemala, for example, specializes in the growth and exportation of raspberries. Mexico now provides much of the lettuce consumed in the U.S., and grapes that appear in American markets in midwinter are likely to have come from Chile.

Older generations of Americans associated foodborne illness mostly

with travel to exotic destinations. They even had a name for it: traveler's diarrhea. But now it is the *food* that does the traveling, coming to us from virtually every corner of the world. And it comes with "bugs" previously rare or even unknown in industrial countries—or, at least, reserved as the perils of overseas travelers.

It's no picnic. Getting products from a grower in Chile to consumers in New Orleans or New York City requires vast, complex transportation and distribution systems. Such systems distribute food, but they also distribute disease-causing microorganisms widely and efficiently. At the same time, the intricacy of the process greatly complicates the tracking of outbreaks of foodborne illness.

"Outbreak scenarios," as epidemiologists call the circumstances surrounding an epidemic, are changing drastically. At one time the typical

outbreak scenario involved the proverbial potato salad at the church picnic—improperly stored food consumed locally by a relatively small number of closely related people. Today, however, the typical scenario is much more likely to involve the contamination of mass-produced or widely distributed foods and the subsequent illness of large numbers of people—sometimes in the thousands—across state and even national borders. Take, for example, a shipment of lettuce grown in Central America—contaminated with *E. coli* via the untreated water used to irrigate the fields—and shipped to a central distribution point in the western U.S. The bacteria-laden produce is then distributed to all of the wholesaler's customers—fast-food chains, supermarket chains, and any number of smaller vendors—with the result that a widespread outbreak of gastrointestinal upset (or serious *E.*

Cartons of produce await shipment on a loading dock in an Oakland, California, warehouse. An enormous transportation network distributes fresh foods from around the globe—and any pathogens they may carry— to every corner of the U.S.

249

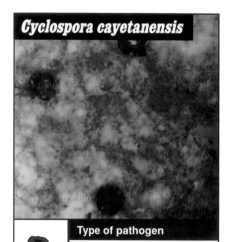

Cyclospora cayetanensis

Type of pathogen

A little-known parasite, possibly transmitted by water or food contaminated with feces.

Symptoms

Watery diarrhea; loss of appetite; weight loss; bloating; excessive gas; stomach cramps; nausea; vomiting; fatigue; muscle ache; low-grade fever.

Associated foods

Fresh fruits; imported raspberries and American-grown strawberries have been implicated in recent documented cases.

Duration

A few days to a month or longer.

Some complications

Symptoms may recur and may be more severe in persons with compromised immune systems.

Treatment

Trimethoprim-sulfamethoxazole.

Photo by Bradley A. Connor, M.D.

250

coli-related disease, depending upon the strain) ensues. Imagine the problems epidemiologists face as they try to track such an outbreak among thousands of persons with vastly different diets who've never shared so much as a single meal.

The case of the contaminated raspberries. A situation much like the one described above was responsible for a huge outbreak in 1996. More than 1,400 consumers in 20 states, the District of Columbia, and two Canadian provinces developed symptoms that included cramping, abdominal pain, severe diarrhea, nausea, mild fever, and fatigue. The cases were diagnosed as infection with a little-known parasitic disease called cyclosporiasis. Up to that time *Cyclospora* infection had rarely been contracted within the U.S. Most cases reported in North America had occurred in people who acquired the parasite while traveling overseas; only three small outbreaks (encompassing only 45 confirmed cases) had been reported in the U.S.

To public health authorities an outbreak of disease due to an organism not commonly found in the U.S. was cause for serious concern. The CDC promptly investigated and ultimately found that raspberries from Guatemala—a country where *Cyclospora* is endemic—were the source of the parasite. Pooling of berries from a number of growers into batches that were sent to the U.S. and Canada by a small number of exporters contributed to the outbreak's broad geographic distribution. The CDC traced the raspberries implicated in 25 of 29 clusters (outbreaks in which two or more individuals shared at least one meal or food item at a particular event, such as a luncheon or conference) to one Guatemalan exporter per event; the berries had arrived in 39

shipments to eight importers between May 1 and June 4, 1996. Each shipment contained berries from as few as 2 or as many as 30 farms, and 6 farms were among those most frequently implicated. Since *Cyclospora* is a waterborne parasite, contamination may have occurred as a result of spraying the fruit with insecticides and fungicides mixed with contaminated water.

WE ARE WHAT WE EAT

Americans' growing reliance on imported foods isn't the only reason for the recent increase in foodborne diseases. Changes in our eating habits have also played a part. One of these changes is the transition from the traditional meat-and-potatoes diet to an eating pattern that includes more fresh fruits and vegetables—a shift that has increased consumers' exposure to exotic pathogens. Another is the sharp rise in the number of meals eaten away from home.

Kind to the heart but unkind to the stomach. In the 1950s and '60s, epidemiologists studying eating habits around the world found a clear association between high-fat diets and heart disease. As a consequence, in the 1970s and '80s the American public was bombarded with nutritional advice that emphasized the importance of limiting fats and increasing the intake of fresh fruits and vegetables. Consumers took these recommendations to heart, and consumption of fresh fruits and vegetables increased almost 50% between 1970 and 1994. Following the new dietary guidelines has undoubtedly helped many people reduce their risk of cardiovascular disease—but it has also increased their risk of foodborne illness.

(*continued on page 252*)

FOOD IRRADIATION: AN IDEA WHOSE TIME HAS (FINALLY) COME?

BY ADRIENNE A. HARKAVY

Ever since World War II, when scientists working for the U.S. Army discovered that the exposure of ground beef to X-rays retarded spoilage, food irradiation has captured the imagination of many who see it as a way to help ensure the safety of the food supply. Irradiation was approved in the mid-1960s as a means of sterilizing objects, such as medical and hospital supplies. But it was not until 1986 that the Food and Drug Administration (FDA) approved irradiation of spices, fruits, and vegetables as a means of destroying insects and mold. In 1990 the agency authorized irradiation of chicken in an effort to check the spread of food poisoning due to *Salmonella* and *Campylobacter*. Other approved uses in the food industry include treatment of pork to eradicate the parasite that causes trichinosis and irradiation of dry enzymes used in food processing to control microorganisms. In December 1997 the FDA approved irradiation of fresh meat to control such pathogens as the potentially deadly *Escherichia coli* O157:H7. Application to fish and seafood was under consideration. At least 30 other countries now use irradiation on foods ranging from corn to Camembert.

Here's how irradiation works: Foods to be irradiated are placed in containers that are then exposed to gamma rays generated by a radioactive source. The gamma rays kill bacteria and fungi in the food by shattering the organisms' genetic material.

A great deal of mythology surrounds food irradiation—indeed, Michael Osterholm, state epidemiologist for Minnesota and a leading authority on foodborne disease, characterizes it as "one of the most misunderstood technologies." Irradiation does not *make* food radioactive. Nor, according to the FDA, does it noticeably alter taste, texture, or appearance or add significantly to cost. Most infectious disease specialists and public health experts agree that the benefits have been well established. Concern about the growing incidence of foodborne illness has led both the World Health Organization and the American Medical Association to put their stamps of approval on the process.

Like cooking, irradiation causes slight changes in the composition of food. Researchers at the Center for Consumer Research of the University of California, Davis, found that irradiation may reduce the amount of vitamin C in an orange or the thiamine and riboflavin content of pork or chicken by 0.01% to 1.5%. They pointed out, however, that there are small natural variations in nutritional content between one orange and another, and the slight decreases measured in irradiated produce are well within this normal range of variation. Elsa Murano, a food-safety microbiologist at Texas A&M University, reported that trained experts were unable to find significant differences in taste between irradiated and nonirradiated beef patties. On the matter of palatability, however, not all experts agree. Some say irradiation makes meat more tender, but others maintain it gives certain foods an unappetizing color and texture.

A major roadblock to food irradiation in the U.S. has been the public's fear of the word *radiation*. There are signs, however, that this fear may be abating. According to recent research by the International Food Information Council, consumer suspicion has begun to give way to acceptance as the frequency of outbreaks of foodborne disease has increased.

Nowadays most health and consumer groups opposed to irradiation acknowledge that it doesn't cause food to become radioactive, but they believe the technology poses other health risks. Michael Jacobson, a microbiologist and executive director of the Center for Science in the Public Interest, has declared himself "strongly opposed" to irradiation, contending that it reduces the vitamin B content of foods and poses potential environmental risks. "The problem with irradiation," says Jacobson, "is that it uses an inherently dangerous substance—radioactive cobalt—that could expose workers [to danger] or could get into the environment." A number of experts remain confident that irradiation is a safe and effective way to battle disease-causing microorganisms. As Osterholm contends, food irradiation "provides the greatest likelihood of substantially reducing bacterial and parasitic causes of foodborne disease associated with numerous foods, including fresh fruits and vegetables." Other authorities caution that irradiation should not—and cannot—replace safe agricultural and processing practices. "Irradiation has a place in food safety," says U.S. Secretary of Agriculture Dan Glickman, "but it's not the magic bullet."

Wolfing down meals from fast-food restaurants is a common pastime of American kids. Although outbreaks of foodborne illness have been traced to these establishments, such cases, fortunately, are *quite* uncommon.

(*continued from page 250*)

As Michael Osterholm, chief epidemiologist at the Minnesota Department of Health, Minneapolis, has said, "The heart-healthy diet may be kind to the cardiovascular system, but it's hell on the digestive tract." Osterholm points out that American citizens traveling abroad are always warned to "boil it, peel it, or don't eat it," but in many instances, he notes, they are "consuming the same product here without knowing it." Thus, the more fresh fruits and vegetables people consume, the more likely they are to be exposed to the threat of foodborne disease.

Dining out in droves. As noted above, another reason for the increase in foodborne illness is that Americans are eating so many meals away from home. According to the National Restaurant Association, more than 44% of Americans' food dollars were spent on meals away

from home in 1995—compared with only 25% in 1955. Clearly, eating in restaurants has become a way of life; fast-food restaurants, take-home meals, and salad bars are more popular than ever. At the beginning of the 1990s, an estimated 80% of reported outbreaks of foodborne illness in the U.S. were due to foods eaten outside the home—although CDC officials acknowledge that cases associated with meals away from home are more likely to be recognized and reported than those that originate in home kitchens. Nevertheless, the ease with which foodborne pathogens can be transmitted makes all restaurants potentially hazardous. Even the most elegant establishments can have problems if food is not properly prepared, handled, and stored.

Increased reliance on meals away from home also means that people are doing less cooking—and consequently, they may know little about safe food handling and storage. Particularly in two-income families, less time spent in the kitchen means less time for parents to spend teaching their children about food safety. Moreover, health education in schools these days is more likely to focus on sexually transmitted diseases and teen pregnancy than on kitchen hygiene.

THE GOVERNMENT'S ROLE

Despite the growing health threat posed by foodborne illnesses, the U.S. still enjoys one of the world's safest food supplies. A complex regulatory system that includes local, state, federal, and international agencies oversees the maintenance of food-safety standards. On the federal level alone, six agencies share the responsibility for inspecting food—a division of labor that some food-safety experts claim is part of the problem. The U.S. Department of Agriculture (USDA) oversees the inspection of meat, poultry, and egg products; the Food and Drug Administration (FDA) inspects and oversees the safety of all other food products; and the Environmental Protection Agency sets limits for certain chemicals in food. The Department of Commerce, the Federal Trade Commission, and the National Academy of Sciences also have roles in ensuring the safety of the American food supply. In August 1998 Pres. Bill Clinton signed an executive order establishing the President's Council on Food Safety, which will oversee the food-safety efforts of the various federal agencies. It is hoped the new council will meet the need for a central authority to coordinate the work of the agencies to prevent outbreaks of foodborne disease.

Recent Outbreaks: A Timeline

July 1990

At a Chicago hospital 21 employees come down with cyclosporiasis (infection with the parasite *Cyclospora cayetanensis*—the first U.S. outbreak attributed to this organism) presumably caused by contaminated tap water.

September–October 1994

At least 224,000 people in several states become infected with *Salmonella enteritidis* after eating contaminated ice cream produced in Minnesota.

December 1994

A San Francisco sausage company recalls 10,000 pounds of *E. coli*-infected dry salami after an outbreak that affects 18 people.

October 1996

An *E. coli* outbreak in Washington state, California, Colorado, and British Columbia is traced to unpasteurized apple juice. A total of 70 cases, including one death, are reported.

June–July 1997

More than 100 cases of food poisoning—at least 70 of them linked to *E. coli*-tainted alfalfa sprouts—are reported in Michigan and Virginia.

August 1997

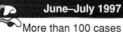

Some 25 million pounds of ground beef are recalled by a Nebraska plant after tests show that some of the meat is contaminated with *E. coli* O157:H7. Seventeen people become ill.

June 1998

After swimming in a kiddie pool near Atlanta, Georgia, 26 children become ill and a two-year-old girl dies as a result of *E. coli* O157:H7 infection probably acquired by swallowing pool water containing fecal matter from an infected youngster.

January 1993

Several hundred people become ill and four children die after a fast-food restaurant in Washington state serves hamburgers contaminated with *E. coli* O157:H7.

November 1994

In Milwaukee, Wisconsin, asparagus and carrots contaminated with *E. coli* cause about 160 people to become ill.

May–June 1996

More than 1,400 consumers in 20 states, the District of Columbia, and two Canadian provinces develop cyclosporiasis as a result of eating tainted raspberries imported from Guatemala.

March 1997

An estimated 260 people, mostly students, become infected with hepatitis A after eating Mexican strawberries served in school lunches in Michigan.

July–August 1997

The largest North American outbreak of *Vibrio parahaemolyticus* infection occurs in Washington state, California, Oregon, and British Columbia. One person dies and more than 200 are infected after eating raw oysters.

April–May 1998

A total of 211 cases of salmonellosis are reported in 12 states, mostly in the Midwest. A breakfast cereal is implicated in the outbreak.

June 1998

An estimated 6,500 people in Illinois become ill with *E. coli* after eating at parties catered by a suburban Chicago delicatessen.

Tips for Avoiding Foodborne Illness

Shopping

- Do not buy dented, cracked, or bulging cans or jars.
- Do not purchase torn or leaking packages.
- Check expiration dates and never buy outdated food.
- Shop for frozen and refrigerated foods last, just before heading to the checkout.

Food Storage

- Unpack perishables first and refrigerate immediately.
- Store poultry, fish, and meats in meat drawer or coldest section of refrigerator.
- Cook or freeze fresh poultry, fish, and ground meats within two days and all other meats within five days.
- Keep meat and poultry in original packaging until ready to use; if storing for more than two months in freezer, overwrap packages in foil, plastic wrap, freezer paper, or plastic bag.
- Store canned goods in a cool, dry place.

Thawing Frozen Foods

- Thaw foods slowly in refrigerator. Make sure juices do not drip onto other foods.
- For faster thawing, place food in a leakproof plastic bag and submerge in cold tap water.
- Meat and poultry thawed in microwave should be cooked immediately.

Preparation

- Wash hands before and after handling raw meat and poultry.
- Clean cutting board often, using a solution of one tablespoon chlorine bleach in one gallon of water.
- Avoid cross-contamination by keeping raw meat, poultry, fish, and their juices away from other foods.
- Marinate meat, poultry, and fish in a covered dish in refrigerator.

Cooking

- Use these cooking temperatures:
  Beef, lamb, and pork: 160° F.
  Whole poultry and thighs: 180° F.
  Poultry breasts: 170° F.
  Ground chicken or turkey: 165° F.

Serving

- Never leave food out on counter or tabletop for more than two hours.
- Keep hot food over heat source and cold food on ice. Platters should be refrigerated until time to serve or heat.
- If eating outside, carry perishables in a cooler and set in shade.

Another recently launched effort in this area is the National Food Safety Initiative, an ambitious program to improve food-safety practices and policies. Its goal is to reduce the incidence of foodborne illness by developing more efficient means of detecting foodborne pathogens and expanding research on such aspects of food safety as risk assessment, training, and education. Proposed tactics for meeting this goal include increasing the number of existing foodborne disease surveillance programs, improving communication and coordination between federal and state agencies in response to outbreaks of foodborne illness, expanding research on how to detect foodborne pathogens, and improving public education about the proper handling of foods.

Seeking problems at the source. As part of the National Food Safety Initiative, the FDA and the USDA have agreed to implement the Hazard Analysis Critical Control Point (HACCP) system. HACCP (pronounced "*hass*-up") is a preventive approach to identifying potential problems in food production that could affect food safety. In the HACCP system, food companies analyze their production and distribution processes and pinpoint "critical control points" at which contamination could occur. Once these critical control points have been identified, risk-reduction measures can be put into effect. Manufacturers and processors then monitor these control points, keeping detailed records to give inspectors a clear view of how well the companies are complying with food-safety laws.

In December 1997 the FDA put HACCP regulations into effect for seafood, and in 1998 the USDA was scheduled to follow with HACCP regulations for meat and poultry. In addition, the FDA will formulate preventive measures for the production of fruit and vegetable juices. The USDA and the FDA will also join forces to implement HACCP for eggs and egg-based products.

The new regulations combine voluntary testing with USDA inspection. Meat and poultry plants will conduct microbiological testing for *E. coli* on a daily basis. The USDA will inspect poultry plants and record the rate of *Salmonella* present in poultry to permit plant-to-plant and within-plant comparisons. Under current HACCP policies the seafood industry is responsible for maintaining its own safeguards. There is no mandatory seafood testing, onsite inspection, or laboratory testing for bacteria, viruses, toxins, or parasites. Overall, however, HACCP represents a significant step toward helping federal agencies provide consistent actions, avoid duplication of effort, and promote continuity throughout the regulatory system. According to Tom Billy, administrator of the Food Safety and Inspection Service of the USDA, "By January 2000, all plants will be required to have HACCP in place."

> # Carelessness anywhere in the food chain... can enable pathogens to survive and grow.

254

At a 1997 news conference, U.S. Agriculture Secretary Dan Glickman (left) and Health and Human Services Secretary Donna Shalala meet the fearsome germ "BAC" (short for "bacteria"), mascot of the Fight BAC! food-safety campaign sponsored by the Partnership for Food Safety Education.

In addition to federal efforts, many of the major agricultural states have set strict safety standards, enforced by their own comprehensive inspection systems. California, for example, which raises more than half the produce sold in the U.S., spends more than $40 million each year to regulate and monitor pesticide use.

Other measures. Other preventive measures are under consideration, including the pasteurization of all fresh fruit and vegetable juices and the use of chemical disinfectants on fresh produce. Food irradiation, which government officials project could be used to eliminate pathogens in up to 40% of foods consumed in the U.S., is another technology that could be instrumental in the fight against foodborne pathogens. (*See* Sidebar: "Food Irradiation: An Idea Whose Time Has [Finally] Come?")

WHOSE RESPONSIBILITY?

Although federal, state, and local governments continue to examine ways to reduce the risk of foodborne illness, food safety is not solely their responsibility. Rather, farmers, producers, shippers, manufacturers, retailers, and, particularly, consumers must take steps to ensure that food is safe. Carelessness anywhere in the food chain—from production and transportation to preparation and food service—can enable pathogens to survive and grow.

The USDA and the FDA have issued consumer tips for the safe handling of food (*see* table, page 254). Consumers who follow these practices can reduce their risk of contracting foodborne diseases. Since virtually any food can be a vehicle for pathogens, purchasing food from reliable sources, handling food properly at home, and exercising vigilance when eating out are practices that will become increasingly important in the battle against foodborne illness.

FOR FURTHER INFORMATION

Book

Scott, Elizabeth, and Sockett, Paul. *How to Prevent Food Poisoning: A Practical Guide to Safe Cooking, Eating, and Food Handling.* New York: John Wiley & Sons, 1998.

Organizations

National Center for Infectious Diseases
1600 Clifton Rd
MS C-12
Atlanta GA 30333
Web site: http://www.cdc.gov/ncidod/diseases/foodborn/foodborn.htm
The Partnership for Food Safety Education
Suite 500
800 Connecticut Avenue NW
Washington DC 20006-2701

Web sites

The *"Bad Bug Book"*
http://vm.cfsan.fda.gov/~mow/intro.html
CliniWeb: Food Poisoning
http://www.ohsu.edu/cliniweb/C21/C21.613.415.html
Food Safety and Food Preservation
http://www.foodpres.com
National Food Safety Initiative
http://vm.cfsan.fda.gov/~dms/fs-toc.html

OVERCOMING INFERTILITY:
THE STATE OF THE ART

BY SAID T. DANESHMAND, M.D., AND ALAN H. DECHERNEY, M.D.

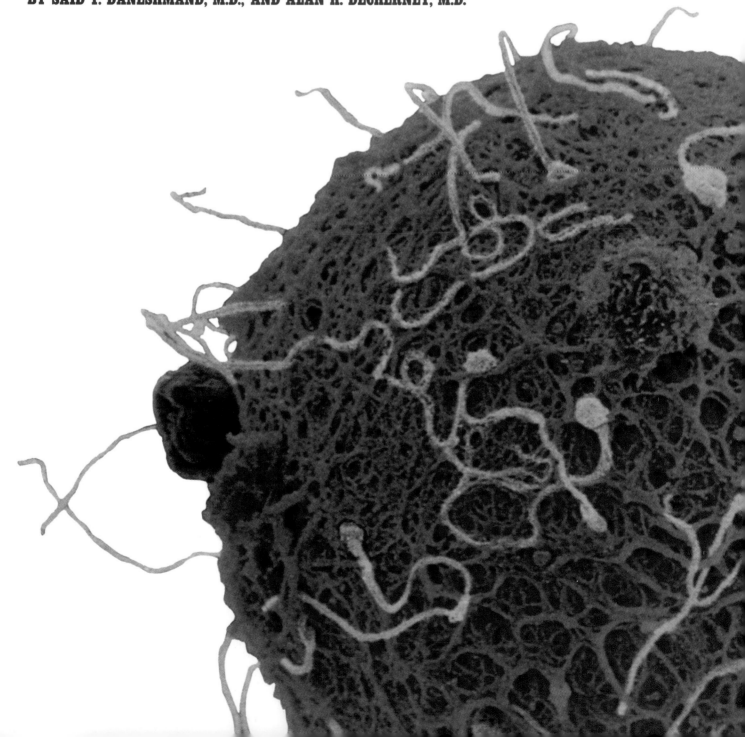

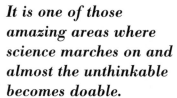

The conception of a child is commonly perceived as the ultimate manifestation of the union between a man and a woman. Indeed, pregnancy and childbirth are among the most emotionally charged and deeply meaningful chapters in a couple's life. It is certainly not surprising then that those who find that they are *unable* to conceive may view their situation as a major life crisis.

Multiple sperm surround a single human egg.

Jason Burns—Ace/Phototake

Giorgio Amendola—Imago 2000

Rosanna Della Corte of Canino, Italy, was 62 years old when she gave birth to her son Riccardo, shown here at age three.

Said T. Daneshmand is a Fellow in the Division of Reproductive Endocrinology and Infertility, University of California, Los Angeles, School of Medicine.

Alan H. DeCherney is Professor and Chairman, Department of Obstetrics and Gynecology, UCLA School of Medicine; Editor, Fertility and Sterility; *and Past President of the American Society for Assisted Reproduction.*

The high value that society places on parenthood and the intense desire of most affected couples to overcome their infertility have been catalysts for a revolution in reproductive technologies. That revolution began exactly two decades ago, in July 1978 in Cambridge, England, with the birth of Louise Brown—the first successful in vitro fertilization (IVF) embryo-transfer baby. Since then, an ever-enlarging spectrum of assisted reproductive technologies, or ARTs, have offered thousands upon thousands of couples around the world the chance to have their own families. Among other successes, ARTs have enabled women with blocked fallopian tubes to circumvent their anatomic problem and men with sperm counts so low that fatherhood was considered out of the question to fertilize an egg from their partner with just a single sperm. Advances in the implantation of donated eggs have shattered the barriers of the reproductive life span. Women well past menopause are now able to achieve pregnancy and give

birth; in 1997 a woman just three months short of her 64th birthday delivered a healthy baby girl.

Today more couples than ever before are seeking medical evaluation and treatment for infertility. In the United States, the estimated number of office visits for fertility problems now exceeds two million annually. As the new millennium approaches, reproductive technologies are continuing to burgeon, making it ever more possible for those who previously had no hope of producing offspring to realize their fondest dream. Along the way, not surprisingly, these seemingly miraculous technologies have also spawned many an emotional, ethical, and legal conundrum.

DEFINING THE PROBLEM

Difficulty in achieving pregnancy is surprisingly common, affecting approximately one couple in 10, or somewhere between 10% and 15% of the population, depending on whose statistics are used. *Infertility*, sometimes termed *subfertility*, is defined as (1) the inability of a couple to achieve conception after one year of unprotected intercourse, or (2) the inability of a woman to carry a pregnancy to a live birth. The chance that a normal fertile couple will conceive within any one-month period is approximately 20–25%; in a given population, 85% of couples who have regular intercourse will conceive a child within a year.

Historically infertility was considered a "female problem." In fact, the cause is as often in the man as it is in the woman. In about 10% of cases, reduced fertility is attributed to both the male and the female; another 10% of infertile couples suffer from infertility due to unexplained causes.

Female infertility may be caused by ovulatory, cervical, and uterine factors, as well as by advanced age. Repeated abortions followed by dilatation and curettage can cause intrauterine scar formation and thereby interfere with implantation of the fertilized egg. The presence of adhesions (rubbery or filmy bands of scar tissue) in and around the fallopian tubes interferes with the ability of the tube to take up the egg after it has been released from an ovary; it can also affect movement of the sperm through the tube. Congenital anatomic deformities of the uterus may contribute to infertility by precipitating recurrent miscarriages. Another cause of infertility is gonadal dysgenesis, a condition in which the ovaries form but contain no eggs.

The causes of male-factor infertility include problems with sperm production, blockage of the sperm-delivery system, the presence of antibodies against sperm, testicular injury, anatomic aberrations, and the presence of a varicose vein around the testicle (varicocele)—all of which can affect sperm quality or quantity. If, in the past, male infertility was given considerably less attention than female infertility, that was often because little could be done about it.

Factors that can have deleterious effects on reproductive capacity in both men and women include previous and current alcohol consumption and drug use, as well as a number of general medical problems. A history of sexually transmitted diseases (STDs) in either partner is also important. The impact of smoking on reproduction is considerable. Cigarette smoke is known to contain hundreds of toxic substances, the negative health effects of which are well documented. By interfering with the production of sperm, smoking can adversely affect male fertility. In women, smoking can affect different stages in the reproductive process, from the pickup of the egg by the fallopian tube to the growth and development of the fetus.

NORMAL REPRODUCTIVE FUNCTION

In order to appreciate the factors responsible for female or male infertility, one must know something about the normal reproductive anatomy and physiology of each sex.

Female. The basic reproductive anatomy of a woman comprises structures that are entirely internal. (*See* diagram this page.) The vagina is a passage that leads from the outside of the body to the cervix, which is the opening of the uterus. The uterus is a muscular organ lined by a mucus-secreting membrane called the endometrium. It is in the endometrium that the fertilized egg (embryo) implants and grows into a fully developed fetus. At the superior portion of the uterus lie two openings (ostia), which lead to the two

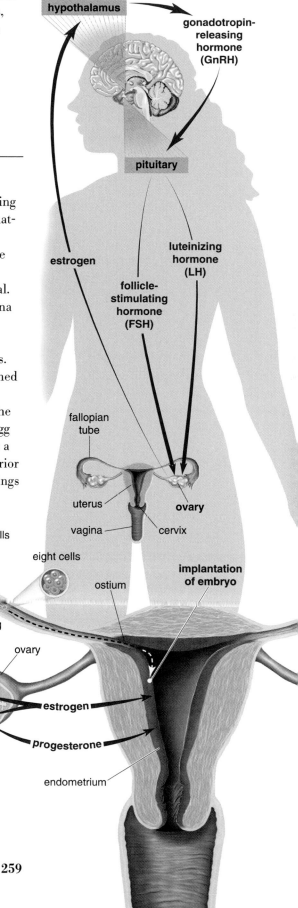

259

fallopian tubes. At the far end of each fallopian tube are the structures known as the ampulla and the fimbria, consisting of thin muscular layers with extensive folds. These regions are responsible for picking up the egg (ovum) after it has been released from the ovary, and it is here that sperm meet the egg and that fertilization and early embryo development occur.

Directly adjacent to the fallopian tube fimbriae lie the ovaries, which are round or oval structures measuring approximately 1.5–2 centimeters (0.6–0.8 inch) in diameter. Egg development occurs in the ovaries under the control of hormones that are released from the pituitary gland at the base of the brain. These hormones, follicle-stimulating hormone (FSH) and luteinizing hormone (LH), are regulated by the release of another hormone, gonadotropin-releasing hormone (GnRH), produced by the hypothalamus. Through receptors on the ovaries, the hormones initiate the growth of follicles, fluid-filled structures in which the maturing ova (oocytes) grow.

Oocytes mature into oogonia, or primitive eggs. The oocyte, nestled within the ovary, is surrounded by cells known as granulosa cells; the entire complex is called a primordial follicle. As the surrounding granulosa cells grow in number, the developing follicle matures to a secondary, then a tertiary, follicle. Eggs within the follicles are surrounded by a hard shell, the zona pellucida, which is composed of proteins that are synthesized and secreted by the oocyte.

The monthly menstrual cycle is extremely important to a woman's fertility. In the follicular phase, FSH, released from the pituitary, stimulates egg development, and developing follicles release estrogen to begin preparing the uterus for implantation of an embryo. The ovulatory phase follows when a surge in circulating LH causes the release of the oocyte from the ovary around midcycle. The final luteal phase occurs after ovulation and is marked by the formation of a structure known as the corpus luteum. This structure releases progesterone as well as estrogen, the two hormones that prepare the endometrium to receive an embryo.

Male. A man's reproductive system is both internal and external. (*See* diagram at left.) The testes, the two coiled tubules located within the scrotal sac, are the structures within which sperm and the primary male hormone, testosterone, are produced. Testosterone, a steroid hormone derived from cholesterol, is essential for the development of the external genitalia and vital to sperm production (spermatogenesis). Within each testis are germ cells (also known as gametes, or immature sperm cells) and stromal (structural) cells. Leydig cells, found between the tubules of the testes, are a third type of cell important in the synthesis of testosterone and production of sperm.

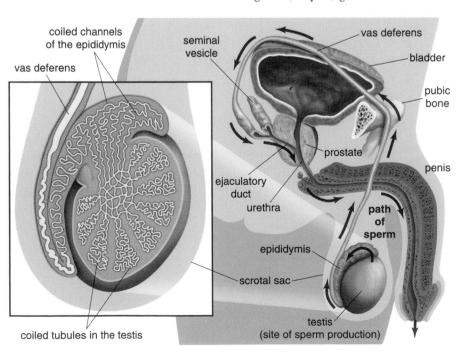

coiled channels of the epididymis

vas deferens

coiled tubules in the testis

seminal vesicle

prostate

ejaculatory duct

urethra

epididymis

scrotal sac

testis (site of sperm production)

vas deferens

bladder

pubic bone

penis

path of sperm

The hormone GnRH is released by the hypothalamus, stimulating the pituitary to secrete FSH and LH into the man's bloodstream. Blood LH levels are the primary regulator of the rate of testosterone synthesis and release. Both FSH and LH are required for spermatogenesis; deficiencies in either hormone cause abnormalities in sperm production.

Under the influence of Leydig cells and Sertoli (stromal) cells, germ cells develop into mature sperm. Sperm development begins with the division of very immature cells, called spermatogonia. Sperm maturation is an ongoing process lasting about 72–74 days; for about 50 of those days, sperm mature in the testes, after which they do so within the long ductal system.

As sperm mature, they pass from the testes through the coiled channels of the epididymis, an organ that provides nourishment to the sperm. Sperm become motile (capable of movement) after 18–24 hours within the epididymis. After traveling through the epididymis for about 14 days, the sperm move into the vas deferens, the tubal structure that connects the epididymis with the seminal vesicles via a common ejaculatory duct. The seminal vesicles are pouchlike glands that produce most of the ejaculatory fluid. Mature sperm (spermatozoa) are stored in the vas deferens until ejaculation.

Spermatozoa are about 60 micrometers (0.0024 inch) long, are subdivided structurally into a head and a tail, and resemble tadpoles. Fluid from the seminal vesicles combines with a thick secretion from the prostate gland to manufacture semen, which carries the sperm. On contact with the egg's zona pellucida, sperm release enzymes that break down this surrounding structure, which allows fertilization to take place. Spermato-

zoa are able to survive for two to three days in the female reproductive tract. The period during which an egg can be fertilized by a sperm ranges from 12 to 24 hours.

EVALUATION OF THE INFERTILE COUPLE

Both partners seeking treatment for infertility are usually seen together by the physician. Taking a thorough medical history of both partners is the first step.

Age considerations. The age of either member of the couple can be an important determinant of the success of fertility treatment. Among men, advancing age is associated with a drop in circulating testosterone levels and a decrease in the level of functioning of the testicles. Compared with their younger counterparts, older men also produce fewer and less-motile sperm.

Numerous studies have shown that female fertility begins declining when a woman is in her mid-30s, about 10 years before menstrual irregularities (continued on page 264)

> Difficulty in achieving pregnancy is surprisingly common, affecting approximately one couple in 10.

Reason for Seeking Infertility Treatment*

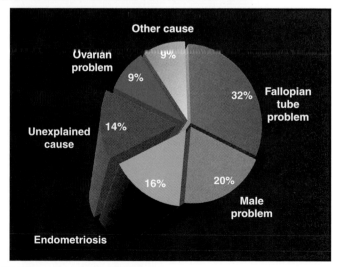

*Based on 45,906 ART procedures carried out in 1995.
Source: *The Assisted Reproductive Technology Success Rates in the United States: 1995 National Summary and Fertility Clinic Reports*, Centers for Disease Control and Prevention, 1997.

261

CAN MEDITATION
MAKE YOU FERTILE?

BY HENRY DREHER

Couples struggling with infertility often say they are on a psychological roller coaster—a breathless ride of rising expectations and dashed hopes. Not only do they contend with the sadness of being unable to conceive, but they typically endure arduous cycles of expensive high-tech medical treatments. The ride doesn't stop until treatment has succeeded or the couple has found peace of mind in another solution.

Although there is little question that infertility causes emotional distress—one study found that infertile women were as depressed as patients with cancer and HIV/AIDS—some scientists now believe that distress may be a cause of infertility. Preliminary data further suggest that a powerful set of psychological treatments, including relaxation techniques, cognitive therapy, training in coping skills, and group support, may increase the odds that infertile women will conceive. Psychologist Alice D. Domar established the Mind/Body Program for Infertility at the Beth Israel Deaconess Medical Center, Boston, in 1987 to "give infertile couples their lives back." Yet "a surprising number of women who enter mind-body treatment for infertility" receive an unanticipated benefit, Domar reports. "They become pregnant."

Domar's research has shown that women who averaged over three years on the infertility roller coaster were markedly less anxious and depressed at the completion of the 10-week program; six months later fully one-third not only were happier but were expecting. A separate study conducted by researchers at the University of British Columbia evaluated a similar group of infertile women who did not participate in a therapeutic mind-body program; only 18% of those women had conceived within six months.

The women who participate in the Mind/Body Program for Infertility, affiliated with the Division of Behavioral Medicine of Harvard Medical School, attend weekly two-and-a-half-hour sessions in which they practice relax-

*Health book writer **Henry Dreher** resides in New York City, is the coauthor (with Alice D. Domar) of* Healing Mind, Healthy Woman *(New York: Henry Holt and Co., 1996), and contributes regularly to the periodicals* Advances in Mind-Body Medicine *and* Natural Health.

ation, learn to restructure negative thoughts, share grief and anger with others in the same circumstances, and, ultimately, reclaim their ability to enjoy life. (The program focuses on women, but male partners are invited to attend 3 of the 10 sessions. Easing the strain on couples is a key element in Domar's approach.) Many participants had had no success with assisted reproductive technologies; after mind-body therapy, however, medical treatment finally worked.

In 1999 Domar and her colleagues will complete a five-year clinical trial sponsored by the National Institute of Mental Health comparing the outcomes of infertile women who participate in her program with those of women who do not. The trial should yield an answer to the question: Can mind-body treatments help reverse infertility?

Some of Domar's patients are already convinced. Molly, a 37-year-old pediatric oncologist, had taken fertility drugs, undergone five intrauterine inseminations and two in vitro fertilization (IVF) procedures, and finally endured a complicated ectopic pregnancy (conception outside the uterus). "After three years of this, I crashed," recalls Molly. She entered Domar's program, and her transformation occurred in a matter of weeks. "One Sunday, in the middle of the program, I woke up and the change was undeniable," says Molly. "Remember the scene in the movie *The Wizard of Oz* when Dorothy steps out of the black-and-white house into a world of color? Well, that's what happened to me. I woke up and my depression was gone." Several weeks later, at her last group session, Molly was thrilled to announce that her third IVF cycle had been successful. Although she cannot prove that the birth of her healthy son, Greg, was a direct result of her therapy, she believes that her emotional improvement "really did change my chemistry."

Much of Domar's most recent research has focused on the link between severe depression and fertility. In what at first glance might seem like a contradictory finding, close to 60% of women who scored high on a depression-rating scale at the start of the mind-body program went on to become pregnant. Why would the women who were initially the most depressed be the most likely to conceive? Domar speculates that depression may have played a pronounced physiological role in their infertility and that the program, which includes well-established behavioral methods for alleviating depression's debilitating symptoms, could have altered their biological milieu to favor conception.

"Depression may hinder one or several biological factors crucial to fertility, including maturation of the egg, ovulation, and implantation," says Domar. "When we treat women's stress and subsequent depression, we stand a chance of helping them become fertile."

Someday mind-body programs for infertile couples may be widely available, but for now Domar and her colleagues recommend that women and their partners practice mind-body techniques on their own. The following are some of the key elements of such a program.

• Develop a daily practice of relaxation. If learned properly and practiced regularly, any number of techniques will be helpful—including deep breathing, meditation, mindfulness, progressive muscle relaxation, guided imagery, yoga, T'ai Chi ch'uan (tai qi), among others. Domar emphasizes that it's important for couples to make *relaxation* their goal; if instead the focus is on "getting pregnant," they may find that it is difficult, if not impossible, to relax. There are many books and audio- and videotapes available at bookstores that provide concrete instruction in the various relaxation techniques. A selection of audiotapes can be ordered from the Mind/Body Medical Institute, Beth Israel Deaconess Medical Center, Suite 1A, 110 Francis St, Boston MA 02215; phone: 617-632-9530; fax: 617-632-7383; descriptions of the

There is no question that women struggling with infertility benefit from practicing mind-body techniques like meditation and yoga.

Regine M.—The Image Bank/PNI

tapes and an order form are available on the institute's Web site: http://www.med.harvard.edu/programs/mind-body.

• Question and replace negative thought patterns that cause emotional distress. For example, instead of thinking, "We'll never have a child," a couple should decide that they will find a solution to infertility that fosters peace of mind.

• Share distress with close friends, trusted family members, therapists, clergy. Fellowship is also available through the national nonprofit organization RESOLVE (*see* For Further Information, page 275), which helps couples find support groups, provides physician referrals, runs a telephone help line, and publishes a quarterly newsletter.

• Keep a journal. The book *Healing Mind, Healthy Woman* points out that infertility often evokes intense feelings that "swim below the surface of consciousness" and never get expressed. Recording these feelings in a daily journal enables a woman to "peel away the emotional levels of hurt" and, ultimately, to cope with powerful emotions like anger and sadness instead of being overwhelmed by them.

• Rediscover once-enjoyed activities. Couples should find ways to nurture themselves on emotional, creative, and spiritual levels. Self-nurturance, in fact, may be the most important prescription in the mind-body approach. "About 98% of my patients leave the program with major psychological improvements," says Domar. "That is my goal, to help patients reclaim their aliveness, their joy, their capacity to live life to the fullest."

(*continued from page 261*)
signal the onset of menopause. This factor is of particular importance today, since increasing numbers of women are choosing to delay child-bearing. Since 1970 there has been a 50% increase in the number of American women who have borne their first child after the age of 35 years. The decline in fertility with advancing age is a consequence of both a decline in the woman's ovarian function and a reduction in her ovaries' reserve of eggs. An elevated level of FSH in the blood is an important marker of such ovarian decline.

Concomitant with a woman's increasing age is an increased risk for chromosomal abnormalities in her fetus—most notably, Down syndrome. An increase in the incidence of miscarriages is also seen in older women. This means that even if normal fertilization takes place, the resulting embryo has a decreased chance of implanting normally. The reason for this reduced implantation rate is not entirely clear but probably has more to do with the poor quality of the egg than it does with any abnormality in the older woman's uterine environment. Nowhere is the fact that the uterus is apparently unaffected by age more evident than in the successful pregnancies that have been achieved in older women who have undergone IVF with a donor egg from a young woman (*see below*).

Semen analysis. Sperm number, concentration, motility, and morphology (shape) are usually assessed by means of a microscopic examination of the semen. *Sperm count* is the total number of sperm in the ejaculate; counts vary widely, but values below 20 million are usually considered on the low side (the condition known as oligospermia). Azoospermia is the complete absence of spermatozoa in the ejaculate. This condition can be caused by an obstruction of the genital tract, testicular dysfunction associated with congenital disorders such as sickle-cell disease, or various medical illnesses.

Sperm concentration is the number of sperm per cubic centimeter of semen. Sperm concentrations of 20 million–250 million per cubic centimeter are usually considered normal, but fertilization of an egg can be achieved by men with values well below this range.

Ovulatory assessment. Disordered ovulation is responsible for approximately 25% of female infertility problems. Anovulation (failure to ovulate) and oligoovulation (very irregular ovulatory cycles) are among the most common disorders. There are several tests for determining whether ovulation is occurring on a regular basis.

Progesterone production by the developed corpus luteum increases the body temperature of the woman by about $0.5°$ C ($1°$ F) around midcycle. Thus, the charting of basal body temperature taken first thing in the morning is one way to document ovulation. Another way ovulatory status can be confirmed is by testing the urine for the preovulatory elevation of LH. Sensitive LH test kits, which a woman can use at home, detect the increase in this hormone. Examination of the ovaries by pelvic ultrasound is a noninvasive way for the gynecologist to determine whether ovulation is occurring. A fourth way is to measure progesterone in the blood; an elevated level of the hormone is an indication that ovulation has occurred.

Tubal evaluation. Blockages and scarring of the fallopian tubes, the conduits for the sperm and egg, are other common causes of infertility. A number of conditions can result in such tubal scarring or obstruction. One such condition is untreated pelvic inflammatory disease (PID), infection of the upper reproductive tract, including the tubes; PID often follows STDs such as gonorrhea or chlamydia infection.

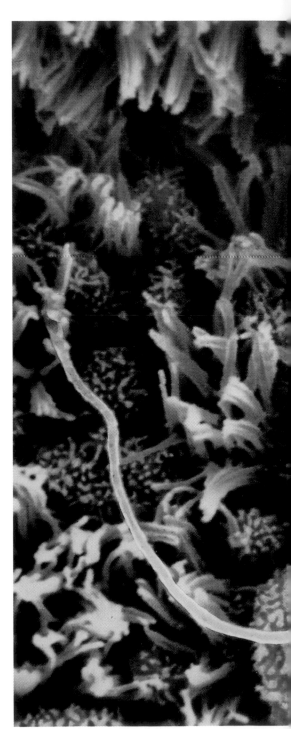

This false-colored scanning electron micrograph shows a single human sperm (yellow) making its way through a fallopian tube lined by ciliated, or fringed (pink), and hormone-secreting (blue) cells.

The traditional test for evaluating the patency (openness) of the fallopian tubes is a radiological exam called hysterosalpingography. Dye injected through the cervix flows into the uterus and then through the fallopian tubes. X-rays are taken, which precisely define abnormalities in the fallopian tubes. Spillage of the dye into the abdominal cavity is an indication of tubal patency. A newer, more direct procedure for evaluating the fallopian tubes is salpingoscopy. A flexible fiber-optic instrument with camera attachments is introduced into the abdominal cavity. This procedure allows detection of subtle abnormalities in the lining of the fallopian tube that can contribute to infertility. Salpingoscopy "scores" are assigned on the basis of the extent of pathology found in the tube; the scores have been shown to be highly predictive of the ability to achieve pregnancy.

The falloposcope is another device that permits visualization of the interior of the entire fallopian tube. A flexible guidewire is introduced through a catheter into the fallopian tube to the point of obstruction. The wire is then removed, and a tiny camera with an outer diameter of no more than 0.5 millimeter (one millimeter is about 0.04 inch), attached to another wire, photographs the area of obstruction and allows the overall quality of the tubal lining to be assessed. This procedure requires minimal anesthesia. In one study 23% of women with normal falloposcopy findings went on to become pregnant. In contrast, women with severe fallopian tube disease had poor chances of becoming pregnant. In the near future a promising refinement in falloposcopy technology could make this diagnostic method a relatively simple office procedure.

Often, microsurgical reconstruction of the fallopian tube eliminates the obstruction and, as a result, the underlying fertility problem. There are also less-invasive ways to unblock obstructed fallopian tubes. One of these is called balloon tuboplasty, which involves the insertion of a small deflated balloon via a catheter through the cervix into the fallopian tube to the point of obstruction. The balloon is then inflated to dilate the tube. Aqueous dissection (flushing with water) is another method for eliminating blockages. The latter is often done during falloposcopy to flush out mucus plugs, another cause of tubal obstruction. When these procedures are successful, ARTs may not be needed.

FURTHER OBSTACLES TO PREGNANCY

Fibroid tumors and endometriosis, both very common conditions, can contribute in direct or subtle ways to infertility.

Fibroids. Uterine fibroids, occurring in one of every four or five U.S. women, are benign tumor growths that originate from the smooth muscle cells within the muscular wall of the uterus. Fibroids can cause excessive uterine bleeding, pain, and a sensation of pressure and may contribute to infertility by interfering with implantation or compressing the opening of the fallopian tubes so that the sperm are prevented from reaching the egg. Occasionally, excision of fibroids that are protruding into the endometrial cavity is necessary to correct the problem.

Improved pregnancy rates have been reported after the removal of fibroids. None of the studies showing improved rates, however, has compared this treatment with no treatment, which makes it impossible to

Louise Brown... is... just one of the more than 300,000 healthy test-tube children in the world, including her younger sister, Natalie.

determine with certainty whether removal of the lesions was responsible for the patient's improved fertility.

Endometriosis. Endometriosis is a condition in which the lining of the uterus, which is normally shed during menstruation, grows outside the uterine cavity. It is estimated to affect one in 10 women of reproductive age in the U.S. Common symptoms are pain before, during, and after the menstrual period, pain during sexual intercourse, and spotting (bleeding between periods). But some women experience no symptoms. Originally, the association between endometriosis and infertility was based on the finding that women with endometriosis who had undergone therapeutic insemination with donor sperm had low pregnancy rates when compared with women unaffected by endometriosis who had the same treatment.

Endometriosis is classified as minimal, mild, moderate, or severe. The condition is diagnosed and the stage assessed by laparoscopy, a procedure that has revolutionized the practice of gynecology. Laparoscopy is usually an outpatient procedure performed under general anesthesia. In most cases a 5–10-millimeter incision is made just below the umbilicus (belly button), after which the abdominal cavity is distended with carbon dioxide gas. The examiner then inserts a narrow lighted tube that allows visualization of the entire reproductive anatomy. Depending on the nature and extent of the endometrial growths, laparoscopic surgical procedures may be undertaken at the same time, using instruments that are guided into the abdominal cavity through additional small incisions in the belly. The goal of surgical therapy is to excise or destroy all endometrial growths without damaging adjacent tissues.

Medical treatment—the use of various drugs—is an alternative to surgery. Agents used in the treatment of endometriosis include GnRH agonists, which act on the pituitary in much the same way as the body's own GnRH; various progesterone preparations; danazol, a testosterone derivative; and nonsteroidal anti-inflammatory medications such as ibuprofen or naprosyn. Medical therapy has the advantage of being able to treat lesions that may not have been detected visually. Further, it avoids the complication of postoperative scarring.

Treatment of endometriosis—whether by drugs, surgery, or a combination of both—often alleviates the infertility problem, and the woman is then able to conceive normally and carry a fetus to term, usually without complications. Some women, however, even after treatment, may still be unable to conceive. They are then appropriate candidates for one of the ARTs.

IVF: 20 YEARS ON

On July 25, 1998, Louise Brown, the world's first test-tube baby, celebrated her 20th birthday. A singular "miracle of technology" back in 1978, today she is "a blonde, blue-eyed, boisterous" young English woman—just one of the more than 300,000 healthy test-tube children in the world, including her younger sister, Natalie. Since Louise's birth, there have been a number of crucial refinements that have both simplified the IVF technique and increased its efficiency.

Initially, IVF was developed for women with absent or irreparably damaged fallopian tubes, but now the method's indications have expanded to include patients with endometriosis, unexplained infertility, immuno-

Louise Joy Brown, the world's first baby conceived outside her mother's body, is shown shortly after her birth at Oldham (England) General Hospital on July 25, 1978 (inset), and at 18 years of age (bottom).

267

logic infertility, and infertility secondary to low male sperm counts. IVF is also used whenever egg donation is indicated.

The first pregnancies achieved by IVF in humans were produced with

(Right) Eggs retrieved from a woman undergoing IVF are separated in the laboratory. **(Below)** Petri dishes containing mature eggs and fresh semen are placed in a special incubator that maintains ideal environmental conditions for fertilization.

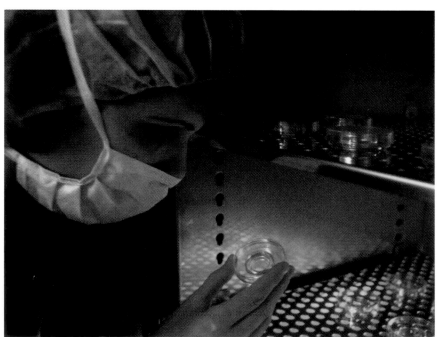

eggs from a woman's unstimulated natural cycle. Nowadays infertile women begin treatment by taking fertility drugs that hyperstimulate the ovaries to produce numerous mature eggs. Once several follicles have matured, a synthetic form of human chorionic gonadotropin (HCG) is administered to induce ovulation and the release of eggs. The eggs are recovered with a needle guided through the vaginal cavity by ultrasound and then placed in a petri dish (*not* a test tube) with sperm from the partner. The dish is placed in a special temperature-controlled incubator.

Eggs that are fertilized become zygotes, which start dividing and become embryos within 36 hours. One embryo or more are transferred to the uterus. If implantation takes place, then embryo development will occur just as in a normal pregnancy. The success rate in terms of live births per IVF cycle attempted (often called the "take-home-baby rate") was 19.6% in 1995. This compares quite favorably with the chances for a normal fertile couple to achieve a pregnancy in any given month (20–25%).

TURNING BACK THE CLOCK

The woman's age seems to have a statistically significant impact on the outcome of IVF. IVF attempts in women older than 40 years of age account for 10–15% of all such procedures; the clinical pregnancy rate for this group, however, is only 8%. But those odds can be raised by means of a couple of fairly recently developed techniques.

Donor eggs. With this method pregnancy rates as high as 38% are common. Donated eggs are usually (*continued on page 270*)

LUCKY SEVEN

BY JOHN CARLSON

D. Fineman ©1998 Sygma

March 1998: Kenny and Bobbi McCaughey with their seven bundles of joy, aged four months.

The soft-spoken 28-year-old Bobbi McCaughey told her husband to sit down while she gave him the news. "I'm pregnant," she said, "but not just with one." Kenny McCaughey knew there was a possibility of multiple births. His wife had been taking a fertility drug in hopes of becoming pregnant with the couple's second child. "How many?" he asked. "Seven," she replied.

Suddenly Kenny, a billing clerk at a Chevrolet dealership in the small town of Carlisle, Iowa, and Bobbi, a part-time seamstress, were in a position to make history. Never before had a woman successfully given birth to seven babies at one time. But the McCaugheys were not interested in making history. They were simply interested in seeing to it that all of their babies were born healthy.

In 1995, when their first attempt at pregnancy failed, the McCaugheys sought help from a fertility specialist. Bobbi was given the drug Metrodin, which stimulates eggs to ripen within the ovaries. It worked; she became pregnant with their first daughter, Mikayla. When the decision was made to have another child, the McCaugheys didn't hesitate to turn again to medical science and Metrodin.

Although they were advised by doctors that aborting several of the fetuses would give the remaining ones a better chance, the McCaugheys wouldn't hear of it. "Whatever happens is God's will," Bobbi told her doctors.

Once they had made their decision, Bobbi's sole job was to stay off her feet, take the best possible care of herself, and hope to carry her babies for at least 30 weeks. (A full-term pregnancy is about 38 weeks.) Doctors who knew of the pregnancy thought such a goal was unlikely, probably even impossible. As John P. Elliott, co-director of maternal-fetal medicine at Good Samaritan Regional Medical Center, Phoenix, Arizona, said, "When you look at the statistical chances that she would be successful, you're literally talking about winning the lottery."

But on Nov. 19, 1997, Bobbi hit the jackpot; in her 30th week, she delivered four boys and three girls, all healthy. The cesarean birth, aided by a team of more than 40 doctors, nurses, and technicians at Iowa Methodist Medical Center, Des Moines, lasted a grand total of six minutes. The birth weights of Kenneth, Alexis, Natalie, Kelsey, Brandon, Nathan, and Joel ranged from 1.1 kilograms (2 pounds 5 ounces) to 1.5 kilograms (3 pounds 4 ounces). Bobbi and Kenny, along with countless others worldwide, declared the birth a "miracle," and so it seemed. The last time septuplets had been born was in 1985, in California, and only three survived.

In contrast, the McCaughey Seven are thriving. Between Jan. 3 and March 1, 1998, all of the septuplets were taken home. Ever since then, the McCaughey living room has been a virtual baby assembly line, with a small army of volunteers—local homemakers, students, factory workers, and farmers—lending Bobbi and Kenny a hand around the clock. Thanks to the generosity of corporations and the public, the family has a supply of diapers, infant formula, and baby food to last the septuplets through babyhood. In late 1998 the family expected to move into a much larger house that was being built for them gratis.

The McCaugheys refuse most interview requests. And they have taken great care to protect Mikayla from the swarm of media attention, vowing that she will not be "the forgotten one in the family." To coincide with the septuplets' first birthday, a book about them was scheduled for publication in November 1998. A television movie was also planned. What's it like having seven eight-month-olds? "An absolute delight—and a blessing," the proud parents affirm. "Sure, we get tired," said Kenny, surrounded by his seven infants. "But this is a wonderful thing. Just look around. These babies are the greatest gift imaginable."

John Carlson *is a reporter for the* Des Moines Register.

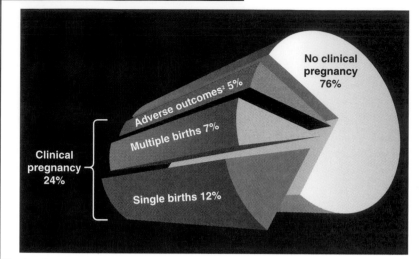
improve clinical pregnancy rates in older women is called assisted hatching. One of the prerequisite processes that occurs before implantation is that the developed embryo must break out of, or "hatch" from, its hard protein shell, the zona pellucida. Scientists have found that in older women some embryos fail to hatch and implant properly and that this circumstance contributes to IVF failures.

In assisted hatching the zona pellucida is either pierced with small holes or a small portion of it is dissolved with an enzyme. The procedure appears to be most effective in women over 38 years of age.

VARIATIONS ON THE IVF THEME

Gamete intrafallopian transfer, or GIFT, is a variation of IVF that is used when a woman has at least one normal fallopian tube. After the ovaries have been stimulated and mature oocytes collected, the latter are mixed with sperm and then, under laparoscopic guidance, placed in the unobstructed fallopian tube. Fertilization then occurs naturally— inside the body (in vivo)—rather than in the laboratory. Unlike standard IVF, GIFT requires anesthesia.

Zygote intrafallopian transfer, or ZIFT, is another IVF variation—one that is generally reserved for women who have cervical damage but at least one patent fallopian tube. As in IVF, oocytes are removed and fertilized in the laboratory. At the zygote, or pronuclear, stage, *i.e.*, before the fertilized egg divides, it is transferred to the unblocked fallopian tube.

ZIFT and IVF have an advantage over GIFT in that fertilization has already occurred. In 1995 GIFT accounted for 6% of total ART procedures and ZIFT for 2%.

(continued from page 268)
obtained from young donors and fertilized by sperm from the infertile woman's partner; one or more of the resulting embryos are transferred to the recipient's uterus, which has been primed with hormones for implantation. In 1995 the Society for Assisted Reproductive Technology (SART) reported a 36.6% clinical pregnancy rate and a 29.3% delivery rate for IVF achieved through egg donation. Although the success of egg donation in IVF pregnancies does not diminish appreciably with the advancing age of the recipient, there is a higher incidence of obstetric complications, including the development of high blood pressure in the mother, as well as abnormal growth of the fetus.

Egg donation is appropriate not only for older women but for those with suspected abnormalities of the oocyte or ovarian failure. The latter condition is common in women who have undergone either chemotherapy or radiation treatment for cancer.

Assisted hatching. Another development in the IVF technique that can

(Opposite page, top) An ultrasound scan shows multiple follicles ready for ovulation in a woman who has taken fertility drugs. (Bottom) An assisted reproduction team uses an ultrasound probe to locate mature ova for retrieval.

270

SPERM INJECTION BREAKTHROUGH

Intracytoplasmic sperm injection (ICSI) is a promising new treatment for men with very low sperm counts or sperm that for some other reason are unable to fertilize an egg. The first child conceived by this method was born in 1992. ICSI involves the direct injection of a single sperm into the cytoplasm (cell material surrounding the nucleus) of an egg that has been retrieved for IVF. If a man has an obstruction in the genital tract that prevents sperm from moving through the genital ducts, sperm can be taken directly from the epididymis with a needle, a procedure known as microsurgical epididymal sperm aspiration (MESA). Eggs that are successfully fertilized are placed in the

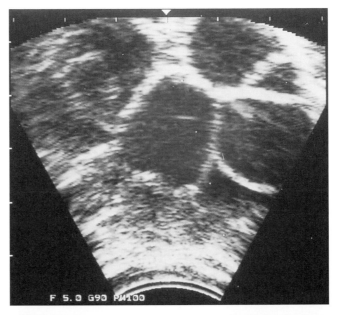

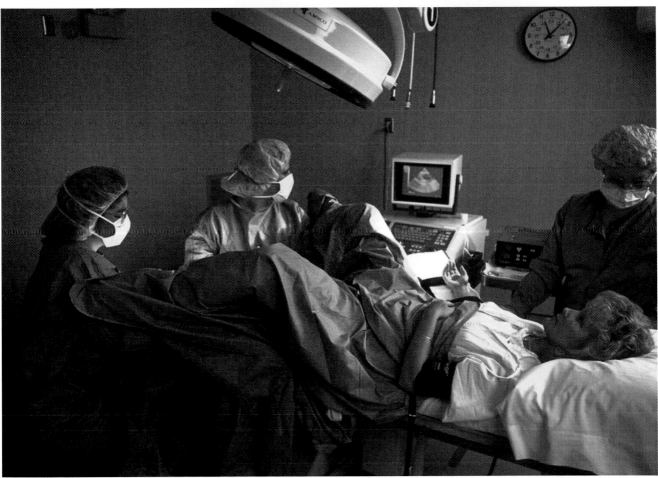

A glass pipette is used to place a single spermatozoid into the cytoplasm of an egg; this state-of-the-art technique makes it possible for men with very low sperm counts to produce offspring.

A British fertility clinic scientist holds a cylinder containing frozen human embryos; in 1996, 3,300 such embryos were discarded in the U.K. when a five-year legal limit on their storage was reached.

Findlay Kember—AP/Wide World

woman's uterus. ICSI success rates vary; recent surveys by SART in the United States and the Human Fertilisation and Embryology Authority in the United Kingdom found take-home rates of 19% and 15%, respectively.

THE FREEZING SOLUTION

Refinements in IVF techniques have substantially increased pregnancy rates. Thus fewer fresh embryos need to be transferred at one time. The American Society for Reproductive Medicine recommends that no more than three or four embryos be transferred; in the U.K. the maximum number allowed by law is three. Because it is common for a dozen or more eggs to be harvested and fertilized in a single IVF cycle, leftover embryos are often available. As the success of IVF has increased, the technology to preserve these extra in vitro-fertilized eggs has evolved. Cryopreservation, a sophisticated freezing technology, now allows embryos to be stored for periods of many years. This means that if the first IVF cycle does not lead to a

pregnancy, a future cycle can be performed without repeating the ovarian stimulation. Using cryopreserved embryos instead of starting the IVF process over from scratch yields higher overall pregnancy rates with less expense and risk to the woman.

Despite these pluses, embryo cryopreservation can raise legal and ethical quandaries in regard to the ownership of embryos and the length of time that they are kept in frozen storage. Such medicolegal dilemmas have frequently come up when couples part or when one partner dies. Given these inevitable situations, it would be highly desirable to have the capability to store unfertilized gametes (eggs and sperm). Cryopreservation of sperm (in liquid nitrogen), in fact, is a relatively straightforward procedure and is already widely available.

The outcome of attempts to freeze unfertilized human eggs (at various stages of development) thus far has been disappointing. Nonetheless, egg cryopreservation remains an active area of research. Scientists have been able to freeze rodent oocytes and later return them to the female's body, and there have been isolated reports of human oocytes that have been frozen and subsequently thawed, fertilized, and returned to the woman's uterus, resulting in a viable pregnancy. At the present time, however, these procedures are not standardized and have not been replicated with enough frequency to be considered reliable. A key barrier to the freezing of human oocytes has been the fragility of the cytoplasmic contents at reduced temperatures.

Still another way some women might be able to overcome infertility is through ovarian cryopreservation. Since a woman's reserve of eggs declines from approximately one million at birth to zero at menopause, this would offer a means of preserving fertility in women who, for example, were undergoing treatment for cancer. An experimental ovarian freezing procedure, first carried out in sheep, was developed by Roger Gosden, a fertility specialist at the University of Leeds, England. Success in sheep led Gosden to remove the ovaries from a handful of human cancer patients before they were to undergo aggressive treatment, in hopes that a portion of the cryo-preserved organ could be surgically replaced once the women were in remission. (At the time of this writing, none of the patients had had their ovarian tissue reimplanted.)

Of course, it would also be feasible for women to delay childbearing—for whatever reason—by this method. As Bernadine Healy has pointed out, ovarian cryopreservation would effectively "equalize men and women in terms of their potential reproductive life span." The ability this technique would afford raises some very difficult questions—for example, is there an age at which society should say that people are too old to have a child?

PREIMPLANTATION GENETIC DIAGNOSIS

Preimplantation genetic diagnosis (PGD) is a still-experimental procedure that allows couples with known hereditary diseases to have eggs tested before fertilization or to have embryos assessed for genetic abnormalities before transfer to the uterus. The method involves analysis of a single cell (or two) after fertilization, when the embryos have divided only to about an eight-cell stage. Such early-stage diagnosis allows selective transfer of unaffected embryos and thus avoids the need for therapeutic abortion later in pregnancy. Down syndrome (trisomy 21), Marfan syndrome, Huntington's and sickle-cell diseases, and X-linked genetic diseases (including Duchenne muscular dystrophy, cystic fibrosis, and hemophilia A) are among the conditions that could be avoided with PGD and the use of the currently available techniques of sex selection.

TOO MUCH OF A GOOD THING?

IVF. GIFT. ZIFT. ICSI. MESA. Assisted hatching. Cryopreservation. PGD. What's next? Just as these recent advances in reproductive technology and molecular genetics have brought about a new age in the treatment of infertility, they have also raised knotty ethical questions, sparked heated debates, and aroused fears about the future.

An ongoing concern of couples undergoing treatment for infertility, the doctors who treat them, and society-at-large is the high prevalence of multiple births resulting from ARTs. More than one-third of IVF pregnancies result in twins and triplets and 1% in even higher-order multiples. Of all ART births in 1995,

Is there an age at which society should say that people are too old to have a child?

273

More than one-third of IVF pregnancies result in twins and triplets and 1% in even higher-order multiples.

37% were multiples (including twins), compared with a multiple-birth rate in the general population of only 2%. Multiple pregnancies are extremely risky; the babies who survive gestation are almost always born prematurely and at very low birth weights. These babies are further predisposed to physical, mental, and developmental health problems, as well as the neurological disorder cerebral palsy.

As already noted, owing to the success of current ARTs, it is no longer necessary to transfer large numbers of fertilized eggs in the hope that a single one will "take." Thus, it is theoretically possible to lessen the chances of multiple pregnancies. In fact, however, many U.S. clinics do not comply with the three-to-four-embryo-transfer guideline, and in 1996 a record number of multiples (in this case, three, four, or more)—6,000 babies—were born, which represented a 19% increase over the number born in 1995.

One solution to the multiples problem is a highly controversial procedure known as selective fetal reduction. The method allows one embryo or more to be eliminated during the first trimester of pregnancy; an injection of potassium chloride administered through the abdominal wall (or vaginally) stops the fetal heart. This procedure, however, is unacceptable to many couples; the McCaugheys, the Iowa couple who had septuplets in November 1997, for example, refused it even though they knew the risks faced by Bobbi, the mother, and the babies she was carrying. (*See* Sidebar: "Lucky Seven" on page 269.)

A British study reported in *The New England Journal of Medicine* (Aug. 27, 1998) found that the chances of pregnancy and birth are related to the number of eggs *fertilized*—not necessarily the number of embryos transferred. When four eggs or more are fertilized, the chance of a birth is not diminished by transferring only two embryos, whereas transferring more than two increases the risk of multiples.

Another concern that many ethicists share is that science has created and will continue to create increasingly frightening and confusing options in human reproduction. Recent developments in animal cloning, for example, have kindled ongoing debates and anxiety about the potential application of such technology in humans. On the other hand, some scientists now believe that the production of "genetically engineered" humans would be a great boon to society because it would mean that the vast majority of genetic diseases could be eliminated.

It cannot be disputed that recent advances in assisted reproduction have produced near miracles for some. But there is also little question that ARTs can be costly and physically and emotionally enervating for those who undergo them. Furthermore, despite the breathtaking array of treatments now available, four out of five couples who seek help for their infertility remain childless.

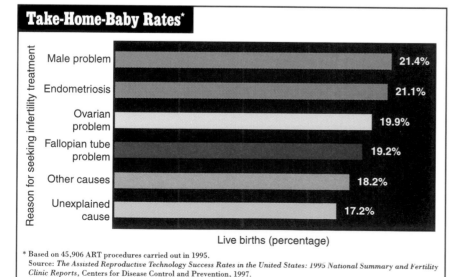

Take-Home-Baby Rates*

Reason for seeking infertility treatment

- Male problem — 21.4%
- Endometriosis — 21.1%
- Ovarian problem — 19.9%
- Fallopian tube problem — 19.2%
- Other causes — 18.2%
- Unexplained cause — 17.2%

Live births (percentage)

* Based on 45,906 ART procedures carried out in 1995.
Source: *The Assisted Reproductive Technology Success Rates in the United States: 1995 National Summary and Fertility Clinic Reports*, Centers for Disease Control and Prevention, 1997.

Floridians Robin (left) and Dana Teagarden with their IVF triplets: (from left) son Austin, daughter McKenzie, and son Micah.

FOR FURTHER INFORMATION

Books

Bialosky, Jill, and Schulman, Helen, eds. *Wanting a Child: Twenty-two Writers on Their Difficult but Mostly Successful Quests for Parenthood in a High-Tech Age.* New York: Farrar, Straus, & Giroux, 1998.

Kearney, Brian. *High-Tech Conception: A Comprehensive Handbook for Consumers.* New York: Bantam Books, 1998.

Jarrett, John C., M.D., and Rausch, Deidra T., Ph.D. *The Fertility Guide: A Couples Handbook for Informed, Rational, and Effective Fertility Treatment.* Santa Fe, New Mexico: Health Press, 1998.

Peoples, Debby; Ferguson, Harriette Rovner; and Domar, Alice D. *What to Expect When You're*

Experiencing Infertility: How to Cope with the Emotional Crisis and Survive. New York: W.W. Norton & Co., 1998.

Silber, Sherman J., M.D. *How to Get Pregnant with the New Technology.* New York: Warner Books, 1998.

Wisot, Arthur, M.D., and Meldrum, David R., M.D. *Conceptions & Misconceptions: A Guide Through the Maze of in Vitro Fertilization & Other Assisted Reproduction Techniques.* Point Roberts, Washington: Hartley & Marks, 1997.

Other publication

The Assisted Reproductive Technology Success Rates in the United States: National Summary and Fertility Clinic Reports was issued in 1997 by the Centers for Disease Control and Prevention, the Society for Assisted Reproductive Technology (SART) of the American Society for Reproductive Medicine (ASRM), and RESOLVE to help couples struggling with infertility make

informed choices about treatment. An online version of the report is available at http://www.cdc.gov/ nccdphp/drh/arts/index.htm. A print version can be obtained by calling RESOLVE (888-299-1585).

Organizations

American Society for Reproductive Medicine (ASRM)
1209 Montgomery Hwy
Birmingham AL 35216-2809
205-978-5000
Web site: http://www.asrm.org/
RESOLVE
1310 Broadway
Somerville MA 02144-1779
617-623-0744
Web site: http://www.resolve.org

Web sites

The Obstetrics and Gynecology Network (OBGYN.net)
http://www.obgyn.net/
Women's Health Interactive Infertility Center
http://www.womens-health.com/inf_ctr/

COULD YOU CATCH

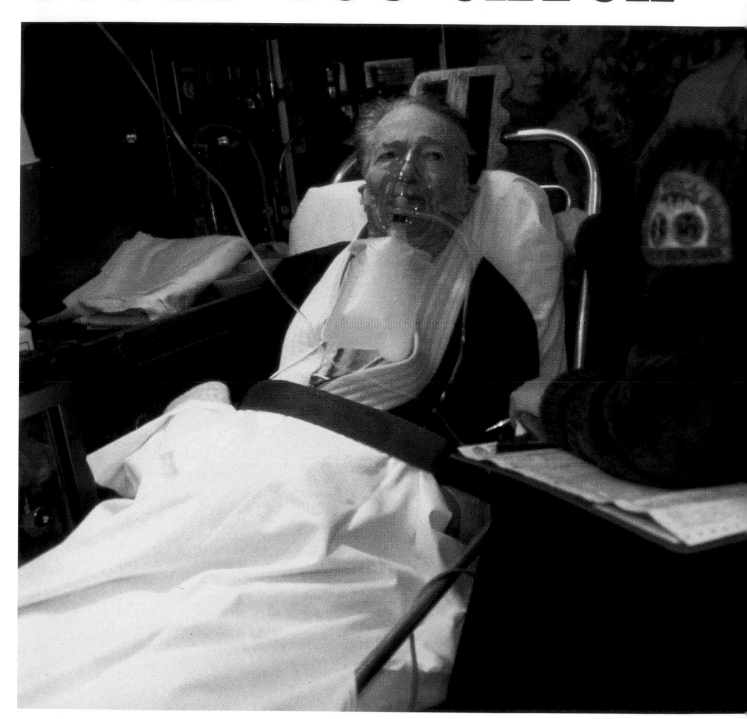

A HEART ATTACK?

Alon Reininger—Contact Press Images/PNI

At the heart of heart disease is a mystery: what really causes it? True, some risk factors are well known. High blood pressure. High cholesterol. Smoking. Diabetes. But half of all heart attacks occur in the absence of any of these. Do some heart attacks simply come out of the blue? Scientists may once have believed this was so—but no longer. Over the past several decades, the evidence has mounted, slowly but inexorably, that there is a link between atherosclerosis—the buildup of fatty artery-blocking deposits—and infection with fairly common microbes.

It took 40 years, but American physician Tom Grayston would eventually help to uncover one of the strongest of these links. Grayston started out in medicine in the early 1950s as a member of the newly established U.S. Epidemic Intelligence

BY STEVEN DICKMAN

277

(Below) Western Ophthalmic Hospital/Science Source-Photo Researchers; (bottom) Alfred Pasieka—Science Source/Photo Researchers

(Right) In the initial stages, trachoma, a leading cause of blindness in many parts of the world, manifests itself as conjunctivitis—redness and inflammation of the mucous membrane that lines the inner surface of the eyelid. (Below) The bacterium responsible, *Chlamydia trachomatis,* is also the cause of a common sexually transmitted disease.

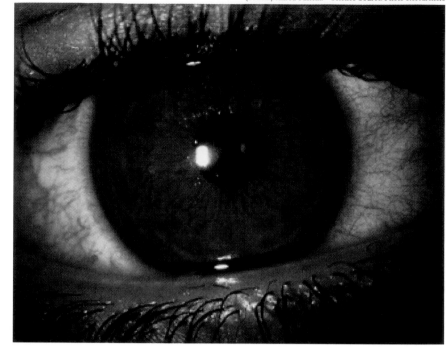

Steven Dickman is a Cambridge, Massachusetts-based freelance writer who specializes in the biological and biomedical sciences. A Knight Science Journalism Fellow at the Massachusetts Institute of Technology in 1992–93 and former Munich, Germany, correspondent for Nature, *he is a regular contributor to* Science, Discover, *and other magazines.*

(continued from page 277)
Service (a branch of the Communicable Disease Center, forerunner of the Centers for Disease Control and Prevention, or CDC), whose mission was to track the transmission of infectious diseases around the globe.

In 1957 Grayston shipped out to Taiwan. He was under contract to set up a microbiology and epidemiology laboratory for the U.S. Navy in the capital city of Taipei. It was during his three-year tour of duty in Taiwan that Grayston first encountered the bacterium chlamydia, a microorganism that would occupy—and preoccupy—him for the rest of his life. Not only did he lay the groundwork for those who eventually would implicate chlamydia in the development of heart disease; Grayston and other microbiologists ultimately helped to expand the very definition of infectious disease.

THE EYES HAVE IT

Geographically, this story may begin in Taiwan, but anatomically, it starts in the human eye. The eye disease known as trachoma, little known in the West, is the leading infectious cause of blindness in less-developed countries. It is caused by the chlamydia species *Chlamydia trachomatis.* (If the name chlamydia sounds familiar, it should. Genital chlamydia infection, which is also caused by *C. trachomatis,* is by far the most common sexually transmitted disease in North America and Europe.)

Trachoma starts out inconspicuously enough. A few *C. trachomatis* organisms infect the mucous membrane of a child's eyes. The bacteria slip into cells in the membrane, or conjunctiva, reproduce themselves, and then attempt to spread. The youngster's eyes become red and irritated. In most cases the immune system responds by producing specialized cells that attack and kill the bacteria. The bacterial swarm slows

278

and then stops, and the victim's eyes clear up. But a few bacteria loiter, settling quietly into the conjunctiva. Many years later the bacteria emerge from this dormant state and begin once again to reproduce and spread. The immune system again launches a defense against the intruder.

The casualties of this battle are the eyes themselves. The repeated influx of immune system cells swells the conjunctiva, scarring it. The scars contract, which causes the upper eyelid to dry and turn inward. Normally, the eyelid functions like a windshield wiper. But as scars form, the eyelid begins to scrape the cornea (the curved, transparent membrane that covers the front part of the eye) in some areas and fails to cover it in others. Without the sweeping action of the eyelid, the tears cannot do their job of keeping the conjunctiva moist and clearing the eye of irritants. Eventually, a profusion of blood vessels clouds the cornea, and the scars thicken. Without treatment, infected individuals can go blind as early as age 30. In some cases blindness occurs later, at 50 or even 70 years of age.

PATIENCE PAYS OFF

Grayston's work in Taiwan strengthened the all-important link between trachoma and *C. trachomatis*. His assignment there was to search for infectious viruses, screening volunteers from all walks of life, and to try to develop vaccines. His primary research tool was the throat culture, a procedure in which organisms swabbed from a subject's throat are grown and identified in the laboratory. At the urging of a Taiwanese medical resident, however, Grayston also took samples from the eyes of some volunteers. And it was a good thing he did. Soon after he arrived in Taipei, word came from China that a researcher there had for the first time

How Atherosclerosis Develops

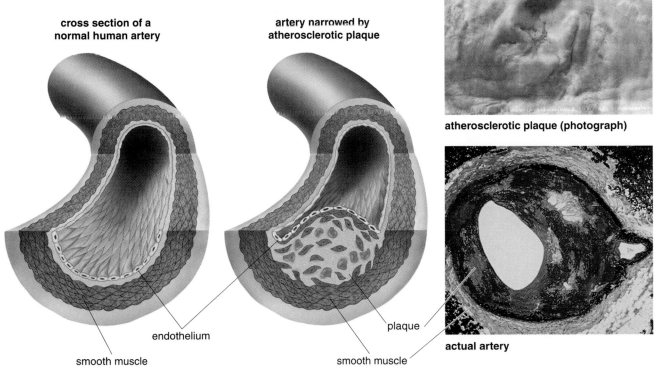

cross section of a normal human artery

artery narrowed by atherosclerotic plaque

atherosclerotic plaque (photograph)

endothelium

smooth muscle

plaque

smooth muscle

actual artery

(Top) Science Pictures Limited/Science Source-Photo Researchers; (bottom) Custom Medical Stock Photo

279

managed to grow *C. trachomatis* in the laboratory—a major breakthrough. Although chlamydia had long been associated with genital and eye infections, it was not until the bacterium could be reliably grown that research on prevention and treatment could begin in earnest.

Grayston, now 74 but still leading the globe-trotting life of a senior scientist, remembers this turning point. "We took the eye specimens we already had…and were able to grow chlamydia," he says. His research team immediately began a set of experiments that became what he considers probably their most significant contribution. They demonstrated that trachoma is not a single infection. For the disease to develop, he explains, "you had to get infected and reinfected and perhaps reinfected again."

Demonstrating the part played by reinfection took patience. Grayston and his colleagues had to infect monkeys, wait for the animals' infections to heal, and then infect them again. Watching for the telltale signs of trachoma to appear in the monkeys took three to five years. Publication of their findings (in 1967) had to wait even longer.

But the results were worth the wait. For one thing, they helped establish Grayston as a chlamydia researcher par excellence. For another, the natural history of the infection, with its long lag time, planted a seed in the minds of Grayston and his colleagues: "The tendency for chlamydia to be involved in chronic disease became important in our thinking."

A MYSTERIOUS STRAIN

During the 1960s Grayston traveled to Taiwan repeatedly to collect samples of chlamydia from the eyes of Taiwanese children. He analyzed the samples at the University of Washington, where he became professor of preventive medicine in 1960 and 10 years later the founding dean of the School of Public Health and Community Medicine. Grayston and his team "typed" the bacteria, using a process analogous to blood typing. Just as human blood falls into several different categories, chlamydia organisms also fall into categories. Most of the samples Grayston examined were of familiar types.

But one, which he named TW-183 (TW for Taiwan), was *not* familiar. "We realized that this strain was not *trachomatis*," says Grayston. That seemed to leave only one possibility. Only one other species of chlamydia, *C. psittaci*, had been identified. Unlike *C. trachomatis*, this species preferred to live in the lungs of humans and could cause pneumonia. *C. psittaci* had a peculiar quirk: it was carried by birds. Humans acquired it through contact with infected birds. Grayston assumed that TW-183 must be a strain of *C. psittaci* that just happened to infect the eyes.

But things were not that simple; this new strain of chlamydia posed some discomfiting problems. *C. psittaci* had never before been found in the eye, and TW-183 did not seem very much at home there. Grayston's team inoculated the eyes of monkeys with TW-183, but the organism did not cause conjunctival infection, as *C. trachomatis* did. Rather, it triggered a mild inflammation and then "went away," Grayston remembers. Over the next few years, he and his colleagues repeatedly tried to identify TW-183. "Whenever a new technique for typing became available," he says, "we'd pull [a sample of TW-183] out of the freezer and test it."

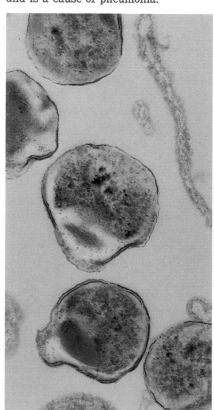

Chlamydia psittaci, shown in this electron micrograph, is a strain that is carried by birds. This bacterium can live in the lungs of humans and is a cause of pneumonia.

Dr. Kari Lounatmaa—Science Source/Photo Researchers

In 1969 Grayston's colleague Wang San-pin developed a new and easy-to-use blood test for TW-183. Now, for the first time, Grayston's team could easily check blood samples collected from volunteers to see if they had ever encountered the bacterium. If so, their immune systems would have mounted a response to it, producing chlamydia-specific antibodies. (Antibodies are proteins manufactured by the immune system to protect against bacteria and other pathogens.)

Without delay, the scientists used the new test to look for TW-183 antibodies in blood collected from families in which some members had trachoma and others were uninfected. The result "blew our mind," says Grayston. "We found lots of antibody, but it was not related to eye disease." In fact, of the two groups, more people who did *not* have trachoma were positive for antibodies against TW-183. Obviously then, the TW-183 strain was a common cause of infection but probably not a cause of trachoma.

Further testing revealed just how widespread TW-183 was—much more so, in fact, than the trachoma-causing strains of chlamydia. "We found it in everyone," marvels Grayston. "American servicemen, Chinese bargirls, [Taiwanese] aborigines." Moreover, the antibodies became more prevalent with age.

CHLAMYDIA'S CRYPTIC LIFE CYCLE

Chlamydia passes most of its existence in a sort of time capsule. The bacterium itself—in all three forms, *C. trachomatis*, *C. psittaci*, and TW-183—normally exists as a hard-shelled pellet called an *elementary body*, or EB. The chlamydia EB is a spore that is thought to be able to survive virtually indefinitely outside a living cell. EBs are impervious to heat, ultraviolet light, and even large doses of radiation. They float constantly between cells or in the air.

Chlamydia organisms keep a very low profile. Unlike many other disease-causing bacteria, they do not produce the toxins (poisonous substances) that are a primary characteristic of illnesses like cholera. Instead, they persuade "host" cells to invite them in, and then they take over the cell. In this behavior they are more like viruses—which also rely on the host-cell machinery to survive—than bacteria. Once an EB successfully infiltrates a cell in a human or other animal, its life cycle begins. It inhabits a tiny balloonlike compartment inside the cell called a vacuole. Typically, cells monitor the contents of their vacuoles and dispose of undesirable materials by squirting them with acid.

But the chlamydia EB has evolved a defense against this threat. It sends a signal to the cell to protect, not destroy, the contents of the vacuole it inhabits. Then, under cover of this protection, the EB transforms itself into something more treacherous: a noninfectious particle called the *reticulate body*, or RB. The RB reproduces quickly and efficiently. The vacuole becomes distended, filling more and more of the cell. Then, just as the cell is ready to burst, the RBs transform themselves back into EBs, which then infect new cells and start the cycle again.

As if this insidious life cycle is not threatening enough, it became clear in the early 1980s that chlamydia has yet another method of inhabiting cells. The textbooks euphemistically call this alternative life cycle "cryptic." In plain language that means that researchers do not know where the bacteria reside within the cell. All

"We found [the new strain] in everyone," marvels Grayston. "American servicemen, Chinese bargirls, [Taiwanese] aborigines."

281

(Below) James Marshall—Corbis; (bottom) Dr. Kari Lounatmaa—Science Source/Photo Researchers

(Above) Crowded enclosed spaces like this subway car provide ideal conditions for the spread of *Chlamydia pneumoniae* (below right), a common bacterium known to cause coldlike symptoms. Its possible role in heart disease is a subject of heated debate.

they know is that the cells appear by all measures to be uninfected. Then, even many years later, if conditions change—if, for example, the infected person becomes immunocompromised or undergoes surgery—the chlamydia can emerge from hiding and begin to infect new cells.

THE FINNISH CONNECTION

During the course of the 1970s, Grayston and others accumulated more and more evidence that TW-183 was indeed a new species of chlamydia. Its pear-shaped elementary bodies, for example, looked different from the round ones of *C. trachomatis*. Then a fortuitous thing happened. In 1978 Pekka Saikku, a Finnish physician and microbiologist, went to Grayston's Seattle lab to learn how to test blood for chlamydia antibodies. He was interested in the possibility that *C. trachomatis* might be a

cause of pneumonia. Saikku, it turned out, was trying to solve a mystery of his own.

For several years Finnish researchers had been collecting blood samples from people with pneumonia and other, less-serious respiratory infections. Saikku had been able to show that some form of chlamydia was involved in these illnesses. But in at least one case, it was highly unlikely that the strain causing the infection was *C. psittaci*. The reason for this was simple; some of the blood specimens had been collected during outbreaks of respiratory infection in northern Finland at a time—the dead of winter—when there are no birds around. And since birds are the only known long-term carrier of *C. psittaci* infection, Saikku reasoned that the infection he was investigating had to be a respiratory version of another chlamydia species, one that, like *C. trachomatis*, can be transmitted from one human to another.

The antibodies from the Finnish blood samples, however, matched none of Grayston's extensive collection of *C. trachomatis* strains. It was Wang who suggested testing TW-183 against the antibodies in the Finnish blood to see if the "mystery" strain was the cause of the respiratory infections. When Saikku

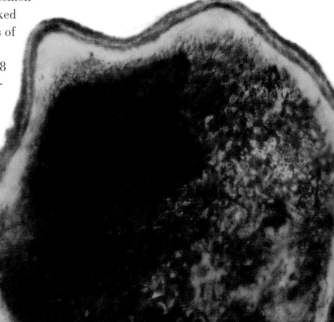

282

tested the antibodies against TW-183, the samples from one outbreak responded strongly. It was a turning point—a match between the mysterious chlamydia strain and an equally baffling group of respiratory infections. The excitement Grayston must have felt at the time has left no trace in his memory 20 years later. He recalls no celebration, no rejoicing—simply the thought, "Well, that explains a lot of things."

The logic was irrefutable. TW-183 was a respiratory agent that caused coldlike symptoms. It could spread in the form of microdroplets emitted by infected individuals when they coughed or sneezed. A person could even be exposed as a result of sharing the air in a confined space like an elevator with someone who was infected. No wonder, then, that so many people had antibodies against the bacterium.

So TW-183 earned a new name, *Chlamydia pneumoniae*, and it earned Grayston and Saikku a place in history as the scientists who discovered it. But a connection between *heart disease* and a bug that causes *colds* never occurred to them. Nor did it occur to anyone else in the medical mainstream. The suggestion that chlamydia could be at the heart of heart disease would come instead from a persistent Finnish doctor.

A HYPOTHESIS CAN BE INFECTIOUS, TOO

In recent decades several studies have uncovered links between infectious agents and chronic diseases. Stomach ulcers, long attributed to spicy foods, excess acid, and psychological stress, are now widely accepted to be the result of infection with the bacterium *Helicobacter pylori*—a theory that earned its chief proponent, Australian physician Barry Marshall, nothing but derision when he initially suggested it in the early 1980s. Liver cancer has been linked to infection with the hepatitis B virus and cervical cancer to human papillomavirus. A herpesvirus has been implicated in Kaposi's sarcoma, a skin cancer sometimes seen in people with AIDS.

That infection might have a role in heart disease was first suggested by animal studies. In the 1970s researchers at Cornell University's College of Veterinary Medicine, Ithaca, New York, showed that a virus that causes leukemia in chickens also induces atherosclerosis-like lesions (deposits of fatty substances and cells) inside the birds' arteries. Ever since, a growing trail of evidence has pointed to a potential role for viruses in heart disease. In one study, for example, scientists found that the rate of restenosis—reclosure of arteries successfully cleared of obstruction—was dramatically higher in angioplasty patients who had antibodies against cytomegalovirus (CMV), another of the herpesviruses, than in those who lacked antibodies. In another study CMV was found to be associated with thickening of the carotid arteries (the vessels in the neck that supply blood to the brain).

Chlamydia, though, was not yet under suspicion. Surprisingly, the suggestion of a link between this bacterium and heart disease first came from someone outside the chlamydia research community—a Finnish doctor, Villi Valtonen, who was not even a heart specialist.

At the time, Valtonen, now chair of the infectious disease department at the Helsinki University Central Hospital, was regarded by many as a crackpot. Grayston recalls that he "believed that every [health problem] is caused by infections." Heart attacks, Valtonen proposed, were

> It was a turning point—a match between the mysterious chlamydia strain and an equally baffling group of respiratory infections.

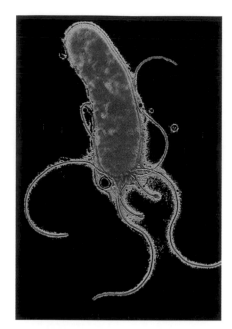

precipitated by a newly acquired bacterial infection. But which bacterium? In 1988 he sought help from Maija Leinonen, Saikku's colleague and wife, who had developed a specific test using antibodies that could identify chlamydia. Valtonen took Leinonen two groups of blood samples, one from patients who had recently suffered a heart attack and the second from patients who had chronic coronary heart disease but had not recently had a heart attack.

Leinonen recalls, "My technician called me down to the lab one afternoon at five o'clock and said, 'What kind of samples are these? I've never seen results like this before.'" She checked the samples herself. The blood specimens were from the patients who had had heart attacks, and around 70% were carrying antibodies against some form of chlamydia, most of which turned out to be *C. pneumoniae* antibodies. Except for the respiratory disease patients Saikku had tested, no group had ever been found to be more than 10% positive for antibodies against *C. pneumoniae*. Leinonen immediately called Saikku, who was on one of his regular visits to Seattle, and woke him up to tell him the news.

Saikku was skeptical. "There must be something fishy," was his first thought. But the results held. Both the chronic heart disease patients and the recent heart attack victims were more likely than non-heart patients to have antibodies against chlamydia.

CULPRIT OR BYSTANDER?

By 1998 some 20 published studies had found a similar correlation between chlamydia and heart disease. That there is an association between the two is no longer in question. The data, in Grayston's words, "are overwhelming." But, he hastens to add, "Is that association meaningful? We don't know." As internist Loïc Capron at the Paris hospital Hôtel-Dieu observes, in the long run chlamydia may turn out to be "a red herring…the wrong answer to a very good question."

Grayston, Saikku, and others have developed the following scenario, though it is by no means accepted as dogma among cardiologists. An infection with *C. pneumoniae* begins, perhaps without any symptoms, in the lungs. The bacteria are picked up by circulating white blood cells. In theory, these immune system cells have been summoned to destroy the pathogen. In practice, however, they allow it to stow away and hitch a free ride to a more hospitable locale: the artery walls.

For some reason bacteria love to burrow into the cells that line the arteries. Chlamydia has a tendency to seek out long-lived cells, and the muscle cells in the arterial wall fit the bill perfectly. Once ensconced in the arterial muscle, the bacteria hunker down, cryptically perhaps, and wait. And wait. And wait. "It's a dormant, silent infection," says Saikku. The bacteria are protected from the immune system, he says, because they are inside cells. Many years later, in response perhaps to inflammation or the beginnings of an atherosclerotic lesion (plaque), the bacteria begin to reproduce again. It is when plaques grow—whether spurred on by bacteria or by something else—that they become dangerous. Sometimes they break off and block a coronary blood vessel (one supplying blood to the heart muscle). The result is a heart attack.

A similar kind of reactivation happens in trachoma. A child infected in, say, the Middle East will immigrate to the United States and live for 50 years with no eye problems. Then the trauma of cataract surgery brings on a bout with trachoma.

But there is another possible explanation—that *C. pneumoniae* is not a disease-causing culprit but merely an innocent bystander. As Julius Schachter of the University of California, San Francisco, explains it, with age everyone may develop little lesions—something like abrasions or nicks—on the insides of the arteries. The lesions are capable of trapping any microbe passing by in the bloodstream, including chlamydia. Chlamydia bacteria, therefore, could be found in conjunction with atherosclerotic plaques even though they have nothing to do with plaque formation. This "bystander hypothesis" is also consistent with the observation that by age 70 most people have antibodies against *C. pneumoniae*. So why doesn't everyone have a heart attack?

Unfortunately, it is impossible to test directly whether chlamydia causes heart disease. For one thing, it would require a 50-year-long experiment. But more important, it would be unethical. Physicians cannot just infect otherwise healthy people with a potentially harmful bacterium. Instead, they must find their research subjects in individuals who are already infected. Or they must work with animals. So far, neither group has yielded an answer.

THE TRIBULATIONS OF TRIALS

The antibiotics known as the macrolides are especially effective in killing chlamydia and have been widely used in the treatment of genital chlamydia infection. Not surprisingly, as evidence of a connection between chlamydia and heart disease has mounted, cardiologists in several countries have begun testing these drugs in heart patients.

In one of the most noteworthy of these trials, cardiologist Sandeep Gupta and his colleagues at St. George's Hospital Medical School in London measured the level of antichlamydia antibodies in male heart attack survivors. They then gave the macrolide antibiotic azithromycin (Zithromax) to one group who had a high level of antibodies. Two other antibody-positive groups served as controls; one received a placebo, and the other received no treatment at all. The investigators found that the men in the control groups had a fourfold increased risk for a heart attack or other "event" such as the severe chest pain known as angina. In patients who received the antibiotic, however, the rate of subsequent cardiovascular events was the same as among men who, at the outset, had no detectable antibodies against the bacterium.

In another notable trial Enrique Gurfinkel and colleagues at the Favaloro Foundation in Buenos Aires, Argentina, treated about 100 heart patients with the macrolide roxithromycin for 30 days. The investigators found that in the first month after treatment—but not after three or six months—patients in an untreated control group had a significantly higher likelihood of heart attacks and other cardiovascular events than did those who received the antibiotic.

Still, these studies have failed to convince many experts. One outspoken critic is Stephen Epstein, former chief of cardiology at the National Heart, Lung, and Blood Institute. Now at the Washington Hospital Center in Washington, D.C., Epstein is investigating links between atherosclerosis and CMV. Both of the

In recent years scientists have shown that bacteria cause or contribute to many disorders not previously considered infectious. (Opposite page, top) *Helicobacter pylori,* now accepted as the cause of stomach ulcers. (Bottom) Scanning electron micrograph of a kidney stone; a 1998 study implicated a class of tiny bacteria in the formation of these and other abnormal calcium deposits.

(Above) Researchers have created atherosclerosis-like lesions in rabbits' arteries by infecting the animals nasally with *C. pneumoniae*. (Below, center) Electron micrograph of plaque deposits inside a human coronary artery showing suspected *C. pneumoniae* bacteria (red).

In addition to small drug doses and comparatively few subjects, the studies in question labor under another handicap; macrolides kill other bacteria besides chlamydia, including *H. pylori*, the ulcer "bug," implicated by some scientists as a factor in heart disease. "No one can say with any certainty that they actually treated *C. pneumoniae*," says Siobhan O'Connor, an infectious disease specialist at the CDC. The most charitable word any chlamydia expert uses about the Gupta and Gurfinkel trials is "preliminary."

When researchers want satisfying proof of a hypothesis about humans, they typically turn to animal research. Animals, especially mammals, resemble humans enough that conclusions drawn from animal studies usually hold for humans as well. At the same time, animals have shorter life spans, can be infected at will, and, perhaps most important, can be sacrificed at the appropriate moment in order to see what a microbe is doing to their bodies.

above-mentioned trials are "seriously flawed" in his opinion. "None of these studies is like the big cholesterol trials in which thousands of patients were treated over several years," he explains. Only when trials include substantial numbers of subjects do most scientists consider the findings truly meaningful.

Nor is Grayston convinced. In fact, he goes even farther than Epstein, dismissing the positive effect of Gupta's study as nothing more than "some kind of accident." The trial was ill-conceived, he contends, not least because Gupta treated patients with no more than 500 milligrams of antibiotic per day, a dose that Grayston characterizes as "homeopathic," which is an ironic way of saying "insignificant."

The research on chlamydia has largely centered on rabbits and mice. Rabbits infected with the bacterium have a tendency to develop lesions similar to atherosclerotic plaques. Saikku and others have demonstrated that the plaques shrink if the animals are treated with azithromycin. Grayston, meanwhile, showed that in a strain of mice prone to atherosclerosis, the course of the disease is accelerated by *C. pneumoniae* infection.

As with the human studies, the experts are by no means in agree-

286

ment about the significance of these findings. Microbiologist Robert Molestina, at the University of Louisville, Kentucky, says that compared with the human studies, the results in animals are more clearly indicative of a cause-and-effect relationship. But Gerald Byrne, a chlamydia researcher at the University of Wisconsin, is more cautious, pointing out that "rabbits don't really get atherosclerosis." Even if positive results continue to flow from animal experiments, claims Byrne, scientists will find no proof that chlamydia *causes* atherosclerosis. Instead, he predicts, they will see *C. pneumoniae* "contributing, aiding, and abetting."

There is nothing Grayston would like to see more than the definitive trial demonstrating exactly what part chlamydia plays in heart and artery disease. That study, says Epstein, "will never be done." There is just no ethical way to do it.

But if a drug exists that might work in reducing heart attack risk, and if that drug has few known side effects—as is the case with the macrolide antibiotics—then wouldn't it be better for more people to be taking it? In fact, people already are. Clinicians this author interviewed at a recent infectious disease conference said that more and more cardiologists are prescribing macrolides for patients who have had one heart attack and may be at risk for a second. One Boston-area specialist quoted a colleague as saying, "If they're harmless, why not?"

Except that they are not harmless. The more frequently physicians prescribe a particular antibiotic, the more quickly drug-resistant strains will evolve. Furthermore, says cardiologist Joseph Muhlestein of the LDS Hospital in Salt Lake City, Utah, who has performed several recent clinical studies on *C. pneumoniae* and heart

disease, "there are risks we do not know. We need definitive proof that this will be more helpful than harmful."

WIZARD: WILL IT WORK?

In search of that proof, scientists in North America and Europe have enrolled more than 3,000 men and women with heart disease in WIZARD (the acronym stands for Weekly Intervention with Zithromax for Atherosclerosis and Related Disorders). Patients will receive a three-month course of treatment with either azithromycin or a placebo and then will be monitored for heart attacks, angina, and other cardiovascular events. The trial, which is being sponsored by Pfizer, the manufacturer of azithromycin, has advantages over the previous studies in that it is larger and the follow-up will be longer, up to three and a half years. The first results may be available as early as 2000.

In Grayston's view, however, even three months' treatment is far too short. Cardiologists have got the idea, says Grayston, "that they can give antibiotics and knock the bug out. The thing about chlamydia is, whether it is in the genital tract, the eye, the lung, or the heart, you do not *eradicate* it with a short course of antibiotic....You may reduce inflammation in the plaque but it's going to come right back."

The duration of the WIZARD trial is not up to cardiologists, or even to Pfizer. The company would probably prefer to treat for a longer period simply because, should the treatment turn out to prevent heart attacks, it would boost the sales of azithromycin. Instead, the Food and Drug Administration (FDA) set the limits of the treatment period. Grayston,

who helped design WIZARD, explains that unless Pfizer first tests the drug to make sure it does not cause cancer, the FDA will approve only a three-month trial. If azithromycin were to be tested on mice and some of them developed tumors, Pfizer might have to face having a multi-million-dollar product pulled off the market. So WIZARD will remain a three-month trial. "Maybe they'll get an effect you can see," ruminates Grayston. "Then if they see it wearing off, it will be good evidence that you've got to treat longer."

IN JOHN SNOW'S FOOTSTEPS

The frustrations of WIZARD bring the graying Grayston back to his days as an enthusiastic recruit in the "epidemic police." As much as he would like to solve the mystery of heart disease—the number one cause of death in the U.S.—he knows from his public health training that scientific inquiry must sometimes take second place to practical concerns.

If antibiotics prove effective in preventing heart disease, he says, "it's like taking the handle off the pump in the place where the cholera was"—a reference to the historic action of the 19th-century physician John Snow, who stopped a deadly cholera outbreak in London by closing a public water pump in a neighborhood where the disease was rampant. Snow suspected that cholera was waterborne, although it had not yet been proved and many doubted his hypothesis. When the removal of the pump handle stopped the outbreak and thus saved hundreds of lives, Snow was vindicated. As Grayston observes, "You sometimes jump ahead to improve human health even though you may not know exactly why."

AT THE HEART
OF HEART RESEARCH—

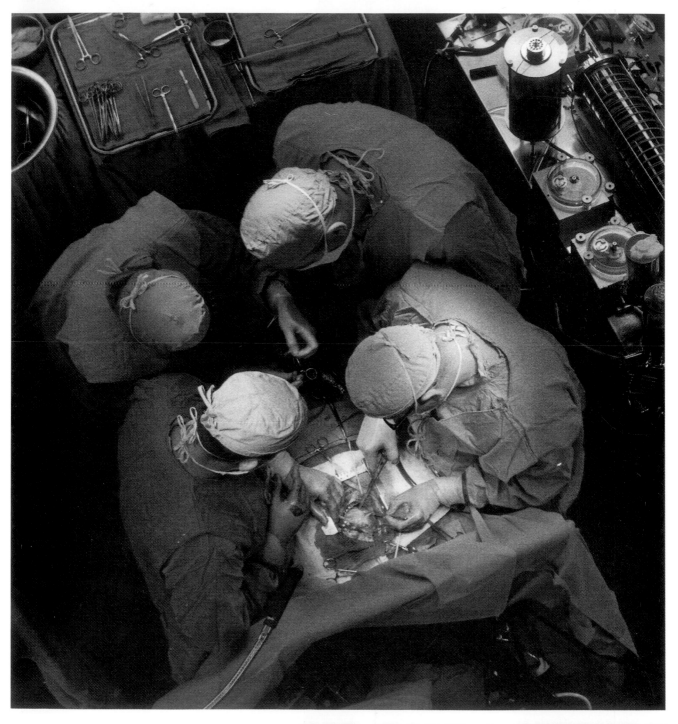

FOR HALF A CENTURY

ifty years ago a heart attack meant certain death for a third of all victims. Survivors were typically hospitalized for six weeks, treated with painkillers, and then told to go home and stay in bed for six months. Many never resumed a normal life. Today, thanks to a half century of biomedical research, the average hospital stay for a heart attack is 10 days, and patients can return to normal activities within weeks. The average rate of death from heart attack has dropped by more than half.

Since 1948 the institution now known as the National Heart, Lung, and Blood Institute (NHLBI), a branch of the U.S. National Institutes of Health, has been at the forefront of the fight to prevent and treat heart disease. Research conducted and supported by the institute has led—among other things—to the identification of heart disease risk factors; means of detecting, treating, and preventing high blood pressure (hypertension) and elevated cholesterol levels; and the development of many types of open-heart surgery, balloon angioplasty to open blocked arteries, tests for diagnosing various heart conditions, devices to improve heart function, and thrombolytic ("clot-busting") drugs.

But although 50 years of efforts have contributed to a dramatic

This article is adapted from a special issue of Heart Memo, *published by the National Heart, Lung, and Blood Institute in honor of the agency's 50th anniversary.*

reduction in deaths, heart disease remains the number one killer of Americans, taking more than 700,000 lives each year. Public awareness of the benefits of a healthy diet, adequate exercise, weight control, and smoking cessation has grown

(Opposite page) National Heart, Lung, and Blood Institute/ National Institutes of Health; (below) CNRI/Science Source-Photo Researchers

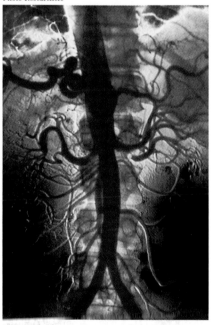

(Above) An angiogram showing the abdominal aorta and its branches supplying the kidneys, liver, and legs. (Opposite page) Open-heart surgery in the 1950s, using an early version of the heart-lung machine.

significantly. Persuading the public to adopt heart-healthy habits, however, remains a challenge.

Today an estimated 58 million Americans have some form of cardiovascular—*i.e.*, heart and/or blood vessel—disease. High blood pressure is the most common of these

conditions, affecting 50 million people. Coronary heart disease (narrowing of the coronary arteries, which supply blood to the heart muscle) is second in prevalence, affecting 13.9 million. And stroke (damage to a portion of the brain that occurs when a vessel ruptures or becomes blocked) is the third most prevalent cardiovascular disorder.

ADVANCES WITH AN IMPACT

In 1948 when Congress established the National Heart Institute (NHI), forerunner of the NHLBI, the institute's mission was to conduct and coordinate cardiovascular disease research and make grants available for research projects. A short time later the NHI took control of the then newly initiated Framingham Heart Study (one of the longest-running and most comprehensive epidemiological studies—still going on today), which, among other contributions, led to the identification of definitive risk factors for coronary heart disease.

The NHI also supported research to develop biomedical devices, including artificial heart valves to replace diseased or damaged ones and heart-lung machines to aid in open-heart surgery. New imaging techniques were introduced in the 1950s and 1960s, including radionuclide angiography, a technique that made it possible to visualize the beating heart. Cardiac catheters, tiny flexible tubes that can be threaded into the arterial system, were devel-

289

National Heart, Lung, and Blood Institute/National Institutes of Health

This device was developed in the mid-1960s to assist in the pumping action of the heart's left ventricle when that chamber has been damaged by disease.

oped to infuse a contrast medium, or dye, for imaging the heart and coronary arteries.

The 1960s brought many more advances, and toward the end of the decade, a discernible decline in deaths from heart disease was seen. Technological progress enabled heart valve replacement and arterial bypass surgery to become "routine" procedures. Research to develop an artificial heart began in 1964 and continues today; devices to assist the pumping action of the left ventricle (the heart chamber most commonly damaged by heart disease), a total artificial heart, and other mechanical devices continue to be tested in NHLBI-supported clinical trials.

The first successful heart transplant operation took place in South Africa in 1967; a team from the Stanford University Medical Center began performing the procedure in the U.S. the following year. Coronary care units (CCUs) began appearing in American hospitals in the 1960s.

In the late 1970s advances in imaging techniques allowed researchers to use cardiac catheters to insert tiny balloons into narrowed arteries to open blockages, a procedure called percutaneous transluminal coronary angioplasty, or balloon angioplasty. In 1995 the NHLBI-funded Bypass Angioplasty Revascularization Investigation compared the success rates of angioplasty and coronary artery bypass surgery in unblocking blood vessels. The study found that the

rates were similar for both procedures—except in people with diabetes, who fared better with bypass surgery.

In 1991 the institute began the National Heart Attack Alert Program to improve the diagnosis and treatment of acute heart attack. The program seeks to reduce the amount of time between the onset of an attack and the start of treatment. The goal is to treat heart attacks within 30 minutes after the patient gets to the emergency room. In 1998 the program was expected to evaluate the results of a large community intervention project, the Rapid Early Action for Coronary Treatment study.

HYPERTENSION MATTERS, CHOLESTEROL COUNTS!

The National High Blood Pressure Education Program—a partnership of the institute, professional and volunteer health agencies, and state health departments—was launched in 1972 to reduce death and disability from hypertension, a condition known as the "silent killer" because it can exist and progress virtually without symptoms. Periodically, the program disseminates updated national guidelines for the treatment and prevention of hypertension. A November 1997 report by the program's joint national committee showed that deaths from stroke, the most devastating outcome of high blood pressure, had declined nearly 60% since the inception of the program. Very recent data, however, show some alarming trends: a slight upturn in stroke incidence, an increase in both end-stage kidney disease and heart failure, and a leveling off of the death rate for patients with heart disease—all of which are influenced by blood pressure; all of these changes are indications that hypertension education efforts need to be stepped up.

In the late 1960s data from the Framingham study showed a link between heart disease and elevated blood cholesterol levels, and researchers set out to see if lowering blood cholesterol could lower the risk of heart disease. In 1984 the NHLBI-sponsored Lipid Research Clinics Coronary Primary Prevention Trial demonstrated that reducing cholesterol could indeed lower the risk of both heart disease and heart attack. Another large clinical trial—the Multiple Risk Factor Intervention Trial—also supported cholesterol lowering and smoking cessation to prevent heart disease. These findings led to the creation of the National Cholesterol Education Program in 1985—a pioneering program that for nearly a decade and a half has been spreading the word about the risks of high cholesterol and the lifestyle measures that can help to reduce or control cholesterol levels.

SUCCESS WITH DRUGS

Remarkable advances have been made in the pharmacological treatment of cardiovascular disease. The first drugs to treat high blood pressure were introduced in the early 1950s. The thiazide diuretics, one class of medications that reduce blood pressure by removing water from the body, followed after NHI-funded research in 1957 showed the effectiveness of the first such drug, chlorothiazide.

During the late 1970s and early 1980s, two new classes of drugs—the calcium channel blockers and the angiotensin converting enzyme (ACE) inhibitors—were added to the arsenal of antihypertensive drugs, previously limited to diuretics and beta-blockers. Other studies at that time showed that thrombolytic agents could reduce the damage from heart attacks. In the 1990s clot-busters such as streptokinase and tissue plasminogen activator (t-PA) were approved for emergency treatment of heart attack and stroke.

In the summer of 1991, two clinical trials showed the positive effect that drug treatment was having in the war against heart disease. The Systolic Hypertension in the Elderly Program demonstrated that low doses of diuretics could significantly reduce the risk of stroke and heart attack in people over 60 with isolated systolic hypertension. (In this type of hypertension, the systolic blood pressure—the top, or upper, number in the blood-pressure reading—is high, but diastolic pressure—the bottom number—is normal.) A month later the Studies of Left Ventricular Dysfunction trial found that deaths from and hospitalization for congestive heart failure (weakening of the heart muscle accompanied by fluid accumulation in the body) could be markedly reduced if patients were treated with ACE inhibitors.

Reducing cholesterol [can] indeed lower the risk of both heart disease and heart attack.

A technician monitors the heart-lung machine during a triple coronary-artery bypass operation.

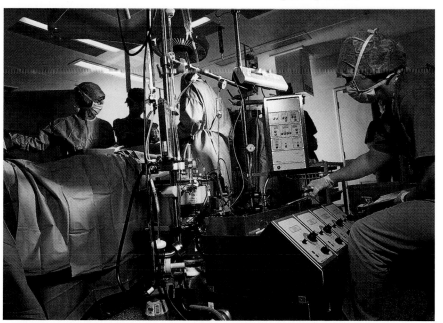

During the 1990s several studies demonstrated that one class of cholesterol-lowering drugs, the statins (lovastatin, pravastatin, etc.), could reduce the risk of heart attack and death in people with high cholesterol. The subjects included individuals who had already had heart attacks as well as persons at risk who had never had an attack. The findings of a study released in 1998 indicated that these drugs may even reduce the risk of heart attack in those with average cholesterol levels and no history of coronary heart disease.

TARGETING SPECIAL POPULATIONS

In the early 1980s epidemiological studies began to reveal that race and ethnicity affect people's risks of developing cardiovascular disease. African-American men, for example, were shown to be at higher risk for hypertension than their white counterparts. This information spurred the NHLBI to begin targeting specific audiences with its public education messages, an effort that eventually developed into the Minority Outreach Program.

Responding to the rapid growth of the Latino population, the NHLBI recently launched a special initiative aimed at this group. Salud para Su Corazón ("For the Health of Your Heart") produces educational materials in English and Spanish designed to raise awareness of cardiovascular risk factors in the Latino community and promote heart-healthy lifestyle changes.

In the past decade the NHLBI has begun to increase its focus on pediatric cardiovascular disease, and several clinical trials, including the Women's Ischemia Syndrome Evaluation, begun in 1996, are examining the ways in which heart disease in women differs from similar illness in men.

THE "BLOOD" AND "LUNG" IN NHLBI

The NHLBI's scope extends beyond the heart to include blood and respiratory disorders. NHLBI-sponsored studies of blood-transfusion techniques and blood products have had a substantial impact on the safety of the blood supply. In the late 1960s NHLBI-sponsored research led to the first screening test for hepatitis B in donated blood. Blood diseases like hemophilia and sickle-cell disease also come under the institute's purview. In 1997 the Stroke Prevention Trial in Sickle Cell Anemia showed that regular blood transfusions can dramatically reduce the risk of stroke in susceptible children with this genetic disorder.

The National Asthma Education and Prevention Program was initiated in 1989 to address the growing problem of asthma in the U.S. It has issued professional guidelines and patient education materials and has

A smiling Spanish-speaking heart helps raise awareness about heart disease risk factors in the Latino community.

Giving blood is a way of giving the gift of life to someone who needs it. The National Heart, Lung, and Blood Institute has done much to ensure the safety and adequacy of the American blood supply.

promoted basic research into the underlying causes of the disease. The latter effort includes the Collaborative Study of the Genetics of Asthma, an investigation seeking asthma-susceptibility genes. Emphysema too has been a concern of the institute. A study of lung-volume-reduction surgery to treat patients in the late stages of the disease was launched in 1996 by the NHLBI in cooperation with the Health Care Financing Administration.

THE *NEXT* 50 YEARS

In one important area of ongoing research, scientists are seeking ways to grow new tissues to help treat heart disease. Studies have shown, for example, that growth factors can stimulate the development of new blood vessels around a blocked artery. One day patients may be able

Researchers are just beginning to identify genes that may determine who is likely to develop hypertension or heart disease.

to "grow" new vessels rather than undergoing bypass surgery. It may even be possible for those with heart failure to produce healthy new tissue to replace damaged heart muscle.

Researchers are just beginning to identify genes that may determine

who is likely to develop hypertension or heart disease. This cutting-edge research may eventually lead to gene therapy treatments and, perhaps, cures for certain heart diseases. Before gene therapy can become a reality for heart patients, however, a great deal more needs to be understood about how to repair defective genes. Of course, 50 years ago gene therapy was undreamed of. The NHLBI plans to spend the next 50 years—and beyond—finding innovative ways to prevent, treat, and cure diseases of the heart, lungs, and blood.

FOR FURTHER INFORMATION

NHLBI home page:
  http://www.nhlbi.nih.gov/nhlbi/
  nhlbi.htm
Framingham Heart Study Web site:
  http://www.nhlbi.nih.gov/nhlbi/
  fram/

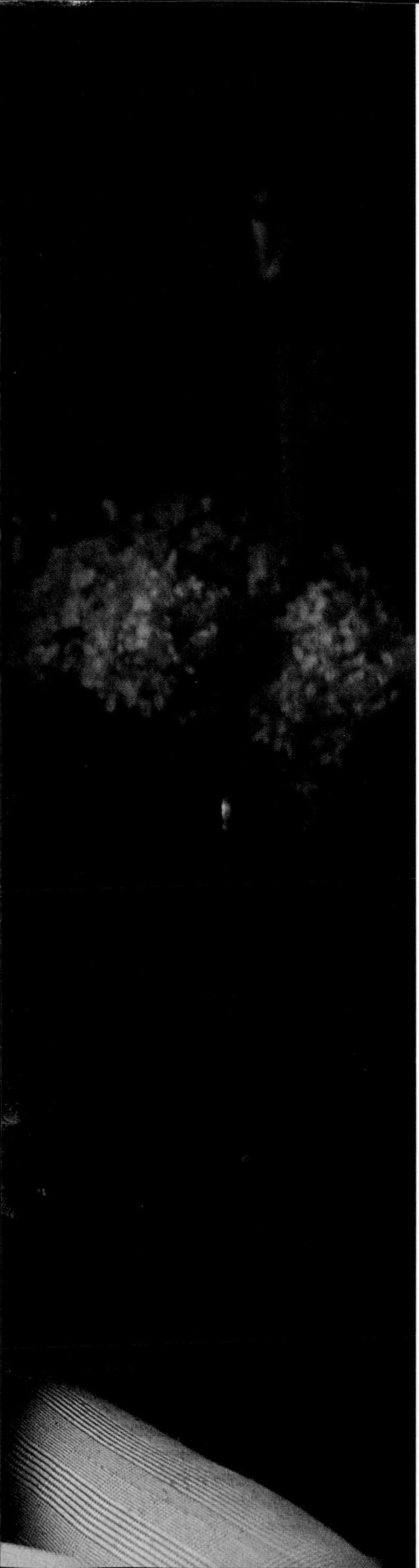

CONTEMPLATING SENIOR CITIZENSHIP

For some years I have been giving thought to the matter of age and aging. This is partly because of the great recent, current, and prospective increase in the older population—a major change, especially impressive in the U.S., to which two key factors have contributed. One is the imminent arrival in the older age brackets of the large number of people born in the immediate aftermath of World War II—the baby-boom generation, as it is less-than-attractively called. The other is the improvement in health care,

BY JOHN KENNETH GALBRAITH

Richard Schultz—Matrix

When doctors told him it would be wise to give up skiing, Galbraith complied—his "only major concession to age."

John Kenneth Galbraith is the Paul M. Warburg Professor of Economics Emeritus at Harvard University. An internationally known economist residing in Cambridge, Massachusetts, Galbraith has also had a distinguished career in American and international politics. He is the author of many acclaimed books, including: American Capitalism *(1952),* The Affluent Society *(1958),* The Liberal Hour *(1960),* Ambassador's Journal: A Personal Account of the Kennedy Years *(1969), and* The Good Society *(1996). On Oct. 15, 1998, he turned 90.*

(continued from page 295)
both in provision for its cost, however still imperfect, and in medical and surgical knowledge and treatment. A further factor that should not be ignored is the drop in tobacco use, which, perhaps surprisingly, will increase medical costs. Cigarette smokers tend to die early and, on the whole, rather inexpensively, whereas nonsmokers live to experience the lengthy and expensive medical care so often required by the old.

My further interest in aging is more personal. I write these lines from a certain measure of experience; this year (1998) I celebrate, if that is the word, my 90th birthday. Thus, I have the authority, greater or lesser, of one who is there.

I should perhaps first note that apart from the aftermath of a fall in 1997—an injured shoulder, hip, and what in polite language is called a pelvis—I am in good health. Over the past half a century, I have not greatly changed my daily routine—breakfast in bed, an often dreary session with the *New York Times*, writing until lunch, exercise (for a long time swimming, now walking), attention to a large correspondence consisting mostly of requests to do or give something. Then a drink, dinner, and whatever commands the evening.

UNRETIRING ATTITUDE

I retired from active teaching at Harvard 22 years ago, when I was 68 years old. This was more formal than real. I live in Cambridge, close to Harvard Yard; after "retirement" the university—faculty, students, and functions—continued to require of me about the same effort as it had previously. Much work for somewhat less money. I thought I would have more time for writing; retirement

There should be no…assumption that because one is old, one must withdraw or find a lesser place on the social scene.

made little difference. For many years my wife, Catherine, and I escaped every winter to Switzerland, where I wrote in the morning and skied in the afternoon. Eventually I was told by doctors that I must stop the skiing. That has been my only major concession to age.

Regarding the larger problem of the aging and the aged, as I have observed it, there are two critical concerns, closely related. The first is how the individual should respond to the mature years. The second is how the larger community, including the government, should respond to the needs of the old. I have rather strong views on both.

In the greatest possible measure, the individual response to growing older should be governed by preference and personal decision. For most older people the dominant, indeed controlling, factor is the matter of work. If this is enjoyed (and therewith the income), the individual should be allowed to exercise his or her preference as long as possible. In modern life an increasingly large proportion of the population—executives (and their financial acolytes), lawyers, authors, teachers, government workers, assorted intellectuals—has that choice. Anything that

thwarts it, specifically an arbitrarily established mandatory retirement age, should be strongly resisted. Although diminishing capacity and aptitude do come with age, they should be acted upon in the specific case. The choice between working and not working, to repeat, must always consider the individual circumstances.

For those for whom work is an unpleasant, repetitive drudgery, required retirement can be anticipated with pleasure. But even here the opportunity for continuing work and income should be available if it is preferred. In the modern—and, one trusts, civilized—community, a leisured existence should be open to the old; it should not be imposed. What is especially important, a point to which I will come presently, is that there should be no social assumption that because one is old, one must withdraw or find a lesser place on the social scene. If advice is to be given, it should not be to work or to retire but to enjoy!

WEALTH, HEALTH, AND POWER

Turning now to the responsibility of the society for the less-well-off elderly, two things are vital: one is income, the other is medical care. For the great majority of aging citizens, there comes a time when income declines, then dries up, and when health care costs become oppressive. Protection here is partly the reward of individual foresight and restraint. But inescapably some public provision of income and medical care for the old is essential—a prime social responsibility. So it is in all the economically advanced countries, starting with Germany under Bismarck more than a century ago.

From 1961 to 1963 Galbraith served as U.S. ambassador to India, under Pres. John F. Kennedy. (Left) He boards the plane in New York that will take him to his embassy post in Bombay. (Above) In March 1962 Ambassador Galbraith is covered with colored powders during a springtime "Holi Day" celebration in New Delhi.

In the United States, Social Security, Medicare, and Medicaid are now fully established government responsibilities. Although the provision of health care is far from adequate—too many of the elderly poor fail to receive needed medical attention or are dependent on charitable help—it is nonetheless widely accepted that there is a basic public responsibility here—especially in the case of Social Security.

All elderly persons should be aware of the reasons for this acceptance. It is partly, one cannot doubt, the compassionate attitude of the

citizenry and their elected politicians. But much more comes from the political role of the old. Here are increasing numbers of voters; here is an increasingly compelling voice. The modern old are a major political force. There should be no hesitation in bringing that power to bear. Certainly no member of Congress today—eccentric ideologists possibly apart—would mount a serious attack on Social Security. A lifetime of effort rightly earns its appropriate social rewards.

THE RIGHT TO DO NOTHING

How those retired from long years of compelled effort, enjoyed or tedious, should spend their time is perhaps the most discussed question among and concerning the old these days. Lurking always is the thought that older people should be engaged in an occupation that serves some socially compassionate need—charitable work, church work, varied forms of help to the young, and much more. All this is good; it is useful; it gives a sense of purpose to those already living in what some may call the declining years. The rule, however, is clear: what is done during retirement from formal lifetime activity should be a matter of individual choice; the old should not, by custom or social pressure, be denied full liberty of choice. If that choice is to do nothing, then that is wholly permissible. All should know of the lines of verse on the gravestone of a British charwoman, which were brought to my attention (as I recall) by John Maynard Keynes:

Don't mourn for me now, don't mourn for me never,
For I'm going to do nothing for ever and ever.

298

Pursuit of purely personal enjoyment should provoke no criticism and certainly no self-criticism. On the other hand, if community or other social service gives satisfaction, that certainly should be pursued. So too should any other lawful chosen form of involvement. The ability to decide as to the manner of one's life is what retirement and provision for it are meant to ensure. I place great value on the choice I have made, which seeks not to admit of age. I do not—nor should anyone—impose this choice on others.

THE STILL SYNDROME

I come finally to a common and damaging public attitude toward the aged and the aging. That the passing of years has its adverse physical and mental effects one cannot deny. Physical strength declines; mental acuity diminishes. So also memory. My own memory of names is highly unreliable. But I have taught myself not to worry; I can always ask or look things up. My writing—I've written around a dozen books since I retired—still attracts favorable comment. But I've also discovered that I have a special sense of delight in something I've said before. Moreover, I enjoy getting the revenues from my books; I rejoice slightly in the thought that my publisher will not get them.

There are diverse problems in getting old, but there is one that is particularly bad. That is the way we are reminded daily, sometimes hourly, as to the inevitability of our decline. This I have previously discussed, including in a review I wrote for the professionally reputable medical journal *The New England Journal of Medicine* (Aug. 18, 1994) of the volume entitled *The Oldest Old*

We are reminded daily, sometimes hourly, as to the inevitability of our decline.

(Oxford University Press, 1993). It is what I call the Still Syndrome.

The Still Syndrome is the design by which the young or the less old daily assail the old. "Are you still well?" "Are you still working?" "I see that you are still taking exercise." "Still having a drink?" As a compulsive literatus I am subject to my own special assault, "I see you are still writing." "Your writing still seems pretty good to me." The most dramatic general expression came from a friend I hadn't seen for some years: "I can hardly believe you're still alive!"

Everyone who is older should have his or her response to the Still Syndrome. Mine, to which I resort regularly, is to call attention to the speaker's departure from grace and decency: "I see that you are *still* rather immature." I urge all of my age or near it to devise some equally adverse, even insulting, response to the Still Syndrome and to voice it relentlessly.

Steven Senne—AP/Wide World

(Opposite page, top) The author of well over a dozen books on world affairs and economics, as well as two popular novels, Galbraith has long been acclaimed for his lucid writing style. (Opposite page, bottom) Professor Galbraith greets Mother Teresa at Harvard University commencement exercises in June 1982. (Below) Answering a question at the John F. Kennedy Library in Boston in May 1998, the internationally respected octogenarian economist still captivates his audiences whenever he lectures.

WELCOME TO ELLIS ISLAND:
A PICTURE ESSAY

TEXT BY JOHN PARASCANDOLA, PH.D.

PHOTOGRAPHS BY STEPHEN WILKES

On Jan. 1, 1892, Ellis Island —an abandoned munitions storage facility in Upper New York Bay and the former site of a U.S. Army fort— opened as a federal immigration depot. A 15-year-old Irish girl named Annie Moore became the first person to enter the country through the new port of entry. The Ellis Island depot was established at the beginning of the peak period of immigration into the U.S.; in the first year of its operation, nearly half a million newcomers were processed there. By 1924, when the flow of immigrants was slowed by more restrictive laws, some 12 million people had passed through Ellis Island.

Under legislation enacted in 1891, the processing of immigrants, previously performed by the states, was taken over by the federal government. The new law mandated the medical inspection of all new arrivals and assigned this task to the Marine Hospital Service, an agency that traced its origins to a 1798 act providing federal health care for merchant seamen. Beginning in the late 19th century, the system of

Aerial view of Ellis Island in Upper New York Bay, formerly the principal U.S. immigration reception center. The public health and hospital facilities were housed on the island's south side (foreground). (Opposite page) A trunk that presumably held all the worldly possessions of a long-ago immigrant remains behind in this room of one of the now-dilapidated hospital buildings.

Archive Photos

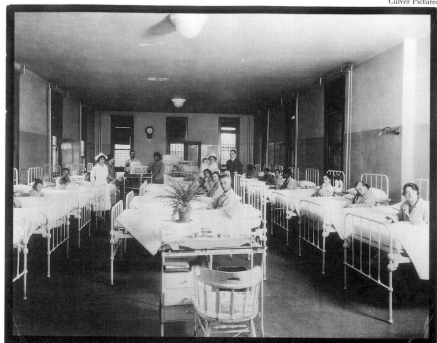

hospitals established for this purpose was assigned public health responsibilities such as quarantine, and in 1912 it was renamed the U.S. Public Health Service (PHS).

The 1891 immigration law stipulated the exclusion of "all idiots, insane persons, paupers or persons likely to become public charges, persons suffering from a loathsome or dangerous contagious disease," and criminals. First- and second-class passengers on steamships arriving in New York Harbor were examined by physicians in the privacy of their

John Parascandola is U.S. Public Health Service Historian, Department of Health and Human Services, Rockville, Maryland. He is the author of The Development of American Pharmacology: John J. Abel and the Shaping of a Discipline *(1992) and the recipient of numerous awards and honors, including the Surgeon General's Exemplary Service Award (1989 and 1996).*

(Top) The women's ward of the hospital on Ellis Island (*c.* 1920), with nearly every bed occupied; (right) the same room in ruins today. (Above) This door to the hospital's linen storage area has weathered the decades of abandonment in somewhat better repair than most of the public health complex.

cabins, but the "huddled masses" in steerage disembarked at Ellis Island for medical inspection and processing. The uniformed PHS physicians who performed this function constituted, in many cases, the immigrants' first contact with their new country, and no doubt many were intimidated by the unintentionally martial quality of a process that they little understood.

The medical scrutiny began as the immigrants ascended the stairs to the Registry Room in the main building. A PHS physician at the top of the stairs watched newcomers for signs of heart trouble, difficulty in breathing, or physical disabilities. The immigrants then formed lines and proceeded through the Registry Room. Given the volume of people flooding U.S. shores in the late 19th and early 20th centuries, the examinations were necessarily brief and superficial. Physicians checked scalps for lice or

scabs, the latter a symptom of favus, a contagious skin disorder. Eyes were carefully scrutinized for signs of trachoma, an infectious eye disease that can lead to blindness. The presence of favus or trachoma or the diagnosis of certain other infectious diseases such as leprosy, tuberculosis, syphilis, or schistosomiasis (a parasitic infestation) could result in an individual's being refused entry into the country. Disabilities, mental or physical, that might interfere with the ability of the immigrant to earn a living were also grounds for exclusion.

If a newcomer's condition aroused concern during the line inspection, the doctor made a chalk mark on the shoulder of the person's garment, signaling the need to detain that individual for further examination. The marks, letters of the alphabet, symbolized the suspected condition—"G" for goiter, for example, or

"X" for mental deficiency. Most immigrants filed through the medical inspection in less than an hour.

As historian Alan Kraut pointed out in his book *Silent Travelers: Germs, Genes, and the "Immigrant Menace"* (1994), despite the large number of immigrants to be processed, the public pressures to exclude the "unfit," and the cultural bias that some PHS physicians may have shared with many of their fellow Americans, most doctors consciously refused to allow the agenda of the immigration restrictionists to influence their medical assessments. Most of the newcomers passed the medical inspection. Only about 20% were detained for more detailed examination, and no more than about 2% were denied admission into the country. Those excluded were returned to their homelands—at the steamship company's expense.

(*continued on page 307*)

A uniformed Public Health Service physician checks for the highly contagious eye disease trachoma, using a buttonhook to evert the eyelids of just-arrived immigrants; in the days before antibiotics, trachoma, a bacterial infection transmitted by flies, was a common cause of blindness. (Opposite page) Ivy now grows in the corridor that formerly connected the hospital's contagious disease wards.

304

Brown Brothers

Decaying, cracking, crumbling, rusted, and mildewed: every building, room, and furnishing of the hospital complex bears the signs of decades of disuse; patients were last treated here in the late 1930s. (Opposite page) Just off the boat (*c.* 1921), immigrants must have their scalps inspected for vermin.

(continued from page 304)

Because arriving immigrants sometimes required hospitalization, the PHS erected several hospital buildings, including, among other facilities, psychiatric and communicable disease wards. The psychiatric ward was intended primarily for the temporary detention of those who were suspected of being mentally ill. Immigrants with acute contagious diseases (*e.g.*, children with measles) might be detained until they had recovered.

The doctors, nurses, and other health professionals on Ellis Island treated a wide variety of medical conditions, from broken arms to tuberculosis. Occasionally, a woman would arrive in an advanced state of pregnancy—more than 350 babies were born on Ellis Island.

Today the abandoned hospital buildings, designated one of the 11 "most endangered historic places" by the National Trust for Historic Preservation, are in an advanced state of dilapidation. Preservationists from New York and New Jersey, along with the National Park Service, are leading a campaign to save them. Plans call for the structures not to be restored to their original condition but simply to be preserved in their present state as a reminder of a poignant chapter of American history. ✿

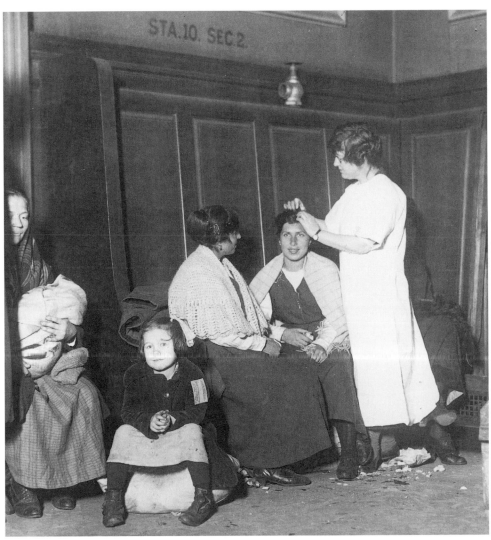

Culver Pictures

(Below) Brown Brothers; (bottom) Culver Pictures

(Left) Physical exams of female immigrants are carried out by a female doctor and nurse (*c.* 1915). The X's on the left shoulders of male immigrants awaiting eye exams (below; *c.* 1912) indicate that they are suspected of being mentally deficient.

WELCOME TO O'HARE INTERNATIONAL...

BY RICHARD D. MOYER

Mateo, an emigrant from the Philippines who is joining his wife in Chicago, gets off his plane at Chicago's O'Hare International Airport. He must now see an Immigration and Naturalization Service (INS) officer, to whom he presents his immigration visa, his Filipino passport, and various other supporting documents, including his medical examination form. The form indicates that he has been examined by a physician in his home country and has been found to be in good health. Because he has met all the medical requirements, which include having no contagious diseases, Mateo clears immigration without ado.

The requirement that would-be immigrants like Mateo undergo a medical examination before gaining entry into the United States was established more than a century ago, when Congress gave the Public Health Service authority to monitor the health of all people entering the country. That meant that persons with severe mental illness and certain contagious diseases could be denied entry for reasons of health.

Today all those who wish to take up residence in the U.S. must be examined in their home countries by an authorized physician. The purpose of the exam is to identify individuals with conditions that might be a threat to the public health. Those conditions presently include tuberculosis (TB), HIV infection, infectious Hansen's disease (leprosy), syphilis and certain other sexually transmitted diseases, mental disorders with associated harmful behavior, substance abuse, and lack of proof of required vaccinations. The exam consists of a brief medical history, a physical examination, an observation for physical or mental disorders, and a check of vaccination records (and vaccination if needed). For people 15 years or older, the exam also includes a chest X-ray for TB and blood tests for syphilis and HIV (those younger than 15 are tested only if there is reason to suspect infection).

If the exam shows that an immigrant has one of the aforementioned conditions, he or she will need special permission (a waiver) to enter the U.S. For example, before Maria, a Guatemalan who has had infectious TB, can enter the U.S., she must present documentation that she has received treatment and is no longer contagious. Once she is in the U.S., she must see a doctor for medical follow-up; failure to comply with the waiver's requirements could result in her deportation.

What happens when an international traveler arrives in the U.S. and appears to be sick? In these situations several federal agencies—including the INS, the U.S. Customs Service, and the Centers for Disease Control and Prevention (CDC)—cooperate. The CDC's Division of Quarantine has quarantine stations to handle such cases at the Atlanta, Georgia; New York City; Miami, Florida; Chicago; Los Angeles; San Francisco; Seattle, Washington; and Honolulu international airports.

Although it happens rarely, the division has the authority to detain, medically examine, or conditionally release persons who might have a "quarantinable" disease such as cholera, diphtheria, plague, yellow fever, TB, or a viral hemorrhagic fever (e.g., Ebola). If, for example, Goran, an Eastern European, arrived in the U.S. with a rash and fever, he would be taken to the airport quarantine station and kept in isolation until a local doctor was consulted. If necessary, Goran would be taken to a local hospital for treatment. Likewise, a U.S. citizen returning from a trip abroad and suspected of having a serious communicable disease might be held in the quarantine facilities until his or her need for isolation and treatment could be determined. John, for instance, was returning from Peru when that country was in the grip of a cholera epidemic; because he was feeling ill and feverish upon arrival at Miami's international airport, he was detained briefly—until a stool test indicated that he had traveler's diarrhea, an unpleasant malady but not a contagious one.

With these processes working together, *most* serious contagious diseases are effectively kept out of the U.S., and the public-at-large can rest fairly well assured that its health is being protected.

Richard D. Moyer *is Chief of the Medical Screening and Health Assessment Branch, Division of Quarantine, National Center for Infectious Diseases, Centers for Disease Control and Prevention, Atlanta, Georgia. This sidebar was prepared with assistance from Susan Temporado Cookson, M.D., Pamela S. Coplan, and Ava W. Navin of the CDC's Division of Quarantine.*

(Above) A woman arranges blocks as part of an intelligence test. Immigrants suspected of being mentally deficient were detained and required to undergo further testing. (Opposite page) A solitary shoe remains behind, a reminder of all those who passed through these now empty rooms.

(Above) An oven that was used for sterilizing hospital mattresses. (Opposite page) A former storage and refuse room. An effort is now under way to "stabilize" the existing structures of the ramshackle hospital complex so that the public can view this historically important side of Ellis Island.

Index

This is a one-year index. Index entries are set in lightface type, *e.g.,* air pollution. Additional information on any of these subjects is identified with a subheading and indented under the entry heading. The numbers following headings and subheadings indicate the page number on which the information appears. The abbreviation *il.* indicates an illustration.

AIDS, *or* acquired immune deficiency syndrome
    doctor-activists **142**
    humor therapy **212**
    pandemic infectious diseases **9**
air pollution
    children and asthma *il.* **77**

All entry headings are alphabetized word by word. Hyphenated words and words separated by dashes or slashes are treated as two words. When one word differs from another only by the presence of additional characters at the end, the shorter precedes the longer. In inverted names, the words following the comma are considered only after the preceding part of the name has been alphabetized. Examples:

        Lake
        Lake, Simon
        Lake Charles
        Lakeland

Names beginning with "Mc" and "Mac" are alphabetized as "Mac"; "St." is alphabetized as "Saint."